MAKING LAWS FOR CYB

Making Laws for Cyberspace

CHRIS REED

OXFORD

UNIVERSITY PRESS

OXFORD
UNIVERSITY PRESS

Great Clarendon Street, Oxford, OX2 6DP,
United Kingdom

Oxford University Press is a department of the University of Oxford.
It furthers the University's objective of excellence in research, scholarship,
and education by publishing worldwide. Oxford is a registered trade mark of
Oxford University Press in the UK and in certain other countries

© Chris Reed, 2012

The moral rights of the author have been asserted

First Edition published in 2012

Impression: 1

Crown copyright material is reproduced under Class Licence
Number C01P0000148 with the permission of OPSI
and the Queen's Printer for Scotland

British Library Cataloguing in publication Data
Data available

Library of Congress Cataloguing in Publication Data
Library of Congress Control Number: 2012932661

ISBN 978–0–19–965760–5
ISBN 978–0–19– 965761–2(pbk)

Printed in Great Britain
on acid-free paper by
CPI Group (UK) Ltd, Croydon, CR0 4YY

Links to third party websites are provided by Oxford in good faith and
for information only. Oxford disclaims any responsibility for the materials
contained in any third party website referenced in this work.

Prologue

It was over thirty years ago that I first began thinking about law and computing technology, and for nearly twenty-five years I've taught and written about nothing else. Cyberspace arrived, and the subject became even more fascinating as the global clash of legal cultures flooded its way onto my desktop. I've also been fortunate in advising companies trading in cyberspace—an internet lottery, online banking and e-payment ventures, e-signature schemes, internet telephony, and of course a range of more general e-commerce activities. I've even dipped my toe into the law-making process for the EU and the UK.

And yet . . .

For the last twenty years or so I've been dissatisfied with the state of the laws that I've been teaching, writing about, and advising on. Far too much of my time, and that of my students and clients, seems to have been wasted in discovering what the law is and what it was intended by its lawmaker to mean. Those who have advised clients will understand this particularly well. The client has no real interest in what the law says, or even what its technical meaning is. What the client wants is advice on the best way to achieve its aims, whilst also acting in a lawful way. And yet the law was so complex and hard to understand that only a small proportion of my time could be spent on that useful advice, because it took so long to get to grips with the law itself.

Worse, I gradually came to the understanding that in cyberspace it was almost impossible to act lawfully. Hundreds of lawmakers clamour for the attention of the cyberspace actor, and clearly not all of them can be obeyed. The sheer cacophony of legal noise obscures the right way to behave, even if there is some law-making consensus about what is and isn't right.

This offends my sensibilities, as a lawyer and as a thinking human being. An important purpose of law is to create order in human relations, so that individuals can interact with each other on a rational and reasonably certain basis. But the system of laws which claim to govern cyberspace is so chaotic that it fails to fulfil this purpose. The best that the would-be law-abiding cyberspace actor can manage to achieve is not to offend the most powerful—Ruritanian laws can safely be ignored here; the Utopian authorities are unlikely to take enforcement action if we do X, even though Utopian law doesn't favour X; and so on. The situation is highly unsatisfactory.

For 2009–11 I was fortunate to be awarded a Leverhulme Major Research Fellowship, to allow me to concentrate uninterruptedly on this problem. I believed that I understood most of the ways in which lawmakers had gone wrong, and could produce a technocratic manual which explained how to avoid these pitfalls in future law-making.

As I happens, I was mistaken. What we have in cyberspace, or at least so I now believe, is not a set of disparate technical flaws in our law-making. Instead, I see a small number of fundamental and related defects in the way laws, in general, are devised. The effects of those defects are less apparent in laws as they govern our physical world activities, but in cyberspace they result in a system of laws which is so far from ideal that it imperils the very enterprise of law itself. If, as I believe, it is important that cyberspace should be a lawful space, then it is essential to know what these defects are and how they might be remedied. What follows is my best effort at explaining these matters.

Acknowledgements

First, the Leverhulme Trust, whose generosity made this work possible. Few people in any field of endeavour are granted the opportunity to work uninterrupted for a long period on a project of their own choosing, and I am conscious of the privilege.

Second, my employer Queen Mary University of London, and in particular its Centre for Commercial Law Studies. Any project which I have thought academically desirable and which was financially viable has been actively encouraged. This is true academic freedom, and I know of few other universities who would have been equally supportive.

I must also mention my academic colleagues in the Centre's Institute for Computer & Communications Law, all of whom have made helpful criticisms of my thinking in this area. In particular, Professors Ian Walden and Christopher Millard have taken the time to comment on parts of this book, and I am most grateful for their thoughtful comments. I must also acknowledge the work of my PhD student, Sofia Casimiro, whose research on re-casting copyright in terms of economic and intellectual uses of works, rather than enumerated rights, helped in developing my ideas on this topic.

Andrew Murray from the London School of Economics and Chris Marsden from the University of Essex have also read parts of the book, and their input has reshaped my thinking as I responded to their comments. Lilian Edwards from the University of Strathclyde has encouraged me by saying and writing unwarrantably nice things about some of the thinking here which I published as articles, and that helped enormously.

From the practising side of the profession, Mark Lewis, now partner at BLP, gave me the chance to advise on a number of cutting-edge cyberspace projects during our time together at the various incarnations of Tite & Lewis, and has constantly exhorted me to raise my academic game. I hope this book meets at least some of his expectations. Graham Smith, partner at Bird & Bird, has rigorously dissected elements of my thinking through our work together for the Society for Computers & Law—he will doubtless disagree with many of the ideas here, but without his help they would have been far woollier and less well supported.

Outside the field of law I also need to thank my friend Graham Higgins. Although a graphic artist by profession, he foolishly expressed an interest in the ideas I was working on, and took the role of the lay commentator whose apparently naive questions I struggled to answer. At least I spared him from reading the footnotes.

And finally Jilly, who in the kindest and most supportive way kept my nose to the grindstone for the two years it took to write this book.

Contents

III. RESPECT-WORTHY LAWS

IV. LAW-MAKING

Table of Cases

Tables of Legislation

EUROPEAN LEGISLATION

Regulations

Directives and Proposals for Directives

Introduction

This book is about how to make the right kinds of laws for cyberspace. The kinds of laws which will make cyberspace a lawful space. Currently cyberspace is full of laws, but that is far from the same as being a space where cyberspace users act lawfully.

My concern is not with that small group of cyberspace users who act in ways which are widely accepted to be morally wrong, and in contravention of the laws of pretty much every country. Spammers, scammers, virus writers, and child abusers make extensive use of cyberspace, but dealing with these problems is not a matter of making better laws. Here, the issue is one of enforcing laws in a difficult environment, where the wrongdoer's identity and location may be hard to determine and where evidence is difficult to gather.

Instead I want to examine the situation of the vast majority of cyberspace users who would wish to act lawfully. Does the current state of law in cyberspace make it possible for them to do so? If not, why not, and what is the cure?

My contention is that lawmakers, sometimes inadvertently and often despite their best efforts, have failed in their law-making endeavour. They have proceeded on the assumption that the law-making techniques which have (perhaps) served well in the physical world can be transposed to cyberspace. As I hope to demonstrate, this is not so. There needs to be a fundamental shift of perspective, from the lawmaker's desires to the activities, attitudes, and aims of cyberspace users. Only by making that shift will the rule of law become widespread in cyberspace.

The inquiry in this book is undertaken not from an idealist point of view but rather in a spirit of pragmatism, or perhaps even utilitarianism or positivism:

Idealists tend to regard governance through law as a series of restraints on the power of government to interfere in the moral lives of ordinary citizens. Positivists typically regard law as an instrument for the pursuit and attainment of collective goals.[1]

Determining the appropriate set of individual rights which cyberspace users should have, and how states should be constrained from diminishing those rights, is a matter of politics and not well-suited to a hardened commercial lawyer such as myself. However, I think there is no dispute that individual rights, whatever their scope, cannot flourish in an environment where the rule of law is absent.

The collective goal that I have in mind is that cyberspace should be a socially useful space. The internet has pervaded our lives to such an extent that it is fast becoming as important to us as our physical transport infrastructure. Lawless driving reduces the

[1] Sean Coyle, 'Positivism, idealism and the rule of law' (2006) OJLS 257, 288.

utility of the roads, and for the same sorts of reasons we have the right, collectively, to expect lawful behaviour in cyberspace.

As Fuller has shown,[2] there are a number of guiding principles to which lawmakers should aspire. Failure to achieve them to a sufficiently high level 'results in something that is not properly called a legal system at all'.[3] Without a functioning system of laws, cyberspace has the potential to become unusable by that majority of individuals whose motives are not nefarious. This is a real danger unless the laws which cyberspace users are expected to comply with are the kinds of laws which will actually command obedience.

---

[2] Lon Fuller, *The Morality of Law*, rev. edn (New Haven: Yale University Press, 1969), Ch 2.
[3] Ibid, 39.

PART I

CYBERSPACE AS
A LAWFUL SPACE

1

Command and Control

In the middle of the 1990s the World Wide Web arrived, and the internet was suddenly visible to the public. Almost immediately a debate began about how the internet should be regulated. The US authorities had already taken action against some internet activities on national security grounds[1] and the introduction in 1995 of the bill which became the US Communications Decency Act 1996[2] raised fears that national governments would rush to assert their right to control all aspects of online communication.

This debate focused on two interlinked issues: whether it was proper for any national government to claim to apply its laws to the transglobal communications mechanism which was the internet; and whether such laws could actually be enforced against online activities.

Cyberlibertarianism[3]

One side of the debate argued that the sphere of jurisdiction for a national lawmaker is that community against which it has the right[4] and ability to enforce its laws, traditionally delimited primarily by the borders of that state's territory. As a consequence, claims to apply those laws to cyberspace, which is outside the territorial jurisdiction, were said to be of doubtful legitimacy. Additionally, making laws which had no realistic prospect of enforcement would risk diminishing the legitimacy of the entire national system of laws.

In February 2006 John Perry Barlow set out the cyberlibertarian position in strong rhetorical terms. His online manifesto, *A Declaration of the Independence of Cyberspace*,[5] opens with a war cry:

---

[1] See Bruce Sterling, *The Hacker Crackdown: Law and Disorder on the Electronic Frontier* (New York: Bantam Books, 1994); *Steve Jackson Games Inc v United States Secret Service*, 816 F Supp 432 (WD Tex, 1993), 36 F 3d 457 (5th Cir, 1994).

[2] 47 USC § 230.

[3] In this discussion and that of cyberpaternalism I adopt the terminology devised by Murray—see Andrew Murray, *Information Technology Law: The Law and Society* (Oxford: Oxford University Press, 2010), Ch 4.

[4] Derived from the voluntary submission of members to those laws—this issue is explored in more depth in Ch 6.

[5] John Perry Barlow, *A Declaration of Independence for Cyberspace* (1996), <http://w2.eff.org/Misc/Publications/John_Perry_Barlow/barlow_0296.declaration.txt>.

Governments of the Industrial World, you weary giants of flesh and steel, I come from
Cyberspace, the new home of Mind. On behalf of the future, I ask you of the past to leave us
alone. You are not welcome among us. You have no sovereignty where we gather . . .

I declare the global social space we are building to be naturally independent of the tyrannies
you seek to impose on us. You have no moral right to rule us nor do you possess any methods
of enforcement we have true reason to fear.

A few months later Johnson and Post published their seminal article, 'Law and
Borders'.[6] Although they expressed doubts whether national laws could in practice
be enforced in cyberspace,[7] their argument concentrated mainly on the question of
legitimacy. Briefly summarized their proposition was as follows:

1. Law-making is the exercise of power over those persons whom the state can
   control:

   Control over physical space, and the people and things located in that space, is a defining attribute of sovereignty and statehood. Law-making requires some mechanism for
   law enforcement, which in turn depends on the ability to exercise physical control
   over, and impose coercive sanctions on, law-violators.[8]

   If states attempt to control those who reside in other jurisdictions, this conflicts with that other state's monopoly right to exercise power over its citizens.

2. Although states have a claim to regulate conduct which has effects in the state's
   territory, online activities have no greater effect in any one state than in the
   remainder of the world. Thus a claim to apply national law merely on the
   ground of effects lacks legitimacy.[9]

3. The legitimacy of a state's law-making power derives from the consent of the
   governed and their role in the law-making process. Imposing national laws on
   cyberspace extends their ambit to those who have not so consented and who
   have no way to participate in the law-making process, for example through
   elected representatives.[10]

4. National borders give notice to individuals that they are entering a space to
   which different laws apply. These borders do not exist in cyberspace, so that
   cyberspace users do not receive the notice to which they are entitled that their
   activities are now subject to a particular state's laws.[11]

---

[6] David R Johnston and David G Post 'Law and Borders—The Rise of Law in Cyberspace' (1996)
48 Stanford LR 1367.

[7] 'efforts to control the flow of electronic information across physical borders—to map local regulation
and physical boundaries onto Cyberspace—are likely to prove futile, at least in countries that hope to
participate in global commerce. Individual electrons can easily, and without any realistic prospect of
detection, "enter" any sovereign's territory. The volume of electronic communications crossing territorial boundaries is just too great in relation to the resources available to government authorities' (ibid,
1372).

[8] Ibid, 1369.

[9] Ibid, 1369, 1375.

[10] Ibid, 1369.

[11] Ibid, 1370.

As territoriality plays such a fundamental role in legitimizing a states' law-making, Johnson and Post conclude that the a-territorial nature of the internet precludes any state from making a legitimate claim to regulate it:

Because events on the Net occur everywhere but nowhere in particular, are engaged in by online personae who are both 'real' (possessing reputations, able to perform services, and deploy intellectual assets) and 'intangible' (not necessarily or traceably tied to any particular person in the physical sense), and concern 'things' (messages, databases, standing relationships) that are not necessarily separated from one another by any physical boundaries, no physical jurisdiction has a more compelling claim than any other to subject these events exclusively to its laws.[12]

Their answer to the question 'Who, then, *should* regulate?' was that the internet would develop its own governing institutions, whose legitimacy would derive from the consent of the internet users to whom the new rules would apply. Even though 'established authorities will likely continue to claim that they must analyze and regulate the new online phenomena in terms of some physical locations',[13] the existence of a legitimate law system[14] for cyberspace would counter those claims.

The history of moves towards self-governance in online worlds such as LambdaMOO and Second Life[15] suggests that the development of self-governance is slow and chancy. What is certain is that states and their courts moved very much faster, asserting that their laws applied to cyberspace activities and enforcing them against those over whom the state had some measure of control. It soon became clear that as a matter of fact, territoriality did not limit the role of national law in cyberspace, and the necessary acceptance of that fact seems to have conferred legitimacy on states to make laws for cyberspace.

The cyberlibertarian argument is now seen very much as the product of its time. With the benefit of ten years' experience, Goldsmith and Wu were able to demonstrate that order in cyberspace is only possible if that order is based on national laws.[16] Thus, for example, eBay's commercial success demands that there be an

---

[12] Ibid, 1376. See also 1390:

Governments cannot stop electronic communications from coming across their borders, even if they want to do so. Nor can they credibly claim a right to regulate the Net based on supposed local harms caused by activities that originate outside their borders and that travel electronically to many different nations. One nation's legal institutions should not monopolize rule-making for the entire Net.

[13] Ibid, 1390.

[14] This useful term is borrowed from Aernout Schmidt, 'Radbruch in Cyberspace: About Law-system Quality and ICT Innovation' (2009) 3 Masaryk University Journal of Law and Technology 195, of whom more in Ch 10. 'Legal system' implies a formal legislator and territorial boundaries, whereas 'law-system' merely describes the set of laws which *in fact* apply to a particular activity, whatever their individual origins.

[15] See Jennifer L Mnookin, "Virtual(ly) Law: The Emergence of Law in LambdaMOO" (1996) 2.1 *Journal of Computer-Mediated Communication*, <http://jcmc.indiana.edu/vol2/issue1/lambda.html>; Chris Reed, 'Why Must You be Mean to Me? Crime and the Online Persona' (2010) 13 New Criminal LR 485.

[16] 'Public goods and related virtues of governmental control of the Internet are necessary across multiple dimensions for the Internet to work, and as a practical matter only traditional territorial governments can provide such goods' (Jack Goldsmith and Tim Wu, *Who Controls the Internet? Illusions of a Borderless World* (New York: Oxford University Press, 2006), 142).

enforceable law of contract and state mechanisms for the detection and punishment of fraud.[17]

For the purposes of this book, what is particularly interesting about both the Johnson and Post proposition and the Goldsmith and Wu refutation is their common emphasis on the law as a system of *control*. For Johnson and Post, the law's primary role is to enable the state, or some person granted privileges by the state such as a copyright owner, to control how others behave.[18] Goldsmith and Wu's fundamental assumption (explicit in their title, *Who Controls the Internet?*, though for the most part implicit) is similar: that the role of national law is to coerce cyberspace users into conformity by controlling their behaviour, and imposing sanctions if they refuse to do so. They espouse the teachings of Hobbes, that 'human beings require "the terror of some power" to force them to behave'.[19]

Cyberpaternalism

The opposing school of thought took the position that not only was it perfectly possible for national laws to regulate cyberspace, but also that it was entirely appropriate for them to do so. The starting point here is Reidenberg's 1996 article 'Governing Networks and Rule-Making in Cyberspace'[20] which he developed more fully in 'Lex Informatica'[21] two years later.

Reidenberg's insight was that cyberspace is not only regulable, but that it is particularly open to regulation through the technology of the network itself. He described the rules embodied in this technology as the Lex Informatica:

> In the context of information flows on networks, the technical solutions begin to illustrate that network technology itself imposes rules for the access to and use of information . . . In effect, this set of impositions on information flows through technological defaults and system configurations offers two types of substantive rules: immutable policies embedded in the technology standards that cannot be altered and flexible policies embedded in the technical architecture that allow variations on default settings. Lex Informatica has a number of distinguishing features that are analogous to a legal regulatory regime and support its role as an important system of rules for an Information Society.[22]

He also identified the overlap between network rules and rules of law, and that national law may be used to modify the content of those network rules, either directly or by imposing liabilities on key actors, such as internet service providers (ISPs), which induce them to modify the network rules to avoid liability.[23]

---

[17] Ibid, Ch 8.

[18] Johnson and Post (n 6). See particularly 1369, 1371–6, 1384–5, and 1392–5.

[19] Goldsmith and Wu (n 16), 135, citing Thomas Hobbes, *Leviathan*, Ch 18 (1651).

[20] Joel Reidenberg, 'Governing Networks and Rule-Making in Cyberspace' (1996) 45 Emory LJ 911.

[21] Joel Reidenberg, 'Lex Informatica: The Formulation of Information Policy Rules through Technology' (1998) 76 Tex L Rev 553.

[22] Ibid, 568.

[23] See also James Boyle, 'Foucault in Cyberspace: Cyberspace, Sovereignty and Hardwired Censors' (1997) 66 U Cin L Rev 177.

This line of thinking is most fully worked out in Lessig's book *Code and Other Laws of Cyberspace*.[24] He argues that the internet is 'evolving from an unregulable space to one that is highly regulable',[25] and that it is doing so via modifications to the code architecture which controls the way in which the internet operates. Lessig sets out four modalities of regulation: Law, Social Norms, the Market, and Code Architecture.

Each of these exerts control, in different ways, over actors in cyberspace. None of them is fixed, and all are subject to regulation by the nation state.[26] And of these four, code is the most powerful because its constraints cannot be evaded.

As a constitutional lawyer, Lessig's primary focus is on the extent to which the shaping of code can properly be left in private hands, and on identifying the role which the state should play in shaping and constraining the development of code:

We live life in real space, subject to the effects of code. We live ordinary lives, subject to the effects of code. We live social and political lives, subject to the effects of code. Code regulates all these aspects of our lives, more pervasively over time than any other regulator in our life. Should we remain passive about this regulator? Should we let it affect us without doing anything in return?[27]

His answer is, of course, a clear 'No', and this establishes a fundamental role for national law in the regulation of cyberspace.

There is, though, one point on which both the cyberlibertarians and the cyberpaternalists agree. This is that law is about control. Its aim is to instruct people how to behave, and to provide an incentive for obedience by sanctioning those who do not comply. Code is a regulator, like law, because it too controls behaviour—indeed, Lessig goes so far as to assert that 'the invisible hand of cyberspace is constructing an architecture that perfects control'.[28] The assumption is that any law which is sufficiently likely to be enforced[29] will necessarily force humans to behave in the ways required by the lawmaker, and that the constraints of code are inescapable.

If this assumption were true, it would merely be necessary for the lawmaker (or the coder) to identify the online behaviours which are to be allowed and prohibited, and then craft the law (or mandate the crafting of code) so as to constrain those behaviours accordingly. But is it true?

---

[24] Lawrence Lessig, *Code and Other Laws of Cyberspace* (New York: Basic Books, 1999). A second edition was published as *Code 2.0* in 2006 and contains additional examples and more detailed working out of Lessig's theory. In my view, though, the additional detail tends to some extent to obscure the argument, which remains unchanged, and so for that reason all references here are to the first edition.

[25] Ibid, 25.

[26] Ibid, 91.

[27] Ibid, 233.

[28] Ibid, 6. This perceived trend towards perfect control of behaviour, and as a consequence perfect regulability by law, is a pervasive theme in the book and is even more salient in *Code 2.0*. Chapter 12 examines how far code is likely to achieve the control which Lessig foresees.

[29] Goldsmith and Wu argue that comprehensive enforcement is not necessary so long as the risk of enforcement is sufficient to influence the human actor: 'We do not conclude from the persistence of occasional bank robberies that laws against theft are ineffective, or even suboptimal. Often, the law accepts small evasions because achieving perfect legal control, though possible, is too expensive' (Goldsmith and Wu (n 16), 67).

Law as a System of Control?

The view of law as a coercive system reflects Austin's philosophy:

> Being liable to evil from you if I comply not with a wish which you signify, I am *bound* or *obliged* by your command, or I lie under a *duty* to obey it.[30]

This assumes that, given freedom of choice, we would behave otherwise than the law demands and it is only the fear of the law's sanctions which persuades us to comply. As a system of control, law must work mainly through deterrence because there can never be enough resources to detect and sanction even a small proportion of the breaches which would otherwise occur.

This is not, though, how law actually works. Take for example, the law of murder. Few seriously argue that the deterrent effect of the law, which universally imposes the greatest permissible penalty on murderers, has any real effect on the number of murders committed. Indeed, it seems likely that the whole of the criminal law, the most likely element of any law system to be effective as a means of control, has in fact little or no deterrent effect:

> Does criminal law deter? Given available behavioural science data, the short answer is: generally, no.[31]

Instead, humans conduct their lives in accordance with a set of social norms, in the belief (if the norm is one which they expect to be part of the law) that the content of the law matches those norms.[32]

This lack of deterrent effect should be unsurprising. The vast majority of readers of this book have never committed a murder, a fraud, or a burglary, and would be equally unlikely to do so were the criminal law abolished. The criminal law certainly punishes conduct which contravenes its rules, but does little to deter such conduct.

Hart's *Concept of Law* argues convincingly that it is more appropriate to understand law as a subset of the social rules by which members of a society order their lives, identifying the subset by means of secondary rules about their source and the

---

[30] John Austin, *Lectures on Jurisprudence*, 3rd edn (London: John Murray, 1869), Vol. I, Lecture I, 91.

[31] Paul H Robinson and John M Darley, 'Does Criminal Law Deter?' (2004) OJLS 173, 173. See also Tom R Tyler and John M Darley, 'Building a Law-abiding Society: Taking Public Views about Morality and the Legitimacy of Legal Authorities into Account when Formulating Substantive Law' (2000) 28 Hofstra L Rev 707, 713:

> research findings suggest that people's compliance with the law is, at best, weakly linked to the risks associated with law-breaking behavior. As a result, social control strategies based primarily on a deterrence model of human behavior have, at best, had limited success.

[32] See ibid, 715, reporting on the authors' survey (John M. Darley, Kevin M. Carlsmith, and Paul H. Robinson 'The Ex Ante Function of the Criminal Law' (2001) 35 Law & Soc Rev 165) of citizens' knowledge of particular legal rules which were written with the expectation of guiding their conduct: 'their belief in the law's commands . . . closely matched their own judgments of what the law *should* be, suggesting that they were using their own moral intuitions to predict the legal rule, rather than any real knowledge of the legal code's rules'.

rule-making capacity of their maker.[33] Only a minority of these legal rules aim at the kinds of control envisaged by the cyberlibertarians and the cyberpaternalists. Most of the rules of contract law are facilitative rather than prescriptive,[34] and the tort of negligence does not aim to control the way people drive but rather to compensate their victims if the driver falls short of the standards which constitute the social norm.[35] These are merely examples taken from the wide variety of types of law, the majority of which do not take the form of coercive orders backed up by sanctions.[36]

We therefore need to abandon the focus on control and adopt a more expansive view of law-making and regulation, as 'the intentional activity of attempting to control, order or influence the behaviour of others'.[37] This is a far closer match to the way that we all, as humans, actually experience law.

Once we recognize that law achieves its aims of control, ordering, and influence primarily via its normative effects, rather than via enforcement, we are also forced to recognize that we cannot focus our attention solely on the activities of the lawmaker. Social norms reflect the consensus of a community about how its members should behave, and those norms which are given the status of law are developed at least as much by the community as by the lawmaker.

This is the insight which Murray terms 'network communitarianism'.[38] By applying network and systems theories to cyberspace regulation he identifies that the cyberspace user is not a mere passive recipient of orders from lawmakers, or the constraints of the market, social norms, and architecture. Instead there is a continuous communication between the individual and these constraints which limits and reshapes them:

> Regulation is a process of discourse and dialogue between the individual and society. Sometimes society, either directly through the application of norms, or indirectly by distilling its opinions, norms or standards down to laws wishes to force a change in the behaviour of the individual. But sometimes it is the regulatory settlement itself which is challenged by society when there is no longer any support for it . . . In network communitarian theory the power to determine the regulatory environment does not rest with the regulator alone.[39]

The Limits of Control in Cyberspace

It is inevitable that most lawmakers, invested as they are with the authority to issue commands and prescribe sanctions for disobedience, will see the products of their

---

[33] HLA Hart, *The Concept of Law*, 2nd edn (Oxford: Oxford University Press, 1994), Chs IV and V.

[34] The obvious exception being those rules which make contracts unenforceable if contravened, such as some consumer protection provisions.

[35] Negligence is a particularly clear example because the standard of care required is that which is expected of members of society generally—in other words, the social norm lies at the core of the legal rule.

[36] Hart (n 33), Ch III. For a more extensive analysis of the functions which law performs see Joseph Raz, *The Authority of Law*, 2nd edn (Oxford: Oxford University Press, 2009), 169–72.

[37] Julia Black, 'Critical Reflections on Regulation' (2002) 27 Austl J Leg Phil 1, 25.

[38] Helpfully summarized in Murray (n 3), 66–70. The concept is fully worked out in Andrew Murray, *The Regulation of Cyberspace* (Abingdon: Routledge-Cavendish, 2007).

[39] Murray (n 3), 68–70.

law-making as instruments of command and control.[40] Many of the defects in the laws for cyberspace arise because of this blindness to the limits on their ability to exercise perfect control over cyberspace users.

Perhaps the most important limit on control is that laws do not automatically establish norms.[41] In most cases the activity which the law attempts to regulate has already developed a set of norms, and if these are strongly entrenched then it is probable that they will continue to regulate behaviour with the consequence that the law will be widely disobeyed. The US experiment with Prohibition in the 1920s is perhaps the best-known example of this phenomenon. Successful laws normally either entrench existing norms, clarifying any uncertainties or ambiguities,[42] or reinforce developing norms, as was the case for the UK law mandating the wearing of seat belts in cars.[43]

There are numerous examples of laws which, because they conflict with established cyberspace norms, have failed to control the actions of cyberspace users. Probably the best-known example is copyright as it applies to the file sharing of digital music.

Once the bandwidth to permit downloading of music became widely available, users began to rip their CDs into MP3 format and share those MP3 files with others online. This was seen by them, though not of course by the music industry, as entirely acceptable behaviour. It is probable that file sharing became the norm partly because the music industry resolutely refused to make its music available in downloadable form, and partly because the global norms embedded in copyright law were ambiguous on whether file sharing was unlawful. Although UK copyright law has never contained an exception permitting private copying per se, much private copying is allowed under the US fair use exception[44] and most civil law copyright systems contain an explicit exception for private copying.[45] Cyberspace norms develop within the entire body of cyberspace users, not merely those of any one state, and so it is unsurprising that the more restrictive UK copyright position did not influence the general norm.[46]

---

[40] The main exceptions are likely to be the rule-makers in co-regulatory systems, such as those commonly adopted for the financial services sector, where the process of rule-making occurs through dialogue between the regulator and the regulated community—see Julia Black, 'Talking about Regulation' (1998) Public Law 77.

[41] Except in those cases where the law establishes a new activity and simultaneously sets out the norms to be followed when engaging in that activity—for example, a law introducing a new social security benefit.

[42] eg the UK Sale of Goods Act 1893, which largely codified the existing case law. That case law was itself a recognition and adoption of mercantile custom over the preceding century and a half.

[43] UK Motor Vehicles (Wearing of Seat Belts) Regulations 1982, SI 1982/1203.

[44] 17 USC § 107.

[45] See eg French Intellectual Property Code Art L122-5(1) and (2).

[46] Indeed, it seems probable that the UK social norm, as opposed to the legal norm in UK copyright law, was already that private copying is permissible. The arrival of the audiocassette in the 1970s led to widespread private copying of vinyl LPs onto tape, and the sharing of those tapes, which produced similar howls of rage from the music industry. The Court of Appeal in *Amstrad Consumer Electronics Plc v British Phonographic Industry Ltd* [1986] FSR 159 accepted that the vast majority of home tape recordings infringed copyright.

The lawmakers' response was to pass new laws, making it clear that file sharing and other online communication of copyright works was an infringement, and introducing penalties for the circumvention of technologies such as Digital Rights Management (DRM) which were intended to prevent copying and file sharing.[47] The music industry pursued a policy of aggressive litigation, first against file-sharing technology providers such as Napster, KaZaA, and Grokster, and then against end-users.[48] Yet, as the music industry's figures show, private copying and file sharing remains the norm.[49] The current strategy is to enrol ISPs as enforcers, requiring them to provide facilities via which the music industry can detect file sharing, and then sanction those persons via technical measures such as bandwidth throttling and temporary disconnection from the internet, as for example in the UK Digital Economy Act 2010's provisions. It seems unlikely, though, that this will be any more successful in shifting the norm. As Murray points out, 'It seems that nothing the lawyers, legislators and code designers do will slow down the growing black market in individual file sharing.'[50]

The case of file sharing is an extreme one, where the rules of law and the social norms of cyberspace are in diametric opposition. For many cyberspace activities there are no strongly established social norms, and it might be thought that here the generalized social norm that laws should be obeyed would apply. However, this will only result in compliance with any particular law if the individual cyberspace user understands that law to be applicable to him in some meaningful way.

This imposes further limits on a lawmaker's ability to control (or order, or influence) the behaviour of cyberspace users. It is not sufficient merely to enact some rule if individuals are not persuaded that the rule is meaningfully applicable to them. There are numerous reasons why laws might fail in this enterprise, but five in particular are worth noting here and will be investigated in more detail later in this book.

The first is simple ignorance. Most individuals have only a general impression of the rules of their own national law,[51] and are likely to be completely ignorant of the multiplicity of foreign laws which claim to apply to their cyberspace activities. This is even true for online businesses with customers in multiple jurisdictions. The costs of discovering the potentially applicable laws of over 190 states, and then analysing their potential application to the business's activities, are so great that such businesses

---

[47] Jessica Litman, *Digital Copyright* (Amherst: Prometheus Books, 2001) sets out a fascinating account of the bargaining process between the copyright interests and the legislators.

[48] See Andrew Murray, *The Regulation of Cyberspace* (Abingdon: Routledge-Cavendish, 2007), 181–200 for an account of this up to 2006.

[49] IFPI, *Digital Music Report 2009: Key Statistics*, <http://www.ifpi.org/content/section_resources/dmr2009.html>, estimates that 16% of European users regularly swap infringing music files online, and that in 2008 the number of infringing music files shared exceeded 40 billion, suggesting an infringement rate for downloads of about 95%. Detailed statistics are not available in the most recent report, which estimates that file sharing among European users has increased to 23%: IFPI, *Digital Music Report 2011*, 14.

[50] Murray (n 48), 199.

[51] See n 32 for an illustration in relation to the criminal law.

tend only to investigate jurisdictions where they perceive themselves as potentially at risk.[52]

Secondly, even if the individual is aware of the law he may understand it as not being addressed to him, and therefore not applicable. This is unlikely for the law of that individual's own country, unless the law appears to be addressed only to a particular sector of activity, but is particularly relevant for foreign laws which claim cross-border applicability. A national law which asserts control over all cyberspace users, irrespective of their online relationship with that country, is unlikely to be taken seriously.

Thirdly, laws which are impossible to obey, or where compliance would be unfeasibly burdensome, will not be perceived as applicable in a meaningful sense. Some laws have demanded action which is impossible because of the technical architecture of cyberspace, as occurred in a number of early cases in 1995 and 1996 where ISPs were required to block access to unlawful content:

In the CompuServe case the public prosecutors considered that certain items available on newsgroups were illegal, and requested CompuServe to block access to these newsgroups. Since CompuServe's software did not initially make it possible to differentiate between German subscribers and others for access to newsgroups, CompuServe suspended access to a number of newsgroups to all its subscribers world-wide, which created wide-spread protests that German standards of morality were being exported. Subsequently, CompuServe restored access to most of these newsgroups except to its German subscribers. No action was apparently taken against other access providers based in Germany, so their subscribers could continue to consult this content, if the access provider chose to carry the newsgroup in question.

In a recent case, the German public prosecutors threatened to prosecute the German internet access providers unless they blocked access to a magazine published on a Web site on a server in the Netherlands which allegedly promoted terrorist violence. Under protest, the access providers did so. However, this meant blocking access to all content on the Dutch server, including harmless content, while the document continues to be available to internet users outside Germany. A number of anti-blocking tactics were also immediately put in place. It is not clear whether the content is contrary to Dutch law—at all events the Dutch authorities have not intervened. The Dutch host service provider has complained that the action of the German authorities constitutes an interference with the free movement of services within the EU.[53]

A more recent example occurred in *Yahoo! Inc v LICRA*,[54] where a French judge ordered Yahoo! to take 'all necessary measures . . . to make impossible' access to Nazi material via Yahoo's auction service, an order which clearly could not be obeyed completely. At a subsequent hearing it was indicated that substantial, rather than full, compliance would suffice to fulfil the order.[55]

---

[52] These risks include the risk of enforcement action, or reputational damage, or the loss of customer confidence.

[53] European Commission Communication, 'Illegal and Harmful Content on the Internet', COM (96) 0487-C4-0592/96 (footnotes omitted).

[54] TGI de Paris, 22 May 2000, Interim Court Order No 00/05308, 00/05309.

[55] TGI de Paris, 20 November 2000, on the basis that expert evidence indicated that it was feasible for Yahoo! to identify the location of around 90% of its auction site users, and this would be enough for

More commonly though, compliance with the law is technically feasible but, for all practical purposes, still impossible because of cost or because it would destroy the business of the company which is required to comply. In 2003 the UK Financial Services Authority demanded that mobile telephone companies should comply with the requirements of the e-Money Directive 2000[56] by registering as e-money issuers. This placed the companies in a difficult dilemma—if they complied, they would be prohibited from continuing to offer telephony services and would thus be in breach of their licence terms as well as being forced out of business.[57] It seems fair to say that it was, in practice, impossible for them to comply with the law's requirements. Certainly they did not believe that the law, as originally drafted, was addressed to them.

Fourthly, cyberspace users may perceive a law to be inapplicable because it appears to regulate a technology, or a method of acting, which has become outdated and is no longer in use. This is a common problem for lawmakers because the pace of legal change is far slower than that of technology and the ways it is used and exploited.[58] Outdated laws also lead to impossibility of compliance—the difficulties which the mobile telephone companies faced in complying with the e-Money Directive were in part because the law was devised to regulate value stored on smart cards, rather than the network and server technologies which were actually used by those companies.[59]

Finally, the extent to which enforcement is practically possible has a real effect on an individual's perception of the applicability of a law. Even though law does not achieve its normative effects primarily through fear of enforcement, a law which is never enforced or is clearly unenforceable sends a message that it is not really intended to be complied with. As we shall see, enforcement is particularly difficult in cyberspace, especially for laws which have cross-border application.[60]

These are all limits on the law's ability to control behaviour. What, though, of code's 'perfect' control? If code could achieve complete control over cyberspace users, their states of mind in respect of those controlling rules would be irrelevant. However, as we shall see in Chapter 12, code is a much more limited modality of

---

substantial compliance. It must be noted, though, that the original order required 100% compliance, which was impossible according to the evidence.

[56] Directive 2000/46/EC of the European Parliament and of the Council on the taking up, pursuit of and prudential supervision of the business of electronic money institutions, OJ L 275/39, 27 October 2000.

[57] See further Ch 8.

[58] See eg the unsuccessful argument put forward in *CBS Songs Ltd v Amstrad Consumer Electronics plc* [1988] AC 1013 that an LP, when copied to tape, became an infringing 'plate' (a term taken from printing technology) under ss 18 and 21 of the UK Copyright Act 1956.

[59] See the original drafting of Art 1(3)(b) in the 1996 proposal for the directive, which defined e-money as being '(i) stored electronically on an electronic device such as a chip card or a computer memory' and '(iii) generated in order to be put at the disposal of users to serve as an electronic surrogate for coins and banknotes' (Proposal for a European Parliament and Council directive on the taking up, the pursuit and the prudential supervision of the business of electronic money institutions, COM (1998) 0461 final, OJ C317, 15 October 1998).

[60] See Ch 4.

regulation than Lessig feared. Technology businesses can use code to control the activities of their customers, but social and market pressure tends to persuade them to abandon those controls.[61] Mandating code controls through law is not simply a matter of issuing orders to technology companies, because they will oppose laws which are likely to damage their businesses or annoy their customers, as is highly likely if the laws conflict with established cyberspace norms. Thus the implementation of the UK's Digital Economy Act provisions requiring ISPs to take technical measures against unlawful file sharing was substantially delayed, partly because of failure to reach agreement between ISPs and right-holders on costs, and also because of a judicial review action by major UK ISPs.[62] There is no doubt that a major factor in the opposition of ISPs was the knowledge that their customers would resent this attempt to control their behaviour.[63]

Escaping Control

In addition to its other defects, a focus on the law as an instrument of control is of little or no help in deciding how to frame laws so that they actually succeed in producing the desired behaviours. Indeed, it almost invites the lawmaker to ignore everything but the desired ends and, subject only to constitutional or other limits on what laws may properly be enacted, issue commands on the assumption that enforcement is all that is needed to ensure compliance.

What needs to be understood is how to make laws which achieve the proper balance between control, deterrence, sanctions, and norm-setting so as to achieve their aims. My contention is that the techniques required are different from those which have so far been used in attempting to regulate cyberspace. The main focus should be not on control, but on the human cyberspace user and the cyberspace communities of which he is a member.

---

[61] A pre-cyberspace example was Lotus's 'key disk' technology, adopted to prevent users running unlicensed copies of the 1-2-3 spreadsheet software and abandoned rapidly as users switched to rival spreadsheet products. More recently, similar pressures persuaded Apple to make its music downloads DRM-free—see Apple press release 6 January 2009, <http://www.apple.com/pr/library/2009/01/06itunes.html>.

[62] 'Digital Economy Act: further delay to illegal downloading measures', *The Guardian*, 28 March 2011. The application for judicial review was rejected in April 2011: *British Telecommunications Plc v The Secretary of State for Business, Innovation and Skills* [2011] EWHC 1021 (Admin).

[63] See eg BT response to the Department for Business, Innovation and Skills consultation, 29 September 2009, para 9:

> If implemented as currently planned, [the proposals] would be likely to result in millions of aggrieved broadband consumers facing rising costs and a poorer internet experience, heavy costs for ISPs resulting from otherwise unnecessary network interventions, continuing unseen infringement taking place in encrypted environments and consequently little improvement in right-holder revenues and in building more constructive relations with consumers. [<http://www.btplc.com/Thegroup/RegulatoryandPublicaffairs/UKPublicAffairs/ResponsestoPolicyConsultations/P2PBTresponse290909.pdf>]

2

The Route to Lawfulness

We saw in Chapter 1 that cyberspace places limits on the use of law to control behaviour. The mere fact that a state has issued commands, in the form of law, is not on its own sufficient to effect changes in the behaviour of cyberspace users.

However, there is still some hope for lawfulness in cyberspace, or at least some approximation to lawfulness. We have already noted in the previous chapter the observation by Robinson and Darley that ordinary citizens order their lives in accordance with what they *believe* the law to be, rather than what it actually is,[1] and Garthoff explains this further:

Strictly speaking, individuals are obligated to do not what the law says they must do, but rather what the prevailing social convention says they are obligated to do . . . Law in particular is needed merely because law is typically the only mechanism by which the relevant convention can be created, sustained, and improved over time; and coercive enforcement of law is typically needed only because it is predictable, given human fallibilities, that a convention solving a moral coordination problem will atrophy over time absent a threat of coercive enforcement. The locus of normative political authority is thus the convention sustained by the law, rather than the law itself, since it is the convention that solves the moral coordination problem and so transmits the normative authority of morality to the social structure in question.[2]

The generalized norm that individuals should act in accordance with the law, as they understand it, is strong. We can thus expect cyberspace users to modify their behaviour in response to laws of which they are aware, and which appear to them to fall within the ambit of that social norm.

The problem is that a substantial proportion of the laws which claim to apply to cyberspace do not look to users like laws which impose a social obligation that they should be obeyed.

Applicability and Legitimate Authority

Clearly there is no obligation, whether social or legal, to obey a law which does not apply to one's actions. Unfortunately, in cyberspace it is extremely difficult to decide

---

[1] Paul H Robinson and John M Darley, 'Does Criminal Law Deter?' (2004) OJLS 173, 175.
[2] John Garthoff, 'Legitimacy Is Not Authority' (2010) Law & Philosophy 669, 680.

which laws *do* apply.[3] This difficulty is compounded by the fact that there are two quite different perspectives on the question of applicability. The first is that of the lawmaker, or the lawmaker's legal institutions such as national courts; the second is based on the attitude of the individual who is attempting to decide whether to obey the law.

From the perspective of the law-making state, applicability is a question of its own national law. Sometimes that law gives clear answers. For example, if a UK-resident e-commerce company sells online to a UK-resident consumer, there is no doubt that the UK Consumer Protection from Unfair Trading Regulations 2008[4] apply to that company's activities. However, it is not obvious from the text of the regulations whether they apply to a non-UK company[5] which sells online to a UK consumer. To answer this question the UK courts would need to consider whether the unfair trading practices complained of took place in the UK, or whether they occurred at the foreign location where the company is resident or where its e-commerce server is situated, which might well be different places. Alternatively the courts might decide that the regulations apply if the unfair practices caused detriment to a UK consumer, even if the practices were undertaken outside the UK. As yet, the courts have not been asked to determine this issue. Thus even when examined from the perspective of the law-making state, the applicability of its laws in cyberspace can be a very uncertain matter.

If it is clear, as a matter of national law, that a particular law does not apply to a particular cyberspace user's activities (though it is rare that any law is clearly inapplicable to *all* cyberspace activities), then the cyberspace user is not obliged by that national law to obey it. Interestingly though, as we shall see in Chapter 5, the social norm that laws should be obeyed might sometimes produce a different result.

This is because that social norm works from the perspective of the person who is potentially subject to the law, rather than from the perspective of the law-making state. A moment's reflection reveals that this must necessarily be so. It is clearly impossible for an individual cyberspace user to investigate the laws of every country in the world, decide which of those laws *might* potentially apply to his cyberspace activities, and then investigate the relevant national law further to discover whether those laws do in fact apply. Were such an investigation to be made, it would often reveal (as in our example of the UK regulations above) that the question of applicability is undecided. Even major multinational corporations find it impossible to

---

[3] See Ch 3.

[4] SI 2008/1277.

[5] If the company is established in the EU then, by virtue of Arts 3 and 4 of the EU Electronic Commerce Directive (Directive 2000/31/EC on electronic commerce OJ L 178/1, 17 July 2000) only those parts of the UK regulations which relate to the contract with the UK consumer will apply, although the equivalent laws of the seller's home state (implementing Directive 2005/29/EC of the European Parliament and of the Council concerning unfair business-to-consumer commercial practices, OJ L 149/22, 11 June 2005, and part of Directive 1999/44/EC of the European Parliament and of the Council on certain aspects of the sale of consumer goods and associated guarantees, OJ L171/12, 7 July 1999) should impose identical obligations on the seller. Note, though, that these are obligations under its home law and not under UK law.

undertake such an enormous exercise. The social norm that laws should be obeyed can only work in respect of laws which the individual believes to be applicable.

Thus the relevant question must be not whether a particular law *claims* to apply, but whether cyberspace users *perceive* that the law applies. They will only have such a perception if they accept that the lawmaker has legitimate authority to make the claim. If users accept the lawmaker's authority, the law may be obeyed because of the generalized social norm. If, though, cyberspace users are ignorant of the law's existence, or believe that it is not properly addressed to them, they will feel no obligation to obey it.

This tells us that if a lawmaker wishes its laws to be obeyed in cyberspace it must convince cyberspace users that it has a legitimate claim to apply its law to them, except perhaps in the unlikely event that it is confident that it can enforce that law against a large proportion of infringers.[6] As Raz makes clear in *The Authority of Law*, 'A common factor in all kinds of effective authority is that they involve a belief by some that the person concerned has legitimate authority.'[7]

It might be thought that the solution for the lawmaker is simply to assert expressly that the law applies in cyberspace, possibly explaining the circumstances when it is intended to apply. Unfortunately this will not do the trick.

We shall see in many parts of this book that there is a clear history of disobeying laws which have been held by their national courts to apply to cyberspace activities. This occurs even among cyberspace users who know of the law's existence and its claims to apply to their actions. The reason for that disobedience is that users have not been convinced that the law in question is *properly*, or *legitimately*, addressed to them. We might put this another way, adopting Raz's terminology, and say that they do not accept that the lawmaker has *authority* over them. This is not legitimacy or authority in its *de jure* meaning, that the lawmaker has the right under the rules of its legal system to make the law and has complied with the procedural requirements for so doing. Instead it addresses the relationship between the lawmaker and those to whom it claims to apply its laws; is the relationship such that this claim ought to be accepted by those persons?

Lawmakers clearly have a legitimate claim, in both senses, to apply their laws to those who are present in their physical territory, and in some circumstances to their citizens even if they are abroad. Claims to apply the law to those who reside elsewhere, even if their activities are accessible online from the state, are necessarily less likely to be perceived as an exercise of legitimate authority. It is not sufficient that a lawmaker's claim to apply its laws is legitimated by its national law; that claim must also convince cyberspace users that it has legitimacy in the broader sense. If it does not, the claim will be rejected and the law will not be obeyed.

This takes us back to the cyberlibertarian argument examined in Chapter 1, that 'no physical jurisdiction has a more compelling claim than any other to subject these

---

[6] See Ch 4.
[7] Joseph Raz, *The Authority of Law*, 2nd edn (Oxford: Oxford University Press, 2009), 29.

events exclusively to its laws'.[8] As a general proposition this must be correct. If there were to be a monopoly lawmaker for cyberspace, it would clearly be wrong for that monopoly to be exercised by a single nation. However, this is not the claim that lawmakers assert. They merely demand that their own laws be obeyed, and are generally indifferent as to the laws of other nations which also claim to be applicable.[9] This, they would say, is a problem for the cyberspace user, not one which national law must solve.

But we have already seen that national laws will only be treated by cyberspace users as applicable to them if they also accept the authority of those laws. Thus it is not correct to say that the problem of compliance with multiple national laws is one which the user must solve. The achievement of lawfulness in cyberspace requires national lawmakers to frame their laws in such a way that their legitimate authority is accepted by users. How this might be achieved is examined further in Chapters 5 and 6.

Respect-worthy Laws

For cyberspace to be a lawful space, more is required than just legitimate authority on the part of the lawmaker. The content of the law is also crucial. This, too, must demand the respect of the cyberspace user if it is to have normative effect, and thus influence the user's behaviour.

Resistance

One way in which laws can fail to achieve such respect is where their content clashes with an already-established cyberspace norm. These conflicts tend to centre around the entrenched norm that information should be free to flow across the internet. Thus national laws which attempt to restrict those flows are often opposed by cyberspace users.

Two examples are worth considering here to illustrate the consequences of attempting to apply laws of this kind.

Our first example is export controls on encryption technology. During the cold war the US introduced controls on the export of both military and 'dual-use' technologies, the latter being those technologies which could be of use for military purposes but were also used in other fields of endeavour. Encryption technologies were included in these controls, which were extended to other parts of the Western world via the CoCom agreement.[10] At that time, any encryption which might be militarily useful required specialized hardware.

---

[8] David R Johnston and David G Post 'Law and Borders—The Rise of Law in Cyberspace' (1996) 48 Stanford LR 1376.

[9] Except where the courts are asked to enforce a foreign judgment based on principles of law which are in fundamental contradiction of the law in the country where enforcement is sought—see *Yahoo! Inc v La Ligue Contre Le Racisme Et L'Antisemitisme*, 169 F Supp 2d 1181 (ND Cal, 2001).

[10] Replaced in 1994 by the Wassenaar Arrangement which is still in operation.

Advances in computing power meant that by the early 1990s high-grade encryption had become possible using software alone. Computer scientists and academic lawyers, among others, wanted to use the internet to share their researches but were informed by those responsible for the export control regimes that doing so would be unlawful.

The reaction of cyberspace users was not one of submission to the law's demands. They saw the export control law as an intolerable interference with their freedom to communicate through cyberspace.[11] Opposition to the law took two forms. An uncoordinated campaign developed which aimed to subvert and ridicule the law. Encryption code was made available for download via websites, an activity which could not be prevented in advance but only sanctioned after it was too late to prevent the export of the code. Philip Zimmermann, the creator of the encryption software PGP which was designed for personal use, was threatened with prosecution once its source code appeared online. He responded by publishing the source code for PGP in a book,[12] which was not classified as technology and therefore fell outside the export control regime. His supporters even produced a T-shirt on which was printed a machine-readable version of the code, though they warned purchasers that the T-shirt should not be taken abroad or allowed to be seen by the wrong kind of foreigner.[13]

Others attacked the law on constitutional grounds. Daniel Bernstein, a graduate student at University of California, Berkeley, challenged the law in the US federal courts arguing that it infringed the Constitutional protections for freedom of speech. In 1999 a Federal Court of Appeals ruled that software source code was a form of protected expression, and that the export control regulations were an impermissible prior restraint on that protected speech.[14]

In addition to this overt opposition, there may have been passive resistance from businesses. During this period I advised a multinational bank on export controls, and the bank took a decision to purchase its encryption software from a country outside the CoCom/Wassenaar area so as to avoid being subject to the control regime. US sellers of encryption software must have been aware that customers were being lost, and are likely to have lobbied the US government for change.

As a consequence of these different forms of pressure the encryption export control regime was gradually relaxed, so that now there are few restrictions on the online dissemination of encryption software. The current US regime is set out in the Export Administration Regulations[15] and the other members of the Wassenaar Arrangement maintain similar regulations.

---

[11] See eg the amicus brief from EPIC and others in *Bernstein v United States Department of Justice*, Part V, <http://www.eff.org/files/filenode/bernstein/971110_epic_amicus.html>.

[12] Philip Zimmermann, *PGP Source Code and Internals* (Cambridge, Mass: MIT Press, 1995).

[13] Robert Gellmann, 'The Latest Weapon in Encryption War: A T-Shirt', *Government Computer News*, 5 February 1996, <http://gcn.com/articles/1996/02/05/the-latest-weapon-in-encryption-war-a-tshirt.aspx>.

[14] *Bernstein v United States Department of Justice*, 176 F 3d 1132 (9th Cir, 1999).

[15] 15 CFR Chapter VII(C).

For encryption controls, cyberspace norms eventually prevailed over the legal norms developed for the physical world. In our second example, the online sharing of digital music recordings, it is not yet clear which will win.

The battle over online music has been described in Chapter 1. It differs from encryption in that the relevant law is not one where a state orders particular behaviour and sanctions those who do not comply. Instead, the law grants rights to individuals, in this case the owners of copyright in music and music recordings, and provides the mechanisms through which those rights can be enforced. This explains why no resolution has yet been reached. The owners of these rights are fighting for the survival of their businesses, or at least their current business model, and are thus likely to continue until all possible avenues have been explored.

What is clear, however, is that there is no sign that the current cyberspace norm, often expressed as 'Music wants to be free',[16] is ever likely to change to comply with the law's copyright norm that sharing music recordings without permission is unlawful. The availability of online services through which music recordings can be accessed without breaching copyright, such as Apples's iTunes and the Spotify streaming service, produces ever-expanding revenue for the music industry[17] but the volume of unlawful file sharing is also increasing.[18] The cyberspace norm appears to be that sometimes music should be paid for, and sometimes it should be free. My view is that, as was the case for encryption controls, it will ultimately be necessary for the law to align itself with the social norm rather than vice versa.

These clashes between cyberspace norms and legal rules are instances of what Murray terms 'regulatory flux'.[19] He explains that there is a continuous process of communication between lawmakers and individuals (and also with the other modalities of regulation, norms, markets, and code in Lessig's terminology[20]) through which each modifies the other to produce changes in the regulatory settlement. Communication by individuals can take the form of disobedience to the law or active opposition:

In any situation there will be an extant, external regulatory settlement that controls the actions, needs or desires of the regulatee. There will also be an internal value set to which the regulatee will refer when making any decisions. The regulatee, by reference to this value set, may choose to accept, or to challenge, the regulatory settlement.[21]

Elements of that internal value set which are widely shared among cyberspace users will tend to establish norms. These may be very different from the norms which are

---

[16] See eg 'Music Wants to Be Free', *The Economist*, 7 February 2007.

[17] On a global basis, revenue from online music constituted 29% of the music industry's income in 2010, up from 25% in 2009 (IFPI, *Digital Music Report 2011*, 6).

[18] Unlawful file-sharing in Europe is estimated at 23% for 2010 (ibid, 14), up from 16% for 2008 (IFPI, *Digital Music Report 2009: Key Statistics*, <http://www.ifpi.org/content/section_resources/dmr2009.html>). Note, though, that it is not clear that the bases for calculation were identical.

[19] Andrew Murray, *The Regulation of Cyberspace* (Abingdon: Routledge-Cavendish, 2007), 25.

[20] Lawrence Lessig, *Code and Other Laws of Cyberspace* (New York: Basic Books, 1999), 85–99.

[21] Murray (n 19), 24.

generally accepted in the geographical areas where users live.[22] Lawmakers cannot simply transpose their physical world laws into cyberspace without considering whether those laws will clash with established cyberspace norms. Clashes tend to produce opposition, and those who oppose laws tend not to accept their authority.

Meaningful law

In many areas of cyberspace activity there are no entrenched social norms, and thus there is little likelihood of the kind of resistance discussed above. This does not mean, though, that a lawmaker is free to enact whatever rules it likes. For a law to be worthy of respect, its content must appear meaningful to the cyberspace user.

The history of law-making for cyberspace is full of examples of failure in this respect. For a law to be meaningful, and thus respect-worthy, it must pass a number of tests.

First, the law must be understandable, and if understood it must appear to the user to be reasonably possible to comply with its requirements.[23] It is rare that a lawmaker sets out to produce a law which cannot be understood or obeyed, but the number of laws which fail to pass this test is surprisingly large. One of the main reasons for such failure is because the lawmaker has adopted a style of law-making which attempts to enumerate the law's requirements in a precisely detailed way, partly as a response to the technically precise workings of the cyberspace technologies and partly by copying the regulatory approaches commonly used for financial services and taxation. It might appear at first sight that a law which sets out its compliance requirements in exhaustive detail would avoid uncertainty, and thus be more understandable and easier to comply with. However, as we will see in Chapter 8, there is a complex trade-off between precision of this kind and understandability, and also between compliance which furthers the law's aims and that which merely ticks the boxes set out in the legislation.

Secondly, the law must appear to be aiming at some sensible end and to have some prospect of succeeding. Failure in this respect was, in my view, the main reason for the opposition to the encryption export controls laws. Encryption software implements mathematical algorithms, normally devised by academics and published in journals and thus not secret.[24] Writing software to encrypt online communications is a complex technical task, but one clearly within the capabilities of the non-CoCom countries to whom export was forbidden. If the aim of the law was to prevent those countries having access to encryption software, its aim was pretty pointless. Additionally, the law had little or no chance of preventing the export of software, which could be transmitted online with little chance of detection and no

---

[22] See eg Murray's analysis of attitudes to indecent and obscene content in cyberspace, ibid, 205–27.

[23] '. . . law has the normative authority of obligation when—and only when—it specifies obligations of individuals that are extra-legally intelligible'. Garthoff (n 2), 681.

[24] The RSA algorithm, which is the foundation of public key cryptography, is published, and thus freely available worldwide, in RL Rivest, A Shamir, and L Adleman, 'A Method of Obtaining Digital Signatures and Public Key Cryptosystems' (1978) 21 *Communications of the ACM* 120.

real prospect of its prevention by the security services. Even the most patriotic cyberspace user found it hard to respect these laws. Much the same criticisms might be levelled at Australia's attempts to apply cinema censorship standards to internet content which, to the outside observer, looks like a hopeless attempt to turn back the tide.[25] Because what has to be achieved is respect for the law by the cyberspace community, the standards used to test the rationality of the law's aims and its likelihood of success must be those of the community, rather than the lawmaker. This perspective shift is particularly difficult for lawmakers who see their activities in terms of command and control.

Thirdly, the content of the law must be a reasonably close match to the way in which the activities which it proposes to regulate are carried out in cyberspace.[26] There are two main pitfalls here. A common source of mismatch is where the law's rules are framed in terms of physical world concepts which either have no analogue, or operate differently, in cyberspace. In those laws which were developed pre-cyberspace it is particularly common to find that the rules focus on aspects of physical property, such as ownership, possession, or copying, and use these as proxies for those activities which the law ultimately aims to control. Thus copyright law has its basis in a right to control the making of physical copies, which until only a few years ago was the only effective way of exploiting a copyright work. Cyberspace operates exclusively through the making of copies of information, though not physical copies. The mismatch is obvious, and copyright law has not yet adapted to cope. Similarly, laws based on unlawful content, such as obscenity laws, often base liability on possession of content, and face the difficulty that the concept of possession is purely metaphysical in cyberspace.

A second source of mismatch is found in those laws which make sense only in terms of a particular model of how the regulated activity will be undertaken, but where that model does not match the way in which the activity operates in cyberspace. This was perhaps to be expected in the application of those laws which were developed before the internet was widely understood, for example in defamation where the author/publisher/distributor model on which the law was based proved unsuitable for the very different way in which information was communicated online. However, a similar mismatch is often found in laws designed with cyberspace in mind, such as e-signature laws, because the lawmaker has adopted a rigid model of how the activity is likely be undertaken but the actual way in which it is carried out in cyberspace turns out to be different. This issue of embedded models of activities is particularly problematic when, as is frequently the case, both the cyberspace technologies and the business models adopted by cyberspace users evolve so rapidly.

This brings us to the final test for meaningfulness, which is that the law must be sufficiently future-proof that it can adapt to technological and business method change. The timescale for law-making is one of decades, at least, whereas the timescale for change in cyberspace is one of months, or at most years. There is a link here

---

[25] See Ch 7.
[26] See Ch 10.

to the issue of excessive precision, because the more precise and detailed a law is, the more likely that some technological change, or change in the way the regulated activity is undertaken as a result, will cause parts of the law to become meaningless, redundant, or impossible to comply with. Almost all attempts to make laws for cyberspace recognize the problem of future-proofing and claim to deal with it by adopting the concept of technology-neutrality. Unfortunately this concept is not well understood, and remarkably few of the laws which claim to be technologically neutral manage to achieve this aim.[27]

Is Cyberspace Special?

Might it be objected that lawmakers face exactly the same problems of engendering respect for their laws in the physical world? In other words, does cyberspace really present a special case?

So far as the physical world is concerned, lawmakers claim mainly to regulate those who are present in the geographical territory of their state. That geographical presence enables lawmakers to use enforcement powers against those who do not voluntarily comply with the law, and this reduces the level of respect required to make the law at least adequately effective. An example might be speed limits on roads, which are widely disrespected across the world. But because they are enforced through speed cameras, radar guns, and other means, the amount of speeding is kept down to a level which each nation finds socially acceptable. If it rises too high, extra spending on enforcement measures is likely to reduce it again. This is not so in cyberspace—even within a single territory the sheer volume of cyberspace activity, coupled with the difficulties of detection and enforcement, can mean that achieving lawful behaviour on the part of cyberspace users demands that the lawmaker either gains their respect, and thus compliance even in the absence of likely sanctions, or adopts some alternative means of practical control instead of relying on enforcement.

Where physical-world laws claim to apply extraterritorially, they apply to very few people outside the territory. No state claims to apply its physical-world laws to the majority of another state's residents. But in cyberspace the exact opposite is true for laws which apply to online activities without geographical limitation. In Korea more than 95.9 per cent of households have internet access, and in the US the figure today must be over 70 per cent.[28] Thus US laws affecting cyberspace claim to apply, potentially at least, to almost the entire Korean population, and Korean laws to over two-thirds of US residents. This scale of extraterritoriality is unprecedented. Even if we were to accept that extraterritoriality is normally only a practical problem for online businesses, the scale of the problem is merely reduced from unimaginable to huge. As an example, in 2009 a third of Australian businesses with ten or more employees purchased some of their supplies online, and nearly 60 per cent sold

---

[27] See Ch 11.
[28] OECD Key ICT Indicators 21 September 2009, <http://www.oecd.org/document/23/0,3343, en_2649_34449_33987543_1_1_1_1,00.html>. The US percentage at that date was 68.7%.

products or services online.[29] Could the US, or Korea, or any other country, expect those businesses to comply with laws they did not respect? Certainly, not even the US has the resources to enforce its laws against those Australian businesses, let alone all the other businesses in the world with an online presence.

We are thus forced to the conclusion that cyberspace is indeed special. If it is to be a lawful space, the national laws which claim to regulate it must achieve compliance through the respect of the law's subjects. No other mechanism to achieve lawfulness exists, not even regulation via code.

We therefore need a different approach to law-making for cyberspace. That approach must achieve respect for the law, and respect has two elements. First, the lawmaker must convince those to whom the law applies that it has legitimate authority to regulate their activities. This generates the potential that the law will be respected, but on its own it is not enough. Additionally, the lawmaker must consider the content of the law to ensure that it imposes obligations on cyberspace users which are meaningful in the context of their online activities.

How these can be achieved is the story set out in this book.

---

[29] Ibid, data as at July 2009. The figures for Australia were 33.3% and 58.2% respectively.

PART II

LAW-MAKING AUTHORITY

3

Extraterritoriality

Laws are invariably more effective when the issues addressed are local issues and governmental authorities are situated close by. Not only is there a much greater respect for the law when it is viewed as reflecting local realities and concerns, but local authorities who know and understand the local population have typically been able to work more effectively with their neighbours to maintain order and resolve conflicts.[1]

Imagine a world where you receive a summons from the Ruritanian prosecuting authorities, claiming that you drove your car in excess of the speed limit. You were actually driving in your home country, where the speed limit is higher, but Ruritania applies its speed limits to all driving, anywhere in the world. Your first reaction would echo that of Mr Bumble: 'the law is a ass—a idiot'.[2] You would have no respect for the Ruritanian law's claim to sanction your past behaviour, nor would you be inclined to obey it for the future.

This is very much the way that users perceived the law in the early days of modern cyberspace. Virtual drivers on the information superhighway[3] discovered that because their online activities were visible in foreign countries they were at risk of breaching the laws in those countries. Millard described the internet as the most heavily regulated environment in the world.[4]

Users of cyberspace understood, or at least thought they understood, that the law was firmly grounded in geography. Of course the laws of their state of residence applied to their activities in the physical world, and perhaps (if they thought about it at all) in the online world. But surely the laws of a foreign country, with which they recognized no connection in the physical world, could not apply to them. It seemed to be wrong in principle that mere cyber-presence in another jurisdiction was enough to trigger the application of that state's laws.[5]

---

[1] Stuart Biegel, *Beyond Our Control* (Cambridge, Mass: MIT Press, 2001), 111.

[2] Charles Dickens, *Oliver Twist* (1838), Ch 51.

[3] A common term for the internet in the 1990s. See eg Jane C Ginsburg, 'Putting Cars on the "Information Superhighway": Authors, Exploiters, and Copyright in Cyberspace' (1995) 95 Colum L Rev 1466; Henry H Perritt, *Law and the Information Superhighway* (New York: John Wiley & Sons, 1996).

[4] Christopher Millard, 'Cyberspace and the 'No Regulation' Fallacy', *Global Telecoms Business Yearbook 1995*.

[5] This is the core of the cyberliberarian argument, examined in Ch 1.

A series of judgments imposing liability under criminal laws,[6] defamation,[7] and copyright,[8] among others, soon made it clear that, wrong in principle or not, this was how laws actually worked online. There were predictions that online activities would be restricted to that subset which was lawful everywhere,[9] and that e-commerce[10] and free speech[11] would be stifled.

Of course, the apocalypse never arrived. Online actors developed risk-management strategies and states took a relaxed view about the need to enforce their laws against online activities emanating from foreign countries, except in what they saw as the most egregious cases. The swift granting of immunities to online intermediaries such as ISPs[12] was particularly helpful in avoiding conflict. Many of the earliest extraterritorial cases had been brought against intermediaries because of their local presence and apparently deep pockets, and also because a successful action against an intermediary would be likely to restrain access to the objectionable content or conduct. Once intermediaries were taken out of the equation the incidence of extraterritorial enforcement activity dropped to a level which made continued use of cyberspace practicable.

Nonetheless, it is still true today that a large proportion of national laws is potentially applicable to foreigners whose only presence in the national territory is via their activities in cyberspace. Does this amount to such legal asininity as to diminish the respect for law which would make cyberspace lawful?

Legitimate Authority and Extraterritoriality

The question arises because laws have always claimed to regulate not only activities within the geographical boundaries of a state, but also activities outside that physical jurisdiction but which nevertheless have effects, of the kind aimed at by the law, within the state territory. In the pre-globalized world the effects doctrine mainly raised issues for multinational corporations and states themselves. Individuals and smaller businesses simply did not undertake activities whose effects might be felt outside the territory where they were acting.

---

[6] eg the German prosecution of CompuServe's local managing director in respect of obscene material hosted by CompuServe USA—see Nathaniel Nash, 'Holding CompuServe Responsible', *New York Times*, 15 January 1996.

[7] *Gutnick v Dow Jones* [2001] VSC 305, [2002] HCA 56 (Australia).

[8] *Playboy Enterprises v Frena*, 839 F Supp 1552 (MD Fla, 1993).

[9] eg Llewellyn Joseph Gibbons, 'No Regulation, Government Regulation, or Self-Regulation: Social Enforcement or Social Contracting for Governance in Cyberspace' (1997) 6 Cornell JL & Pub Policy 475, 479: 'the greatest danger is the balkanization of information (content)'.

[10] See proposal for a European Parliament and Council directive on certain legal aspects of electronic commerce in the internal market, COM (1998) 586 final, 98/0325 (COD), 18 November 1998, 2.

[11] eg Eric J McCarthy, 'Networking in Cyberspace: Electronic Defamation and the Potential for International Forum Shopping' (1995) 16 U Pa J Int'l Bus L 527; Floyd Abrams, 'First Amendment Postcards from the Edge of Cyberspace' (1996) 11 St John's J Legal Comment 693.

[12] See n 48.

In today's globalized world, and especially in cyberspace, things are very different: domestic laws now commonly regulate extraterritorial conduct and transnational litigation has blossomed. No longer limited to the antitrust and commercial contexts, courts apply all sorts of public and private laws to activity occurring abroad. Academics have encouraged the trend, finding the notion that law should be tied to territory to be an archaic remnant of a preglobalized world. In an age of globalization, the argument goes, law should find national and political borders of little significance. The enactment and application of extraterritorial laws have become unexceptional.[13]

Because the effects test is of general application the lawmaker's intention as to extra-territoriality, if any, is irrelevant. The consequence is that potentially any foreign law, including laws made in the pre-cyberspace era, might apply to a cyberspace user.

Why is this problematic so far as respect for the law is concerned? The answer is twofold. First, one consequence of extraterritoriality based on effects is that it often produces disputes between states, or state legal systems. Pre-cyberspace, the most common areas of law which applied cross-border on the basis of effects were environmental laws, dealing with issues such as pollution across national boundaries,[14] and antitrust law, for example in relation to mergers and acquisitions or the trading practices of multinational companies.[15] Disputes arise where the activities in question are lawful in the state where they were undertaken but not in the state where their effects are felt, because the standards set out in the laws of the two states are different. Extraterritorial enforcement action sends a clear message that the other state's laws are inferior, and thus less worthy of respect.[16] In cyberspace, conflicts of this kind are increasingly common.

The second, and more serious, consequence is that unintended and inappropriate application of national laws to cyberspace diminishes the respect of cyberspace users for that country's laws. This is caused by the public pronouncements of courts, and by the mental state which it induces in the minds of users. Because those involved are less likely to be major corporations, and thus less worthy of the political attention which might resolve conflicts, this quiet assault on respect might continue indefinitely.

It seems clear to me that extraterritorial application of laws is rarely problematic if the laws of both states are broadly similar on the point at issue. A cyberspace actor who is engaged in behaviour which is unlawful at home can hardly complain if a foreign state, where those actions have effects, also takes objection to the activities.

---

[13] Austen Parrish, 'The Effects Test: Extraterritoriality's Fifth Business' (2008) 61 Vand LR 1455, 1456.

[14] See examples in Andrew Eckert, R Todd Smith and Henry van Egteren, 'Environmental Liability in Transboundary Harms: Law and Forum Choice' (2008) JLE&O 434.

[15] For an overview see Ronald Cass, 'Competition in Antitrust Regulation: Law beyond Limits' (2010) JCL&E 119.

[16] The economic consequences of extraterritorial enforcement raise political as well as legal issues, which may need to be resolved through international fora such as the WTO—see Nicolas F. Diebold, 'The Morals and Order Exceptions in WTO Law: Balancing the Toothless Tiger and the Undermining Mole' (2008) JIEL 43.

Where, however, the differences represent conflicting public policies, an attempt to apply national law will meet widespread resistance.

Most jurisdictions will refuse to enforce the judgments of foreign courts where the result of the foreign case is repugnant to the policy of the state where enforcement is sought. This is not limited to laws which might be said to have a public political purpose, such as laws preserving freedom of speech or, in the other direction, limiting political expression. In the private law sphere a particularly striking example is the series of US refusals to enforce English defamation judgments against US defendants relating to material which was only available in England via a defendant's website.[17]

US public policy, established in *New York Times v Sullivan*,[18] is that criticism of or commentary on public figures is an exercise of the free speech guaranteed by the First Amendment to the Constitution. For this reason a defamation action by a public figure can succeed only if the plaintiff is able to prove malice on the part of the maker of the statement, in other words either that the maker knew the statement was false or was reckless as to its truth or falsity.[19] The policy embedded in English defamation law is radically different. All a claimant need do is to prove that the statement was defamatory, and it is then for the defendant to raise defences which can include truth. This means that it is for the defendant to prove the statement was true, rather than for the claimant to prove it untrue.[20] Where public figures are claimants in an English action the *Reynolds* defence[21] permits a journalist defendant to avoid liability by proving that the publication met the standards of responsible journalism, in essence that the journalist was not negligent. In other words, in England it is for the commentator to justify his words, whereas in the US it is for the claimant to prove that the comment was unjustified and to prove this to a higher standard which, in the case of public figures, requires proof of more than mere negligence.[22] As a consequence, various US courts have refused to enforce English libel judgments as repugnant to the free-speech public policy of the US Constitution and state laws.[23]

Refusal to enforce on these grounds is not limited to defamation. In the *Yahoo! v LICRA* litigation[24] a US District Court issued a declaration that a French court order requiring Yahoo! to prevent access to Nazi materials via its auction service

---

[17] For a detailed analysis of this issue see Robert Balin, Laura Handman, and Erin Reid, 'Libel Tourism and the Duke's Manservant—an American Perspective' (2009) 3 EHRLR 303:

> under traditional principles of international comity, American courts in the past two decades have declined to grant recognition to, or to enforce, English libel judgments in the United States on the ground that they are contrary to American public policy as embodied in the First Amendment and state constitutions. [Ibid, 305]

[18] 376 US 254 (1964). *Sullivan* considered only the defamation of public officials, but its principles were extended to all public figures by *Curtis Publishing Co v Butts*, 388 US 130 (1967).

[19] *Sullivan*, ibid, 279–80.

[20] This is another point on which the policies of the US and England diverge.

[21] *Reynolds v Times Newspapers Ltd* [2001] 2 AC 127.

[22] *Sullivan* (n 18), 283–8.

[23] See eg *Bachchan v India Abroad Publications*, 585 NYS 2d 661 (NY Sup Ct, 1992); *Telnikoff v Matusevitch*, 702 A2d 230 (Md, 1997).

[24] Discussed in detail at p 44, *Irreconcilable public policies*.

would not be enforceable.[25] More recently in *Sarl Louis Feraud v Viewfinder Inc*[26] the New York Court of Appeals recognized the possibility that it might decline, on free-speech grounds, to enforce a French judgment based on copyright infringement and breach of unfair competition by means of pictures of a fashion show displayed on a website, though the case was remitted to the District Court for further fact-finding. The message from these courts is clear—foreign laws which fall short of US free-speech standards are not worthy of respect.[27]

Judicial refusal to enforce a foreign judgment as repugnant to public policy sends a strong norm-weakening message about that foreign law. The principle of comity theoretically recognizes that national law differences are inevitable and must be accepted, but refusing enforcement sends a contrary message:

> although a difference in relevant laws of the rendering and enforcing countries does not automatically make a judgment based on such laws unenforceable, it might indicate that underlying public policies vary . . . recognition and enforcement of a foreign judgment effectively endorses the foreign law that underlies the foreign judgment; such endorsement requires that the judgment not exceed the public policy limits acceptable to the enforcing country's society. Therefore, courts cannot truly separate the scrutiny of the potential effects of recognition from the content of the underlying foreign law.[28]

A clear judicial statement that a foreign law is bad, and need not be obeyed, must reduce respect for that law.

An equally clear message is contained in the title of New York's Libel Terrorism Protection Act 2008,[29] which enabled defendants to seek a declaratory judgment that a foreign defamation judgment, issued under a law which did not provide at least the same protection for free speech as both the US and New York Constitutions, should not be enforced. The more recent Federal SPEECH Act 2010[30] has a somewhat more conciliatory title, though even this (Securing the Protection of our Enduring and Established Constitutional Heritage (SPEECH) Act) makes it clear that foreign defamation laws are likely to be less worthy of respect than those of the US.

Of course, the fact that extraterritorial application of the law has the potential to weaken the respect of cyberspace users for that country's laws does not make extraterritoriality wrong as a matter of principle. Rather, I would argue that the effects on

---

[25] *Yahoo! Inc v La Ligue Contre Le Racisme Et L'Antisemitisme*, 169 F Supp 2d 1181 (ND Cal, 2001), overturned on appeal on the ground that the first instance court had no jurisdiction to hear the suit because enforcement had not yet been threatened—379 F 3d 1120 (9th Cir, 2004).

[26] 489 F 3d 474 (NY, 2007).

[27] The language of the court in *Feraud*, though otherwise appropriately restrained, was striking in its quotation from the judgment in *Sung Hwan Co v Rite Aid Corp*, 850 NE 2d 647 (NY, 2006): 'public policy inquiry rarely results in refusal to enforce a judgment unless it is inherently vicious, wicked or immoral, and shocking to the prevailing moral sense'.

[28] Marketa Trimble Landova, 'Public Policy Exception to Recognition and Enforcement of Judgments in Cases of Copyright Infringement' (2009) 40 IIC 642, 649 (references omitted).

[29] N CPLR 302, 5304, enacted in response to the judgment in *Ehrenfeld v Bin Mahfouz*, 881 NE 2d 830 (NY, 2007).

[30] 28 USC § 4101-05.

respect should not be ignored by lawmakers. Extraterritorial application should result from a conscious decision of the lawmaker, after considering its potential consequences, rather than as an accidental and unthinking outcome of the effects doctrine:

If the law is used for broader ends than are accepted as legitimate, the cost of securing conformity to the law necessarily will rise . . . When law exceeds the narrow bounds of its generally acknowledged legitimacy, more resources will be required to persuade people subject to the law that it is worth obeying, whether the investment is in the form of convincing people of the law's justice or of compelling obedience through higher sanctions for non-compliance.[31]

Masterly Inactivity?

It is, though, tempting for lawmakers to avoid the difficult analysis of the cross-border application of law to cyberspace activities. The burden of analysing the potential extraterritorial effect of new laws is not trivial. Why should not lawmakers adopt a policy of masterly inactivity, ignoring the question of global reach until it is clear that the law creates problems in cyberspace? Could these problems not be addressed at a later stage once the impact of those laws is known in detail?

Kohl points out:

States have not assumed a right to regulate foreign online activity as readily as might have been expected. Given the vast amount of online activity, the number of cases, at least reported cases, in which States have actually assumed jurisdiction over foreign online activities is astonishingly small. And there are two further aspects the above cases have in common which may explain their relative rarity. First, in all cases there seems to have been a very strong public interest in regulating the activity, so much so as to outweigh the burden imposed on the foreign provider . . . Secondly and more importantly, in all cases, the regulating State had some actual power over the foreign provider.[32]

Thus, in her view, extraterritoriality presents few difficulties for cyberspace users in practice. Nonetheless, there are strong arguments why a policy of masterly inactivity is a bad one.

An objection on legal grounds is that the public international law principle of comity requires that a state should not normally claim to apply its national laws to persons located in another state unless it has the greater interest in so doing.[33] Effects within that state do, of course, permit the state to apply its law without breaching comity. One might argue, though, that comity implies at least some minimal duty to consider the global effects of national laws, rather than just ignoring the question.

---

[31] Ronald Cass (n 15), 122.

[32] Utah Kohl, 'Eggs, Jurisdiction and the Internet' (2002) 51 ICLQ 555, 579 (references omitted).

[33] See eg Restatement (Third) of Foreign Relations Law of the United States, § 403(1) (1987). The US Supreme Court has defined comity as 'the recognition which one nation allows within its territory to the legislative, executive, or judicial acts of another nation, having due regard both to international duty and convenience, and to the rights of its own citizens or of other persons who are under the protections of its law'. *Hilton v Guyot*, 115 US 113, 163–64 (1995).

More forceful is the practical objection that extraterritoriality can lead to unwanted defensive behaviour by cyberspace actors. Because it is unclear whether their behaviour might have effects in some foreign territory, coupled with their almost certain ignorance about the details of the laws of that state (see Chapter 8), cyberspace actors may decide to manage this risk by restricting the content communicated or refusing to supply services to those located in 'problem' jurisdictions.[34]

Because of the differences between UK and English defamation law, examined above, US content providers have sought ways to reduce their liability risk without adopting English standards. Some have gone so far as to block online access from UK IP addresses.[35] If this practice became widespread, the UK would be cut off from a large part of the world's online content. Fear of this risk, together with embarrassment at the international criticism typified by the US judgments and legislation described above, has led the UK government to announce plans for major law reform to end 'libel tourism', particularly in relation to online publication.[36] At the time of writing, a bill is making its way through the UK Parliament,[37] though its reforms may still be insufficient to satisfy the US courts.[38]

Even for activities which carry little risk of defamation liability, cyberspace actors have used 'filtering' technologies and procedural means such as anti-targeting measures[39] to limit access to their websites and services by users who are located in states whose laws are unfavourable to the activity in question. It is generally accepted that global communication and trading is, by and large, a benefit to society. If actors decline to communicate or transact with persons in a particular state because of its laws, that state loses these benefits:

By hindering the speed and accessibility of the Internet, state control over high-level norms will decrease the economic and other expected benefits of participating in the Internet regime.[40]

Schultz takes the contrary view, asserting that 'Safeguarding local values is one of the foundational roles of the state, part of the national (as opposed to universal) social contract.'[41] He argues that it is legitimate for a state to pass laws which potentially apply to the online activities of foreigners because those foreigners have the ability

---

[34] Thomas Schultz, 'Carving Up the Internet: Jurisdiction, Legal Orders, and The Private/Public International Law Interface' (2008) 19 EJIL 799.

[35] 'Libel Threat to Force US Papers Out of Britain', *The Times*, 8 November 2009.

[36] 'Jack Straw Pledges Action to End Libel Tourism', *The Sunday Times*, 22 November 2009. It is likely that this will subsume the consultation on reform of the multiple publication rule, which effectively means there is no limitation period for online defamation—<http://www.justice.gov.uk/consultations/defamation-internet-consultation-paper.htm>.

[37] Defamation Bill [HL] 2010–11.

[38] Andrew R Klein, 'Some Thoughts on Libel Tourism' (2011) 38 Pepp L Rev 385, 389–90.

[39] These might include identifying the geographical location of a user's IP address and denying access to users from some jurisdictions, or requiring the user to self-identify his location and checking that matter via eg a credit card billing address.

[40] Timothy S Wu, 'Cyberspace Sovereignty?—The Internet and the International System' (1997) 10 Harvard Journal of Law & Technology 647, 659.

[41] Thomas Schultz (n 34), 806.

to undertake a de facto partitioning of their use of the internet, and can thus choose to avoid the application of the national law in question.[42]

However, by concentrating on enforcement rather than the substantive rule itself, this response ignores the negative effects of global reach on the normative value of law as a whole. Online actors who adopt a filtering and targeting strategy are deliberately setting out to avoid the application of a law, rather than to comply with it. Because the identification of all the world's national laws which might apply is impossibly difficult, a risk-management exercise must be conducted which acknowledges the likelihood of acting unlawfully in some jurisdictions but ignores it if the risk of enforcement is sufficiently low.[43] National laws with global online application often force otherwise respectable entities deliberately to act unlawfully.[44]

Finally, we need to recognize that law-making is a slow process. If a law has unintended extraterritorial effects in cyberspace which are damaging to respect for the law, the problem is unlikely to be remedied for several years. By then, the damage will have been done.

Avoiding Unintended Extraterritoriality

Thus far we have seen that states have, or at least should have, an interest in limiting the reach of their laws into cyberspace to the minimum extent compatible with their legislative aims. But is this possible? What techniques can they adopt to avoid regulating cyberspace excessively?

Aiming at convergence

If every state's laws applicable to cyberspace activities were substantially identical (in effect if not in wording) to those of other states, the difficulties addressed in this chapter would largely cease to exist. A cyberspace user which complied with its home state laws would also be very likely to be compliant with the laws of other states. If the home state enforced its laws, other states affected would have little need to do so. If it did not, there could be no real objection to another affected state's courts hearing a case, nor to the enforcement of that judgment in the home state.

The existence of cyberspace is already producing this result in some areas of law through a natural process of convergence. The desire to achieve the benefits of global

---

[42] Ibid, 808 ff.

[43] '. . . in the absence of extradition—which is unlikely to be granted with respect to the vast majority of Internet matters—a state can enforce its laws only against in-state actors, against entities with a presence on the territory of the state or with assets there' (ibid, 813).

[44] Amit M Sachdeva, 'International Jurisdiction in Cyberspace: A Comparative Perspective' (2007) 13 CTLR 245, 248:

> the cyber world . . . admits of no territory or polity based borders sufficient to impose a certain set of rules to a certain territorially defined set of persons. This leads each cyberactor to act according to his own legal order (or perhaps no legal order at all), leading to blatant violations of what may be guaranteed rights under other legal regimes.

communication and commerce which the internet brings creates an incentive for lawmakers to eradicate the differences between their own laws and those of other states. To this is added pressure from electronic commerce enterprises and influential policy organizations, who rightly see differences in national law as imposing additional costs on online activity. National governments routinely consult on proposed measures which are likely to raise cyberspace issues, and if a national law proposal differs too greatly from the laws of other states, intense lobbying is likely both at home and from abroad.

A strong driver of convergence is the example of other states' laws, which provide templates for lawmakers who are seeking to regulate a new online activity. The principles of the world's first digital-signature law, from the US State of Utah,[45] were adopted by other countries[46] and are still evident in the provisions of the EU e-Signatures Directive[47] relating to advanced electronic signatures and certification-service-providers. Similarly, the principle that internet intermediaries such as ISPs should generally be immune from liability for the content they host and carry has been adopted very widely.[48]

Convergence of laws can also be achieved through formal processes, such as international treaties or regional programmes of harmonization or approximation. The European Union provides the classic case study for harmonization, which can be effected with comparative speed because the European Treaty requires Member States to implement harmonizing measures which have passed through the legislative process. The degree to which harmonization within the EU has been successful can be seen in the single passport regime for banking and financial services[49] and the introduction in Article 3(2) of the E-Commerce Directive[50] of the general principle that online businesses established in one Member State should not be subject to regulation in another.

---

[45] Utah Digital Signature Act 1996 (Utah Code § 46-3) and Utah Digital Signature Rules (Rule 154-10 of the Utah Commerce, Corporations and Commercial Code), now pre-empted by the Federal Electronic Signatures in Global and National Commerce Act 2000 (E-Sign) 15 USC § 96.

[46] eg German Digital Signature Act (Signaturgesetz) 1997; Singapore Electronic Transactions Act 1998.

[47] Directive 1999/93/EC on a Community framework for electronic signatures, OJ L 13/12, 19 January 2000.

[48] eg Singapore Electronic Transactions Act 1998; US Communications Decency Act 1996 47 USC § 230; US Digital Millennium Copyright Act 1998 17 USC § 512; Directive 2000/31/EC on electronic commerce OJ L 178/1, 17 July 2000.

[49] Directive 2000/12/EC of the European Parliament and of the Council of 20 March 2000 relating to the taking up and pursuit of the business of credit institutions, OJ L 125/1, 26 May 2000.

[50] EU Directive 2000/31/EC on electronic commerce OJ L 178/1, 17 July 2000. See in particular recital 22: Information Society services should be supervised at the source of the activity, in order to ensure an effective protection of public interest objectives; to that end, it is necessary to ensure that the competent authority provides such protection not only for the citizens of its own country but for all Community citizens; in order to improve mutual trust between Member States, it is essential to state clearly this responsibility on the part of the Member State where the services originate; moreover, in order to effectively guarantee freedom to provide services and legal certainty for suppliers and recipients of services, such Information Society services should in principle be subject to the law of the Member State in which the service provider is established.

However, forcing convergence of national law in this way is a lengthy process, particularly for new and fast-moving areas of technology like cyberspace. Success has been achieved in a few areas[51] and calls have been made for treaties in others,[52] but there seems little prospect of an overarching international treaty on the law of cyberspace. The process of negotiating such an instrument is so lengthy a task, requiring such a wide range of political compromises, that it would be likely to require decades rather than years before it is implemented. Cyberspace evolves rather faster than this, so there is every chance that the convention would be overtaken by new technologies well before its text reached the second or third draft.

Even if the political will to begin negotiations on such a treaty existed, which is doubtful, there are two conceptual difficulties which seem insoluble. The first is that there is no consensus, even among academic commentators, about which areas of law make up the law of cyberspace. There are few areas of national law which are incapable of applying to online activities,[53] and the inclusion of many of those areas of law which are clearly relevant would be opposed by states who wish to continue to maintain their national differences.[54]

Secondly, even if these problems were bypassed by confining the treaty to an uncontroversial subset of legal areas, there remains the problem of the principle that there should be broad equivalence between online and offline laws. This policy has been adopted by a number of states,[55] and Chapter 7 will attempt to show that it has real normative importance for the law of cyberspace. If the principle is followed, a treaty on the law of cyberspace necessarily also becomes a treaty on all the national offline laws within its scope. The world is probably not yet ready for such a wide-ranging project of approximation.

This does not mean that it is pointless for lawmakers to adopt a policy that new laws should, so far as possible, converge on any international cyberspace norms which are identifiable. By doing so the lawmaker reduces the number of extraterritorial conflicts and increases the pressure on other states to converge on the norm.

---

[51] eg the Council of Europe Convention on Cybercrime, CETS No 185.

[52] See eg Kevin A Meehan, 'The Continuing Conundrum of International Internet Jurisdiction' (2008) 31 BC Int'l & Comp L Rev 345 (jurisdiction); Ken D Kumayama, 'A Right to Pseudonymity' (2009) 51 Ariz L Rev 427 (privacy); Aaron D White, 'Crossing the Electronic Border: Free Speech Protection for the International Internet' (2009) 58 DePaul L Rev 491, Michael F Sutton, 'Legislating the Tower of Babel: International Restrictions on Internet Content and the Marketplace of Ideas' (2004) 56 Fed Comm LJ 417 (free speech); Rifat Azam, 'E-Commerce Taxation and Cyberspace Law: The Integrative Adaptation Model' (2007) 12 Va JL & Tech 5 (taxation).

[53] Including unexpected areas such as real property law—see *Bragg v Linden Research*, 487 F Supp 2d 593 (ED Penn, 2007).

[54] Through the OECD, national governments have consistently maintained the position that consumption taxes should be payable in the country of consumption, irrespective of whether the supply takes place on- or offline—OECD, *International VAT/GST Guidelines* (February 2006), Ch 1, para 7; Ch 3, para 5. It seems likely also that countries such as France and Germany will wish to maintain the extraterritorial application of their hate speech laws to online speech, as exemplified in *Yahoo! Inc v LICRA*, TGI de Paris, 22 May 2000, and *Töben*, BGH 12 December 2001 1 StR 184/00 LG Mannheim (2001) 8 NJW 624.

[55] See eg Bonn Ministerial Conference Declaration of 6–8 July 1997, principle 22, <http://europa.eu.int/ISPO/bonn/Min_declaration/i_finalen.html>.

Suppose, though, that a state has good reason for departing from the converged norm, but still wishes to ensure that its new law does not have extraterritorial effect. In that case an alternative solution must be found.

Restricting a law's application to cyberspace

Drafting a law so as to limit its online application is not a simple task. It is necessary to produce a definition of those persons to whom it should apply which, at the same time, excludes online actors who are not intended to fall within the scope of the law. The solution seems to lie in identifying an appropriate link to the territory of the lawmaker. Over the years, private international law has developed a body of techniques for such localization,[56] and these can be adapted for this purpose.

As we have seen above, the effects doctrine is one such technique, but a very blunt instrument. It will always be unclear which effects in the jurisdiction will trigger the application of the law, at least until the national courts have considered the matter. Until then, uncertainty about whether the law applies to a user's cyberspace activities will produce the undesirable results explained earlier.

One drafting technique which lawmakers can use is to set out explicitly the effects which will make the law applicable. This was the approach adopted by section 21 of the UK Financial Services and Markets Act 2000, which provides that an invitation or inducement to engage in an investment activity must be either issued or approved by a person authorized under the Act. Without more, this would clearly apply to the websites of almost every financial institution in the world. Section 21(3) therefore states that the prohibition 'applies only if the communication is capable of having an effect in the United Kingdom'.

As yet there are no decisions interpreting section 21(3), but it seems likely that the website invitations of a foreign financial institution which either confines its dealings to residents of its home state or refuses to transact with UK residents would be incapable of having an effect in the UK. The concept of effect is, of course, somewhat imprecise at the margins—for example, a UK resident could evade these restrictions by giving a foreign address and transferring funds from a non-UK account—and thus this approach does not offer complete certainty as to whether the law applies.[57] Nonetheless, section 21(3) is likely to be helpful in reducing the application of this element of UK law to foreign websites.

A more exact method of localization is to frame the law by reference to the presence of persons or property in the territory. This is the approach taken in Article 3 of the New Zealand Model Code for Consumer Protection in Electronic Commerce 2000, which states:

[56] See further Chris Reed, *Internet Law: Text and Materials*, 2nd edn (Cambridge: Cambridge University Press, 2004), Ch 7; Utah Kohl, *Jurisdiction and the Internet* (Cambridge: Cambridge University Press, 2007); Julia Hörnle, 'The Jurisdictional Challenge of the Internet' in Lilian Edwards and Charlotte Waelde (eds), *Law and the Internet*, 3rd edn (Oxford: Hart Publishing, 2009), Ch 3.

[57] In any event, certainty is probably not achievable and has disadvantages of its own—see Ch 8.

The model code has been developed for businesses and/or their subsidiaries based in New Zealand, dealing with both New Zealand and overseas consumers.

This makes it clear that a business which does not have a base in New Zealand is not subject to the code. However, this form of drafting is only a partial solution to the problem of global reach, as it still leaves an overseas online business potentially subject to the statutory and case law provisions of New Zealand consumer law in its dealings with New Zealand citizens.

The same territorial approach is seen in the country of origin regime established by the EU E-Commerce Directive.[58] Under Articles 3 and 4 of the directive an information society service provider established in one Member State may not be made subject to prior authorization under the laws of another Member State in order to do online business there, and the law applicable to its establishment and conduct of business is the law of its home state. The country of reception law continues to apply, however, to contracts with consumers in that state and to a limited subset of activities for which prior authorization might still be required.[59] Establishment means that an enterprise has the use of fixed premises or equipment in the state, and also staff who undertake business transactions with customers in the state, and this provides the territorial link.[60]

However, the directive only solves the global-reach problem on a regional basis, as Articles 3 and 4 apply only to intra-EU online activities. A non-EU e-commerce business will still potentially be subject (at a minimum) to the national laws of every EU Member State with whose residents it does business.

Regulating by reference to the use of property which is physically located in the territory is an equally precise way of delimiting the law's reach. This is the approach recommended by the Commentary to Article 5 of the Organisation for Economic Co-operation and Development (OECD) Model Convention with respect to Taxes on Income and on Capital, which suggests that exclusive (but not shared) use of a server should constitute a permanent establishment. Under Article 7 business income is to be taxed if it arises from a permanent establishment in a state, and the concept is defined in Article 5 by reference to physical location of property or persons.

The UK government has applied this principle to the licensing of online gambling. Section 33 of the Gambling Act 2005 requires a person who provides facilities for gambling to be licensed, but section 36(3) disapplies this obligation unless at least one piece of remote gambling equipment is situated in Great Britain, excluding equipment not supplied by the gambling operator such as the user's own computer.[61]

---

[58] Directive 2000/31/EC on electronic commerce OJ L 178/1, 17 July 2000.

[59] These are set out in the Annex to the directive. It is worth noting that much of the non-sector-specific consumer protection law has been harmonized within the EU, and good progress is being made in sector-specific harmonization (see in particular Directive 2002/65/EC of 23 September 2002 concerning the distance marketing of consumer financial services, OJ L271 p 16, 9 October 2002, harmonizing the consumer protection law for financial services consumers), so that in practice the differences in national laws relating to consumer contracts will become increasingly minor and thus less of a barrier to online commerce.

[60] *Somafer SA v Saar-Ferngas AG*, Case 33/78 [1978] ECR 2183.

[61] s 36(5).

However, those other provisions of the Act which do not relate to licensing can still apply to foreign gambling websites, as do many other provisions of UK gambling law.[62]

A final localization technique is to disapply the law to residents of a specified list of countries. This is the second element of the E-Commerce Directive country of origin scheme, which works by disapplying local regulation to information society service providers established in any other Member State. A similar effect is produced by mutual recognition schemes, such as that for the qualification of providers of electronic signature identity certificates in Article 7 of the EU e-Signatures Directive.[63] This type of 'white-list' approach has also been used in the UK Gambling Act 2005 in respect of advertising controls,[64] though without any formal requirement for there to be mutual recognition of the UK licensing regime by those countries in respect of advertising by UK gambling operators.

Selective enforcement

Earlier in this chapter we saw that the refusal by a court to enforce a foreign judgment because the law involved is repugnant to domestic public policy makes a statement that the foreign law is not respect-worthy. The position is very different, however, if a country refuses to enforce its *own* law against a foreign cyberspace actor. The statement here is not that the law is unworthy of respect by persons generally, but rather that the foreign actor is *not obliged* to respect it in the particular circumstances. In other words, although the law applies in theory to the foreign actor, in practice the state has informed the actor that it can be ignored.

One way in which this can be achieved is through a general principle of national law which defines when a law which, on its wording, applies to a foreign actor, will not be enforced against that person. The best-known example is probably the Due Process provisions of the US Constitution, set out in the Fifth and Fourteenth Amendments. In a long line of jurisprudence originating in the Supreme Court decision in *International Shoe Co v Washington*,[65] these have been interpreted as meaning that it is not permissible for a non-resident defendant to be subject to judicial proceedings unless there is a sufficient connection between the defendant and the jurisdiction (often described as the 'minimum contacts' doctrine). As explained in *CompuServe v Patterson*:[66]

This court has repeatedly employed three criteria to make this determination: First, the defendant must purposefully avail himself of the privilege of acting in the forum state or causing a consequence in the forum state. Second, the cause of action must arise from the defendant's activities there. Finally, the acts of the defendant or consequences caused by the

---

[62] See further Julia Hörnle and Brigitte Zamitt, *Cross-border Online Gambling Law and Policy* (Cheltenham: Edward Elgar, 2010), Ch 3.
[63] Directive 1999/93/EC on a Community framework for electronic signatures OJ L13/12, 19 January 2000.
[64] s 331(1) and (4).
[65] 326 US 310 (1945).
[66] 89 F 3d 1257 (6th Cir, 1996).

defendant must have a substantial enough connection with the forum to make the exercise of jurisdiction over the defendant reasonable.

In the online context, *Zippo Mfg Co v Zippo Dot Com Inc*[67] identified a continuum between 'passive' websites, which are merely visible within the jurisdiction, and 'active' websites which solicit dealings with persons in the jurisdiction. At some fact-dependent point along this continuum, the defendant website owner has sufficient minimum contacts with the jurisdiction to allow the courts to assert jurisdiction.[68]

This type of rule does not provide the 'bright-line' certainty which cyberspace users would prefer.[69] However, it does enable them to make a reasoned risk assessment as to whether they may be subject to US court proceedings. The rule does not completely solve the problem of extraterritorial application of US federal and state laws, but it does reduce the difficulties to a potentially manageable level.

This concept of targeting has been adopted elsewhere, though not normally as a general jurisdictional rule. However, in the EU countries the question whether there is jurisdiction over a dispute arising from a consumer contract is determined by whether the business party targeted sales to the consumer's country.[70] Similarly, the UK courts have decided that a trade mark on a website is only used in the UK, use being the main ingredient for infringement of UK trade mark law, if the website targets UK customers.[71]

Where no such general rule of law exists, it is still possible to achieve a similar effect by announcing a state's enforcement policy in respect of particular laws whose cross-border application is known to be problematic. This is a well-recognized issue in the regulation of financial services advertising. Most countries provide that it is unlawful, and usually a criminal offence, to advertise financial products in their territory unless the advertiser is a regulated person in the jurisdiction or the advertisement is approved by a regulated person.[72] Strictly applied, rules of this kind would potentially subject all financial institutions with a website to criminal liability somewhere in the world.

---

[67] 952 F Supp 1119 (WD Pa, 1997).

[68] For an more detailed explanation of the US approach to jurisdiction and an examination of the post-*Zippo* jurisprudence see Brian D Boone, 'Bullseye!: Why a 'Targeting' Approach to Personal Jurisdiction in the E-Commerce Context Makes Sense Internationally' (2006) 20 Emory Int'l L Rev 241.

[69] Cf the very different approach to jurisdiction in the EU Council Regulation (EC) 44/201 on jurisdiction and the recognition and enforcement of judgments in civil and commercial matters, OJ L12/1, 16 January 2001 (Brussels Regulation), though it should be noted that the apparent certainty of the tests for jurisdiction is largely illusory—see Julia Hörnle, 'The Jurisdictional Challenge of the Internet' in Lilian Edwards and Charlotte Waelde (eds), *Law and the Internet*, 3rd edn (Oxford: Hart Publishing, 2009), Ch 3.

[70] Brussels Regulation (n 69), Art 15(1)(c).

[71] *Euromarket Designs Inc v Peters* [2000] EWHC (Ch) 453; *L'Oreal SA v eBay International AG* [2009] EWHC 1094 (Ch).

[72] See eg UK Financial Services and Markets Act 2000, s 21.

A 1998 report from IOSCO, the International Organization of Securities Commissioners, made recommendations to reduce the scope of this problem,[73] and a review of the implementation of these recommendations in 2001 found that the majority of the nineteen jurisdictions reviewed had issued guidance based on the recommendations:[74]

The recommendation suggested that the assertion of regulatory jurisdiction (ie, the imposition of licensing, registration, reposting and other requirements) be predicated on . . . (2) the offer of securities or services having a significant effect upon residents or markets in a regulator's jurisdiction. In determining whether the offer meets the second test, regulators were to consider whether, among other things,

- the offer targets residents of the regulator's jurisdiction;
- the offeror accepts orders from or provides services to residents of the regulator's jurisdiction; and
- the offeror uses e-mail or other media to 'push' the information to residents of the regulator's jurisdiction.

Conversely, regulators could find the second test was not met if, among other things,

- the offeror clearly states to whom the Internet offer is directed, rather than appearing to extend the offer into any jurisdiction;
- the offeror provides a statement on its website listing the jurisdictions in which it is (or is not) authorized to offer or sell its securities or services; or
- the offeror takes precautions that are reasonably designed to prevent sales to residents in the regulator's jurisdiction (eg, screening addresses and other residency information of respondents).

The US followed the 1998 recommendations very closely,[75] focusing on whether the US had been targeted by the financial advertisement. It also provided further comfort to foreign financial institutions by stating that the test which would be applied was whether the precautions taken to avoid selling to US persons were adequate, rather than whether they were completely effective, so that a failure of those precautions would not automatically subject the foreign institution to US law and regulation.[76]

---

[73] IOSCO, Securities Activities on the Internet (IOSCO, 1998):

14. Regulators should provide guidance on the circumstances under which they will exercise regulatory authority over Internet offers.

15. If an issuer's or financial service provider's offer or sales activities over the Internet occur within a regulator's jurisdiction, or if the issuer's or financial service provider's offshore activities, in fact, have a significant effect upon residents or markets in the regulator's jurisdiction, a regulator may impose its regulatory requirements (eg, licensing and registration requirements) on such activities.

[74] IOSCO, Securities Activities on the Internet II (IOSCO, 2001), 5.

[75] Securities and Exchange Commission, Statement of the Commission Regarding Use of Internet Web Sites to Offer Securities, Solicit Securities Transactions or Advertise Investment Services Offshore (Release Nos 33-7516, 34-39779, IA-1710, IC-23071, International Series Release No 1125) 23 March 1998.

[76] Ibid, part III.C:

In our view, if a US person purchases securities or investment services notwithstanding adequate procedures reasonably designed to prevent the purchase, we would not view the Internet offer after the fact as having been targeted at the United States, absent indications

By contrast, the UK implementation of the recommendations concentrated on how effectively the advertiser had prevented UK residents from seeing the advertisement or responding to it.[77]

Whether enforcement is restricted by rules of law or by policy guidance, there seems to be a consensus that the relevant test for when a law should be enforced is whether a foreign online actor is targeting the jurisdiction. This can be helpful to an online actor which is aware of potential liabilities abroad and wishes to take steps to avoid them. Outside heavily regulated sectors such as financial services, however, cyberspace users have little knowledge of the cross-border risks created by extraterritoriality of law, and online actors may never have considered whom they intend to target. Selective enforcement policies will be of little guidance to them.

Irreconcilable Public Policies

Where the public policies of two states are in fundamental conflict, it is only possible to resolve the clash either by limiting the law's application to cyberspace or by one or other of the states changing its policy. The clash between English and US defamation law is the result of such a fundamental conflict, and the resolution attempted by the 2010/11 bill in the UK adopts both routes. Extraterritorial reach will be limited by adopting a form of single publication rule, which will prevent each access to a website amounting to a fresh publication and thus restarting the limitation period for actions. Stronger protections for free speech will also be embedded in the law, so that a claim against a defendant who is reporting or commenting on a matter of public interest will need to prove that the publication was irresponsible. These changes, if enacted, will not merely result from the political and commercial pressures resulting from the clash with US law. They also reflect changes in UK society, such that the norms embodied in the current defamation law are now seen as inappropriate domestically, as well as in cyberspace. The proper balance between claimant and defendant in defamation litigation does not help define Englishness, which thus makes it possible for the balance to be adjusted.

In some instances, though, public policies are so deeply entrenched that 'surrender' by one country or the other is impossible. The classic example is the series of court proceedings arising from Yahoo!'s online auction service, through which offers to sell Nazi memorabilia were visible to internet users in France.

> that would put the issuer on notice that the purchaser was a US person . . . Additionally, if despite its use of measures that appear to be reasonably designed to prevent sales to US persons, the offeror discovers that it has sold to US persons, it may need to evaluate whether other measures may be necessary to provide reasonable assurance against future sales to US persons.

[77] Financial Services Authority, *Treatment of Material on Overseas Internet World Wide Web Sites Accessible in the UK but Not Intended for Investors in the UK*, Guidance 2/98. This guidance was issued under the Financial Services Act 1986, whose provisions relating to advertising were rather different from those in the Financial Services and Markets Act 2000 which replaced it (see the discussion of s 21(3) above). The guidance has not been withdrawn, and so it may still be helpful in deciding under s 21 whether an online advertisement is capable of having an effect in the UK.

The dispute began when Yahoo! Inc, a US corporation with no assets or staff in France, was sued in the French courts by anti-Nazi groups who alleged Yahoo! had contravened the French laws prohibiting the promotion of Nazism. Liability under those laws was based on publication in France. The court found that the auction site was accessible in France, and therefore held that Yahoo! was in breach. It granted an interim injunction which required Yahoo! to take 'all necessary measures . . . to make impossible' access by French residents to that material.[78] The court was unimpressed by the argument that French customers were served primarily by a French subsidiary, Yahoo.fr, and rejected the argument that Yahoo! Inc's auction site activities took place only in California where the servers were located.

At the hearing to confirm the interim injunction Yahoo! Inc again lost. The French court rejected the assertion that it was impossible to comply with the injunction, accepting expert evidence that filtering on IP addresses combined with other measures would be sufficient to prevent between 70 and 80 per cent of French residents from viewing auctions for Nazi memorabilia, and thus held that Yahoo! could achieve substantial compliance with the injunction.[79]

Yahoo!'s next step was to seek a declaration from a Californian court that the French judgment should not be enforced within the USA as such enforcement would contravene the free-speech provisions of the First Amendment to the US Constitution.[80] The judgment of the court, granting the declaration, set out the conflict between US and French law as follows:

> In a world in which ideas and information transcend borders and the Internet in particular renders the physical distance between speaker and audience virtually meaningless, the implications of this question go far beyond the facts of this case . . . The government and people of France have made a different judgment based upon their own experience. In undertaking its inquiry as to the proper application of the laws of the United States, the Court intends no disrespect for that judgment or for the experience that has informed it.[81]
>
> . . .
>
> What makes this case uniquely challenging is that the Internet in effect allows one to speak in more than one place at the same time. Although France has the sovereign right to regulate what speech is permissible in France, this Court may not enforce a foreign order that violates the protections of the United States Constitution by chilling protected speech that occurs simultaneously within our borders.[82]

This declaratory judgment was overturned on appeal on the grounds that the District Court had no jurisdiction to hear the case because enforcement in the US had not been threatened, though without commenting on the merits of the decision.[83] Yahoo! Inc then resolved the civil litigation by banning the sale of Nazi-related material on its auction sites.

---

[78] *Yahoo! Inc v LICRA*, TGI de Paris, 22 May 2000.
[79] *Yahoo! Inc v LICRA*, TGI de Paris, 20 November 2000.
[80] *Yahoo! Inc v La Ligue Contre Le Racisme Et L'Antisemitisme*, 169 F Supp 2d 1181 (ND Cal, 2001).
[81] Ibid, 1186.
[82] Ibid, 1192.
[83] 379 F 3d 1120 (9th Cir, 2004).

However, this was not the end of the matter. While the appeal in the US was pending, Timothy Koogle, former chairman and chief executive of Yahoo Inc, was pursued in France for the offence of justifying war crimes. His challenge to jurisdiction was rejected by the French court, which noted in its judgment that the Californian declaration recognized the applicability of French law to web pages visible in France.[84] At the subsequent hearing on the merits, however, Mr Koogle was acquitted because he had no personal knowledge of the Nazi material nor control over its offering for sale, and neither he nor Yahoo! Inc had attempted to justify war crimes or crimes against humanity.[85]

This type of aggressive extraterritorial enforcement tends to occur when there is a major disparity between the public policies of the states in question. Thus, as a further example, US states and the federal government have for many years sought to bring actions against online gambling companies established outside the US,[86] and Antigua has succeeded in World Trade Organization dispute proceedings against the US resulting from those actions.[87] Similarly, Germany has enforced its obscenity and anti-Nazi laws against foreign online actors.[88]

There are other areas of controversy, including political speech and the promotion or denigration of religion, where the gulf between states is so wide that we can expect similar cases to occur. Because the policies in question are fundamental to the societies in question, restricting their applicability to cyberspace is unlikely. This would amount to acceptance that the policy is defective. States have a right to adopt policies which clash with those of other states unless they have voluntarily constrained their actions by, for example, entering into treaty obligations. It is even arguable that, in a small number of areas, they might have a moral duty to adopt such policies, perhaps arising from their history as in the case of the anti-Nazi laws of much of Continental Europe.

The solution, if any, lies in the gradual convergence of norms. Cyberspace plays an important role here. National laws which are more restrictive than those of other countries may seem unexceptionable, when viewed from a purely domestic perspective, because things have always been so. But cyberspace users are exposed to the wider, global perspective, which informs them that their activities can be ordered differently. It is worth noting that a great number of anomalous national restrictions on communication, both private and commercial, have been abandoned in recent years.[89] Cyberspace is not the sole cause, but it has played an important part.

---

[84] *Timothy K v Amicale des Déportees d'Auschwitz et des Camps de Haut Silesie*, TGI de Paris, 26 February 2002.

[85] Report at <http://www.out-law.com/page-3319>.

[86] See Julia Hörnle and Brigitte Zamitt, *Cross-border Online Gambling Law and Policy* (Cheltenham: Edward Elgar, 2010), Ch 3.

[87] WTO Dispute DS 285, *Antigua & Barbuda v United States—Measures Affecting the Cross-Border Supply of Gambling and Betting Services*.

[88] As examples, the CompuServe prosecution for obscenity (n 6 above); *Töben* BGH 12 December 2001 1 StR 184/00 LG Mannheim (2001) 8 NJW 624 (enforcement of anti-Nazi laws against Australian defendant).

[89] We have already seen the effects on English defamation law in this chapter, and on US export controls in Ch 2. Examples from other countries might include the replacement of controls on commercial advertising in Germany's unfair competition law.

Making Choices

All the solutions to the problem of extraterritoriality have a common factor. States *could* legitimately enforce their laws against foreign internet activities, but choose not to do so. That choice can be implemented in different ways, most commonly either by defining the scope of the law to exclude foreign defendants or by announcing an enforcement policy which enables online actors to modify their behaviour so as to avoid proceedings under the law. However, such a choice will only be made if states feel it to be justifiable.

By choosing not to apply or enforce its own laws, a state of reception is leaving the regulation of the online activity in question to be managed by the cyberspace user's home state. This requires a degree of confidence that the standards of the home state, though different, are still adequate to protect the interests which the reception state's law seeks to protect. Such confidence is more likely if the relevant laws of the two countries are broadly similar, and this explains why the phenomenon tends to be seen where convergence, approximation, or harmonization have reduced national law differences. We should note, however, that there also needs to be a high level of trust that the home state will enforce those standards, particularly if the effects of the online actor's conduct are felt only in the state of reception.

The normative force of the home state's laws also plays an important part in this choice. If those laws are generally obeyed by its residents, other states will have increased confidence that the standards will be adhered to and that there will be little need to seek enforcement action by the home state. By contrast, enforcement of a state's laws against a foreign online actor makes a negative statement about the laws of the actor's home state, thereby reducing respect for those laws, in just the same way as does a refusal to enforce a foreign judgment on public policy grounds.

States need to recognize that applying their laws extraterritorially has adverse consequences. The most important of these are the negative effects on cyberspace users' respect for the law. These negative effects can be avoided, or at least mitigated, if national lawmakers attempt to make laws whose reach into cyberspace is understood and properly limited.

Because cyberspace is a global phenomenon with no respect for national boundaries, a state which wishes to benefit from unfettered access to cyberspace cannot afford to apply its laws extraterritorially as a general rule. The mantra 'Think Global, Act Local'[90] has a clear relevance for contemporary lawmakers. National laws which differ significantly from those of other states, particularly if those laws are to be enforced against online actors, require the lawmaker to consider their global as well as their local consequences.

---

[90] Thought to have originated in the field of urban planning (see Walter Stephen (ed), *Think Global, Act Local: The Life and Legacy of Patrick Geddes* (Edinburgh: Luath Press, 2004)) but perhaps better known as a slogan from environmentalism (see the obituary of David Brower, founder of Friends of the Earth, *Daily Telegraph*, 8 November 2000).

4

Enforcing Law in Cyberspace

Some readers may still hold the view that law can operate as a system of control. One purpose of this chapter is to convince them that, even if they are right about law in the physical world, their view cannot be true for cyberspace. If law works by controlling individuals, and thus coerces them to alter their behaviour, it follows that any failure to enforce the law reduces the amount of coercion and thus weakens law's control. At some low level of enforcement the law ceases to exert any effective control at all, so that any compliance with it must necessarily be due to some other reason. I shall try to demonstrate that the difficulties of enforcement in cyberspace make it impossible, in practice if not in theory, to achieve that minimum level which would make control a plausible explanation.

The enforcement of a law also plays an important role in engendering respect for that law. If a state consistently fails to enforce a law it sends a message to the law's subjects that the state does not expect them to obey it. This diminishes their respect for that law, often to such an extent that any subsequent attempt to enforce it produces outrage and opposition.[1] Some jurisdictions recognize this as a problem and allow the courts to deny enforcement of such laws on the ground that they have fallen into desuetude.[2]

Where a state wishes to enforce a law but is unable to do so in any consistent and effective way, the message is rather different but equally damaging to respect. Here the state desires that its commands should be obeyed, but is impotent to force individuals to do so. This weakens respect not merely for the particular law but for *all* that state's laws. Power may command respect, but an impotent lawmaker loses all authority.

These problems are not confined to laws which need to be enforced by state authorities. Laws conferring private rights also need respect, and inability by the right-holder to enforce those rights produces the same effects on individuals. We have already noted some of the difficulties faced by copyright proprietors in asserting their rights against cyberspace users, and those issues will be explored further below.

---

[1] A recent, well-known example is the attempt by various US state prosecutors to use antiquated sodomy laws to prosecute for acts of consensual sexual behaviour in private. See Cass R Sunstein, 'What Did Lawrence Hold? Of Autonomy, Desuetude, Sexuality, and Marriage' (2004) Supreme Court Review 27.

[2] For a summary of the US approach see Erik Encarnación, 'Desuetude-based Severability: A New Approach to Old Morals Legislation' (2005) 39 Colum JL & Soc Probs, 149, 152–64.

Enforcement against Individuals

Let us start by examining the difficulties faced in a single attempt to enforce a law against one individual cyberspace user. These difficulties have been analysed extensively by others,[3] and so only a brief account will be given here.

Identification

The first difficulty is one of identification. Most obviously, the identity of the person against whom enforcement is sought needs to be discovered.[4] This is not an easy task. Cyberspace communications are identified primarily by the IP addresses of the communicator and recipient, and any other identifying information is either self-provided or available only from providers of communication services, such as ISPs offering connectivity and/or hosting services. As Lessig has pointed out:

> The absence of self-authenticating facts in cyberspace reduces its regulability. If a state, for example, wants to regulate obscenity or control children's access to 'indecent' speech, the Internet architecture provides no help. Both data and people are unidentified in this world, and while it is often possible to make good guesses, it is also easy to make good guesses impossible.[5]

The problems are most easily understood by working through two hypothetical examples.

First, let us imagine a posting on a discussion board which incites racial hatred, contrary to the UK's criminal law. The UK law enforcement authorities cannot take action against the poster until they discover who he or she is, and his or her geographical location. The posting itself is unlikely to contain these details, as discussion-board users are normally asked to invent a user name to identify their postings. This person posts as 'KuKluxMan'.

Initially the authorities will consider contacting the discussion board administrator. If the board focuses on some legitimate area of discussion then contacting the administrator via the board itself might well produce a helpful response. If, however, the board is aimed at fostering racist discussion, the authorities will suspect that the administrator is likely to want to help hide the identity of the poster, and will thus not respond or will destroy evidence. In this case they need to approach the internet service provider (ISP) which hosts the board and ask for identifying details of the board administrator—it is unlikely that the ISP holds any information which will help to identify KuKluxMan. These details may be as scanty as the administrator's

---

[3] On identification see Terrence Berg, 'www.wildwest.gov: The Impact of the Internet on State Power to Enforce the Law' (2000) BYU L Rev 1305, 1357–8. The cross-border problems are analysed at length in Utah Kohl, *Jurisdiction and the Internet* (Cambridge: Cambridge University Press, 2007).

[4] Some jurisdictions permit claims to be made against unidentified defendants if the identity of the defendant cannot be discovered, but even so a judgment cannot be enforced until identity is known. The normal reason for such litigation is to establish the claimant's rights for use in negotiations with or claims against third parties.

[5] Lawrence Lessig, *Code and Other Laws of Cyberspace* (New York: Basic Books, 1999), 33.

email address and payment card details, so the law enforcement authorities will need to seek further identification from the email service provider or the payment provider.

Once this information about the board administrator is discovered, he or she needs to be persuaded, or perhaps coerced via a warrant, summons or court order,[6] to disclose such identification information about KuKluxMan as exists. This too might be no more than an email address and the IP address from which the posting was made to the board. The email address may or may not link to a physical world identity—for example, both Hotmail and Gmail rely purely on self-identification when an account is created, and have no system for checking whether the identity provided is a true one. The IP address used when posting may[7] link to an identifiable ISP, in which case that ISP can be persuaded or compelled to identify the account holder who used that address, though if there are multiple users of the account (for example family members or visitors) this still does not resolve to an identifiable individual.

Alternatively the authorities may decide to use covert surveillance of the discussion board in order to discover information which will enable them to identify KuKluxMan. This will only be undertaken if it is likely to be impossible to discover this information from the board administrator or the service providers involved, and is subject to quite onerous requirements which safeguard civil liberties.[8]

We can already see that compared with a similar incitement to racial hatred made at, say, a public meeting, the single task of identifying the maker of the statement imposes a far greater burden of effort on law enforcement authorities. And this example assumes that all those involved—the board administrator, hosting ISP, communications ISP, and KuKluxMan himself—are located in the UK. If one or more of them are situated elsewhere identification becomes many times more difficult, and might even be impossible.[9]

In addition to the identity of the person against whom enforcement is sought, the authorities will also need to identify the necessary evidence and its location. This will present exactly the same kinds of difficulties explained above.

As a second example we will examine the enforcement of a private law right. Let us suppose that the owner of the rights in a musical recording is concerned that the recording is being distributed via a peer-to-peer (P2P) network such as Gnutella. To identify those who are making files available, the rights owner will install Gnutella client software and then use that software to make downloads from other users. Once it finds a user whose software is offering the music file in which it owns the rights, it can download the file from that user and thereby discover the IP address of the user.[10]

---

[6] See Ian Walden, *Computer Crimes and Digital Investigations* (Oxford: Oxford University Press, 2007), 234–75.

[7] A poster determined to hide his identity will use an anonymous web surfing service such as that offered by anonymouse.org (a Seychelles organization).

[8] Ian Walden (n 6), 214–34.

[9] Ibid, 310–28.

[10] Because of the way that P2P networks operate, the sole identifying information will be this IP address. See Peter Biddle, Paul England, Marcus Peinado, and Bryan Willman, 'The Darknet and the Future of Content Protection' in Joan Feigenbaum (ed), *Digital Rights Management 2002* (Berlin: Springer-Verlag, 2003) 155–76.

From this the ISP can be identified, and then the rights owner can seek to compel the ISP to identify the user account. Because this is a civil rather than a criminal matter the ISP is unlikely to disclose this information without being ordered to do so by a court, unless there is legislation which requires the ISP to do so on receipt of mere notice.[11]

We can see in both of these examples that the difficulties faced by those trying to enforce the law are caused by the fact that the identity of cyberspace users is not discoverable directly from their communication activities. The information which can identify them resides in the hands of third parties, and in particular the ISPs who provide those users with access to cyberspace. Because these ISPs owe obligations to their subscribers under confidentiality, privacy, and data protection laws, in almost every case the enforcer will need to undertake the burden of securing court orders or search warrants to extract this information. This is a stark contrast to the physical world, where the identity of the person against whom enforcement is sought can often be discovered without needing to go to such lengths.

Cross-border issues

Because cyberspace is a global medium, it is likely that many of the communications which are unlawful will originate from outside the state whose law is at issue. Enforcement of laws cross-border is substantially more difficult than doing so internally.

Enforcement will, of course, only be possible if the law in question actually applies to the foreign cyberspace user's activities. This is often a difficult question to answer because it depends on where, geographically, the act which triggers the application of the law took place. For any cyberspace communication there are at least two possibilities; the place where the sender was located and the place where the communication was received.[12] Unless the text of the law makes it clear where a cyberspace communication occurs, an attempt to enforce the law is likely to result in an expensive test case.

If we return to our examples above, we see that KuKluxMan's posting inciting racial hatred could have amounted to the criminal offence of publishing or distributing material which is intended or likely to stir up racial hatred.[13] This publication or distribution might be treated by the law as occurring at KuKluxMan's location when he posted, at the server which hosts the discussion board, anywhere it was read, or of course all of these. The case of the infringing music file is simpler from the point

---

[11] The UK Digital Economy Act 2010, not yet in force, contains provisions allowing a rights owner to report the IP address of a suspected infringer to an ISP, who is then required to notify the subscriber of the report. The Act contains provisions, which will only be implemented if this system fails to reduce infringement, to require the ISP to implement technical sanctions such as bandwidth throttling or suspension of access. The ISP is obliged not to reveal the identity of the suspected infringer (Communications Act 2003, s 124B, inserted by the Digital Economy Act), so to discover this information and bring enforcement action the rights owner will still need to secure a court order (s 3(8)(c)).

[12] Further possibilities include the locations of any servers operated by intermediaries.

[13] UK Public Order Act 1986, s 19.

of view of location, as P2P networks do not make use of intermediary servers (other than for mere transport of packets). However, copyright law offers a number of choices for enforcement all of which are problematic. The user certainly copied the file, but in his home country not in the country where enforcement is sought, and so has not infringed by copying in the country of enforcement. Did making the file available for downloading amount to secondary infringement by way of incitement or authorization, and if so where did the incitement or authorization occur? If neither of these were demonstrably committed in the country of enforcement, the user has still committed the infringing act of communicating the file to the public, but again the location where this happened is uncertain.

Assuming the enforcer of the law is satisfied that the law applies, the next step is identification of the foreign user. This ceases to be a matter of the national law in question but falls under the law of the user's home state. We have already noted that the user's ISP is likely to be the main source of identity information, and thus any court orders or warrants will need to be served and complied with in the ISP's home state. It is unlikely that a foreign ISP will comply voluntarily with a court order or warrant issued in the enforcer's state, and so these will need to be obtained under the foreign law in question. The courts of that state may well refuse to issue these, particularly if the conduct complained of is not contrary to their domestic law.[14]

Once identified, the user needs to be brought before the courts of the state of enforcement. In civil claims a writ or summons needs to be served outside the jurisdiction with the court's permission, and this imposes an additional cost burden. For criminal matters the user may need to be extradited from his home country to the country of enforcement, and this will only be possible if the offence is sufficiently serious and there is an extradition treaty between those countries. Walden notes that 'Extradition is a complex and often lengthy process, involving, at least in common law jurisdictions, both judicial and executive decision taking',[15] and also that most countries are unwilling to extradite their own nationals.[16]

Once before the court, the user may be able to raise valid objections to the court's jurisdiction over his activities. For our copyright example this is often the same question as the applicability of the law—the user will only have infringed if he committed infringing acts in the territory of the jurisdiction,[17] and the commission of those acts in the territory will permit the court to take jurisdiction. However, national rules of law may limit jurisdiction even here. For example, the US 'minimum contacts' test for taking jurisdiction over an out-of-state resident usually requires evidence of more than a single infringing act.[18] The incitement case is more difficult because jurisdiction may depend on the effects of the actor's conduct in the jurisdiction. This will depend on how the offence is defined by national law[19] and thus reopens

---

[14] Berg (n 3), 1353.

[15] Ian Walden (n 6), 326.

[16] Ibid, 327.

[17] Because of the territorial principle of copyright law, established in the Berne Convention, Art 5.

[18] See Ted Solley, 'The Problem and the Solution: Using the Internet to Resolve Internet Copyright Disputes' (2008) 24 Ga St U L Rev 813.

[19] Utah Kohl (n 3), 91.

the metaphysical discussion above about the geographical location of cyberspace communications.

Finally there is the question of implementing the judgment of the court. If KuKluxMan has been extradited this will present no difficulties as he is in the jurisdiction. If he has been tried in his absence, it is unlikely that the law of his home country will implement the punishment, for example by enforcing an order to pay a fine, so that the conviction will be largely symbolic. If our copyright owner obtains an injunction and an award of damages against the infringing cyberspace user, there is an additional cost of seeking to enforce that award in the infringer's home courts and a real likelihood that enforcement will be refused.[20]

Enforcement at the Macro Level

When viewed at the level of individual cases it is clear that the problems of enforcement can probably be overcome, as against domestic defendants at least, provided sufficient resources are devoted to the case. Cross-border enforcement will of course always be more problematic and substantially more expensive.

However, this perspective is not the appropriate one when considering the matter of cyberspace. A single act of enforcement is no more than symbolic; it makes a statement that the law *could* be enforced more widely, but not that it will or is likely to be. If control is to be achieved through enforcement then the law must be enforced at least to the level that the prospect of further enforcement influences the behaviour of cyberspace users. Is that level of enforcement achievable? To answer this question we need to examine the problem at the macro scale, not that of the individual.

Goldsmith and Wu, arguing from the perspective of law as a system of control, cite the economics work of Becker.[21] Becker's argument is that criminals behave rationally in economic terms, and thus the potential cost of lawbreaking,[22] discounted in accordance with the risk of detection and conviction,[23] needs to be high enough that behaving lawfully is more rational than breaking the law. If enforcement rates are low, the cost of lawbreaking can be raised by increasing the penalties imposed on those actually convicted of crimes.[24] However, as Goldsmith and Wu point out, 'there's an upper limit on what most governments can threaten',[25] unless minor wrongs are to be punished as severely as serious crimes. We should also note

---

[20] See Ch 3.

[21] Gary S Becker, 'Crime and Punishment: An Economic Approach' (1968) 76 J Pol Econ 169.

[22] ie the likely penalty if the offender is apprehended and convicted.

[23] Becker's formulation is somewhat more sophisticated:

> This approach implies that there is a function relating the number of offenses by any person to his probability of conviction, to his punishment if convicted, and to other variables, such as the income available to him in legal and other illegal activities, the frequency of nuisance arrests, and his willingness to commit an illegal act. [Ibid, 177]

[24] Ibid, 183–4.

[25] Jack Goldsmith and Tim Wu, *Who Controls the Internet? Illusions of a Borderless World* (New York: Oxford University Press, 2006), 80.

that actual human behaviour may not follow Becker's model. Research into the effect on unlawful drug use of sanctions for lawbreaking suggests that only 5 per cent of variance in drug use can be attributed to the level of potential penalties.[26]

However, it does seem generally to be accepted that the likelihood of detection and enforcement, irrespective of the level of penalty, has a substantial effect on the behaviour of those subject to the law.[27] If it were possible to enforce the law rigorously enough, control might be achievable.

So, given that states cannot ratchet up the penalties for lawbreaking without limit, and that increased penalties may in any event fail to achieve control of behaviour, we are left with frequent enforcement as the main mechanism of control. Because enforcement of law in cyberspace is more time-consuming and more expensive than in the physical world, we therefore need to understand the size of the problem to see whether effective enforcement is achievable. To put it another way, what is the scale of online lawbreaking compared with that in the physical world?

Child sexual-abuse images

Even in the low-bandwidth days of the mid 1990s the internet was immediately used for the communication of sexual images. Today, high-definition video of sexual content is readily available. There is no reliable data as to the proportion of internet traffic which consists of sexual content, but there is no doubt that there is a lot of it: 'it is indisputable that sexual expression—along with every other kind of expression— is more readily available online than through traditional media'.[28]

A small proportion of this content consists of images of child sexual abuse. There is a clear international consensus that the creation, communication and (in most countries) possession of such images should be a serious criminal offence. This consensus is typified by the Council of Europe Convention on Cybercrime,[29] which as at April 2011 had been signed by forty-three of the forty-seven members of the Council of Europe and also by the US, Japan, South Africa, and Canada. The UK implementation of the Convention is via the Protection of Children Act 1978 as amended, in respect of the making and supply of images of child sexual abuse, and the Criminal Justice Act 1988, s 160 as amended, in respect of their possession.

The physical sexual abuse of children is generally recognized to be a largely 'hidden' activity, with only a small proportion of offences reported to the police or otherwise detected. This is probably because most abuse is undertaken by family members or others in a position of trust or authority. A survey undertaken by the UK National

---

[26] Robert J MacCoun, 'Drugs and the Law: A Psychological Analysis of Drug Prohibition' (1993) 113 *Psychological Bulletin* 497.

[27] Raymond Paternoster, 'The Deterrent Effect of the Perceived Certainty and Severity of Punishment' (1987) 4 Justice Quarterly 173; Daniel S Nagin and Raymond Paternoster, 'The Preventive Effects of the Perceived Risk of Arrest: Testing an Expanded Conception of Deterrence' (1991) 29 Criminology 561–87.

[28] Yaman Adkeniz and Nadine Strossen, 'Sexually Orientated Expression' in Yaman Adkeniz, Clive Walker, and David Wall, *The Internet, Law and Society* (Harlow: Longman, 2000), Ch 9.

[29] European Treaty Series No 185, Art 9.

Society for the Protection of Children in 2009[30] found that 4.8 per cent of 11–17 year olds reported experiencing sexual abuse at some time, which suggests that in any one year between 37,000 and 295,000 UK children experience abuse.[31] We must recognize that these acts of abuse were self-identified, and many will not have constituted the more closely defined criminal offences. Nonetheless we can safely conclude that the number of these crimes committed in the UK each year is likely to be in the hundreds of thousands. There is no reason to believe that physical child sexual abuse is more common in the UK than anywhere else.

Only a small fraction of these offences is prosecuted. In 2007 there were 865 convictions,[32] and if the conviction rate is the same as for other sexual offences, in the region of 60 per cent,[33] this suggests that around 1,440 prosecutions were commenced. In other words, the UK law enforcement authorities are able to detect and prosecute fewer than 4 per cent of physical child sexual abuse offences.

How does this compare with offences relating to child sexual abuse images in cyberspace? In the same year, 2007, there were 967 convictions for possession or supply of child sexual abuse images,[34] which, scaled up, suggests around 1,610 prosecutions, though the conviction rate here is likely to be higher than for offences of actual abuse because there is no need for the children involved to give evidence. These figures are not broken down between physical and digital images, but at most the number of prosecutions for online images cannot have exceeded 1,500.

There is no way of knowing how many offences are committed, but it is possible to estimate the potential demand for such images. This is because the Internet Watch Foundation operates a blocking list of URLs which link to child sexual abuse images.[35] Almost all UK ISPs subscribe to this list, and use it to block requests from their subscribers. In 2009 *The Register* obtained figures from BT, the largest UK ISP with 25 per cent of the market, which indicate that BT blocks between 35,000 and 40,000 such requests each day.[36] Scaled up for the entire market, the annual demand in the UK alone appears to be for between 51 million and 58 million images, each access to which would constitute the commission of a criminal offence.

Walden points out that these figures 'are likely to be substantially over-stated, for a number of technical reasons'.[37] Nonetheless, it is clear that the potential number

---

[30] Summary results available at <http://www.nspcc.org.uk/Inform/research/statistics/prevalence_and_incidence_of_child_abuse_and_neglect_wda48740.html>.

[31] Using the UK population figures for 2009 from the UK Office for National Statistics *Population Estimates* (June 2010), which give a total population of 61.3m, just under 20% of whom are under 16. The lower number is if each child experienced abuse only in one year between the ages of 11 and 17, the higher if they experienced it throughout the period.

[32] Answer to Parliamentary Question, *Hansard*, 13 October 2009, cols 846W and 847W.

[33] UK Ministry of Justice, Criminal Statistics: England and Wales 2008 Statistics bulletin (January 2010), para 107.

[34] *Hansard* (n 32).

[35] The IWF 2009 Annual and Charity Report, at 15, identifies 8,844 such URLs at 1,316 domains only 40 of which are from the UK.

[36] Chris Williams, 'BT Blocks up to 40,000 Child Porn Pages per Day', *The Register*, 7 April 2009, <http://www.theregister.co.uk/2009/04/07/bt_cp_figures/>.

[37] Ian Walden, 'Porn, Pipes and the State: Censoring Internet Content' (2010) 44 The Barrister 16, 17.

of offences in cyberspace is several orders of magnitude greater than the related offences in the physical world. Walden goes on to say that 'the industrial volumes involved would overwhelm any attempt by the police to investigate individual users'.[38] The resources available[39] could not conceivably be stretched to cover such a vastly increased number of investigations and prosecutions.[40] Nor could the courts, the prisons, or the probation service cope. Even if unlimited funds were magically to become available, there are insufficient trained investigators and prosecutors to increase the level of prosecutions even to the 4 per cent estimate for physical child sexual abuse.

Reporting hotlines broadly similar to that of the Internet Watch Foundation exist in thirty-six other countries,[41] mainly in Europe. Some operate a blocking system,[42] but in others reports are investigated by law enforcement authorities[43] who are no better resourced than in the UK. It seems reasonable to conclude that the number of offences committed in cyberspace relating to child sexual abuse images is probably hundreds of times greater than the physical instances of abuse. Any attempt to control a problem of this scale by means of enforcing the law seems doomed to failure.

Copyright infringement by file sharing

We have already seen in Chapters 1 and 2 that the cyberspace technologies have enabled users to copy music recordings and share them online. There is no doubt that the majority of such file sharing infringes copyright, both when the lawful recording is copied and when a copy is downloaded by another user. Rights owners in those recordings can, in theory, take legal action against those users and secure injunctions and awards of damages to enforce their rights. But can such enforcement work to prevent, or even limit substantially, these copyright infringements?

It is, perhaps, instructive to examine the predecessor technology for sharing infringing music recordings, the audiocassette. In the 1970s recorded music was sold on vinyl LPs or on audiocassette, and the arrival of the home audiocassette recorder made it possible for users to copy those recordings and share them with their friends. I was a teenager at that time, and the norm was to possess a number of legitimately purchased LPs or audiocassettes and perhaps twice as many copies made

---

[38] Ibid.

[39] The annual budget for the Police Central e-Crime Unit is only £7.4m over three years—*ACPO e-Crime Strategy* (28 May 2009), 18—and the Unit's work covers a far wider range of cyberspace crimes than child sexual abuse.

[40] The National Policing Improvement Agency, *Guidance on Investigating Child Abuse and Safeguarding Children* (2009), <http://www.npia.police.uk/en/docs/Investigating_Child_Abuse_WEBSITE.pdf>, stresses throughout its 192 pages the need to work within the limits of over-stretched resources.

[41] See <http://www.inhope.org/gns/our-members.aspx>.

[42] eg South Africa, see <http://www.fpbprochild.org.za/Home.aspx>.

[43] eg Belgium, <http://www.stopchildporno.be/en/procedure-en/treatment-of-reports/transmission-of-reports/>; US, <http://www.ncmec.org/en_US/documents/CyberTiplineFactSheet.pdf>.

from recordings purchased by friends. This matches the figures quoted in *CBS Songs Ltd v Amstrad Consumer Electronics plc*:[44]

The sales of sound recordings in 1984 were estimated at 40 million, and the sales of blank tapes at 70 million or thereabouts. Blank tapes may be employed for purposes which do not infringe copyright but on average for every authorized copy of a record there will now be two infringing copies.

The main reasons for the 2:1 infringement ratio were that the recording media were comparatively expensive, perhaps 10–20 per cent of the cost of purchasing a lawful copy, and that it was only possible to make a copy of a recording to which one had physical access.[45]

Nearly thirty years later, the scale of infringement has increased markedly. There are no definitive figures, but even the lowest range of estimates indicates a high level of unlawful copying. The largest numbers come from IFPI (International Federation of the Phonographic Industry), the representative body of the music industry, whose *Digital Music Report 2009: Key Statistics*[46] estimates that 16 per cent of European users regularly swap infringing music files online, that more than 40 billion music files were shared in 2008 in sixteen countries, and that the infringement rate for downloads was about 95 per cent. Research by BBC Radio 4's 'More or Less' programme into the source of the 16 per cent figure suggests that it was substantially overstated and should in fact be 11.6 per cent.[47] This would reduce the 40 billion figure to 29 billion, or just under 2 billion infringing copies per country. As a cross-check, the industry estimates for the UK for 2004 were 4.73 billion[48] which, scaled down on the same basis, would give a figure of 3.43 billion UK downloads annually.

Even with such a wide range of uncertainty, infringement at a level of 2 to 5 billion per annum for the UK represents a substantial increase over the 70 million estimate for 1984 in *CBS v Amstrad*. More users are infringing, and/or they are infringing more often. This is confirmed by the research undertaken by Paul Lamere of Sun Labs in 2006[49] which investigated the iPod music collections of over 5,600 users. The average contents were 3,542 recordings, of which 64 per cent had never been played. It seems almost certain that the majority of these recordings had not been purchased, and thus infringed. Lamere warns us, 'this isn't exactly scientific. These were self-selecting users, who were geeky enough to want to upload their iTunes data

---

[44] [1988] AC 1013, 1048. The case arose from the development of 'high-speed dubbing' in the early 1980s, which permitted tapes to be copied comparatively rapidly. The House of Lords held that Amstrad's twin-deck audiocassette recorder had lawful as well as infringing uses, and thus refused to grant an injunction to prevent its sale.

[45] It was also preferable to have physical access to the original, or at worst a first generation copy, because the analogue tape copying technology rapidly degraded the audio quality for later generation copies.

[46] Avaliable at <http://www.ifpi.org/content/section_resources/dmr2009.html>.

[47] Barry Collins, 'How UK Government Spun 136 People into 7m Illegal File Sharers', *PC Pro*, 4 September 2009, <http://www.pcpro.co.uk/news/351331/how-uk-government-spun-136-people-into-7m-illegal-file-sharers>.

[48] Ben Goldacre, 'Illegal Downloads and Dodgy Figures', *The Guardian*, 5 June 2009.

[49] Paul Lamere, 'What's On Your iPod?', 22 May 2006, <http://blogs.sun.com/plamere/entry/what_s_on_your_ipod>.

to a website. They are probably not your typical iPod user . . .' But taking the industry figures for the UK, revised in accordance with the previous paragraph, and dividing by the online proportion of the population, suggests an average annual download of 879 files per user. Thus the Lamere numbers provide some confirmation that the industry estimates have at least some relationship with actuality.

If the UK figures are representative of the rest of the world, right-holders seeking to enforce their rights would need to commence legal proceedings against 11.6 per cent of the world's population, or at least a substantial proportion of those infringers. Leaving aside cost, there are insufficient courts and lawyers to sustain litigation at this level. But might enforcement through litigation still achieve some benefits in terms of the infringement rate, even if action is taken against only a tiny proportion of infringers?

The music industry has sued individual infringers on this smaller scale. In 2003 the RIAA, the US music industry body, issued just over 1,600 subpoenas against ISPs under the US Digital Millennium Copyright Act 1998. Using the information thus obtained it filed 261 copyright infringement suits against individuals, 64 of which were settled,[50] and the following year it filed nearly 1,000 further suits against individual users.[51] In the UK a small number of judgments have been obtained against individuals,[52] but right-holders have also engaged in 'volume litigation' which consists of sending letters threatening action and offering to settle, without actually taking those who refuse to settle to court.[53] It seems likely that these letters have been sent in their tens of thousands or more.[54]

Bhattacharjee et al investigated the consequences of the RIAA litigation in the US across a population of 2,056 users of Kazaa P2P file-sharing software.[55] Users did indeed react as RIAA had hoped: file sharing was reduced to between 10 and 33 per cent of its pre-litigation level, with the most active file sharers bearing the greatest reduction. Unfortunately the research did not continue long enough to determine whether the volume of file sharing rebounded to its original level once the RIAA campaign had faded from memory; but the music industry figures, which indicate year-on-year increases in file sharing, suggest that this is probably what happened.[56]

---

[50] See David Haubert and Shannon Yavorsky, 'Piracy: DMCA Wars' (2004) Ent LR 94.

[51] Amanda Witt, 'Burned in the USA: Should the Music Industry Utilize its American Strategy of Suing Users to Combat Online Piracy in Europe?' (2005) 11 Colum J Eur L 375, 381.

[52] The best-known of which is *Topware v Barwinska*, PAT.08023 Patents County Court, 18 August 2008 (unreported), see <http://news.bbc.co.uk/1/hi/technology/7568642.stm>.

[53] See Andrew Murray, '*Volume Litigation:* More Harmful than Helpful?' (2009) 20(6) Computers and Law 43.

[54] *PC Pro* reported that the firm ACS Law is sending letters out in batches of 25,000: 'Will you get caught file-sharing?', 10 January 2010, <http://www.pcpro.co.uk/features/354340/will-you-get-caught-file-sharing/2>.

[55] Sudip Bhattacharjee, Ram D Gopal, Kaveepan Lertwachara, and James R Marsden, 'Impact of Legal Threats on Music Sharing Activity: An Analysis of Music Industry Legal Actions' (2006) 49 J L & Econ 91.

[56] This would accord with findings from other areas of law, that changes to the law produce a temporary decrease in lawbreaking because publicity about the changes leads offenders to overestimate the risk of apprehension and punishment, but that this effect rapidly fades away. See H Laurence Ross, *Deterring the Drinking Driver: Legal Policy and Social Control* (Lexington: Lexington Books, 1982).

What this tells us is that what might be described as 'symbolic' enforcement activity does have some effect, but that it probably needs to be sustained continuously to achieve anything more than a temporary reduction in infringing activity. It is worth noting that as a consequence of the RIAA action, file sharing was reduced but far from eliminated. If a UK campaign were similarly successful this would be likely to reduce infringements only to somewhere between 700,000 and 1.7 million annually. And of course, a sustained enforcement campaign is costly, not merely in financial terms but, perhaps more importantly, in souring the relationship between right-holders and their customers. It is worth noting that the music industry seems now to have abandoned its litigation strategy and is concentrating instead on 'education' of users and persuading governments to introduce technical blocking measures which, it hopes, will prove more successful:

the industry favours a preventative and educational approach involving communication with subscribers over the more punitive and less effective alternative of mass-scale individual lawsuits.[57]

The likelihood of this strategy succeeding is at best uncertain, and even the industry itself recognizes that 'consumer education alone, while it has effectively raised awareness of the legal and ethical issues around unauthorized downloading, does not change consumer behaviour'.[58]

The problem of scale

It seems that enforcement, although feasible at the individual level, is in practical terms ineffective at the macro level. The reason for this is the vastly increased scale of unlawfulness in cyberspace. If an unlawful activity can be undertaken in cyberspace, it appears that it is likely to be undertaken far more often and by more people.

This is inherent in the nature of cyberspace. It makes information exchange very easy, by removing barriers such as distance and physical property from the process. As a consequence more information is exchanged, both lawful and unlawful. Thus to copy a friend's CD I no longer need access to that CD; indeed, it is equally easy to copy a stranger's CD.

Even if all those sharing information were in the same country, we would still expect a vast increase in communication. But of course, it is as easy to communicate online with foreigners as with fellow citizens. Thus the scale of the problem increases further. Enforcement is a global issue, although the laws are national.

It is therefore unsurprising that the cost and effort of individual enforcement is overwhelming. The solution to the problem of lawfulness in cyberspace cannot lie here.

---

[57] IFPI, Digital Music Report 2011, 18.
[58] IFPI, Digital Music Report 2010, 7.

Indirect enforcement

The most obvious solution to the problem of scale is to permit enforcement against the intermediaries, such as ISPs, which make this huge volume of communication possible. There are generally no more than a few hundred ISPs in each country,[59] although there will be many other service providers offering hosting, blogging, social networking, or discussion services. Even so, the scale problem reduces dramatically.

A further advantage, from the perspective of enforcement, is that this would enrol[60] the ISPs as policemen of their users' activities. To avoid liability they would need to develop ways of controlling unlawful behaviour by their subscribers, and this should drive down unlawfulness to a minimal level. The system introduced by the UK Digital Economy Act 2010 is an example of such enrolment; detection of copyright infringement is left to right-holders, but once they have identified an IP address as involved in infringing activity the ISP whose subscriber used that address is required to notify the subscriber of the fact and, if the Act's provisions on this point are brought in to force, in the case of repeated infringements impose sanctions on the subscriber which might extend to suspension of internet access. The actual workings of this system are to be set out in a code of practice, whose introduction has been delayed by judicial review,[61] by disagreement about how the costs of the system should be shared, and debate about how far the system is feasible in practice.

Unfortunately there are a number of substantial disadvantages to enforcing laws against intermediaries. These are set out succinctly in the 1995 Report of the US Government Working Group on Intellectual Property Rights:[62]

that the volume of material on a service provider's system is too large to monitor or screen; that even if a service provider is willing and able to monitor the material on its system, it cannot always identify infringing material; that failure to shield on-line service providers will impair communication and availability of information; that exposure to liability for infringement will drive service providers out of business, causing the [National Information Infrastructure] to fail; and that the law should impose liability only on those who assume responsibility for the activities their subscribers (and, presumably, they) engage in on their system.

The working group recommended that no immunity should be granted to intermediaries, however, but the US legislature was convinced by these arguments and introduced liability immunities in the Digital Millennium Copyright Act 1998 (DMCA).

---

[59] And normally only a small number of major players. In the UK, for example, the seven largest ISPs account for 96.5% of the residential and small and medium enterprise broadband market: Ofcom, *Online Infringement of Copyright and the Digital Economy Act 2010: Draft Initial Obligations Code* (Consultation Paper, 28 May 2010), para 3.15.1.

[60] See Julia Black, 'Enrolling Actors in Regulatory Processes: Examples from UK Financial Services Regulation' (2003) Public Law 62.

[61] *BT & Talk Talk v Secretary of State for Business Information and Skills* [2011] EWHC 1021, denying judicial review except in relation to the requirement that ISPs should bear certain costs.

[62] Bruce A Lehman, *Intellectual Property and the National Information Infrastructure: Report of the Working Group on Intellectual Property Rights* (1995), 115–16.

When viewed at a global level, which is of course the only correct perspective when considering cyberspace, there is a further pragmatic argument in favour of immunity. National liability laws are inevitably different, in detail if not in principle. It is unreasonable and impracticable to expect an intermediary to understand the obligations imposed on it by these laws and, as we shall see in Chapter 8, it will often be impossible for the intermediary to comply with them all. The problem could be solved by converging the differences between national laws, but it is unlikely that this will happen soon, if at all. Far simpler, then, to erase the problem by removing intermediaries from the application of those laws through granting immunity.[63]

The principle that intermediaries should not be liable for the unlawful acts of their users, unless they have notice of unlawful content and fail to take action, has been widely adopted in national laws. For indirect enforcement to be possible those laws would need to be modified so as to decrease the scope of the immunity.

There is no international consensus about the proper scope of intermediary immunities. In the US the Communications Decency Act 1996 (CDA) immunity, which primarily protects intermediaries from tort claims based on content, has been consistently upheld in an absolute form.[64] This is because its underlying justification has been held to be the free-speech provisions of the First Amendment to the US Constitution.[65] However, in December 2010 a Florida Circuit Court held in *Giordano v Romeo*[66] that the CDA did not prevent the issuance of an order requiring defamatory information to be removed from a website, but merely immunized the website operator from damages claims by the person defamed. It remains to be seen whether this indirect re-imposition of liability, similar to the approach taken by some European courts as we shall see below, will survive appeal.

The US courts take the same approach to the DMCA immunities from liability when considering copyright infringement. Owners of copyright in content have brought numerous legal actions against intermediaries to test the boundaries of the DMCA but have failed to persuade the courts to overturn the immunity in almost all cases. *Perfect 10 Inc v CCBill LLC*[67] decided that general knowledge that the plaintiff's rights were being infringed was insufficient to ground liability, and that actual knowledge of specific infringing material was necessary. Modifying the material via automated processes in the course of communicating it to users does not take

---

[63] This is the main justification for the granting of immunities under EU law—see Proposal for a European Parliament and Council directive on certain legal aspects of electronic commerce in the internal market, COM (1998) 586 final 18 November 1988, 4.

[64] See eg *Zeran v America Online Inc*, 129 F 3d 327 (4th Cir, 1997). Those few cases where a genuine intermediary has been held liable had unusual facts—see eg *Barnes v Yahoo!*, 570 F3d 1096 (9th Cir, 2009) where liability arose from breach of on oral contract to remove offending material.

[65] The Communications Decency Act was not intended by Congress as primarily a free-speech measure, but the Supreme Court decision in *ACLU v Reno*, 929 F Supp 824 (ED Pa, 1996), *affirmed* 117 S Ct 2329 (1997), which struck down the other provisions of the Act, established the surviving immunity as First Amendment based.

[66] No 09-68539-CA-25 4 (Fla 11th Cir Ct Dec 28, 2010), <http://www.scribd.com/doc/46015195/Giordano-v-Romeo-Injunction-Against-Ripoff-Report>.

[67] 488 F 3d 1102, 1114 (9th Cir, 2007). See also *Corbis Corp v Amazon.com, Inc*, 351 F Supp 2d 1090, 1108 (WD Wash, 2004).

the intermediary outside the DMCA safe harbour, as held in *UMG Recordings, Inc v Veoh Networks Inc*[68] where videos hosted by the defendant were converted to the Flash .flv format to enable them to be streamed to users.[69] Nor does making financial gain from hosting infringing content, provided that the host receives income from all hosted content of that kind and does not receive additional benefit from the unlawful content.[70] The most recent significant decision, *Viacom Intl Inc v YouTube Inc*,[71] makes it clear that it is the responsibility of right-holders, not intermediaries, to search out infringing content, and that in the absence of specific knowledge the intermediary's duties are limited to taking down that material on receipt of proper notice.

By contrast, a trend can be detected in Europe towards reducing the scope of immunities. Although the UK courts initially declined to do this,[72] the same has not been true in other countries. In *Google v Copiepresse*[73] a Belgian court held that Google News, which displays links to news stories on other sites together with the first few lines of the story, was in breach of unfair competition law, and that Google was not entitled to immunity as an intermediary because it operated the Google News service on its own account. By similar reasoning, in *SA Louis Vuitton Malletier v eBay Inc*[74] the Paris Tribunal de Commerce held that eBay's involvement in the business practices of some of its sellers went so far beyond mere hosting of their auction items that it was no longer acting as an intermediary and therefore lost its immunity under the Electronic Commerce Directive.[75]

The recent decision of the Court of Justice of the European Union (CJEU) in *L'Oreal v eBay*[76] confirms that the hosting immunity is not absolute, but depends on the extent of the involvement by the intermediary in determining the content in question. The court made a contrast between intermediaries whose role is merely that of 'providing that service neutrally by a merely technical and automatic processing of the data provided by its customers'[77] and those who play an active role in presenting the content:

Where, by contrast, the operator has provided assistance which entails, in particular, optimising the presentation of the offers for sale in question or promoting those offers, it must be considered not to have taken a neutral position between the customer-seller concerned and potential buyers but to have played an active role of such a kind as to give it knowledge of, or control over, the data relating to those offers for sale.[78]

---

[68] 620 F Supp 2d 1081, 1092 (CD Cal, 2008).

[69] However, influencing content by suggesting options to users can lead to loss of intermediary status, and thus immunity: *Fair Housing Council v Roommates.com*, 521 F3d 1157 (9th Cir, 2008).

[70] *Hendrickson v eBay, Inc*, 165 F Supp 2d 1082 (CD Cal, 2001).

[71] 718 F Supp 2d 514, 516 (SDNY, 2010).

[72] See eg *L'Oreal v eBay* [2009] EWHC 1094 (Ch).

[73] Brussels Court of First Instance (TGI), 13 February 2007.

[74] Tribunal de Commerce de Paris, Premiere Chambre B (Paris Commercial Court), Case No 200677799, 30 June 2008.

[75] Directive 2000/31/EC on electronic commerce OJ L 178/1, 17 July 2000, Art 14.

[76] Case C-324/09, 12 July 2011.

[77] Ibid, para 113.

[78] Ibid, para 116.

Whether eBay's activities went beyond those of a neutral intermediary will not be known until the UK court reconsiders the case and applies these principles.

An alternative European route to the reimposition of liability uses the provisions of the Electronic Commerce Directive which permit court orders requiring the ISP to 'terminate or prevent an infringement'[79] as exceptions to its immunities. In *Rolex v eBay/Ricardo (Internet Auction I)*[80] the German Federal Court of Justice upheld an order requiring eBay to police its auctions to detect and prevent future trade mark infringements, and in *SABAM v Scarlet SA*[81] a copyright collecting society was granted a wide-ranging injunction which required the ISP Scarlet to identify and block access to infringing works requested by any of its subscribers, potentially from any website worldwide. The attitude of the UK courts, which had previously been reluctant to reduce the scope of intermediary immunities, may now be moving closer to that of the civil law countries, at least in the field of intellectual property. In *Twentieth Century Fox Film Corp and ors v British Telecommunications Plc*[82] the court granted right-holders a wide-ranging injunction which required BT to block access by its subscribers to the Newzbin2 website. This was on the basis that over 90 per cent of the content available from that site was likely to infringe copyright,[83] and the small proportion of non-infringing material available from the site was not enough to persuade the court to limit the blocking order to specific URLs.

However, this second route to the imposition of liability has largely been closed by the CJEU. *SABAM v Scarlet*[84] held that the Belgian courts had been wrong to grant a wide-ranging injunction against the ISP Scarlet, ordering it to make it impossible for its customers to send or receive in any way files containing a musical work in SABAM's repertoire by means of peer-to-peer software. Although issuing an injunction was allowed under the Electronic Commerce Directive, such an injunction must not contravene Article 15, which prevents measures which require an ISP to carry out general monitoring of the information which it transmits. This order would have required such monitoring. In addition the court held that an injunction would need to strike a fair balance between a claimant's intellectual property rights, which are not absolute, and other fundamental rights. These are enshrined in the Charter of Fundamental Rights of the European Union and include the freedom of ISPs to conduct a business (Article 16) and the rights of users to protection of their personal data (Article 8) and of their freedom to receive or impart information (Article 11). This injunction did not strike a fair balance between the rights involved.[85]

---

[79] Electronic Commerce Directive (n 75), Arts 12(3), 13(2), and 14(3).

[80] German Bundesgerichtshof, Case I ZR 304/01, [2005] ETMR 25. See also *Hermès International v Feitz*, Case RG 06/02604, Tribunale di Grande Instance Troyes, 4 June 2008.

[81] Brussels Court of First Instance (TGI), 29 June 2007, 24 October 2008.

[82] [2011] EWHC 1981 (Ch).

[83] Ibid, paras 50–3.

[84] Case C-70/10, 24 November 2011.

[85] Where a national legislature has undertaken such a balancing exercise the courts are unlikely to substitute their own view about the proper balance between these interests—see *British*

General legislation on this issue is likely to be some time away, though there is already legislation in the field of copyright infringement.[86] It is by no means obvious how the immunities for intermediaries should be recast, and there are strong arguments against limiting those immunities more than is already the case. MacCarthy has recently undertaken an important analysis comparing the position of immune intermediaries, such as ISPs, with that of payment service providers who do not benefit from any immunity.[87] Two of his findings are particularly relevant here.

First, he challenges the perceived wisdom that intermediaries are the 'least cost avoider', ie the person who would have to spend the least on preventing such losses, and thus the economic case for placing the burden of enforcement on them. From his analysis of the enforcement of US anti-gambling laws via payment intermediaries he identifies a number of unacknowledged costs which have been omitted from the analysis:

- The cost to maintain and enforce an internet gambling coding and blocking scheme that is entirely manual and cannot be automated;
- The cost from over-blocking legal transactions;
- The cost to screen and check the business activity of merchants participating in the payment systems;
- The cost to monitor the use of payment systems for specific illegal activity, where the payment systems are in no better position than anyone else to conduct this monitoring activity;
- The cost to assess complaints of illegality, where the intermediary has no special expertise and is often less familiar with the legal and factual issues than the wronged party and the allegedly bad actor;
- The cost to defend against legal challenges to enforcement actions, where the challenge typically comes in an off-shore jurisdiction; and
- Long-term costs to the United States from taking unilateral action in this area, including the encouragement of copycat regimes in other areas of law and in other jurisdictions.

and concludes that:

The reasonableness of these costs in light of the benefits achieved has not yet been seriously studied. Instead, it seems to be assumed that small compliance costs are justified by large enforcement benefits. Although precision in the estimates of costs and benefits is unlikely in this area, a more disciplined qualitative analysis is required.[88]

Telecommunications Plc v The Secretary of State for Business, Innovation and Skills [2011] EWHC 1021 (Admin), paras 207–18.

[86] See eg UK Digital Economy Act 2010, French Loi favorisant la diffusion et la protection de la création sur internet, 12 May 2009, as modified following the Conseil Constitutionnel Décision 2009-590 DC, 22 October 2009.

[87] Mark MacCarthy, 'What Payment Intermediaries are Doing About Online Liability and Why it Matters' (2010) 25 Berkeley Tech LJ 1037.

[88] Ibid, 1060. See also 1053.

In MacCarthy's view it is likely that there are similar unacknowledged costs in relation to the enforcement of intellectual property laws via intermediaries. For example, Tiffany has engaged in litigation in the US in an attempt to force eBay to police its listings for infringements of Tiffany's trade marks, although the courts have so far rejected its arguments that eBay is a direct or contributory infringer.[89] The evidence in that litigation is that eBay spends at least $20 million annually on fraud prevention and has over 200 employees dealing with infringement issues.[90] MacCarthy argues that:

The fact that eBay and Tiffany were unable to come to an agreement on compensation, despite years of negotiations and discussions, suggests that the full costs of these enforcement efforts exceeded what Tiffany was willing to pay. If Tiffany is a rational actor, willing to pay up to the amount that it would cost it to take its own enforcement actions, the failure to reach an enforcement agreement suggests that eBay is not the least cost enforcer after all.[91]

Secondly, MacCarthy points out that removing immunities from intermediaries introduces national borders into cyberspace, because they must now understand and comply with different laws, depending on the transaction in question, in order to avoid liability. The experience of payment service providers is that a bordered internet does not scale well, with the result that transactions are unjustifiably prevented or delayed.[92] This is related to the justification for the immunities provisions of the Electronic Commerce Directive,[93] as an alternative to the harmonization of national liability laws.

In addition to considering these arguments, lawmakers will also need to decide whether a diminution in the scope of the immunities would frustrate national policies on increasing access to and use of the internet. The uncertainties created by making intermediaries liable for third party content will certainly reduce the amount of content available, and desirable content will be restricted as well as unlawful content because it is not easy, or perhaps not even possible, for an ISP to distinguish the two categories with sufficient certainty. There are also complex moral questions to be decided. From one perspective, intermediaries make possible the communication of illegal content, and should therefore bear some responsibility for it. From a different perspective they are mere innocent carriers, like the mail or telephone services, and play no legally significant role in any wrongdoing.[94] There is no obviously correct answer to this conundrum.

---

[89] *Tiffany v eBay*, 600 F 3d 93 (2nd Cir, 2010).
[90] Ibid, at 98.
[91] MacCarthy (n 87), 1049, and see also 1051.
[92] Ibid, 1108–115.
[93] See n 63.
[94] See MacCarthy (n 87), 1056:

> The focus on parties who had no part in creating the problem and who are not responsible for the illegal activity puts a burden on people who are innocent of any wrongdoing. Burdening innocent people seems unfair, and arguments that justify this approach on the grounds that it is good for society as a whole violate widely accepted moral principles and are unlikely to withstand public scrutiny.

Where Next?

I hope that by now the reader is convinced that people in general, and cyberspace users in particular, do not obey the law because of fear that it will be enforced against them. The fear of enforcement seems to play only a small part in persuading people to obey the laws which govern their physical world activities, and we have seen that the risk of enforcement is far lower for their cyberspace activities. This is because cyberspace encourages far more communication, unlawful as well as lawful, and communication which often crosses national boundaries. Those seeking to enforce the law are thus faced with a volume of law-breaking which is many times greater than in the physical world, so great indeed that it is inconceivable that sufficient resources could ever be found to take action against all, or even a significant proportion of, law-breakers.

If enforcement is not the main reason people obey the law, even in the physical world, then there is little point in lawmakers producing laws for cyberspace which rely on enforcement to secure obedience. Instead they need to understand why cyberspace users obey some laws, but not others, and frame their laws accordingly.

The argument of this book is that laws are obeyed in cyberspace because they achieve the respect of cyberspace users. That respect has two elements: respect for the authority of the lawmaker as a source of rules which should be obeyed; and respect for the content of the law as being worthy of obedience. We therefore need to turn in the next chapters to the question of authority—what are the sources of a law-maker's authority, and when will a cyberspace user accept that authority as a reason for obedience?

5

Sources of Authority

It should by now be apparent that lawmakers are faced with a complex problem. How can they achieve the authority which will allow them to prescribe norms which will actually influence the behaviour of those who are not physically present in the lawmaker's jurisdiction? This problem is not unique to cyberspace—the same questions arise when regulating businesses which conduct transactions across national borders. However, those businesses made a conscious decision to undertake their foreign transactions, and could normally[1] be confident that the only foreign lawmakers they needed to concern themselves about were those which had territorial authority over the counterparty to the transaction or the place where some significant element of the deal, such as delivery, took place.

Cyberspace activities, as we have seen, have the potential to produce effects anywhere in the world. On the basis of those effects, lawmakers can claim the authority to regulate the user's actions. These claims are often not predictable in advance,[2] nor are they restricted to the territories where the user might expect to be subject to such a claim. This potential extension of authority claims to the activities of all cyberspace users is a new problem, and one which needs to be resolved for cyberspace to be a space whose users generally act lawfully.

Applicability and Authority Distinguished

We need to begin by clearing up a potential source of confusion, between the applicability of a national law to a particular cyberspace situation and the authority of that lawmaker's rules so far as cyberspace actors are concerned. After all, if a law is applicable to a cyberspace actor, and is actually enforced against him, it would seem perverse to assert that the lawmaker's rules had no authority so far as the actor was concerned. Conversely, if a law is not applicable to a cyberspace activity there is no obligation to obey that law, and thus no need to defer to the authority of the lawmaker. Seen in this way, applicability and authority appear to be two sides of the same coin.

---

[1] The exception is anti-trust or competition law, whose applicability is based on effects in the market. Even here, though, commercial actors are at least likely to have an advance understanding of the markets which might be affected by their activities.

[2] See Ch 3.

There is an extensive literature which investigates whether a particular legal system's own rules permit it to assert jurisdiction and attempt to enforce its laws against that cyberspace actor.[3] By and large, the consensus is that a cyberspace actor will have an online presence in almost[4] every country. If that presence produces effects in the country this is usually sufficient to allow national courts to take jurisdiction over the actor and apply their national law.[5] If applicability of law means that the lawmaker has authority over cyberspace actors, then every lawmaker has authority over every cyberspace actor. Even without further analysis, we must see that this proposition cannot be correct.

The confusion arises because the problem is being examined from the perspective of the lawmaker. Rules of law have been promulgated in such a way as to make them legitimate in terms of the relevant constitution or other validating rules, and—either expressly or as interpreted by the national courts—those rules apply to the cyberspace actor. From the lawmaker's point of view, these rules should therefore be obeyed by cyberspace actors.

But this perspective, based as it is in the rules of one particular national legal system, is not appropriate to determine the question of authority in cyberspace. A lawmaker has authority in cyberspace if actors are likely to, or at least ought to, obey that lawmaker's rules. This is not a matter which can be decided by national rules of law. Rather, it is a question of the internal state of mind of the cyberspace actor.[6]

When viewed from the actor's perspective there are five reasons why he might not accept a lawmaker's authority. The first of these is that the mere theoretical applicability of a law, determined in accordance with the rules of the state in question, does not necessarily make it binding on a particular person in practice. If the courts of that country do not have jurisdiction over that person then there is no available mechanism for applying the law. In other words, even when viewed from the lawmaker's perspective there is no obligation to obey the law unless both elements, applicability *and* jurisdiction, are fulfilled.

We saw in Chapter 3 that in some cases a state may take a policy decision not to enforce a law against a foreigner acting in cyberspace, even if that law is applicable to the situation and its courts have jurisdiction. Further, we noted in Chapter 4 that enforcement of national laws against cyberspace actors is many times more difficult than enforcing them against those acting in the physical world, so that even if a state has not adopted a non-enforcement policy it will, in practice, only be able to take enforcement action in a small minority of cases. This is the second reason why a lawmaker might lack authority. A cyberspace actor might reasonably take the position

---

[3] See eg Utah Kohl, *Jurisdiction and the Internet* (Cambridge: Cambridge University Press, 2007); Julia Hörnle, 'The Jurisdictional Challenge of the Internet' in Lilian Edwards and Charlotte Waelde (eds), *Law and the Internet*, 3rd edn (Oxford: Hart Publishing, 2009), Ch 3.

[4] China and Singapore, among others, operate a censorship system which limits access of their residents to certain websites, and even in open countries such as the UK some sites may be blocked—for example, sites containing images of child sexual abuse are blocked on a voluntary basis by ISPs via the UK Internet Watch Foundation's list.

[5] Austen Parrish, 'The Effects Test: Extraterritoriality's Fifth Business' (2008) 61 Vand L Rev 1455.

[6] HLA Hart, *The Concept of Law*, 2nd edn (Oxford: Oxford University Press, 1994), 89–91.

that a state which will not, or cannot, enforce its laws against him has no authority to require obedience to those laws.

The third reason is simple ignorance—if you are unaware of a lawmaker's claim to regulate your activities then you cannot have a state of mind which accepts that lawmaker's authority. Ignorance of foreign law is not just common in cyberspace; it is inevitable. This is because it is not practically possible for the cyberspace actor to discover or to understand all the foreign rules of law which claim to apply to his activities. To illustrate this I take the example of laws regulating banking, all of which are likely to prohibit specified activities unless a national banking licence is held. Implicitly this prohibition applies only to dealings with or offers made to persons in the jurisdiction, but because a website is visible almost everywhere in the world this does not restrict the application of the law only to domestic banks. For example, Mongolian banking law appears to contain a number of such prohibitions, including the provision of 'investment, financial consultancy and/or information services' other than by licensed banks.[7] Most non-Mongolian bank websites provide financial information, and because they can be viewed in Mongolia would thus seem to contravene the law.

It is not clear whether the text quoted above is an official translation, and even if it were official it would still not be the *applicable* law, which is of course the version in the Mongolian language. The meaning of that law is found not simply in its Mongolian text, but is only understandable in the context of the Mongolian legal system as a whole, including its banking regulatory system, its contract law, and its criminal and civil procedure laws. Without some understanding of all these, a foreign bank cannot know the precise nature of its obligations under Mongolian law. The same applies to its obligations under the laws of Fiji, Tanzania, Uruguay, and all the other national or state banking laws which, on their terms, claim to be applicable to each bank's website.

Because a bank cannot discover the existence and meaning of these laws without disproportionate effort,[8] it is thus likely to be ignorant of all but those it considers important. Although ignorance of the law is not a defence to enforcement action, it does affect the law's authority. A law of which the bank is ignorant must, by definition, have no normative influence on its actions:

> It is fundamental to recognize that a norm cannot really operate as a norm and be effective without being held, if only transitorily, in the minds of the agents, by this means regulating their behaviour . . .[9]

---

[7] Art 6(1)(11) Banking Law of Mongolia, <http://www.frontier.mn/>.

[8] A proponent of the proposition that applicable foreign rules of law have authority purely because they are laws might argue that their meaning can be discovered by taking professional legal advice. In cyberspace, this requires advice on the laws of every country in the world, because all are potentially applicable. This is grossly disproportionate in both time and money, even for a large commercial concern such as a multinational bank.

[9] Rosaria Conte and Cristiano Castelfranchi, 'The Mental Path of Norms' (2006) 19 Ratio Juris 501, 503.

Fuller tells us that rules made in secret by a lawmaker can have no practical authority for the lawmaker's subjects.[10] The Mongolian banking law is not secret, in that sense, but so far as most cyberspace users are concerned it might as well be, because they have no realistic way of discovering what it says. And of course, viewed from the perspective of a Mongolian cyberspace actor, the same could be said about UK or US banking laws.

A fourth reason for lack of authority is that it may be impossible to comply with the lawmaker's rules.[11] Again we need to make a distinction between theory and practicality. Lawmakers rarely enact rules which they know will be impossible to comply with, though they may do so unintentionally. Unintentional failure is particularly common in the cyberspace application of rules which were devised with the physical world in mind. More usually, though, the impossibility arises because there are multiple national laws which claim to apply to an online activity, and these laws conflict with each other. Although it may be theoretically possible to comply with one, or some, of those rules, it is practically impossible to obey them all. Thus, to continue our example, the only certain way for a bank to comply with all the laws which claim to apply to it is to obtain a banking licence from every jurisdiction in the world. This may not be possible unless the bank physically establishes a branch in every country. So far as I can discover no bank holds a worldwide set of banking licences. Even if it did, it would find that the online activities of some of its branches infringed the laws of other states, unless it reduced its banking activities to that minimum core which is permissible everywhere.[12]

Contradiction is not unique to banking laws. As a related example, US antiterrorism legislation requires SWIFT, the interbank messaging organization, to provide personal data about funds transferors and transferees to the US authorities while EU data protection law forbids SWIFT from doing so.[13] Although both sets of laws were applicable to SWIFT, it had to choose which one to comply with because it could not obey both. Such a choice inevitably rejects the authority of the losing lawmaker, in this case the EU, to govern the cyberspace user's conduct in that particular instance.[14]

The final reason the cyberspace actor might reject the authority of a lawmaker is if he perceives there to be an insufficient connection between his activities and the

---

[10] Lon Fuller, *The Morality of Law*, rev. edn (New Haven: Yale University Press, 1969), 49–51.

[11] This is examined in greater depth in Ch 8.

[12] And even then it might not be possible to be compliant with, for example, national rules on advertising loan interest rates, which require the rate to be calculated using different formulae.

[13] EU Article 29 Data Protection Working Party, 'Opinion 10/2006 on the Processing of Personal Data by the Society for Worldwide Interbank Financial Telecommunication (SWIFT)', 01935/06/EN, 22 November 2006. Negotiations between the EU and the US to resolve this conflict were still in progress as of 2011.

[14] This is not to say that SWIFT denied that the EU had authority to make data protection laws and apply them to SWIFT, nor that those laws had no normative force. SWIFT is owned by the world's banks and is a highly respected organization. No doubt it would have preferred to obey both sets of laws, had the conflict between them not made this impossible. Nor is there any suggestion that SWIFT fails to comply with EU data protection law where there is no such conflict. The rejection of authority applied only to this particular activity.

space over which the lawmaker has authority. Although from the lawmaker's viewpoint each of its rules of law ought to have authority for those to whom the laws apply *de jure*, this is not how the actor will perceive authority to work in cyberspace. The rules of private and public international law subject actors not merely to more than one legal system, but (at least potentially) to every legal system in the world. Thus the lawmaker's viewpoint asserts, in effect, that each cyberspace actor is subject to the collective set of those national laws which are applicable to cyberspace, and that this set of laws constitutes the legal system the authority of whose rules should be upheld. It is hard to argue that such a single, global system of law exists,[15] and impractical for the cyberspace actor to accept it as authoritative. In cyberspace we are faced with a situation where multiple and overlapping systems of rules all claim some degree of authority over our actions, a phenomenon which Santos has described as 'interlegality'.[16] The cyberspace actor must therefore make a selection between these competing claims to authority, and is likely to do so on the basis of his perceived connection with the lawmaker's sphere of authority.

In the physical world the space over which a lawmaker has the right to assert authority, and can do so effectively, is primarily territorial. But the foreign cyberspace actor is not physically present in that territory. He has a virtual presence there, but this is true of all other lawmakers' territories, and so virtual presence is not sufficient by itself to create the necessary connection. I shall argue later in this chapter that the relevant connecting factor is virtual membership of the community over which the lawmaker asserts authority. Unless the cyberspace actor perceives himself as a member of the lawmaker's community, he will not accept the authority of that lawmaker.

These reasons, separately or in combination, explain why a cyberspace actor is unlikely to accept the authority of a lawmaker to regulate his actions merely because the rules of that lawmaker's legal system state that a law applies to the actor. But is the actor wrong to take this position? Is there perhaps a moral argument that all applicable laws should be obeyed?

The argument in favour of this proposition would be that there is a general obligation on all persons to obey the law, and that this duty extends to all the applicable rules of law, whatever their source. In other words, all these laws should be obeyed simply *because* they are laws. No commentator espouses this argument in such unqualified terms, though it appears at first sight to be consistent with Finnis's position that 'if you are to have and retain the quality "law-abiding citizen" you *must*

---

[15] Werner Krawietz, 'The Concept of Law Revised—Directives and Norms in the Perspectives of a New Legal Realism' (2001) 14 Ratio Juris 34, 38: 'From the point of view of a *theory* of norms and action, the legal systems of modern society as a whole in their form, structure and functions could— virtually, at least—be regarded as *one* single information and communication system, although this has not been achieved completely as yet.' See also Benedict Kingsbury, 'The Concept of "Law" in Global Administrative Law' (2009) 20 Eur J Int'l L 23, 29: 'A convincing rule of recognition for a legal system that is not simply the inter-state system has not been formulated, the institutions for "adjudication" are often non-judicial and sometimes absent, and the processes of change are not easily articulated in terms of rules.'

[16] Bonaventura De Sousa Santos, 'Law: A Map of Misreading. Towards a Postmodern Conception of Law' (1987) 14 Journal of Law & Society 279, 298.

perform each action which the law has stated to be "obligatory", whenever and in all the circumstances in which such stipulations are applicable'. However, Finnis includes an important caveat immediately following this assertion:

> This fundamental principle . . . embodies the postulates that each obligation-stipulating law is a member of a system of laws which cannot be weighed or played off one against the other but which constitute a set coherently applicable to all situations and which exclude all unregulated or private picking and choosing amongst the members of the set . . . either you obey the *particular* law, or you reveal yourself as lacking or defective in allegiance to the *whole* [system], as well as to the particular.[17]

It is clear that the global set of legal rules which is applicable to a cyberspace actor was not designed as a coherent set of rules. Rather, that set of rules is a contingent and emergent phenomenon resulting from individual normative directives produced, in the main, at national level.[18] This lack of coherent design means that, in terms of Finnis's argument, there is no overriding moral or normative obligation to obey all of those rules simply because they are rules of law.

The existence of bank websites is empirical proof that such 'unregulated or private picking and choosing' takes place. As explained above the cost of global compliance is prohibitive, even if it were theoretically possible, so that any bank with a website is certainly contravening some other country's banking law. Banks are, as a class, highly averse to the reputational risk of law-breaking and go to great lengths to ensure legal compliance. If a bank is not complying with national laws which on their terms apply to its activities, we can only conclude that it does not accept mere applicability as conferring authority on the maker of those laws. If this is so for banks, it must be at least as true for other cyberspace actors.

Power

If the applicability of national law, determined by the rules of that legal system, does not necessarily confer authority on the lawmaker, can we find the answer in terms of realpolitik rather than formal legalism? Does authority derive from power over the cyberspace user, the power to enforce the lawmaker's rules by imposing sanctions?

This would be the explanation offered by Austin:

> If you cannot or will not harm me in case I comply not with your wish, the expression of your wish is not a command . . . Being liable to evil from you if I comply not with a wish which you signify, I am *bound* or *obliged* by your command, or I lie under a *duty* to obey it.[19]

Austin would conclude that if a state has no means of enforcing a particular law against an online actor then the law does not apply to that actor. For the online actor it is simply not law at all.

---

[17] John Finnis, *Natural Law and Natural Rights* (Oxford: Clarendon Press, 1980), 317.
[18] See Werner Krawietz (n 15) at 40–1.
[19] John Austin, *Lectures on Jurisprudence*, 3rd edn (London: John Murray, 1869), Vol I, Lecture I, 91.

In the early years of the commercial use of cyberspace, e-commerce businesses appeared to subscribe wholeheartedly to the Austinian view. Accepting that they were potentially subject to all the world's laws, they coped by adopting a risk-management approach to the obligations imposed upon them by foreign legal systems. Foreign laws would be ignored unless there was a real risk that they could be enforced by the state in question. Even if enforcement was probable the actor might still decline to comply if the cost of compliance exceeded the likely sanction.[20]

Some academic commentators took the position that the de facto limits on a state's ability to enforce its laws demonstrated that those laws were not truly applicable to cyberspace activities.[21] Certainly the risk of enforcement was low then and, as we have seen in Chapter 4, is likely to be even lower now simply because there is vastly more activity in cyberspace, while state resources available for enforcement have not increased at the same rate. Kohl, reviewing cases where enforcement has been attempted, points out that 'the number of cases, at least reported cases, in which States have actually assumed jurisdiction over foreign online activities is astonishingly small' and that 'in all cases, the regulating State had some actual power over the foreign provider',[22] usually in the form of assets or persons located in the jurisdiction. A cyberspace actor will inevitably pay less attention to a foreign law which it knows is unlikely to be enforced against it.[23]

The view taken by these early actors about the authority of foreign law is clearly illustrated by the action brought in the French courts against Yahoo! Inc, a US corporation, by anti-Nazi groups who alleged Yahoo!'s auction site contravened the French laws prohibiting the promotion of Nazism. Liability under those laws was based on publication in France. A Paris court granted an interim injunction which required Yahoo! to take steps to prevent French residents obtaining access to that material.[24] Yahoo!'s response was that it would comply with this order only if forced to do so by a US court, and a month later it filed a claim for declaratory judgment in

---

[20] See Utah Kohl (n 3), 209–10.

[21] These arguments are helpfully summarized in James Boyle, 'Foucault in Cyberspace: Cyberspace, Sovereignty and Hardwired Censors' (1997) 66 U Cin L Rev 177, 179–84, though note that they do not represent Boyle's own view.

[22] Utah Kohl, 'Eggs, Jurisdiction and the Internet' (2002) 51 ICLQ 555, 579 (references omitted).

[23] A low risk of enforcement does not, however, mean in Austin's terms that the rule ceases to be law:

> The greater the eventual evil, and the greater the chance of incurring it, the greater is the efficacy of the command, and the greater is the strength of the obligation . . . But where there is the smallest chance of incurring the smallest evil, the expression of a wish amounts to a command, and, therefore, imposes a duty. The sanction, if you will, is feeble or insufficient; but still there *is* a sanction, and, therefore, a duty and a command. [John Austin, n 19, 92–3]

See also Jack Goldsmith and Tim Wu, *Who Controls the Internet? Illusions of a Borderless World* (New York: Oxford University Press, 2006), 67–8, pointing out that the threat of sanctions is enough to modify behaviour substantially, even if complete compliance is not achieved.

[24] *Yahoo! Inc v LICRA*, TGI de Paris, 22 May 2000, confirmed with amendments TGI de Paris, 20 November 2000.

a Californian federal court.[25] Before that suit could be heard,[26] however, Yahoo! banned Nazi material from its US auction site, though still maintaining that the French judgment did not apply to it.[27] Some commentators suggest that the main reason for Yahoo!'s compliance was the fear of sanctions against the royalty stream from its French subsidiary company.[28]

And yet it seems to me that obedience to power explains only a small element of the behaviour of cyberspace actors. Imposing sanctions via a new law is rarely sufficient to control unwanted online behaviour because the time, money, and effort required for enforcement is usually grossly disproportionate to the mischief, even if enforcement is possible at all.[29] The *LICRA v Yahoo!* litigation was undertaken by a private representative group, largely as a symbolic activity, and not by the French state. It is noteworthy that France makes little effort to enforce its anti-Nazi laws against the multitude of foreign websites which contain such material.

Further, an analysis of authority in terms of state power to impose its rules offers no explanation at all for why there might be compliance with laws whose makers are in practical terms powerless to secure their enforcement. As Hart has pointed out, obeying the law is very different to obeying the demands of a gunman, even though the gunman also has the power to impose sanctions to enforce his demands.[30]

To begin with, we must recognize that obedience based solely on the power of the lawmaker is likely to disappear if that power is lost. As we saw in Chapter 4, cyberspace has dramatically reduced the power of lawmakers to enforce their laws against foreign cyberspace users. Yet cyberspace users still obey some, but not all, of the laws which apply to them. This tells us that the authority of a law is not dependent solely on the enforcement power of its maker. It is likely that some level of enforcement power is needed if a lawmaker is not to lose all authority, but that authority must derive from a source other than power to enforce the law.

---

[25] Jack Goldsmith and Tim Wu (n 23), 8.

[26] The declaratory judgment was granted in *Yahoo! Inc v La Ligue Contre Le Racisme Et L'Antisemitisme*, 169 F Supp 2d 1181 (ND Cal, 2001), but was overturned on appeal on the ground that the first-instance court had no jurisdiction to hear the suit because enforcement had not yet been threatened: 379 F 3d 1120 (9th Cir, 2004).

[27] 'We removed items we decided are objectionable, but by removing those items we in no way acknowledge the court case. We in no way fulfilled the order that was placed against us' (Scott Morris, Yahoo! spokesman, reported in 'Yahoo! Defies Court Ruling over Nazi Items', CNN, 21 February 2001, <http://archives.cnn.com/2001/TECH/internet/02/21/defiant.yahoo.idg/>).

[28] See eg Joel Reidenberg, 'Yahoo and Democracy on the Internet' (2002) 42 Jurimetrics J 261, 269; Jack Goldsmith and Tim Wu (n 23), at 8; but see contra Utah Kohl (n 3), 206–7 suggesting that the likely response of market forces to reputational damage was the prime motivation. Almost certainly both these considerations played a part in Yahoo!'s decision.

[29] Thomas Schultz, 'Carving Up the Internet: Jurisdiction, Legal Orders, and the Private/Public International Law Interface' (2008) 19 EJIL 799, 813:

> in the absence of extradition—which is unlikely to be granted with respect to the vast majority of Internet matters—a state can enforce its laws only against in-state actors, against entities with a presence on the territory of the state or with assets there.

[30] HLA Hart (n 6), 19–25. For Hart's explanation of the essential features which distinguish the law's commands from those of the gunman see Chs II–IV and summary at 79–80.

Any doubts on this score should be dispelled by the phenomenon of purely voluntary compliance. The approach which e-commerce businesses took towards compliance, based purely on the risk of sanctions, described above, was that of the dot com boom of 1999–2001.[31] The world has moved a long way since then. An online presence is now a core activity for most major corporations, and they commonly treat as normative laws which are unlikely to be enforced against them. Some even comply with laws which are not applicable to them under the national law in question, and where there is thus no risk of sanctions. This acceptance of authority cannot be based on the power of the lawmaker. Conduct of this kind might be termed the Amazon Paradox.

Some readers will be surprised to learn that amazon.co.uk is not a UK entity. It is in fact the trading identity of three Luxembourg corporations, Amazon EU SARL, Amazon Services Europe SARL, and Amazon Media EU SARL. These corporations also trade as Amazon.de and Amazon.fr.

Amazon.co.uk ('Amazon UK') deals online with its customers and is thus an 'information society service provider' under the EU Electronic Commerce Directive.[32] Because Amazon UK is established in an EU Member State, Luxembourg, its online dealings with customers in other EU Member States need only comply with Luxembourg law, with the exception of its contracts with consumers which are subject to the law of the consumer's home state.[33]

But though much of UK law is not applicable to the Amazon UK website, even a cursory review indicates that the website complies with UK advertising regulation and other legal requirements which would only be applicable to it if it were a UK corporation. It is clear that Amazon UK invests substantial time and effort in understanding UK law and ensuring that its amazon.co.uk website complies with it.

Amazon UK's reasons for acting in this way are no doubt a complex mix of commercial, marketing, reputational, and perhaps even moral motives. It is clear, though, that some rules of UK law have authority for Amazon UK simply because they are part of UK law. The fact that the UK authorities have no power to enforce those laws against Amazon is simply not a relevant consideration.

We are therefore faced with a situation in which cyberspace actors treat *some* laws as having authority, but not others. It has not been possible to explain this choice on the basis of the applicability of the law, nor on the basis of the lawmaker's power to enforce compliance. What other explanations might there be?

Legitimacy

One way of describing the internal mental state of a cyberspace actor who acknowledges an obligation to comply with the law of a foreign state might be to say that the

---

[31] For an overview of the boom see Roger Lowenstein, *Origins of the Crash: The Great Bubble and its Undoing* (London: Penguin, 2004).

[32] Directive 2000/31/EC on electronic commerce OJ L 178/1, 17 July 2000.

[33] Ibid, Arts 3(1)–(3), and Annex.

actor recognizes the legitimacy of that state to make laws which direct his activities. However, 'legitimacy' has a range of meanings, only some of which are appropriate here.

The global effects of activities in cyberspace have produced debates on whether it is legitimate for *any* state to claim to regulate cyberspace[34] and, if so, the most appropriate ways to devise and apply such regulation.[35] We studied these debates in outline in Chapter 1. This aspect of legitimacy is of great interest to constitutional lawyers and political theorists, but is unlikely play much part in forming the mental state of a cyberspace actor. The related topic of governance as a means of dealing with overlapping and potentially contradictory national law claims to regulate cyberspace is also important,[36] but again it seems implausible to suggest that a cyberspace actor is influenced by whether the lawmaker's enactments or decisions fit within an accepted theory of how cyberspace should be governed.

Legitimacy might also mean that the lawmaker is an organ of a state whose government is legitimate by international standards, as opposed to being a usurper or a tyrant. This meaning of legitimacy usually implies at least some element of democracy but this is not essential—an absolute monarchy might be a legitimate government, and there is no real doubt that the government of China is legitimate even though China is not a democratic state. However, a cyberspace actor might reasonably deny the legitimacy of, say, the North Korean government and thus its authority to make laws with which he should comply. Legitimacy in this sense is probably a sine qua non for authority but it cannot explain why a cyberspace actor might deny the authority of the UK, or the US, to make a particular law to govern his actions.

A related meaning of legitimacy is that the law in question complies with the requirements of the lawmaker's state for valid law-making. In other words, a law which fails to pass the test imposed by Hart's rule of recognition,[37] perhaps because it is unconstitutional, will be denied authority by the cyberspace actor because it is not a legitimate law. Legitimacy in this sense will also be a sine qua non for authority, but again cannot be the primary reason for denial of authority.

I argued in Chapter 2 that the authority of a law derives from respect for the lawmaker, and also for the content of the law. Respect for the lawmaker arises because the cyberspace actor recognizes that the lawmaker has a legitimate claim to regulate the aspect of cyberspace in question.

It seems, then, that we need to look at legitimacy from the perspective of the cyberspace actor, rather than from that of the lawmaker's legal system. This requires us to abandon the usual jurisprudential focus on whether the rules of a legal system,

---

[34] See eg David R Johnston and David G Post 'Law and Borders: The Rise of Law in Cyberspace' (1996) 48 Stanford Law Review 1367; Jack Goldsmith and Timothy S Wu (n 23).

[35] See eg Lawrence Lessig, *Code and Other Laws of Cyberspace* (New York: Basic Books 1999); Andrew Murray, *The Regulation of Cyberspace* (Abingdon: Routledge-Cavendish, 2007).

[36] See eg Lee Bygrave and Jon Bing (eds), *Internet Governance: Infrastructure and Institutions* (Oxford: Oxford University Press, 2009); Chris Marsden, *Net Neutrality: Towards a Co-regulatory Solution* (London: Bloomsbury Academic, 2010).

[37] HLA Hart (n 6), 100–10.

taken as a whole, have normative force for a person physically located in its jurisdiction or otherwise connected to it by some geographic nexus. Such an approach analyses the question of authority from the perspective of a national legal system, rather than from that of the person who is subject to the law,[38] and as Cotterrell points out, this focus closes off discussion of alternative sources of authority.[39]

The question we need to address is thus: when does a cyberspace actor perceive a foreign lawmaker to have a legitimate claim to regulate his actions? For what reasons? The answer I proposed in Chapter 2 is that such a legitimate claim arises if the cyberspace actor is, either permanently or temporarily, a member of the community which by and large accepts that the lawmaker has authority to make laws which govern it.

Community Membership

It is generally accepted by commentators that a legal system produces rules of law which have authority for the members of the community which that system regulates. Thus, for example, Hart's discussion of the idea of obligation[40] refers throughout to the group or society which, from its internal point of view, accepts the rules as imposing an obligation to act in conformity with them. However, most commentators have in mind the modern nation state and the community of those who reside within its borders; rarely do they ask whether the community might extend beyond the geographical territory of the state.[41]

Raz recognizes the existence of this problem[42] though he does not resolve it directly. However, he does suggest that perceived membership of a community which has a legal system might be one (though not the only) source of respect for the law:

A person identifying himself with his society, feeling that it is his and that he belongs to it, is loyal to his society. His loyalty may express itself, among other ways, in respect for the law of the community.[43]

---

[38] For a detailed (though non-jurisprudential) critique of the failings of methodological nationalism in a globalized world see Ulrich Beck and Natan Sznaider, 'Unpacking Cosmopolitanism for the Social Sciences: A Research Agenda' (2006) 57 *British Journal of Sociology* 1.

[39] '... the price paid for [Kelsen's] clear solution of the authority-validity puzzle is that a diversity of valid, competing legal systems or legal regimes, co-existing in the same social environment yet not integrated, cannot be envisaged' (Roger Cotterrell, 'Transnational Communities and the Concept of Law' (2008) 21 Ratio Juris 1, 6).

[40] HLA Hart (n 30), 82–91.

[41] Thus Hart recognizes that 'We may be doubtful in certain circumstances whether one legal system or another applies to a particular person', but says that these are 'questions of law which arise *within* some system of law (municipal or international) and are settled by reference to the rules or principles of that system' (HLA Hart, n 30, 216). As I have explained above, this is true from the viewpoint of the state but not necessarily so from the internal perspective of the rule-subject.

[42] 'The search for an obligation to obey the law of a certain country is an inquiry into whether there is a set of true premises which entail that everyone (or every citizen? every resident?) ought always to do as those laws require . . .' (Joseph Raz, *The Authority of Law*, 2nd edn (Oxford: Oxford University Press, 2009), 234).

[43] Ibid, 259.

Cotterrell goes further by identifying that globalization has produced 'networks of community' which might act as the basis of regulatory authority.[44]

Because positivist jurisprudence examines the question of authority from the perspective of a legal system it has little more to say about the concept of community. For these purposes the relevant community is defined by the internal rules of the legal system and thus needs no further analysis. For a cyberspace actor, however, the community necessarily transcends state borders and thus their legal systems.

The concept of community has been examined in greater depth by scholars from the natural law tradition. According to Finnis, the authority of a rule-maker comes from the fact that his authority is by and large obeyed by members of the community, and the fact of general obedience creates an obligation that all members should obey those rules:

These normative consequences derive from a normative principle—that authority is a good because required for the realization of the common good—when that principle is taken in conjunction with the fact that a particular person, body, or configuration of persons can, for a given community at a given time, do what authority is to do (ie secure and advance the common good).[45]

The aim which the community is seeking to achieve is the common good. Achieving this aim requires coordination, which creates a need for norms, which creates authority.[46]

Unlike other commentators, Finnis does not assume that the community which is obliged to obey the laws of a particular legal system is necessarily the same as the residents of a state's geographical territory. Rather, the community is a group which is interacting towards a common end, or set of common ends:

political community exists partially (and sometimes primarily) as a kind of business arrangement between self-interested associates . . . partially (and sometimes primarily) as a form of play, in which the participants enjoy the give-and-take, the dissension, bargaining and compromise, for its own sake as a vastly complex and absorbing performance; partially (and sometimes primarily) as an expression of disinterested benevolence, reinforced by grateful recognition of what one owes to the community in which one has been brought up and in which one finds and founds one's family and one's life-plan, and further reinforced by a determination not to be a 'free rider' who arbitrarily seeks to retain the benefits without accepting the burdens of communal interdependence; and characteristically by some admixture of these rationales.[47]

Indeed, Finnis notes that communities can transcend geographical boundaries: 'sharing of aim rather than multiplicity of interaction is constitutive of human groups, communities, societies'.[48]

---

[44] Roger Cotterrell (n 39), 12–13.
[45] John Finnis (n 17), 246.
[46] Ibid, 153.
[47] Ibid, 149.
[48] Ibid, 152.

If we apply these observations to cyberspace it is comparatively easy to decide whether an e-commerce business has made itself part of a foreign community. In metaphorical terms, either it has used cyberspace to transport its shop to the customer's computer, or the customer has travelled online to visit the shop at the business's home location. Which of these is the case is likely to be determined by reference to the marketing activity of the e-commerce business and the quantity of transactions undertaken with foreign customers. For example, a UK-based e-commerce business which places its offline advertising solely in UK print publications or broadcast media and focuses its online marketing on UK users, will see itself as part of the UK community only. If an order is received from a foreign customer, the business will perceive the customer as travelling via cyberspace to the UK, and thus not consider any need to obey that customer's home state laws even if they are, on their own terms, applicable. If orders are received regularly from a particular foreign country then, at some point, the business is likely to see itself as participating in the commercial life of that foreign country as well. This transition is likely to be marked by a change in marketing practices, such as quoting prices in that country's currency and directing online advertising to its residents, and perhaps also by seeking advice as to that country's laws.

Conversely, an e-commerce business which sets out to target customers abroad will consciously be joining the trading community of that country, and thus is likely to perceive those foreign laws as normative whether or not they apply in fact. This may explain the Amazon Paradox. Even though Amazon.co.uk is a Luxembourg corporation its .uk domain name, its advertising, and its customer base connect it so closely to the UK community that it is unsurprising that Amazon feels an obligation to comply with some elements of UK law.

The position is likely to be rather different for a private, non-commercial individual, as opposed to an e-commerce business or a large non-commercial organization. Such a person may have a general desire to respect the law of foreign states but is unlikely to have sufficient knowledge about those laws for them to be authoritative. For individuals, and perhaps small e-commerce businesses as well, a particular foreign law will only have normative force if the actor becomes aware of it, and particularly if a credible threat of sanctions for non-compliance is made.

This is not to say that such actors will inevitably fail to respect foreign laws which apply to a community they have joined via cyberspace unless they are threatened with enforcement. Imagine a US participant on a French discussion board. If relevant to the discussion that person might, through ignorance, post an image of, or link to, Nazi material. But, once alerted to the fact that this contravenes French law, we can see that the US participant might well delete the image or link, and would almost certainly refrain from repeating the conduct.

However, actors who are ignorant of foreign law do not find cyberspace to be a normative vacuum, leaving aside their own national rules of law. There is a widespread awareness that there are laws which apply to their activities, such as copyright or defamation, and often some understanding of the general principles of those laws. To the extent that the norms which are perceived to be established by those laws are considered meaningful and respect-worthy,[49] they are largely obeyed. Furthermore, a great deal of activity in cyberspace takes place in online communities, and these communities all have, or rapidly develop, social norms which guide the online actions of community members.[50] In some cases those norms are formalized and enforcement mechanisms are introduced, so that it might reasonably be argued that the communities have developed their own legal systems. Schultz makes a strong case that eBay is such a community[51] and I have made similar observations in relation to the rules of social networking sites against harassment and other aggressive activity.[52] As is the case for foreign national law, these community rules have authority only for those who have voluntarily become members of the community.

Individualized Authority

The shift of perspective to that of the cyberspace actor rather than the lawmaker opens up a different understanding of the nature of authority in cyberspace. In particular, it shows us that asking the general question whether a lawmaker has authority or not does not produce a meaningful answer. Authority in cyberspace is individualized—a lawmaker's authority may be accepted by actor A, but not by actor B, and actor A will accept the lawmaker's authority only in relation to some of his activities but not for others.

This is very different from, say, the debate over the authority of Germany's Nazi government to make laws.[53] This debate focused on a particular category of laws, those which were thought to go beyond the limits of a state's legitimate claim to regulate its citizens, but did not suggest that those laws might have authority for some citizens but not others. This is because there was a clearly definable category of persons subject to the laws of the state, those resident or present in Germany, and the laws in question either had authority for all of them, or none of them.

Cyberspace community is fluid. Actors move between different communities, often many times in a single day. An online business selling to a German resident is, at that moment, a temporary member of the community of those resident in Germany. But if the next sale is to an Argentinian customer we need to recognize that the seller has left the German community, whose rules no longer apply, and joined the Argentinian community, accepting the authority of a different set of rules.

[49] Copyright is a special case, because the norms of copyright law are widely perceived as being inappropriate for the digital world and thus lacking in authority for the majority, perhaps even almost all, cyberspace users—see Ch 7. Readers who doubt this should examine their own infringing online behaviour and ask themselves if they perceived their actions as wrongful.

[50] See further Andrew Murray (n 35), 126–64.

[51] Thomas Schultz, 'Private Legal Systems: What Cyberspace Might Teach Legal Theorists' (2007) 10 Yale JL & Tech 151.

[52] Chris Reed, 'Why Must You Be Mean to Me?—Crime and the Online Persona' (2010) 13 New Criminal Law Review 485, 496–505.

[53] See HLA Hart, 'Legal Positivism and the Separation of Law and Morals' (1958) Harvard LR 598; Lon Fuller, 'Positivism and Fidelity to Law' (1958) Harvard LR 630; HO Pappe, 'On the Validity of Judicial Decisions in the Nazi Era' (1960) 23 MLR 260.

Furthermore, even whilst temporarily a member of the German community it is clear that our online business will not accept the authority of all its laws. For example, the authoritative laws in relation to its corporate management will be those of its state of establishment, not of Germany. Thus each cyberspace actor will accept the authority of a subset of the world's national laws at any moment, and the content of that subset will change as the actor moves between communities.[54]

Lawmakers who wish to influence behaviour in cyberspace need to understand this different way in which authority works. How they should use that understanding in framing their laws is the subject of the next chapter.

---

[54] This possibility of choice between rule-sets existed before the advent of the internet but was only available to multinational corporations—see Bonaventura De Sousa Santos (n 16), 293:

> [The] historical interplay between geocentric and egocentric legality cannot be definitely decided in favour of geocentric legality. Some recent trends in legal development seem to witness the emergence of new legal particularisms, that is to say, forms of egocentric legality that, by creating personal legal 'enclosures', empty or neutralise the conditions for the application of the law of the land.
>
> . . . we are witnessing the emergence of a new particularism which echoes the personalistic laws of the ancient and medieval world described by Weber. Like the old status groups, each multinational corporation or international economic association has its own personal legal quality and carries its law wherever it goes. [at 294]

The near universal accessibility of cyberspace now requires every person with an online presence to make similar choices as to which legal rules should be treated as personally authoritative.

6

Authoritative Law-making

How can a lawmaker achieve the respect of cyberspace actors for its authority to govern their activities? The fact that a law claims to be applicable, even though that claim is legitimate under the national law in question, is insufficient. Fear of enforcement may secure obedience, though not necessarily respect, but a state's ability to enforce its laws against foreign cyberspace actors is severely limited.

To begin with, the lawmaker needs to understand the way in which a cyberspace actor is likely to decide which lawmakers (or more accurately, which laws produced by a particular lawmaker) he will respect, and which not.

A Subject Rule of Recognition

We saw in Chapter 5 that some foreign laws are likely to have authority for at least some cyberspace actors, even if on their own terms they do not apply to their activities. We have also seen that some laws which *do* apply on their own terms have no authority. The risk of a law's enforcement against the actor is relevant to its authority, but not conclusive. The cyberspace actor is clearly selecting a subset of foreign laws and accepting an obligation to comply with them.

I suggest that what is happening here is that cyberspace actors frame their conduct according to a rule of recognition, albeit an unconscious or unstated rule. They decide whether a foreign rule of law forms part of that subset of the global system of laws to which the actor needs to conform, and they do so through a rational process rather than capriciously. This is not to say that the actor undertakes a formal calculus, or even engages in the decision process consciously. In the physical world we do not consciously ask each time why we are obeying a law, though if queried we would probably be able to identify our reasons for doing so.

Hart's concept of a rule of recognition, addressed to officials tasked with applying the law, identifies whether a rule is part of the system of law to which those officials belong. By contrast, the rule of recognition used by cyberspace actors is addressed to themselves as rule-subjects, not to the official charged with applying the rule. Hart appears to accept that there can be rules of recognition used by others than officials: 'a person who seriously asserts the validity of some given rule of law, say a particular statute, himself makes use of a rule of recognition *which he accepts as appropriate for identifying the law*'.[1]

---

[1] HLA Hart, *The Concept of Law*, 2nd edn (Oxford: Oxford University Press, 1994), 108 (emphasis added).

Raz argues that although there is no independent moral obligation to obey the law,[2] there are two reasons why a person might in practice obey. The first is for prudential reasons, either to avoid sanctions which that legal system is able to impose or because of other kinds of disadvantage which might result from disobedience.[3] The second is that the subject has such a degree of respect for the legal system that the fact of respect imposes at least a prima facie moral obligation to obey the laws of the system.[4]

Adopting Raz's approach would suggest that what we might term the subject rule of recognition has two limbs: foreign laws have authority for a cyberspace actor if the risk[5] of their enforcement (or other adverse consequences) is sufficiently great that a prudent actor would follow them; and they also have authority if the actor has sufficient respect for that foreign legal system to create a moral obligation to comply with its laws, or at least some of them. This chimes with Cotterrell's thinking on the sources of authority for transnational law:

> As regards the nature of law's authority, legal theory can recognize that this authority has two aspects. It resides partly in law's legitimated power of command (*voluntas*)—often guaranteed by the police and military power of a state—and partly in the principled character (*ratio*) of legal doctrine; that is, in the moral meaningfulness of that doctrine for the communities it regulates . . . Hence it opens the possibility for seeing transnational networks of community as producing or inspiring their own law or, at least, being in a position to give or refuse legitimacy to forms of regulation addressed to them or developed with reference to them. One might begin to develop a sense of legal authority and validity as given or refused, in some way, by networks of community that are not restricted to homogeneous nation-state populations (ie, subjects or citizens of the state).[6]

This notion of respect for the law chimes with our everyday experience. We obey the laws which we believe are properly addressed to us, and we do so because we subscribe to the social norm that such laws should be respected and thus obeyed.

However, at first sight the idea that notions of respect might influence corporations seems implausible. Surely corporations are rational profit-maximizers whose ultimate decision-making criterion is the effect of that decision on the corporation's profits?[7] If so, complying with a non-applicable foreign law as Amazon UK does would seem irrational, because it incurs the costs of compliance without any corresponding benefit in avoiding the costs of that law being enforced against it. There are two answers to this objection.

The first is that corporations consider not only immediate costs and benefits but also those which could arise in the future. Thus a corporation might rationally decide to respect a foreign legal system if it believed that this would increase the chance that

---

[2] Joseph Raz, *The Authority of Law*, 2nd edn (Oxford: Oxford University Press, 2009), Ch 12.

[3] In cyberspace the most obvious disadvantage is the risk of reputational damage, which might also have been a factor in Yahoo!'s decision (see Ch 5) to bar Nazi material from its auction site.

[4] Joseph Raz (n 2), Ch 13.

[5] Measured as a combination of the risk that the law will be enforced, and the size of the sanction if it is enforced.

[6] Roger Cotterrell, 'Transnational Communities and the Concept of Law' (2008) 21 Ratio Juris 1, 13.

[7] Utah Kohl, *Jurisdiction and the Internet* (Cambridge: Cambridge University Press, 2007), 209.

the residents of that country would buy its products or services. The same would be true if it thought that doing so would improve its relationship with that state's regulatory authorities if, for example, it were later to establish a subsidiary there. Respect for a legal system might impose an obligation to comply with its rules, but there is no requirement for that respect to derive from moral, as opposed to economic, considerations.

Secondly, and perhaps more pertinently, it is by no means clear that corporations are in all respects rational profit-maximizers. Although research into corporate decision-making has been unable to reach a consensus on the process, it has identified that decision-making purely on the basis of formal rationality tends not to achieve rational control over the world.[8] Thus corporations often make decisions which appear irrational if assessed on purely economic grounds:

Normative research has engendered an increasing consensus among researchers as to what kinds of decision making should be called rational. At the same time, empirical research has found ample evidence of decision-making processes that appear irrational by the normative standards.[9]

Managers construct a narrative to explain their decisions,[10] and these narratives are often based on incorrect perceptions about the world.[11] They encompass not merely the corporation itself but also its environment.[12] That environment is not determined objectively: 'an organization's environment is an arbitrary invention of the organization itself'.[13] It should thus not surprise us if a corporation which has a cyberspace connection with a foreign state constructs a narrative in which that state is so important a part of the environment that the corporation should respect the state's laws.[14]

This last point may help us to understand the second limb of my proposed rule of recognition more fully. We have already noted that the cyberspace actor cannot attempt successfully to comply with all the laws which claim to be applicable, so that

---

[8] Tony J Watson, *In Search of Management: Culture, Chaos and Control in Managerial Work* (London: Routledge, 1994), 138–9.

[9] Nils Brunsson, 'The Irrationality of Action and Action Rationality: Decisions, Ideologies and Organizational Actions' (1982) 19 *Journal of Management Studies* 29, 30 (references omitted).

[10] David Sims, 'Between the Millstones: A Narrative Account of the Vulnerability of Middle Managers' Storying' (2003) 56 *Human Relations* 1195; Tony J Watson (n 8).

[11] John M Mezias and William H Starbuck, 'Studying the Accuracy of Managers' Perceptions: A Research Odyssey' (2003) 14 *British Journal of Management* 3.

[12] 'The organization cannot be responsive to the tidal wave of information potentially available to it . . . organizations create their own environments by paying attention to some information from out there while ignoring other information. This subset of information from outside the organization's boundary becomes the environment, the perception of the outside world upon which all subsequent decisions are based' (John White and David M Dozier, 'Public Relations and Management Decision Making' in James E. Grunig (ed), *Excellence in Public Relations and Communication Management* (Hillsdale NJ: Lawrence Erlbaum Associates, 1992), 91, 92).

[13] William H Starbuck, 'Organizations and their Environments' in Marvin D Dunnette (ed), *Handbook of Industrial and Organizational Psychology* (Chicago: Rand McNally, 1976), 1069, 1078.

[14] The currently fashionable focus on Corporate Social Responsibility (see Catherine Pedamon, 'Corporate Social Responsibility: A New Approach to Promoting Integrity and Responsibility' (2010) Company Lawyer 172) might be a further inducement to the construction of such a narrative.

he will therefore need to choose which legal systems to respect, and thus which rules to comply with.[15] If the actor has, albeit remotely and perhaps temporarily, made himself part of the community which is subject to that legal system, that legal system is likely to play a significant part in the actor's decision-making narrative so far as legal compliance is concerned.

Transnational lawmakers

The subject rule of recognition provides a useful explanation for why, and when, actors in both the physical world and cyberspace accept the authority of rules of transnational law. A traditional analysis of authority from the lawmaker's perspective, under which one is either subject to the full rule-set or not subject at all to the rules of that lawmaker, can only explain transnational law's authority if it is accepted as forming one or more legal systems which are independent of the nation state. Linarelli makes the case for such a legal system with some force,[16] but admits that it is not conclusive. Many would disagree with him.

Some of the bodies from which transnational law emanates, such as UNCITRAL, UNIDROIT, and the OECD, have membership which is limited to state representatives. Thus it might be argued that their authority is delegated or at least derives from the authority of states as lawmakers. But this is not true of purely private bodies such as the International Chamber of Commerce, whose Uniform Customs and Practice for Documentary Credits has for many years been recognized as the primary source of the law governing these transactions. ICANN, a non-state corporation though with state representation in its governance structures, is the effective source of law for many important elements of cyberspace.

---

[15] See Rosaria Conte and Cristiano Castelfranchi, 'The Mental Path of Norms' (2006) 19 Ratio Juris 501, 508:

> autonomous cognitive agents need internal reasons, ie, goals, for doing something; their actions are intentional and motivated, and follow some decision. Hence, the question is, on what basis do the norms aim to be adhered to by competing (within the decision-making process) with other active goals, stemming from personal desires, needs, and so on? Why should agents decide to conform to a recognized norm?

[16] John Linarelli, 'Analytical Jurisprudence and the Concept of Commercial Law' (2009) 114 Penn St L Rev 119. Linarelli argues that the implicit entrenchment of the state as the sole source of law-applying institutions is a defect in positivist thinking (at 195), and that:

> A cosmopolitan conception of legal positivism, one which removes the state as an enabling condition for a legal system, would require that five conditions be met: (1) acceptance by the participants in the legal system of the rules of the system as valid, binding, and authoritative; (2) systemic qualities of normative consequence within the putative legal system that make the normative order the system represents intelligible or comprehensible to the participants; (3) secondary rules and secondary rule officials, though they can be distributed across different state and non-state hierarchies; (4) shared agency between secondary rule officials demonstrating sufficient mutual responsiveness and joint commitment to a legal system; and (5) primary rules dealing with issues that legal systems usually deal with, such as property, contract, and dispute resolution. [130]

See 201–11 for his analysis suggesting that transnational commercial law largely meets these five criteria.

The laws emanating from these bodies, with only a few exceptions,[17] aim to regulate the international dealings between members of a *community*. Even if they are not enacted as state law, they can derive authority from the agreement of the community that these rules are appropriate to govern their transactions. As a consequence, those who choose to become members of the relevant community subject themselves, through that choice, to the authority of the transnational rules which govern the community.

This, according to Linarelli, is the source of the normativity of transnational commercial law. In the traditional positivist conception the law's subjects are members of a community which is regulated by a state's legal system, simply by virtue of their geographical presence in the state's territory. By contrast, transnational commercial law obtains its normative force from the voluntary submission of participants to the system's rules:

In a normative community that is not determined by state boundaries, the internal reflective attitude exists in both norm givers and norm users, towards both secondary and primary rules. . . . Role or identity seems to be key in understanding the practical authority of rules in normative communities not formed by political borders. For example, if a person accepts a role or identity of a merchant, then the law merchant rules relevant to that merchant grouping apply to her.[18]

Or, to put this in my terms, the rule of recognition used by transnational traders is that membership of a trading community obliges a trader to respect, and thus acknowledge the authority of, the rules which that community accepts as governing its dealings.

Cyberspace legal systems

Early commentators predicted that cyberspace would develop its own legal system, but we saw in Chapter 1 that this failed to materialize. Viewed at the level of cyberspace as a whole what we currently have is a patchwork of national law rules supplemented by a number of international instruments, such as the Council of Europe Convention on Cybercrime, the OECD Guidelines on the Protection of Privacy and Transborder Flows of Personal Data, or the UNCITRAL Model Law on Electronic Commerce. This rule-set is clearly a substantial distance from being describable as 'the' legal system for cyberspace. Its application to cyberspace is often purely contingent, based on effects in the relevant jurisdiction which may not have been intended or even foreseeable, and it lacks the degree of coordination and design[19] which we would expect to see in the rules emanating from a legal system. The development of a true legal system for cyberspace will require consensus about

---

[17] Such as the various Hague Conventions in the field of private international law.

[18] John Linarelli (n 16), 196. See also 202–3 and 210.

[19] Except where the national rules have converged on the basis of a designed model, such as the transnational instruments listed above.

the content of that system's rules, and such consensus is unlikely to be reached for many years, if at all.[20]

However, we have seen the development of systems of regulation for specific areas of cyberspace activity, and some of these look very like legal systems. The clearest example is perhaps the regulation of domain names through the ICANN system, and in particular its Uniform Domain Name Dispute Resolution Policy.[21] These rules apply only to the top-level domains (most importantly .com, .org, and .net) over which ICANN asserts its authority, but the country-level domain systems have adopted very similar principles in their own regulations. Registrars sign up to the ICANN rules when seeking authorization, and registrants of domain names enter into contracts with registrars which oblige them to submit to the dispute resolution system. Trade mark owners who wish to contest a domain name registration sign up to the rules when submitting their complaint. There is thus a web of contractual obligations which makes the system effective, and which applies to all those who voluntarily agree to take part. The system runs in parallel to national trade mark law, but the volume of complaints submitted to the WIPO element of the system alone (over 20,000 as at June 2011[22]) suggests that it provides a more accessible dispute resolution system than conventional litigation.

Another example, which has to an extent developed more organically than the top-down ICANN model, is the set of rules which regulates the global eBay trading community. These rules are set by eBay itself and, like the ICANN system, work through a web of contractual obligations. Here, the content of the rules has evolved over time to align with the expectations of eBay users. Buyers often have fewer rights than under their domestic sale or consumer protection laws—in essence, a right to a refund only if they have paid via PayPal and if the item purchased is either not received or not as described by the seller.[23] Because the sums involved are usually too small to justify litigation, particularly if the sale takes place cross-border, eBay's rules are in practice the primary legal system for its participants.[24]

In both these cases the joining of the relevant community, and the consequent voluntary subjection to its rules, is formalized by contracts. These contracts are justiciable under the relevant state laws, and so it might be thought that the ultimate source of authority for the community's rules is in fact state law. This is not how these systems work in practice, however. Enforcement of ICANN's rules is achieved by

---

[20] The range of activities which are possible in cyberspace is as diverse as those undertaken in the physical world, and for many of those activities the achievement of a transnational consensus on the appropriate norms seems very distant. Norms relating to electronic contracting and, perhaps, electronic signatures may already have become part of the transnational commercial law system, and a consensus on the appropriate norms to regulate online crime seems to be building around the Council of Europe Convention on Cybercrime, CETS No 185. By contrast, national norms regulating free speech and content liability are intransigently divergent.

[21] <http://www.icann.org/udrp/udrp-policy-24oct99.htm>.

[22] <http://www.wipo.int/amc/en/domains/statistics/cases.jsp>.

[23] For the UK these are set out at <http://pages.ebay.co.uk/help/policies/buyer-protection.html>, but largely identical policies are applied by the other eBay sites.

[24] Thomas Schultz, 'Private Legal Systems: What Cyberspace Might Teach Legal Theorists' (2007) 10 Yale JL & Tech 151.

removing a registrar's authorization or transferring a domain name, both of which are effected directly through the workings of the system rather than indirectly via court order. eBay's decisions on disputes between buyers and sellers are similarly implemented internally, by refunding the buyer and issuing a chargeback to the seller's PayPal account. The main role of the contracts is to protect the system against claims in national courts by dissatisfied subjects of decisions,[25] rather than to make those decisions enforceable.

Subsets of national law

For both ICANN and eBay the rules of the system have authority for a cyberspace actor because of his voluntary choice to join the relevant community. This choice is often also available for national legal systems. The nature of the cyberspace technologies allows an actor a high degree of control over the global reach of his online activities so that, for the most part, the undesired application of the rules of a particular legal system can be avoided through technological means.[26] Thus whether a particular rule of law is authoritative for a cyberspace user is decided by his technological and operational choices, which determine whether he has joined the community regulated by that lawmaker.

However, the fact that a cyberspace user has, for the moment, become part of a foreign national community does not mean that he accepts the authority of *all* that community's laws. The user has temporarily joined the community for a particular purpose, such as doing business, communicating information or storing or accessing data. The only national laws which are likely to have authority for the user are those which relate to carrying out that purpose.

In Chapter 5 we noted that Amazon UK has made itself part of the UK trading community, and thus complies with the UK's laws relating to trading even though most of those laws are not applicable to it. However, Amazon is not a UK employer in respect of its Luxembourg-based employees, nor is it a UK-registered corporation for company law purposes, nor is it a member of the UK taxpayer community in the same way as UK-established corporations.[27] Cyberspace actors do not generally become full members of the foreign communities with which they interact, and so for them the only authoritative elements of foreign law are those subsets of national law which are applicable to their interactions with the local community.

---

[25] Such as the litigation in *Bragg v Linden Research Inc*, 487 F Supp 2d 593 (ED Pa, 2007). In that case Linden had terminated Bragg's Second Life account in accordance with its terms and conditions, and was sued by Bragg on the basis (*inter alia*) that this had deprived him of his rights in land contrary to the applicable Californian real property laws. The case was settled, so we will never know whether the court would have upheld the terms and conditions in Linden's favour, or indeed whether it would have decided that Second Life 'land' fell within the scope of real property laws.

[26] See Thomas Schultz, 'Carving Up the Internet: Jurisdiction, Legal Orders, and the Private/Public International Law Interface' (2008) 19 EJIL 799.

[27] At least in respect of its online trading, for taxes other than VAT. The Amazon Group has a number of UK premises and staff and owns at least two UK corporations (Amazon.com.uk Ltd and Amazon. co.uk Ltd), and the activities of these corporations within the geographical territory of the UK are likely to be subject to UK tax law.

Authority and Law-making

Governments are naturally concerned when they discover that the activities of foreign cyberspace actors have effects in their state which are unlawful. There are often strong political pressures to do 'something', usually taking the form of enacting a new law. The history of such attempts to control foreign cyberspace users is one of consistent failure.[28]

An important reason for this failure is the natural assumption by lawmakers that merely asserting their authority to regulate is sufficient to give their laws actual authority for all cyberspace users. This is not so. In cyberspace, authority derived from respect for the foreign legal system is the primary currency. Thus if a state wishes to influence the behaviour of cyberspace actors it needs to frame its laws in such a way that their authority is accepted by actors, and thus secure compliance primarily because of respect for the law.

Over-assertion of authority

Let us revisit our imaginary example from Chapter 3, where the state of Ruritania enacts a new road traffic law which expressly applies its speed limits to all driving, anywhere in the world. Foreign recipients of a summons from the Ruritanian authorities would, after their initial puzzlement, be likely to laugh. A national law which purports to direct the behaviour of cyberspace actors who recognize no connection with that jurisdiction will probably elicit a similar reaction.

And yet, this is what states largely do at present, though often without perhaps realizing it. Just as cyberspace activities potentially have effects everywhere, so do the tendrils of national laws reach out into cyberspace and influence attitudes to those laws and their makers. Laws whose reach into cyberspace is undefined make a claim on cyberspace users that their authority should be recognized.

National lawmakers might be tempted to accept the proposition that respect for a foreign legal system is engendered by becoming a virtual member of that system's community, but still choose to enact laws which claim to apply to all cyberspace actors. Their reasoning would be that those laws will tend to be complied with by actors who interact with residents of the state, thus becoming community members, and that non-compliance by the remainder can simply be ignored. This fails to recognize the effects of over-assertion of authority on the internal mental state of cyberspace actors.

---

[28] The US Communications Decency Act 1996 47 USC § 230 and the Australian Broadcasting Services Amendment (Online Services) Act 1999 are well-known examples from the field of online content control. This is not to say that national enforcement authorities cannot enforce their content control laws against foreign infringers—there are numerous example of successful enforcement, see eg David Bender, 'Personal Jurisdiction against Websites' (1999) 547 PLI/P at 67; European Commission Communication, 'Illegal and Harmful Content on the Internet', COM (96) 0487-C4-0592/96. The point is that these enforcement actions failed to convince the wider cyberspace community to follow those national rules, even though a few individuals were forced to comply.

Respect is not a one-way but a mutual relationship, and if the state does not respect the cyberspace actor there is a likelihood that the actor will reciprocate. Laws which apply without distinction to all cyberspace actors, and which are thus clearly unlikely ever to be complied with by, or enforced against, the majority, are likely to be dismissed as mere propaganda. They will not be perceived as serious attempts by the state to influence the behaviour of those individuals which the state has the right, as seen from the perspective of the cyberspace actor, to regulate, and will thus lose their normative force.[29] A further defect in this scattergun approach to law-making is that it fails to consider the likely response of the cyberspace actor who *does* respect the legal system, who may well respond in a way which is very different from what the lawmaker intended. This too can erode the lawmaker's authority because it suggests incompetence.

A clear example of a law which failed in both these ways is the 2002 amendment to the EU Sixth VAT Directive.[30] Prior to the amendment, non-EU suppliers of online services to consumers could lawfully do so without charging Value Added Tax. Supplies of information such as music downloads are services for VAT purposes, and so the VAT regime created a strong incentive for those services to be supplied from outside the EU with a consequent loss of tax revenue to EU Member States. The solution set out in the amendment was to require non-EU suppliers of online services to consumers to register with the tax authorities in the EU jurisdiction of their choice, and then to identify the EU country from which each consumer customer originated and charge VAT at the rate of the consumer's country of residence. A VAT return was due to the country of registration, identifying the proportion of supplies to each EU Member State, on the basis of which the country of registration was to distribute the tax between the Member States where the supplies were made.

The burden of identifying customers, charging differential VAT rates, and keeping records would have been extremely onerous, and it was also clear that the EU authorities had little hope of enforcing the law.[31] Thus few, if any, online suppliers chose to

---

[29] '. . . a general disregard of the rules of the system . . . may be so complete in character and so protracted that we should say, in the case of a new system, that it had never established itself as the legal system of a given group, or, in the case of a once-established system, that it had ceased to be the legal system of the group' (HLA Hart (n 1), 103, and see also 117–19 for extended discussion of this issue).

[30] Council Directive 2002/38/EC of 7 May 2002 amending and amending temporarily Directive 77/388/EEC as regards the value added tax arrangements applicable to radio and television broadcasting services and certain electronically supplied services, OJ L 128 p 41, 15 May 2002.

[31] The discussion of enforcement on p 9 of the Explanatory Memorandum strikes a rather forlorn note:

> From the perspective of the non tax compliant business, failure to meet legitimate obligations carries several direct and serious risks. Not the least of these is that an incurred liability for VAT does not resolve itself simply by its concealment or failing to report it to the correct tax administration. Failure to comply with self-assessment obligations does nothing to reduce or remove a debt owing in respect of taxation. Rather, it exposes the business to additional penalty and interest charges which only serve to cause the liability to escalate further.
>
> For an operator, even one located outside the EU, to risk exposure to significant and unresolved tax debts in the world's largest marketplace cannot be considered prudent business practice. Neither does the debt lapse over time but continues to hover over the business and

comply voluntarily. Even if they respected the EU as a legal system, they had no respect for this particular law.

Those suppliers who wished or needed to comply with EU VAT law took a different route. They created a permanent establishment in a chosen EU Member State and made the supplies from that establishment. This had the advantage that supplies to all EU consumers were made at the VAT rate of the country of establishment, which was of course chosen to be the EU Member State with the lowest VAT rate. Effectively the law directed the missing taxes to Luxembourg, which was far from what had been intended.

The aims of the law were twofold: to persuade foreign suppliers of online services to collect VAT; and to share that VAT between the EU Member States. What the law actually achieved was to turn most of those online suppliers into law-breakers, and to direct the VAT paid by the remainder to a single EU Member State. It is hard to argue that the EU's law-making authority was not thereby reduced.

If national law is to respect the cyberspace actor, and thus achieve voluntary compliance through its normative effects, it needs to correlate with the actor's understanding of the limits on a state's legitimacy in regulating cyberspace.[32] In the same way that an actor ought to respect the relevant laws of a state whose community he has joined, the state ought to refrain so far as is possible from attempting to regulate those who are not part of its community.[33]

This principle is very close to that set out in the Due Process provisions of the US Constitution, the Fifth and Fourteenth Amendments. We saw in Chapter 3 that the

---

even, in certain circumstances, passes on to a subsequent purchaser of the operation. The presence of such a liability is furthermore hardly likely to assist in access to legitimate capital or funding sources. Normal accepted standards of statutory auditing or due diligence examinations would be expected to detect failure to comply with tax obligations in a significant jurisdiction such as the EU. The risk of punitive tax assessments is also high.

Moreover, in certain cases, sanctions under civil or criminal law may attach to the managers or owners of the business. Moreover, existing Community provisions in relation to mutual assistance and recovery ensure that a tax debt in one Member State is effectively enforceable anywhere in the Community.

Legitimate operators will moreover wish to ensure that they have access to legal protection and remedies in respect of infringements of copyright or other intellectual property rights. To this end, they will also wish to ensure that they respect their own legal and regulatory obligations.

Although all of the foregoing are strong forces in favour of opting for compliance, they are however not enough in themselves and, particularly for remote suppliers, there is a need to develop tools of direct enforcement on which tax administrations can call . . . Developing the necessary tools and procedures is a part of the maturing process for e-commerce and there are good indications that this will be achieved.

[32] Austen Parrish (n 5), 1490.

[33] This accords with Post's 'presumption of a-territoriality':

a law's reach is confined and bounded ultimately by the network of those who have participated in its adoption and consented to its application. If that network is itself bounded or defined by physical geography, the presumption of territorial reach and the power of the territorial agent is well founded; if not, not. [David Post, 'The "Unsettled Paradox": The Internet, the State, and the Consent of the Governed' (1998) 5 Ind J Global Legal Stud 521, 542].

line of jurisprudence deriving from *International Shoe Co v Washington*[34] holds that a non-resident defendant can only be subject to judicial proceedings if there is a strong connection between the defendant and the jurisdiction.[35] At an appropriate point on the continuum between 'passive' and 'active' websites, explained in *Zippo Mfg Co v Zippo Dot Com Inc*,[36] a defendant website owner has sufficient connection with the jurisdiction to allow the courts to assert jurisdiction. I would suggest that this is also likely to be the point at which the defendant perceives that it has become a member of that jurisdiction's community.

The European rules on jurisdiction tend to adopt a 'bright-line' approach based on geographical factors,[37] and thus are unable to take account of community membership. However, there are a number of techniques which lawmakers can adopt to match the reach of their laws to the expectations of cyberspace actors.[38] These include limiting the application of the law to activities which have a physical connection with the state's territory[39] or adopting a published non-enforcement policy for online activities which do not have sufficient connection with the jurisdiction.[40]

It is also possible for the courts to take account of the principle when interpreting national law. There are signs that this is beginning to occur in English defamation jurisprudence, though implicitly rather than expressly. The earliest online defamation cases simply applied the rule that defamation occurs in the place where the defamatory material is read,[41] and thus allowed foreign claimants to sue foreign defendants in the English courts so long as the claimant had some minimal reputation

---

[34] 326 US 310 (1945).

[35] *CompuServe v Patterson*, 89 F 3d 1257 (6th Cir, 1996) explains the test as follows:

This court has repeatedly employed three criteria to make this determination: First, the defendant must purposefully avail himself of the privilege of acting in the forum state or causing a consequence in the forum state. Second, the cause of action must arise from the defendant's activities there. Finally, the acts of the defendant or consequences caused by the defendant must have a substantial enough connection with the forum to make the exercise of jurisdiction over the defendant reasonable.

[36] 952 F Supp 1119 (WD Pa, 1997). See further Brian D Boone, 'Bullseye!: Why a "Targeting" Approach to Personal Jurisdiction in the E-Commerce Context Makes Sense Internationally' (2006) 20 Emory Int'l L Rev 241.

[37] Typified by the EU Council Regulation (EC) 44/201 on jurisdiction and the recognition and enforcement of judgments in civil and commercial matters, OJ L12/1, 16 January 2001 (Brussels Regulation). This 'bright-line' approach produces less certainty than might be imagined—see Julia Hörnle, 'The Jurisdictional Challenge of the Internet' in Lilian Edwards and Charlotte Waelde (eds), *Law and the Internet*, 3rd edn (Oxford: Hart Publishing, 2009), Ch 3.

[38] See Ch 3 and the discussion below.

[39] eg s 36(3) of the UK Gambling Act 2005, which disapplies the obligation to hold a UK gambling licence unless at least one piece of remote gambling equipment is situated in Great Britain, excluding equipment not supplied by the gambling operator such as the user's own computer.

[40] As is done in relation to online financial and securities advertising in a number of countries—see eg Securities and Exchange Commission, *Statement of the Commission Regarding Use of Internet Web Sites to Offer Securities, Solicit Securities Transactions or Advertise Investment Services Offshore* (Release Nos 33-7516, 34-39779, IA-1710, IC-23071, International Series Release No 1125), 23 March 1998.

[41] Following the reasoning in *Godfrey v Demon Internet* [2001] QB 201 and *Gutnick v Dow Jones* [2001] VSC 305, [2002] HCA 56 (Australia).

in England to be damaged.[42] More recently, however, the courts have recognized that bringing proceedings in England where neither of the parties is from England can be an abuse of process if there is little prospect that the outcome of the trial will vindicate the claimant or provide an appropriate remedy.[43] The fact that neither of the parties forms part of the English community clearly plays some part in reaching these decisions, and where there is evidence of community involvement by a claimant the court is unlikely to find an abuse of process.[44]

The problem with the US rules on jurisdiction and the UK limitation of scope by means of abuse of process is that their application to a particular cyberspace actor can only be known after legal proceedings have commenced. The substantive law in question still appears to claim authority over the cyberspace actor, even if that claim is softened by the chance that, on closer examination, it will turn out that the state does not in fact make that claim. From the actor's perspective, a law which makes its claims to authority clear at the outset is far more likely to command the appropriate respect than one which does not.

Making laws to command respect

Any lawmaker which has read this far should by now be aware that its laws are only likely to be obeyed by foreign cyberspace actors if either they believe there is a real prospect of enforcement against them, or if they respect the lawmaker's claim to authority over them because they are members of the community it regulates. Fear of enforcement is less likely to secure obedience than respect because the benefits from non-compliance may outweigh the low risk of enforcement.

How, then, can the lawmaker restrict its assertion of authority to those who have joined its community via cyberspace? We have seen that relying on the rules of jurisdiction alone is unlikely to be successful.

The primary task involved is to define a line which can distinguish those cyberspace actors who join the lawmaker's community from the other users of cyberspace. This is not a way of thinking to which lawmakers are accustomed. It is normal practice simply to identify the behaviour to be regulated and then enact the law accordingly, assuming that it will apply to those resident in the lawmaker's territory and leaving it to the courts to decide how far the law should apply to those outside

---

[42] See eg *Berezovsky v Michaels and ors* [2000] UKHL 25, [2000] 2 All ER 986, though note in particular the dissenting judgment of Lord Hoffmann.

[43] *Dow Jones & Co Inc v Jameel* [2005] EWCA Civ 75:

> If the claimant succeeds in this action and is awarded a small amount of damages, it can perhaps be said that he will have achieved vindication for the damage done to his reputation in this country, but both the damage and the vindication will be minimal. The cost of the exercise will have been out of all proportion to what has been achieved. The game will not merely not have been worth the candle, it will not have been worth the wick. [para 69 per Lord Justice Phillips MR]

See also *Lonzim plc v Sprague* [2009] EWHC 2838 (QB); *Atlantis World Group v Gruppo Editoriale L'Espresso SPA* [2008] EWHC 1323 (QB).

[44] See eg *Lewis and ors v King* [2004] EWCA Civ 1329; *Mardas v New York Times Co* [2008] EWHC 3135 (QB).

the territory. To the extent that laws restrict their extraterritorial application, this is usually designed to avoid clashes with other national legal systems.[45]

There are signs though that lawmakers are beginning to recognize the need to change their thinking. Section 21(3) of the UK Financial Services and Markets Act, discussed in Chapter 3, provides that the prohibition on issuing an invitation or inducement to engage in an investment activity, other than by or under the approval of a person authorized under the Act, 'applies only if the communication is capable of having an effect in the United Kingdom'. This provision is aimed primarily at cyberspace advertising of investments, though it will also apply to the small quantity of print advertising which circulates in the UK via foreign publications.

However, this drafting goes only part of the way to identifying the cyberspace community which is likely to accept the UK's claim to regulate it. Online investment businesses will understand that only the UK courts are capable of deciding whether their advertising is capable of having an effect in the UK, and will recognize that there is a risk that the courts will so decide even if the business did not believe itself to have joined the UK community. It requires but a little further thought to realize that the only cyberspace actors which the UK should want to regulate are those whose intention is to induce UK residents to invest, or who actually secure investment by residents. Redrafting in terms of the actor's intentions would make a clear distinction between advertisers to the UK community and the remainder of cyberspace investment activity.

The US Children's Online Privacy Protection Act 1998[46] delimits its scope by reference to the intention of providers of websites and online services. If these providers undertake commerce in the US and target their websites to children, then the Act's provisions apply to the provider.[47] This targeting approach matches the US rules on jurisdiction,[48] and is also likely to match closely the understanding of service providers about whether they are dealing with the US community.

Attempts to wrestle with this issue can also be seen at the transnational level, in the Commentary to Article 5 of the OECD Model Convention with respect to Taxes on Income and on Capital, discussed in Chapter 3. Here the line is drawn by reference to persons or physical property located in the jurisdiction, which provides a very clear division between those cyberspace actors over whom authority is asserted and the remainder. However, only a minority of cyberspace activities involve physical property, and so in most cases the lawmaker will need to adopt a less precise technique.

It seems to me that the most successful way of drawing this line is likely to be by reference to the apparent intentions of the cyberspace actor, as manifested through his actions. If the actor does not intend to become a temporary member of the lawmaker's community he is unlikely to respect the authority of that community's

---

[45] As an example, although the UK Insolvency Act 1986 gives liquidators and the courts power to unravel certain pre-insolvency dealings, the settlement and security rules of designated financial systems (many of which will be non-UK systems) are given precedence over that power by the Financial Markets and Insolvency (Settlement Finality) Regulations 1999, SI 1999/2979.

[46] 15 USC § 6501.

[47] 15 USC § 6501(2) and (10).

[48] See Ch 3.

laws, and this technique thus matches closely the subjective internal state of mind of the actor which, as we saw in Chapter 5, is what the lawmaker needs to influence to achieve respect. It also has the advantage of being very closely related to the existing legal concept of 'targeting', though used here to delimit the scope of the law in advance rather than as an *ex post facto* test to decide if it should be applied.

Once the lawmaker has decided how to draw this line, it needs to be incorporated into the law itself. The two main techniques for doing so, restricting the law's application in cyberspace or announcing a policy of selective enforcement based on the dividing line, have been explained in Chapter 3. We also saw there that if the content of the law converges on established cyberspace norms, if they exist in the field, an over-assertion of authority is less likely to reduce respect for the law.

It is important to recognize that drawing this line is not an end in itself. Its purpose is to limit the lawmaker's claim of authority to those who ought, by virtue of joining the community, to recognize it. If the line is not set according to this principle there is a real risk that the law's authority will not be accepted by cyberspace users.

One of the clearest illustrations of failure in this respect is found in EU data protection law. Article 4(1)(c) of the 1995 Directive[49] draws a line between those cyberspace processors of personal data to whom the law claims to apply and those to whom it does not, apparently by reference to physical property located in the jurisdiction. Thus the directive's obligations apply only to a controller who is not established on Community territory where the controller:

for purposes of processing personal data makes use of equipment, automated or otherwise, situated on the territory of the said Member State, unless such equipment is used only for purposes of transit through the territory of the Community.

However, the EU's Article 29 Data Protection Working Party has explained that the proper interpretation of this wording gives the application of the law far wider scope than at first appears. It is unsurprising that 'it is not necessary for the controller to exercise ownership or full control over such equipment for the processing to fall within the scope of the Directive'[50] because otherwise it would be easy to devise information processing structures to evade the application of the law. Few cyberspace users would expect, however, that the proper meaning of 'equipment', read in the light of the other language versions of the directive, is in fact 'means',[51] which extends to non-physical processes carried out by the controller in the territory of a Member State. Adopting this meaning, the Working Party has concluded that 'equipment' can include tracking cookies or scripts and other software, originating from the controller and running on the Member State resident's own computer.[52]

---

[49] Directive 95/46/EC on the protection of individuals with regard to the processing of personal data and on the free movement of such data, OJ L281/31, 23 November 1995.

[50] Article 29 Data Protection Working Party, 'Opinion 8/2010 on Applicable Law', 0836-02/10/EN, WP 179, 16 December 2010 ('WP179'), 20.

[51] Ibid, 20.

[52] Article 29 Data Protection Working Party, 'Working Document on Determining the International Application of EU Data Protection Law to Personal Data Processing on the Internet by non-EU Based Web Sites', 5035/01/EN/Final, WP 56, 30 May 2002, 10–12.

The Working Party's opinion does not assert that simple web forms amount to 'equipment', but on the reasoning set out they would also appear to be means used for collecting personal data, and the HTML code for the form is certainly down-loaded to the user's computer and thus processed in the user's territory.

There must be real doubt whether this wide assertion of authority matches the internal mental states of non-EU collectors of personal data. From their perspective the EU resident has chosen to visit their website, which is 'located' where they are resident and not in the EU. Cookies and scripts are merely technology which assists the visitor to obtain the information and services provided by the website. Why should a foreign lawmaker claim to control these activities, any more than if the user had travelled physically outside the EU to obtain services from a foreign supplier? As Kuner notes:

the existence of jurisdictional assertions with a tenuous link to the forum (such as based on data processing by cookies on a website) and the resulting low chance of enforcement may cause controllers to regard data protection rules as a kind of bureaucratic nuisance rather than as 'law' in the same category as tax laws, employment laws, etc.[53]

Cyberspace users who do not regard the directive as 'real' law are unlikely to respect it or accept its authority.

The Article 29 Working Party has recognized that this interpretation of Article 4(1)(c) makes excessive claims of authority over foreign data controllers[54] and has therefore proposed that the primary test for applicability of EU law to foreign controller should be via a:

targeting of individuals, or 'service oriented approach': this would involve the introduction of a criterion for the application of EU data protection law, that the activity involving the processing of personal data is targeted at individuals in the EU. This would need to consist of substantial targeting based on or taking into account the effective link between the individual and a specific EU country. The following examples illustrate what targeting could consist of: the fact that a data controller collects personal data in the context of services explicitly acces-sible or directed to EU residents, via the display of information in EU languages, the delivery of services or products in EU countries, the accessibility of the service depending on the use of an EU credit card, the sending of advertising in the language of the user or for products and services available in the EU.[55]

Unfortunately it is still proposed to retain the means/equipment provisions, though in modified form, as a backup measure to counter the risk of the EU becoming a 'data haven' for the processing of non-EU personal data. Unless this backup is devised carefully, it risks losing the advantages to be gained from moving to a targeting approach.

---

[53] Christopher Kuner, 'Data Protection Law and International Jurisdiction on the Internet (Part 2)', (2010) 18 Int JL & IT 227, 236.

[54] WP 179 (n 50), 29.

[55] Ibid, 31.

Competing Claims to Authority

The analysis in this chapter tells us that lawmakers should, so far as possible, avoid the situation where the cyberspace actor is subject to competing claims to law-making authority. If this is not achieved the cyberspace actor will use the subject rule of recognition to determine which claims are accepted and which must be rejected.

In some instances, though, the lawmaker may not be able to frame its law so as to avoid a conflict with other lawmakers' claims. Here it is faced with the choice of asserting its authority, or abandoning the planned law-making. How is this choice to be made?

Murray's concept of 'regulatory gravity'[56] may be of some assistance here. This is a refinement of his concept of the regulatory matrix, through which communications between lawmakers, individuals, norms, markets, and code produces a regulatory settlement.[57] These nodes are not all equal—some have far greater influence on the outcome of the regulatory settlement than others or, in Murray's terminology, possess more regulatory gravity. Thus the subjects of regulation encompass both comparatively powerless cyberspace actors such as individuals, but also very powerful actors such as Google, Facebook, and eBay. This latter group derives its power from its role as gatekeepers, enabling access by individuals to information and services in cyberspace:

internet gatekeepers are uniquely powerful regulators of all online activity. Arguably they are more powerful than any single state or state-based regulator as they uniquely have full regulatory control over that part of the network which they manage. As the cyberlibertarians pointed out fourteen years ago no government can claim such control. Internet gatekeepers are therefore uniquely powerful within cyberspace due to their positions at the nexus points between communications networks; this gives them considerable ability to control and therefore considerable gravity. This explains why they are effective as regulators . . .[58]

One potential source of conflicting claims to authority is thus the rules, often in the forms of terms of service, which these gatekeepers impose on cyberspace actors as a condition of using their services. These claims to authority are particularly powerful because they are based on the actor's voluntary accession to the gatekeeper's community.[59] By contrast, an actor's membership of a national lawmaker's community is often temporary and contingent on, for example, unsolicited dealings with residents of the lawmaker's state. An online seller is thus more likely to obey eBay's rules than those of, say, UK law, because eBay has greater regulatory gravity for such sellers unless they are also UK residents.

It seems obvious, too, that state lawmakers possess different levels of regulatory gravity for each cyberspace actor. Our UK seller may agree that UK sales law has

---

[56] Andrew Murray, 'Nodes and Gravity in Virtual Space' (2010) 5 Legisprudence 195.

[57] See Ch 1, text to n 39.

[58] Andrew Murray (n 56, 220).

[59] Ibid, 221: 'Either power is legitimately transferred from an already legitimate regulator or legitimacy is recognized by the regulated community.'

greater authority than eBay's rules, but is likely to give more weight to eBay's rules than those of US sales law. eBay.com will recognize US law as having greater authority for it than UK law because eBay.com is a US corporation; eBay.co.uk will give more weight to the authority of UK law than eBay.com, but cannot ignore the authority of US law because it is owned by eBay.com.

In resolving its dilemma, our lawmaker therefore needs to identify the competing claims to authority in its field of law-making, and then assess its regulatory gravity in relation to those other claimants from the perspective of the group of cyberspace actors to which it intends to apply the law. If our lawmaker's regulatory gravity is strongest, its law-making authority is likely to be accepted by those cyberspace actors. If not, its authority is likely to be rejected, thus rendering its law-making activities at best pointless, and at worst likely to reduce the normative force of its other law-making claims to authority.

PART III

RESPECT-WORTHY LAWS

7

Cyberspace Communities and Cyberspace Norms

In Part II I argued that laws are unlikely to be obeyed by cyberspace actors if they do not accept the lawmaker's authority to govern their cyberspace activities. Actors are faced with competing and overlapping claims to authority, and will therefore need to choose between them. If there is a non-trivial prospect of the law being enforced against the actor, this may be sufficient to cause its authority to be accepted. In other cases though, and these will be by far the majority, a lawmaker's authority will only be accepted if the cyberspace actor has become a virtual member of the community which that lawmaker regulates.

But this does not mean that the cyberspace actor will accept the authority of *all* the laws emanating from that lawmaker. In the same way that the actor has to choose between the competing claims of lawmakers, so the actor also has a choice as to which individual rules of law he accepts as imposing binding obligations. If a law requires the impossible or even the impracticable, or conflicts with other obligations which the actor accepts as binding or with established cyberspace norms, or demands behaviour which has no apparent connection with achieving the law's aims, or has been outdated by technological change, its authority is likely to be rejected. In other words, we must look not merely at the source of the law but also its content. For want of a better term I describe the content of those laws which are likely to be accepted as 'meaningful'. Meaning has to be assessed from the perspective of the actor. Unfortunately, many law-making attempts in cyberspace have failed to achieve such meaningfulness.

Suppose that the lawmaker restricts its law-making to the community (as extended into cyberspace) which it has a legitimate claim to regulate. This alone is not enough to ensure that its laws will be complied with. The lawmaker still faces the challenge of ensuring that the content of the rules it imposes on that community are accepted by its members as imposing meaningful obligations upon them.

One promising strategy is to take the existing legal norms which regulate that community and transpose them so that they also apply to the extended cyberspace community. Those norms are already accepted as meaningful by the lawmaker's physical world community, and so if they can be transposed successfully there is a strong chance that the extended cyberspace community will recognize their meaningfulness as well.

As we shall see, though, it is not always possible to transpose norms in a way which is meaningful to the cyberspace actor. Even if this approach is potentially feasible, success requires an understanding of the techniques which need to be used to ensure normative equivalence between the obligations imposed on physical world members of the community, and those imposed on offline members.

Lawmakers also need to understand that a cyberspace actor is likely to be a member of multiple communities. These will include not only the actor's 'home' physical world community, but also purely cyberspace communities. Many of these latter communities have developed their own internal norms. If a cyberspace actor is a member of one or more communities which impose normative obligations on him, and which he accepts as meaningful, he is less likely to recognize the meaning, and thus the authority, of conflicting normative obligations which another lawmaker attempts to impose. This is not to say that a lawmaker is limited to making laws which match existing norms in cyberspace—after all, one of the functions of law is to establish or reinforce norms by giving them the greater authority which derives from the lawmaker's status, and also from the consequent possibility of their enforcement via the mechanisms of the legal system. Nonetheless, a lawmaker who decides to make laws which are in such conflict must recognize the difficulties it faces in persuading cyberspace actors to accept the authority of those laws.

Transposing Offline Legal Norms to Cyberspace

The principle that the legal norms which regulate the physical world should, where possible, regulate cyberspace as well, is widely accepted by lawmakers. The concept is more usually expressed by saying that there should be equivalence of legal treatment between online and offline activities. The first public statement to this effect appears in the Bonn Ministerial Conference Declaration of 6–8 July 1997, which declared in its principle 22:

Ministers stress that the general legal frameworks should be applied on-line as they are off-line. In view of the speed at which new technologies are developing, they will strive to frame regulations which are technology-neutral, whilst bearing in mind the need to avoid unnecessary regulation.[1]

This statement referred to the general body of existing law, as it was thought that when purely cyberspace issues were identified they would require cyberspace-specific law-making on a case-by-case basis. However, within a few years lawmakers began to view the principle as more widely applicable, leading to a law-making approach under which all laws and regulations should, so far as possible, be equivalent online and offline. In other words, the legal principles which regulated an online activity should be the same as those which applied to the equivalent offline activity.[2]

---

[1] <http://europa.eu.int/ISPO/bonn/Min_declaration/i_finalen.html>.

[2] See eg Communication from the Commission to the Council, the European Parliament, the Economic and Social Committee, and the Committee of the Regions, 'Principles and Guidelines for the Community's Audiovisual Policy in the Digital Age', COM (1999) 0657 final, note 17: 'identical services should in principle be regulated in the same way, regardless of their means of transmission'.

Equivalence between offline rules and those which are to apply in cyberspace is important if the lawmaker wishes to take advantage of the normative force which those offline rules already possess. If the rule imposes a different set of obligations for cyberspace actors, then the fact that the authority of the cognate rule is accepted in the physical world is less likely to influence whether the cyberspace actor accepts the new rule's authority. Worse, lack of equivalence might persuade the cyberspace actor that the obligations of the new rule are meaningless for him; his expectation is that the rule in cyberspace will be the same as it is offline, and if it is not the same this throws doubt on the competence of the lawmaker.

It is worth noting here that the concepts of equivalence and technology neutrality are by no means synonymous. Equivalence guides the lawmaker as to the principles of law which should apply to cyberspace activities and thus shapes the substantive rules of any law. Technology neutrality addresses the choice between the available substantive rules which could be used to implement those legal principles, and aims at future-proofing the law by ensuring that developments in technology do not make its rules outdated. This latter issue is examined in Chapter 11.

What does 'equivalence' mean?

The first problem with adopting a principle of equivalence is that the term does not have a clear meaning in the context of law-making. Schellekens identifies two main ways in which it has been used.[3] The first is as an overarching policy statement that there should be broad equivalence of treatment for offline and online activities while remaining agnostic as to how such equivalence should be achieved. As Schellekens points out, this tells us nothing about what the law should say:

The law is a black-box and its output must meet certain requirements. It is for lawyers to figure out how the requirements can be met.[4]

The alternative usage is that the principle acts as a substantive guideline for the application of existing law or the creation of new law. However, this guideline is by no means clear.

One possible meaning is that the *same* rule has to apply to both online and offline situations. In other words, the search is for a single rule which applies to all situations. We might describe this as *equivalence of form*. The dangers of seeking equivalence in this purely formal sense are well known from the cases which applied pre-cyberspace laws to online activities. The problem which these cases highlighted was that differences between online and offline technologies and practices often result in the effect of a rule being very different as between them. As an example, the established offline rule in defamation law was that a publisher is liable to the person

---

[3] Maurice Schellekens, 'What Holds Off-Line, Also Holds On-Line?' in Bert-Jaap Koops, Miriam Lips, Corien Prins, and Maurice Schellekens (eds), *Starting Points for ICT Regulation: Deconstructing Prevalent Policy One-liners* (The Hague: TMC Asser Press, 2006), 51, 56–7.

[4] Ibid, 57.

defamed, as well as being liable to the author.[5] Applying this rule to cyberspace without modification produced the result that the host of an internet resource, such as a website or newsgroup, was liable for defamatory content of which the host had no knowledge and which it could not discover without taking unusual precautions.[6] The effect of the rule is very different for an offline publisher, who rarely publishes material which has not first been reviewed by representatives of the publisher such as editors.

The alternative way of using the principle as a substantive guideline is to seek to achieve *functionally equivalent* legal treatment of an activity, irrespective of whether the activity takes place online or offline. This approach seeks equivalence of application of the rules, in other words that the obligations imposed on the subject of the rules should be broadly equivalent in burden once allowance has been made for the differences between the online and offline versions of the activity.

Meaning and authority

Adopting a policy of equivalence between online and offline law can enhance the meaningfulness of laws in cyberspace. Such a policy makes a normative assertion about the ways in which online actors are expected to behave. The standards to which they are be held are the same as the standards offline. The meaningfulness of those standards is already accepted by the offline element of the lawmaker's community, and this enhances the prospect of their acceptance by the online part of that community.

A normative statement of this kind also helps to counter the natural human tendency to treat cyberspace as somewhere 'other' where different, and usually lower, standards of behaviour are permissible. This tendency is well documented, and we know that many users of online discussion sites engage in a degree of aggression and casual abuse which they would not show face-to-face,[7] while those who would never dream of making multiple physical copies of a music CD for friends are perfectly happy to engage in file sharing.[8] If online and offline law were radically different, it would be necessary for users to make a complex mental switch when going online. Human beings already have difficulty in comprehending all the legal rules which apply to their offline activities, and it is unrealistic to expect them to learn a separate set of rules to govern their online lives.

---

[5] Indeed, publication is the 'material part' of the cause of action, rather than the writing itself: *Hebditch v MacIlwaine* [1894] 2 QB 58, 61 per Lord Esher MR.

[6] For an example from the UK, see *Godfrey v Demon Internet Ltd* [1999] 4 All ER 342, though in that case the claim was carefully drafted to apply only to publication which occurred subsequent to the defendant receiving notice of the presence of the defamatory material in a newsgroup which it hosted.

[7] Anirban Sengupta and Anoshua Chaudhuri, 'Are Social Networking Sites a Source of Online Harassment for Teens? Evidence from Survey Data', NET Institute Working Paper #08-17, September 2008, <http://www.NETinst.org>; Tanya Byron, *Safer Children in a Digital World: Report of the Byron Review* (2008), para 3.63, <http://www.dcsf.gov.uk/byronreview/>.

[8] Steven A Hetcher, 'The Music Industry's Failed Attempt to Influence File Sharing Norms' (2004) 7 Vand J Ent L & Prac 10.

However, a policy of equivalence can only be successful in achieving this normative effect if there is a close match between the policy and reality. This does not, of course, mean that there must never be a difference between online and offline law. But those differences need to be kept as few as possible, and to be justified, if the policy is to have any meaning.

How easy it is to achieve equivalence depends very much on the way in which the law in question is framed. Laws which address the mental states of actors, or the outcomes of their behaviours, tend to require little adaptation to achieve equivalence. By contrast, laws which address the ways in which behaviour is undertaken can pose difficult challenges for lawmakers, because the cyberspace technologies tend to incentivize actors to undertake those behaviours very differently.

Adopting a policy of equivalence also highlights unstated assumptions in the law, and these assumptions often prove not to hold when an activity is translated into cyberspace. It is usually impossible to achieve equivalence here unless the law is reformed on the basis of accurate assumptions.

Mental states and the outcomes of behaviour

Many of the legal rules which are designed to regulate everyday human activities are expressed in terms of the mental state of the actor when engaged in the activity in question. The reason these rules require little or no modification to be applied to online activities in an equivalent way is that a user's mental state will generally be much the same whether acting online or offline.

Criminal law rules often define offences in terms of the intention of the defendant, and there has been no real difficulty in applying general purpose rules, such as those against harassment, to online actors who are simply using the internet as a new vehicle to engage in criminal conduct.[9] Problems have arisen, however, where an essential element of the offence involves the mental state of the *victim* as opposed to the defendant. Because computer and communications technologies permit automated decision-making, it may not be possible to identify a human victim who has the required mental state. In the UK this issue arose in relation to the offence of fraud, which required a victim to have been deceived. The initial approach to resolving this problem was via piecemeal amendment of specific offences,[10] but the Law Commission identified that this was not a satisfactory solution and recommended complete reform of the law of fraud.[11] The UK Fraud Act 2006 deals with the problem by redefining the offence in terms of the defendant's intention only,

---

[9] See Chris Reed, 'Why Must You Be Mean to Me?—Crime and the Online Persona' (2010) 13 New Criminal Law Review 485.

[10] See eg UK Value Added Tax Act 1994, s. 2(6):

> intent to deceive, includes a reference to furnishing, sending or otherwise making use of such a document, with intent to secure that a machine will respond to the document as if it were a true document.

[11] UK Law Commission, *Fraud*, Law Com No 276, Cm 5569, 2002.

thereby producing a single rule which works in an equivalent way both online and offline.[12]

Mental states also play a role in non-criminal rules. Contract formation is an obvious example, requiring the reaching of an agreement between the parties.[13] The means of communication used to form this agreement, whether online or offline, are irrelevant, and thus the main legal difficulties in this area have arisen under legal systems which impose formal requirements for such agreements to be legally valid contracts.[14]

An example of achieving equivalence in terms of the outcomes of behaviour is the requirement under the Electronic Commerce Directive for businesses to identify themselves and give an offline address and contact details.[15] This is simply the extension of the long-standing offline principle that traders should be identifiable, as seen in the requirements for company registration and the UK Business Names Act 1985, s 4(1). At the EU level the need for offline as well as online sellers to be identifiable is set out in the Distance Selling Directive.[16] The additional obligations imposed by the Electronic Commerce Directive simply apply these offline principles to online traders to ensure that there is a common minimum of information disclosure in cross-border trade. If reverse equivalence were needed, the directive's provision could be extended to offline cross-border traders without any special modification for the use of offline communication.

Behaviours and technology

By contrast, where legal rules target the behaviour of actors, irrespective of their intentions or the outcomes of that behaviour, achieving functional equivalence between their online and offline application can be more difficult. In the early days of public use of the internet, when the courts had no choice but to apply the existing offline rules, many examples of non-equivalent effects became apparent. The reason for this is often that online and offline activities are undertaken in such different ways that it may be almost impossible to assess the application and outcome of the rules on a comparable basis. In defamation, for example, many jurisdictions have amended their laws to introduce new rules which apply only online. These rules attempt to achieve equivalence of application by conferring some degree of immunity on an online host of defamatory material[17] or by redefining the term 'publisher' to exclude some categories of online actor.[18] However, the result may well have been

---

[12] See also Council of Europe Convention on Cybercrime (2001, in force 2004), Art 8 for a similar approach.

[13] Or, more precisely, the objective appearance of the formation of an agreement.

[14] See further Chris Reed, 'Electronic Commerce' in Chris Reed (ed), *Computer Law*, 7th edn (Oxford: Oxford University Press, 2010), Ch 4.2.2.

[15] Directive 2000/31/EC on electronic commerce OJ L 178/1, 17 July 2000, Art 5.

[16] Directive 97/7/EC on the protection of consumers in respect of distance contracts, OJ L 144/19, 4 June 1997, Art 4.

[17] See eg Directive 2000/31/EC on electronic commerce OJ L 178, 1, 17 July 2000, Art 14.

[18] See eg US Communications Decency Act 1996, 47 USC § 230.

to favour online publishing over offline in some circumstances.[19] Given the substantial operating differences between online hosting and offline publishing, it is far from clear what equivalence of treatment between them might be. Defamation law focuses on behaviour—publishing—rather than the outcome of that behaviour—reputational damage. It is this focus on the behaviour of publishing, which in cyberspace potentially encompasses a far wider range of activities than in the physical world, that makes equivalence difficult to achieve.

Laws regulating behaviour do not transpose easily to cyberspace because when an activity is moved online, aiming to achieve the same purposes as offline, the technology both encourages the actor to do this in new ways and constrains him from replicating all the features of the offline activity. To illustrate this, let us take the example of Georgina who publishes a hard-copy specialist-interest magazine. She does this as a labour of love, not seeking to make a profit, and the 500 recipients of the magazine, all of whom are in Georgina's country, pay an annual subscription which covers the cost of production and mailing.

When she transforms the magazine into a website, the internet technologies encourage Georgina to make a number of changes in the way she communicates with her readers. She will probably begin by making access free of charge, because she no longer has to print and mail the physical copies. There will be some small costs for web hosting, but these can easily be covered by incorporating advertising links onto her web pages. Advertising was previously not possible because the magazine had too small a circulation. One consequence of incorporating advertising is that if her readers find the advertisements attractive and click through from them to the advertisers' sites, Georgina may find that she begins to make a profit, transforming her activity into a business. As Georgina is no longer charging, the website can be open to the whole world. It is therefore likely to be viewed from many other countries by those sharing the special interest.

The range of content made available is also likely to increase. In the offline magazine, Georgina could only include text and images of which she had copies. Now she can link to all kinds of material hosted on other websites, incorporating them virtually as part of her own offering. The website will allow her to host audio and video clips, something which was not possible in a hard-copy magazine. Website hosting services often provide tools for creating discussion fora, and if Georgina uses these she will be hosting material provided by her users, probably unmoderated unless she is prepared to devote substantially more time to the project.

The technology also constrains Georgina from, among other things, restricting website access to her existing 500 subscribers. There is no easy way of doing this,[20] and in any event why should she wish to do so given the advantages of allowing

---

[19] For example, a host does not lose its US Communications Decency Act immunity even when it knows the nature of the content: *Zeran v America Online Inc*, 129 F 3d 327 (4th Cir, 1997), at 330–1; *Barrett v Rosenthal*, 146 P 3d 510 (Cal Supr Ct, 2006), at 514, 525, whereas an offline distributor of defamatory material becomes liable for its content once knowledge of its defamatory nature has been acquired—see eg *Cubby Inc v CompuServe Inc*, 776 F Supp 135, 140 (SDNY, 1991).

[20] Password-protecting the website will only work until a subscriber shares his password with another, and there is no simple way of identifying who is in fact accessing a website, whatever technology is used

free access? Similarly, she cannot easily limit access to UK-based users, and as we have seen the technology encourages her to make the website accessible worldwide.

Although, from Georgina's perspective, she is doing much the same things as she was before, the effect of copyright law on her behaviours will be very different. In her offline magazine Georgina will generally[21] infringe copyright in any materials she includes in it unless she has permission from the right-holder, for example the author of the text and the owner of copyright in photographs. This is because making copies and distributing copies are infringing acts.[22] However, when Georgina starts her website she can 'include' materials on other websites in her offering simply by linking to them, so that she does not need to make copies or host them on her website. Now there is real uncertainty whether she is infringing copyright.[23] Copyright law addresses behaviours such as copying or communicating works to the public. All Georgina's website contains, even in the case of inline links,[24] are the addresses of those materials via which the user's web browser can download them direct from the websites which host them. She engages in no copying herself. Also she does not communicate those materials directly, but rather points to the location from which someone else will communicate them. Any complaint here is really that Georgina has made the materials accessible in a way which the right-holder did not intend,[25] and potentially also that she is taking unfair advantage of the right-holder's work for her own benefit without making payment.[26] These are not the same as the behaviours which copyright claims to regulate.

Unstated assumptions

Achieving equivalence is also difficult if the law contains unstated assumptions. Once these assumptions are unmasked they often prove not to hold true in cyberspace. This is particularly likely where the law assumes that there should be a particular balance of interests, but is framed in terms of behaviours rather than impairment of those interests. It is also likely where the law assumes that those engaging in behaviour can be categorized into distinct groups, each of which can be subject to a different set of rules.

The law of copyright engages the interests of three groups: creators of works, consumers of works, and those who act as intermediaries in making works available.

---

to control access—see Chris Reed, *Internet Law: Text and Materials* 2nd edn (Cambridge: Cambridge University Press, 2004), Ch 5.

[21] Public domain materials present no copyright problems and so are not considered here.

[22] These are Berne Convention rights, and so almost all countries will have equivalent rules.

[23] For a more detailed explanation of how linking works, technically and in terms of infringement, see Chris Reed, 'Controlling World-Wide Web Links: Property Rights, Access Rights and Unfair Competition' (1998) 6.1 Indiana Journal of Global Legal Studies 167.

[24] eg web page code which results in the display of images to accompany the text, but where those images are hosted on a different server and the code merely points to their location. Technically, this results in the user's web browser requesting a copy of the image from the hosting server, and displaying it on the user's screen in the format prescribed by the web page code.

[25] Chris Reed (n 23).

[26] See eg *Google v Copiepresse*, Brussels Court of First Instance (TGI), 13 February 2007.

What the balance between those interests should be is assumed, but never stated, by the rules of law as they apply to the physical world. If we return to Georgina's example we see that if the right-holder's protected interests are defined narrowly, in terms solely of controlling making copies of the work and disseminating those copies, then any linking from Georgina's website does not really affect those interests at all because the right-holder still controls those matters.[27] This would mean that the application of the offline rules to the website produced equivalent effects, and no modification of the rules is required. If, though, the protected interests of the right-holder include control of all forms of dissemination of the work, it appears that Georgina's website does affect those interests. There is no consensus about which of these analyses of the right-holder's interests is the correct one.

The uncertainty about interest balancing is also illustrated by the difficulties which copyright faces in relation to private copying of works in cyberspace. In most of the civil law jurisdictions private copying is a permitted exception to the right-holder's exclusive rights.[28] Offline copying of a book or a CD requires physical contact between the copier and the work to be copied, and this therefore limits the extent of private copying. Once the work is accessible in digital form online, however, anyone with an internet connection can copy it without needing to move from their desktop. This produces a dramatic increase in the quantity of private copies made, an increase which is so large that it seems likely to destroy the current music industry business model.[29]

This qualitative change in the consequences of private copying has inevitably led to a debate about whether the rule should be changed online. Schellekens points out[30] that the two sides of the debate focus on different interests; proponents of change argue that the interests of right-holders are being damaged, and that the private copier has no interests to protect, whereas opponents identify the interests in protecting the private life of the users of works and in freedom to communicate information as paramount. This debate had not been necessary offline because private copying was economically *de minimis* and, in practice, not something which could be controlled effectively.

---

[27] Even if expressing the interests of the right-holder in this way includes an interest in controlling the ways in which the work is combined with other works, an interest which would be affected by inline linking, the right-holder has the ability to control this matter through the way in which the hosting website makes the linked material available. Failure to exercise such control suggests that the right-holder does not object to inline linking, and thus that the interest is not adversely affected—see Chris Reed (n 23), at 193–99.

[28] Natali Helberger and P Bernt Hugenholtz, 'No Place Like Home for Making a Copy: Private Copying in European Copyright Law and Consumer Law' (2007) 22 Berkeley Tech LJ 1061.

[29] IFPI, *Digital Music Report 2009: Key Statistics*, <http://www.ifpi.org/content/section_resources/dmr2009.html>, estimates that 16% of European users regularly swap infringing music files online, and that in 2008 the number of infringing music files shared exceeded 40 billion, suggesting an infringement rate for downloads of about 95%.

[30] Maurice Schellekens (n 3), at 63–5.

The EU is attempting to deal with this issue in a way which will achieve online and offline equivalence of effect. Article 5(2)(b) of the EU Copyright Directive[31] permitted Member States to maintain their private copying exceptions under more restrictive conditions than previously, and the Explanatory Memorandum to the proposal for the directive[32] explains the factors to be taken into account in determining the appropriate balance, which include compensation for right-holders and respect for the three-step test set out in Article 9(2) of the Berne Convention. A consultation by the European Commission on the exception has been in progress since 2004[33] and the Belgian and French courts have reconsidered the appropriateness of the balance, deciding that the three-step test is the paramount statement of the balance and that national law needs to be interpreted in that light.[34] The UK plans to widen its copyright exceptions to, so far as is possible, remove those 'areas where copyright restricts activity to no direct commercial benefit',[35] and by the time this book is published should have produced detailed proposals on this issue.[36] But it is worth noting that these efforts have not yet produced a consensus on the proper scope of private copying. The problem is clearly an intractable one, precisely because the revelation of the unstated assumption about the balance of interests has generated argument over whether that assumption is the correct one for the future.

A further unstated assumption in much of offline law, that it is possible to divide actors into clear categories and regulate these categories separately, is also challenged by cyberspace. The cyberspace technologies are highly flexible in operation, and this tends to lead to a blurring of category boundaries, and often to their complete collapse.

Categorization is hard to resist because it is a fundamental part of legal analysis. Lawyers are trained to review an activity, identify potentially applicable categories under the existing law, and then assign the activity to its most appropriate category. This analytical method enables the lawyer to advise which rule-set from the existing law applies to the activity.

Where the most similar existing category is not a good fit for a new cyberspace activity, in spite of the apparent similarities, this is a defective method for determining the appropriate legal solution. In the first instance an inappropriate offline rule

---

[31] Directive 2001/29/EC of the European Parliament and of the Council of 22 May 2001 on the harmonization of certain aspects of copyright and related rights in the information society, OJ L167/10, 22 June 2001.

[32] COM (97) 628 final, 10 December 1997, see in particular 37–9.

[33] See <http://ec.europa.eu/internal_market/copyright/levy_reform/index_en.htm>.

[34] *Test Achats v EMI Recorded Music Belgium and ors*, Brussels Court of Appeal, 9 September 2005, case 2004/AR/1649; *Studio Canal and ors v S Perquin and Union federale des consommateurs Que choisir*, Cour de Cassation, 28 February 2006.

[35] Government Response to the Hargreaves Review of Intellectual Property and Growth, August 2011, 7, <http://www.ipo.gov.uk/ipresponse-full.pdf>.

[36] These will include:

   proposals for a limited private copying exception; to widen the exception for non-commercial research, which should also cover both text- and data-mining to the extent permissible under EU law; to widen the exception for library archiving; and to introduce an exception for parody. [Ibid, 9]

will be applied, even though it is not properly adapted for the new activity. Following this, the error will be compounded when it becomes clear that a new rule is necessary, because the search for a new rule will inevitably start from the existing categorization, which was wrong in the first place. The tendency is always to regulate a new activity by modifying an existing legal regime, rather than subjecting it to a *de novo* analysis with a view to developing a new and appropriately fitting rule-set.

This is precisely what occurred with the EU regulation of e-money. When the concept of e-money was first mooted in the early 1990s it was clear that it did not exhibit any of the characteristics which would subject it to existing financial services regulation, and was thus an almost completely unregulated activity in most jurisdictions.[37] In Europe there was strong pressure to regulate this new phenomenon,[38] resulting in the e-Money Directive 2000.[39]

The drafters of this directive perceived the closest existing model to be that of payment systems operated by deposit-taking banks, and therefore imported many characteristics from the regulation of those institutions into the new law on e-money. Their aim was expressly to achieve some degree of regulatory equivalence, described in the recitals to the directive as being to 'preserve a level playing field between electronic money institutions and other credit institutions issuing electronic money'.[40] However, the effect was to impose an unworkable business model on e-money issuers which probably restricted the further development of e-payment services.[41] A new directive was enacted in 2009 and came into force in 2011,[42] and this new legislation abandons the deposit-taking bank analogy in favour of a more generic model of payment service regulation which was developed in the light of modern, online payment services.

The problems which a focus on categorization creates for achieving equivalence can be seen particularly clearly in respect of the legal regulation of search engines. Gasser identifies[43] a large number of strands which make up the regulatory debate

---

[37] See Chris Reed and Lars Davies, *Digital Cash: The Legal Implications* (London: Centre for Commercial Law Studies Report, 1995). The exceptions were those few countries which already regulated payment services as a generic activity, such as the Netherlands.

[38] Though not in the US, which took the position that regulation should be delayed until the nature of the phenomenon became clearer: Federal Reserve Bank Governor Kelly, 'Developments in Electronic Money and Banking', Cyberpayments '96 Conference, Dallas 1996, <http://www.federalreserve.gov/boarddocs/speeches/1996/19960618.htm>.

[39] Directive 2000/46/EC of the European Parliament and of the Council of 18 September 2000 on the taking up, pursuit of and prudential supervision of the business of electronic money institutions, OJ L 275/39, 27 October 2000.

[40] Ibid, recital 12.

[41] See the analysis of the defects of the original directive in Proposal for a directive of the European Parliament and of the Council on the taking up, pursuit and prudential supervision of the business of electronic money institutions, amending Directives 2005/60/EC and 2006/48/EC and repealing Directive 2000/46/EC, COM (2008) 627 final, 9 October 2008, 2.

[42] Directive 2009/110/EC of the European Parliament and of the Council of 16 September 2009 on the taking up, pursuit and prudential supervision of the business of electronic money institutions amending Directives 2005/60/EC and 2006/48/EC and repealing Directive 2000/46/EC, OJ L267/7 10 October 2009.

[43] Urs Gasser, 'Regulating Search Engines: Taking Stock and Looking Ahead (2006) 8 Yale JL & Tech 201 at Part III.A.

about search engines. All these strands derive from the categorization of search engine activities in terms of known, and mainly offline, activities. The debate on infrastructure regulation places search engines in the category of utilities and argues for or against their regulation along the same lines as telecoms and water companies.[44] The ownership debate divides quite clearly between those who place search engines in the same category as ISPs and online communication network operators[45] and those who see them as intentional copiers and republishers of others' material.[46] The content debate contains a wide variety of categories for its participants to use. A common divide is between those who categorize search engines with newspapers, broadcasters, and other free-speech facilitators[47] and those who view them as executive arms of the pornography industry.[48] To add a further example not listed by Gasser, the web-crawling and deep-linking activities of search engines have been categorized by some courts and some commentators as trespasses to physical property.[49] The fact that search engines can, with little effort, be fitted into *all* these categories is surely a clear indication that *none* of them provides an appropriate rule-set with which to attempt to achieve equivalence.

Categorization problems also arise when there are two distinct offline categories, each with its own rule-set, but conducting the activity online converges the categories so that it is no longer obvious which the online activity fits into. The potential to apply both rule-sets can produce contradictory rules, and inevitably makes the starting point for achieving equivalence entirely opaque.

The problems this creates for lawmakers are illustrated particularly clearly in the EU's recent attempt to clarify the application of television regulation to online audiovisual content. Most countries place constraints on the types of content which can be included in television programmes, but do not apply those constraints to audiovisual material made available via a website.[50] The Audiovisual Media Services

---

[44] For a comprehensive review of this line of discussion see Viva R Moffatt, 'Regulating Search' (2009) 22 Harv JL & Tech 475.

[45] Matthew D Lawless, 'Against Search Engine Volition' (2008) 18 Alb LJ Sci & Tech 205; Jane Strachan, 'The Internet of tomorrow: the new-old communications tool of control' (2004) 26 EIPR 123.

[46] This group is sub-divided on the question whether search engine activities do, or ought always to, fall within a copyright exception like fair use. For a review, see Jonathan Band, 'Google and Fair Use' (2008) 3 J Bus & Tech L 1.

[47] Seth F Kreimer, 'Censorship by Proxy: The First Amendment, Internet Intermediaries, and the Problem of the Weakest Link' (2008) 155 U Pa L Rev 11; Ben Allgrove and Paul Ganley, 'Search Engines, Data Aggregators and UK Copyright Law: A Proposal' (2007) 29 EIPR 227.

[48] See the discussion of US attempts to control the availability of pornography to children in Jonathan P Wentz, 'Ashcroft v ACLU: The Context and Economic Implications of Burdened Access to Online Sexual Speech' (2007) 17 Geo Mason U Civ Rts LJ 477.

[49] See eg *eBay v Bidder's Edge*, 100 F Supp 2d 1058 (ND Cal, 2000); John D Saba Jr, 'Internet Property Rights: e-Trespass' (2002) 33 St Mary's LJ 367.

[50] A notable exception is Australia whose government is renewing its efforts to introduce internet content filtering via what has been described as the Great Australian Firewall. A plan to require ISPs to provide a 'clean feed' of internet content, using a blacklist maintained by the Australian Communications and Media Authority, was announced in December 2007 by the Telecommunications Minister Stephen Conroy, <http://www.abc.net.au/news/stories/2007/12/31/2129471.htm>, with a provision that residents could opt out of the 'clean feed' to receive unrestricted content. In October 2008 it was reported

Directive of 2007[51] aimed to maintain the regulatory control for television programming, whether delivered by traditional broadcasting or provided online, and also to ensure that a less onerous regulatory regime applied to 'television-like' on-demand online content whose provision 'would lead the user reasonably to expect regulatory protection'.[52] This is a clear policy that there should be equivalence between the regulation which applies to offline television and that which applies to similar content services provided online.

However, the difficulties in achieving equivalence are substantial and have produced an unusual law. The recitals to the directive would normally state the reasons why particular provisions are included. Instead they make lengthy statements about what its provisions *hope to* achieve. This is perhaps in recognition that the nature of the technology makes it unlikely that they will in fact achieve those aims.

As examples, recital 16 states:

the definition of an audiovisual media service should cover only audiovisual media services, whether television broadcasting or on-demand, which are mass media, that is, which are intended for reception by, and which could have a clear impact on, a significant proportion of the general public . . . but should not cover activities which are primarily non-economic and which are not in competition with television broadcasting, such as private websites and services consisting of the provision or distribution of audiovisual content generated by private users for the purposes of sharing and exchange within communities of interest.

There was clearly no way to translate this optimistic statement into law, and so the definition which decides whether or not an online activity is subjected to the regulatory regime is that its operator 'has editorial responsibility for the choice of the audiovisual content of the audiovisual media service and determines the manner in which it is organized'.[53]

Similarly hopeful statements are that the regulation should not apply to emails or to 'websites that contain audiovisual elements only in an ancillary manner, such as animated graphical elements, short advertising spots or information related to a product or non-audiovisual service',[54] nor to online versions of newspapers and magazines.[55] The concept of 'television' is to include 'near video-on-demand' online services, but not actual video-on-demand.[56] Finally, 'In the context of television broadcasting, the notion of simultaneous viewing should also cover quasi-simultaneous viewing because of the variations in the short time lag which occurs between the

---

that the government had modified its plans to require mandatory filtering of certain categories of content,<http://www.heraldsun.com.au/news/mandatory-censorship-on-web/story-0-1111117883306>. The proposals have not yet received legislative approval at the time of writing.

[51] Directive 2007/65/EC amending Directive 89/552 on the coordination of certain provisions laid down by law, regulation or administrative action in Member States concerning the provision of audiovisual media services, OJ L298/23, 18 December 2007. The predecessor legislation, Directive 89/552, had established the regulatory regime for the preceding 20 years.

[52] Ibid, recital 17.

[53] Ibid, Art 1(1)(d).

[54] Ibid, recital 18.

[55] Ibid, recital 21.

[56] Ibid, recital 20.

transmission and the reception of the broadcast due to technical reasons inherent in the transmission process', although the actual definition refers only to simultaneous viewing.[57]

This is not the place to discuss the merits and defects of the directive,[58] and only time will tell whether the hopes expressed in its recitals are matched by the decisions of the courts and the ways in which the online audiovisual content sector develops. The important point here is that the difficulties in framing the law arise because it is firmly grounded in a categorization labelled 'television broadcasting', whilst convergence resulting from the nature of the cyberspace technologies has made that categorization, at best, problematic.

In this case the online version of the activity has not merely converged the categories but has actually merged them. In effect they have ceased to exist as separate categories so far as the online world is concerned. As a consequence, any attempt to categorize the online activity is a pointless exercise. If equivalence is sought, it can only be achieved by reforming the offline law to abolish or modify its categories in a way which is compatible with the online world. This is the route taken in the most recent revision of the EU communications regulation regime, which has abandoned the distinction between voice and data carriage, in large part, in an attempt to achieve online and offline equivalence.[59]

Routes to meaningful equivalence

The normative advantage of applying the same legal principles to all elements of a lawmaker's community is clear. It matches the expectations of the law's subjects, that the law will be consistent for activities which they perceive to be equivalent, irrespective of whether they are undertaken offline or online. The difficult question is how the lawmaker can achieve this aim.

A potentially effective technique is to lay down general principles of law and then create specific rule-sets to deal with the particular difficulties which arise online in an attempt to achieve functional equivalence in the application of those principles. This approach is widely used to regulate online banking and financial services. The UK Financial Services Authority (FSA) adopted this technique in its policy document 'New Regulator for a New Millennium',[60] which explained how it intended to apply the Financial Services and Markets Act 2000 to online activities. Gkoutzinis summarizes the policy as follows:

---

[57] Ibid, recital 24 and Art 1(1)(g) (definition of television broadcasting).

[58] See Andreas Breitschaft, 'Evaluating the Linear/Non-linear Divide: Are There Any Better Factors for the Future Regulation of Audiovisual Media Content?' (2009) Ent LR 291; Stephen Ridgway, 'The Audiovisual Media Services Directive: What Does it Mean, Is it Necessary and What Are the Challenges to its Implementation?' (2008) CTLR 108; Neal Geach, 'Converging Regulation for Convergent Media: An Overview of the Audiovisual Media Services Directive' (2008) 1 Journal of Information, Law and Technology (JILT), <http://www2.warwick.ac.uk/fac/soc/law/elj/jilt/2008_1/>.

[59] See Katrina Dick, 'The Emergence and Regulation of VoIP' (2004) CTLR 157.

[60] UK FSA (London, January 2000).

This policy means that the FSA will not discriminate in its approach on the basis of delivery channel alone, unless the risks to the statutory objectives justify it. Nevertheless, non-discrimination does not suggest the imposition of the same requirements on all delivery channels, since the risk may differ but it does require the FSA to be able to justify any differences by reference to the features of the specific medium.[61]

The Act itself made no special provision for online activities but has been amended numerous times since its enactment to introduce detailed online rules,[62] and further detailed regulation has been introduced in the FSA Handbook. There seem to be no complaints from the sector that the policy is not working to achieve equivalence.

However, as will be explained in Chapter 8, this technique is only appropriate where there is a regulatory community which can engage in dialogue with the regulator over the content, application, and enforcement of the detailed rules. If the law is addressed to cyberspace actors generally it is improbable that they will understand how such highly detailed and complex law implements the general principles. The likely effect, as we shall see, is that even if the general principles are accepted as meaningful and thus authoritative, actors will nevertheless fail to find meaning in the detailed obligations, and thus fail to obey them.

The approach which lawmakers have most commonly adopted is to devise a new rule for online activities, applying the offline rationale in a different way to take account of online differences.[63] One example of an attempt to achieve equivalence in this way is the case of electronic signatures. In the common law world, manuscript signatures simply perform evidential functions, and so the common law jurisdictions have experienced no difficulty in translating the rules for online signatures in a way which achieves equivalent effect.[64] However, in civil law jurisdictions signatures often have a formal significance which derives from the physical action of writing one's name on paper. Because this physical action cannot be replicated online, those jurisdictions have experienced substantial difficulty in modifying their laws to enable electronic signatures to achieve legal equivalence to those made by hand.[65]

To solve this difficulty the EU e-Signatures Directive[66] introduced the concept of an 'advanced electronic signature' which, if supported by a qualifying identity

---

[61] Apostolos Gkoutzinis, 'The Prudential Supervision of Internet Banking in the United Kingdom: Is the 'Basel Approach' Finding its Way Through National Regulations' (2002) 17 JIBL 249, 254.

[62] See eg Financial Services and Markets Act 2000 (Financial Promotion) (Amendment) (Electronic Commerce Directive) Order 2002, SI 2002/2157; Financial Services and Markets Act 2000 (Regulated Activities) (Amendment) (No 2) Order 2002, SI 2002/1776; Financial Services and Markets Act 2000 (Financial Promotion) Order 2005, SI 2005/1529.

[63] See Schellekens (n 3), 70 for a discussion of the rationale for adopting this approach.

[64] See Chris Reed, 'What *Is* a Signature' (2000) 3 JILT, <http://www2.warwick.ac.uk/fac/soc/law/elj/jilt/2000_3/reed/>.

[65] See Minyan Wang, 'The Impact of Information Technology Development on the Legal Concept: A Particular Examination on the Legal Concept of "Signatures"' (2007) Int JL&IT 253, 259–63 (Germany and China); Stephen Mason, 'The International Implications of Using Electronic Signatures' (2005) CTLR 160, 164 (France).

[66] Directive 1999/93/EC on a Community framework for electronic signatures OJ L13/12, 19 January 2000.

certificate issued by an appropriate person, would be legally equivalent to a hand-written signature.[67] The intention of this measure was clearly to establish equivalence of outcome between online and offline signatures, and there is no doubt that it did so in purely legal terms. As a matter of law, throughout the EU such electronic signatures are legally equivalent to manuscript signatures.

But equivalence of legal effect is not enough on its own. The directive's legal solution was far from equivalent to manuscript signatures in terms of its practicability. Manuscript signatures require no technology more complex than a pen, and are easy and cheap to apply to a document. By contrast, advanced electronic signatures require expensive technology, major changes to the ways that users interact with each other, and detailed legal and technical advice before they can be adopted.[68] The minimal adoption of advanced electronic signatures by cyberspace actors demonstrates this failure very clearly.[69] The lesson to be drawn here is that an attempt to achieve functional equivalence must not consider just the purely legal effects of a rule. It must also encompass the effects of the rule on how the activity is undertaken.

We also saw earlier that many rules of offline law contain unstated assumptions about interest balancing, or about the categorization of activities, which make it difficult or impossible to transpose their general principles to cyberspace. It is clear that achieving functional equivalence by creating cyberspace-specific rules is a challenging task for lawmakers.

The most effective way of achieving equivalence is for the lawmaker to devise a new formulation of the rule which is equally applicable to both online and offline activities. This would result in both equivalence of form and functional equivalence. However, there is clearly a risk that the offline effects of the rule might be altered unintentionally, and so this approach can only be successful as part of a full review of the law,[70] or where or a completely new rule is being formulated.[71] Reformulation is likely to be easy if the general principle focuses on the intentions or beliefs of the actor, or on the outcomes to be achieved by the actor. For other laws it is likely that fundamental assumptions about interest balancing or categorization will need to be reviewed and most likely abandoned.[72] We have seen examples of this from the laws

---

[67] Art 5(1).

[68] See the discussion in Chris Reed, 'How to Make Bad Law: Lessons from the Computer and Communications Sector' (Queen Mary School of Law Legal Studies Research Paper 40/2010), Part 2, <http://papers.ssrn.com/sol3/papers.cfm?abstract_id=1538527>.

[69] See Jos Dumortier et al, *Study on the Legal and Market Aspects of Electronic Signatures* (KUL, 2003), <http://ec.europa.eu/information_society/eeurope/2005/all_about/security/electronic_sig_report. pdf>; Report from the Commission to the European Parliament and the Council on the operation of Directive 1999/93/EC on a Community framework for electronic signatures, COM (2006) 120 final, 15 March 2006, 5–8.

[70] As was the case eg for the UK Fraud Act 2006, discussed above.

[71] eg the UK Terrorism Act 2006 created a new offence of disseminating terrorist publications, and s 2(2) states that this includes transmitting the publication electronically.

[72] Such an overturning of assumptions can also be required because of policy decisions made to encourage the development of cyberspace, such as the scheme of country-of-origin regulation established by Arts 3 and 4 of the Electronic Commerce Directive. As a consequence German unfair competition law, which placed severe limits on advertising and other competitive activity by traders, ceased to apply to online sellers based in other EU Member States but remained in force for German sellers. The assumption that

relating to fraud, defamation, payment services, and telecommunications regulation, all of which identified that the assumptions underlying the offline law needed to be modified if equivalence was to be achieved.

As cyberspace permeates more and more activities, *ab initio* law reform is likely to increase. Because such reform tends to produce laws which are both functionally *and* formally equivalent, we may eventually see a decline in the approach of using heavily modified offline rules to govern cyberspace. The principle of equivalence is clearly of more than symbolic value, and a rule whose wording applies equally well both online and offline is likely to convey more meaning to cyberspace actors, and thus be more likely to achieve respect from them, than two different rule-sets whose combination of application and outcome merely aspire to be equivalent.

Internal Norms of Cyberspace Communities

Cyberspace is not a community in itself. But it has made it possible for a host of communities to come into existence. These communities transcend geographic boundaries and overlap and interact with each other in complex ways. Cyberspace users might be merely passive participants, reading and viewing the contributions of others, or might take a very active role in the life of the community. Multiple community membership is common.[73]

Online communities rapidly develop a set of norms which governs the ways that members participate.[74] Some are purely social, so that breach of the norms is sanctioned by disapproval and ostracism. Where the platform through which the community interacts has an 'owner', these norms might become incorporated in the terms for membership of the platform, which can provide stronger sanctions for breach such as suspension or termination of membership.[75]

eBay presents an interesting case study here.[76] The original intention was that buyers and sellers should deal with each other according to the norms of fairness and

---

the law would regulate all selling in Germany was no longer true, and so the unfair competition law was swiftly reformed to impose equivalent obligations on German sellers to those which their home law imposed on foreign sellers—Gesetz gegen den unlauteren Wettbewerb (UWG) of 3 July 2004 (BGBl. I 2004 32/1414).

[73] eg I am an active member of the online aviation, ukulele playing, luthier, and cyberspace law communities, and from time to time drop in on other communities as a passive consumer or researching observer. Most readers of this book will have a similarly diverse portfolio of communities in which they are involved.

[74] For examples see Jennifer L Mnookin, 'Virtual(ly) Law: The Emergence of Law in LambdaMOO' (1996) 2.1 *Journal of Computer-Mediated Communication*, <http://jcmc.indiana.edu/vol2/issue1/lambda.html>; Dmitri Williams et al, 'From Tree House to Barracks: The Social Life of Guilds in World of Warcraft' (2006) 1 Games and Culture 33; Thomas Schultz, 'Private Legal Systems: What Cyberspace Might Teach Legal Theorists' (2007) 10 Yale JL & Tech 151.

[75] This has occurred eg for both YouTube and Second Life, and I have explored the ways in which their rules deal with bullying and harassment in Chris Reed, 'Why Must You Be Mean to Me?—Crime and the Online Persona' (2010) 13 New Criminal Law Review 485.

[76] A useful short history of the development of norms in eBay is in Jack Goldsmith and Tim Wu, *Who Controls the Internet? Illusions of a Borderless World* (New York: Oxford University Press, 2006), 130–45.

openness, which had developed rapidly among eBay users. To make this process possible as the community of traders and buyers grew, a feedback system was introduced so that each participant had a reputation, based on the experiences of their trading partners. Further growth produced the need for a dispute resolution system, and ultimately the community's trading norms were entrenched in the eBay terms to which buyers and seller have to sign up to become members.[77]

Because eBay controls both the trading platform and the primary payment mechanism, through its ownership of PayPal, buyers and sellers operate under a set of norms which run in parallel to the trading rules of national laws. These can be summarized as follows:

1. Sellers must maintain a good trading reputation; if they fail to do so their fees for selling increase, and ultimately their accounts can be suspended or revoked.

2. Sellers must deliver the goods they sell. If they fail, the payment transaction will be reversed by eBay/PayPal.

3. The goods must be substantially as described by the seller. eBay runs a mechanism for mediating and determining disputes over this, and if the goods were not as described the payment is reversed.

States are naturally concerned to protect their citizen consumers who transact online, and some states have expended substantial effort in devising consumer protection laws for online sales. As an example, a proposal for an EU directive on consumer rights[78] is, at the time of writing, making its way through the legislative process. This directive will consolidate the main EU directives on the topic and update their provisions to take account of e- and m- (mobile) commerce. The law will, of course, apply to all eBay sales by businesses to EU consumers, and consumers will have the rights, *inter alia*, to prior information about the seller and charges, a right to withdraw from the contract, and rights to receive goods of appropriate quality. None of these are provided for in the eBay rules.

And yet, for all practical purposes, this directive is almost irrelevant to sales made via eBay. The law will only be enforceable through court action, either directly by the buyer or as a representative action by consumer protection organizations. Most sales are low value, so that court action is uneconomic. Few eBay sellers are economically significant enough to merit collective enforcement action. So far as most buyers are concerned, the de facto regulation of their sales relationship is via the eBay rules, not via the law.

If the EU lawmaker's aim is to secure that EU consumers have these rights when buying online, merely passing a law to that effect is unlikely to achieve that aim.

---

[77] For ebay.com, <http://pages.ebay.com/help/policies/user-agreement.html>, and for ebay.co.uk, <http://pages.ebay.co.uk/help/policies/user-agreement.html>. All the eBay User Agreements, so far as is possible under the national laws which apply, impose the same trading obligations on sellers and buyers.

[78] COM (2008) 614, 8 October 2008.

The lawmaker needs to recognize that there are at least three communities of traders who sell to EU consumers, and that the approach to each has to be different.

The first community consists of sellers who are established in the EU and who sell direct to consumers. The largest of these, sellers such as Amazon, are already careful to comply with the law and to provide the prescribed rights to consumers. Smaller community members may be unaware of the precise consumer rights which the law provides, but will usually wish to respect the law because it is their own national law. Here, education and persuasion will gradually be effective.

The second community, which is still comparatively small, is the group of non-EU traders who sell direct to EU consumers. The likely effect of the EU's laws on those traders will be minimal. Most of their trade is with customers in their own countries, under different legal norms for consumer protection. There is almost no risk of the EU law being enforced against them, and so consumers will be limited to the rights which the trader provides for its own national customers.

The third community consists of those small EU-established sellers who use trading platforms like eBay, together with any foreign sellers (irrespective of their size) who do the same. For the reasons explained above, the law is unlikely to be complied with fully by these sellers.[79] A more effective way for the EU lawmaker to achieve its aims, so far as this community is concerned, would be to engage with eBay and other trading platforms in an attempt to persuade those platforms to incorporate the legal norms into the rules for buyers and sellers. If this could be done, buyers would receive a refund if the seller did not respect their consumer rights, and would therefore have effective recourse rather than needing to engage in slow and expensive court proceedings.

The difficulty is, of course, that organizations such as eBay have little incentive to change a system which, from their perspective at least, works perfectly well. In theory lawmakers could impose change, perhaps by making trading platforms secondarily liable for the activities of their trading members, but this would be a radical modification to the way consumer protection laws operate and might well have unexpected and undesirable consequences.[80] For example, online selling might move to offshore platforms to which the law did not apply, and who could thus charge lower fees. As we will see below, there are strong arguments that the law can only be used effectively to change community norms, which is effectively what would occur here, if the change is made gradually and incrementally.

---

[79] Though the law does have at least some impact. In relation to the right of withdrawal, eBay explains the consumer's rights to sellers (see <http://pages.ebay.co.uk/help/policies/business.html#returns>), and some (but not all) business sellers do offer consumers the right. However, there is no eBay enforcement mechanism if sellers do not do so, or fail to comply with their offer, which leaves the consumer with redress through the courts alone.

[80] One such consequence, which would occur because a trading platform will inevitably apply the same rules to all its members irrespective of their national location, is that foreign consumer purchasers from EU-based traders would benefit from these rights, even though as a matter of EU law they do not always do so currently. Of course, this might not be undesirable.

Community norms and copyright

Although there is a gap between the expectations of consumers and the rights which small-business cyberspace sellers believe they should offer, this gap is not wide enough to threaten the normative principle that consumers should have at least some rights. This is far from true for copyright. The legal norms set out in the international framework of copyright law have very little connection with the norms under which cyberspace users make use of protected works.

The digital technologies have put the power to copy and make other uses of works into the hands of pretty much every cyberspace user, and as a consequence a wide range of copyright-using communities has developed. As just one example, there is a substantial community on YouTube of collectors of 78 rpm records.[81] The majority of these videos consist of the playing of a record, sometimes merely showing the record turning on its turntable but in other cases accompanied by a montage of stills and video clips which relate to the music. It is likely that the vast majority of these videos infringe copyright, either in the recording itself, the accompanying images or video clips, or both. However, there are no indications in the introductions by those who post videos, or the comments responding to them, that the community ever considers that its activities might be unlawful.

YouTube also hosts a community, or perhaps more accurately a collection of sub-communities with overlapping membership, which consists of amateur musicians. Members record their performances, in many cases of songs in which copyright subsists, and post them for comment by other members of the community. The social norm here, at least to begin with, was that a non-commercial video recording of a song was perfectly permissible. However, as YouTube became more and more successful, right-holders began to issues notices to YouTube under the US Digital Millennium Copyright Act 1998 in respect of allegedly infringing content.[82] Although the main aim of right-holders was to secure the removal of direct copies of recordings in which they owned the rights, notices were also issued for a number of cover-version recordings. This resulted in increased awareness of the conflicting legal norm, but discussions of the issue by community members indicate that the community norm has not been supplanted. Responses vary between grudging acceptance of the need to comply whilst disagreeing that the law is right, and active opposition.[83]

Probably the largest community whose norms conflict with the law of copyright is that of file sharers. We saw in Chapter 1 that the norm here is to make copies of music recordings available to others online, and so long as this is not done for profit it is not seen as wrongful, even though most members are likely to know it is unlawful.

---

[81] A YouTube search for '78 rpm' in July 2011 returned over 66,000 videos.

[82] A short explanation of this issue is usefully set out in Electronic Frontier Foundation, 'A Guide to YouTube Removals', <https://www.eff.org/issues/intellectual-property/guide-to-youtube-removals>. The process used by rights owners for identifying infringing content is, as would be expected, highly automated and leads to a high level of erroneous notices—see *Lenz v Universal Music*, 572 F Supp 2d 1150 (ND Cal, 2008).

[83] See eg <http://www.ukuleleunderground.com/forum/archive/index.php/t-25142.html>.

The volume of this activity is so great that it is destroying the music industry business model, and all attempts to change the norm through strengthening the rights of copyright owners appear to have been ineffective.

Why are these community norms so different from the long-established principles of copyright law? I would suggest, though admittedly this is purely speculative, that cyberspace users have started from their understanding of the norms which governed their activity in the physical world. Collectors regularly gather together to admire each other's collections, and amateur musicians play for each other and for friends. Teenagers in particular, though adults also of course, have for years met to listen to music recordings and have lent their records and CDs to friends. These activities were not impinged on by copyright law. Initially at least (though this is probably no longer true for file sharing) users considered that their activities in cyberspace were merely online analogues of their physical-world activities, and thus should be governed by the same rules. If they thought about copyright at all they would consider that its application to their activities was an accidental result of the way the cyberspace technologies work, rather than an intended consequence by the lawmakers. Any breach of copyright would be merely 'technical', and thus not morally wrong even if unlawful.

A second, and probably more important, reason is that the legal copyright norm has never become entrenched as a social norm in the same way as, say, most criminal laws. Tyler, writing about social attitudes to copyright pre-cyberspace, notes that:

one crucial problem is the lack of a public feeling that breaking intellectual property laws is wrong. In the absence of such a conception, there is little reason for people to follow intellectual property laws.[84]

Part of the reason for this is that intellectual property laws do not match the public's conception of fairness, for example that they should have to pay for something only once.[85] There also appears to be some doubt whether intellectual property laws are viewed as having legitimate authority to direct the lives of ordinary citizens:

People need to believe that the rules established serve reasonable social purposes and are not simply efforts to create profits for special interest groups, such as large corporations. Again, the key to developing an effective strategy in this area is to understand better how the public currently views copyright laws. Are such laws regarded as illegitimate efforts by corporations to enrich themselves at public expense?[86]

Jensen takes this last point and analyses it at length in relation to cyberspace actors.[87] He points out that the law of copyright was developed in order to regulate relations between those involved in the exploitation of creative works, only to a limited extent to regulate relationships with creators, and hardly at all in relation to the use of works

[84] Tom R Tyler, 'Compliance with Intellectual Property Laws: A Psychological Perspective' (1997) 29 NYU J Int'l L & Pol 219, 226.
[85] Ibid, 228.
[86] Ibid, 233.
[87] Christopher Jensen, 'The More Things Change, the More They Stay the Same: Copyright, Digital Technology, and Social Norms' (2003) 56 Stan L Rev 531.

by the general public. Because the law was not developed for 'ordinary' people, they do not perceive it as imposing meaningful obligations on them:

> Voluntary compliance with intellectual property laws in general and copyright laws in particular suffer from a perceived lack of procedural fairness and public mistrust. The process of drafting copyright legislation often amounts to little more than negotiations among narrow interest groups; without a seat at the bargaining table, the public has no meaningful opportunity to participate in the legislative process. This process fosters the (often accurate) perception that copyright law is designed by and for the benefit of a small circle of vested interests. This widespread sense of unfairness—that copyright protections exist for the benefit of Microsoft and Disney—undermines voluntary compliance with copyright law.[88]

This sense that copyright has little meaning for the ordinary citizen has been compounded by the way in which the operation of the law remained hidden from them, before the digital technologies and cyberspace expanded the scope of copyright to cover the everyday activities of members of the public:

> groups such as authors and publishers formed relatively small communities of repeat players. As such, they knew the rules of the game and knew that, as repeat players, following the rules in one transaction would affect their success in future interactions with other players. In this context, constructing a widely embraced normative justification for copyright law was unnecessary to ensure that the commercially significant players obeyed the law. Under any circumstances, the game went on outside the view of the ordinary consumer of copyrighted works, who remained unsocialized in any 'copyright culture' that developed among those involved in the business of making and selling copyrighted works.[89]

So we need to ask how lawmakers can, or should, react when facing entrenched social norms which are in radical opposition to the norms set out in the law.

Law-making and cyberspace norms

The experience of file sharing tells us that a law is less likely to be accepted as meaningful, and thus less likely to be obeyed, if there is an established norm which tells people that they should behave in a different way from that which the law demands. Cyberspace is full of such norms.

Lawmakers who wish to do more than merely make a symbolic statement therefore need to recognize the constraints which cyberspace norms place on their law-making. This is not to say that lawmakers can never successfully enact laws which conflict with established norms—after all, one important function of law is to set norms for a community. However, a lawmaker who is unaware of those norms, or fails to understand their strength, is likely to produce laws whose content will not be respected.

The critical issue seems to be the size of the gap between the established social norm and the legal norm which the lawmaker wishes to substitute for it:

> just as social norms can have a law-reinforcing aspect, legal rules can reinforce social norms. However, this feedback loop can be short-circuited if social norms diverge widely from legal rules.

---

[88] Ibid, 540.
[89] Ibid, 543.

This often occurs when legislation changes a legal rule without directly affecting the underlying norms of conduct. Copyright presents a somewhat different situation. Although the legal rule that holds infringers liable for unauthorized copying has remained the same, new technology has changed the context in which the rule against unauthorized copying operates. Under either circumstance, the effect is to decouple the *is* of the positive law from the *ought* of its normative content. As a consequence of this discrepancy between *is* and *ought,* attempts to reform social norms are most likely to fail where the gaps between legal rules and social reality are at their widest. Where unlawful conduct is unlikely to connote that the lawbreaker is blameworthy or antisocial, the normative meaning of the legal rule fails to provide a selective incentive to obey the law . . . Thus, even in cultures where a general norm of law-abidingness is firmly entrenched, discrepancies between legal rules and social norms can persist more or less indefinitely if the gap between laws and norms is unusually wide.[90]

In such circumstances the lawmaker needs to narrow the gap. This can be achieved (if it is achievable at all) either by changing the social norm to be closer to that of the law, or by converging the law more nearly with the social norm.[91] The canny lawmaker will doubtless attempt both of these.

One way of shifting the social norm in the direction of the law is via education. If cyberspace actors can be convinced that their conduct is morally wrong, rather than merely unlawful, enough of them may change their behaviour in the direction of the legal norm to start change in the social norm. Rights holders have attempted to do this by equating file sharing with crimes against physical property, such as theft, which are widely accepted as being morally wrong.[92] The UK's Digital Economy Act 2010 seems to be aimed more at changing the cyberspace file-sharing norm than at enforcing the existing law, through its primary mechanism of warning letters to ISP customers whose accounts have been used for file sharing.[93] This is certainly how the industry sees the law as working:

The solution to P2P piracy, now being adopted and debated in countries around the world, is the so-called 'graduated response' model requiring responsible steps by ISPs to help address piracy on their networks. Graduated response is a proportionate approach that involves a system of educational notifications and warnings, culminating in deterrent sanctions for those who refuse to stop infringing.[94]

Lawmakers might also benefit from taking a gradualist approach which aims to move the social norm to match the desired legal norm by means of incremental change to the law. Kahan has found that if the law's condemnation of an activity is greatly in excess of that which a decision-maker, such as a judge or prosecutor, feels towards the activity, the decision-maker is likely to seek to mitigate the difference by enforcing the law less rigorously. However, if the law's condemnation is only a little

---

[90] Christopher Jensen (n 87), 562.
[91] Dorothea Kubler, 'On the Regulation of Social Norms', (2001) 17 JL Econ & Org 449, 452–3; Tom R Tyler (n 84), 234.
[92] Christopher Jensen (n 87), 557–60.
[93] Communications Act 2003, s 124, inserted by Digital Economy Act 2010, s 3.
[94] IFPI, Digital Music Report 2011, 18.

stronger than that of the non-legal norm then the decision-maker's respect for the law is usually enough to ensure that the law is enforced more rigorously.[95]

We saw in Part II that the social norm that the law should be respected is a strong one. If the law's demands are not greatly in excess of those made by an existing cyberspace norm, it seems plausible that respect for the law among cyberspace actors might on its own be enough to move the norm gradually in the lawmaker's desired direction.

Certainly this gradualist technique is worth trying. Our experience of law in cyberspace to date is that where a lawmaker goes head-to-head with an entrenched cyberspace norm it is usually the norm which prevails.

---

[95] Dan M Kahan, 'Gentle Nudges vs Hard Shoves: Solving the Sticky Norms Problem' (2000) 67 U Chi L Rev 607.

8

Three Ways to Make Meaningless Law

We saw in the previous chapter that a law may not be accepted by a cyberspace actor as imposing a meaningful obligation on him if there is an already-established norm which imposes a contradictory obligation. If that norm cannot be ousted by the law, as seems to be the case for copyright law, then the law will fail to achieve its function of influencing the mental state of the actor to accept its obligations. Fortunately for lawmakers there are few cyberspace norms which are so strong as this.

It is far more common that a law fails to impose a meaningful obligation because the law's subject simply cannot understand what that obligation consists of. Lawmakers rarely intend this to happen, but it is surprising how often they achieve it. A cyberspace actor who accepts the lawmaker's authority to regulate the activity in question might still take the view that a lawmaker who is unable to explain the obligations it wishes to impose in a particular law cannot reasonably expect those obligations to be complied with.

When asking if a law imposes meaningful obligations it is important to recall that the relevant viewpoint is that of the cyberspace actor, and not the lawmaker. We have seen that the scope for a lawmaker to impose its will on cyberspace actors is extremely limited, so that by and large laws work (if at all) in cyberspace because actors accept their normative force and thus obey them. A law whose meaning is not understood by those to whom it is addressed can have little normative force.

How, then, do lawmakers fail to make meaningful law? One common fault is to make the law so complex that it can only be understood by specialist professional advisers, if indeed even they understand it fully. In effect such laws are addressed to the advisers, and not to the cyberspace actor. But this way of law-making assumes that a cyberspace actor is able to secure advice on all its legal obligations. This is not so. In the same way that the global reach of cyberspace multiplies the problems of enforcing the law, so it multiplies the difficulty of taking advice. Only the largest corporations can in theory afford to take legal advice about every national law to which they might be subject, and in practice such corporations do not do so because the costs are disproportionate to the risk of enforcement. 'Ordinary' cyberspace actors do not even have this theoretical possibility to obtain advice, so that at best they will comply with a law whose authority they accept in accordance with their lay understanding of its meaning. If they cannot understand it, they cannot comply.

A second type of potentially meaningless law is a law which contradicts some other obligation to which the cyberspace actor is subject. Internal contradiction within laws is not unknown, and these kinds of law are particularly likely to be seen as lacking in meaning for the actor. More commonly the conflict is with the provisions of some other law. Whichever is the case, it is impossible for the actor to be certain which ought to be obeyed, and this robs one or other obligation of its meaningfulness, perhaps even both.

The final type of meaninglessness which will be examined in this chapter is perhaps a surprising one. It arises when a lawmaker attempts to state the law with complete precision. On first consideration it might be thought that precise law is highly desirable—after all, it is a common complaint that the law is obscure or ambiguous. As we shall see, though, absolute precision is rarely if ever achievable, and failed attempts at precision regularly lead to over-complex and contradictory laws, lacunae where it is unclear whether the law imposes any obligation at all, and other undesirable consequences.

Over-complexity

Some minimum level of complexity is inevitable in any legal rule. The law of theft could be summarized, for most countries, as prohibiting taking another's property with the intention that the taking be permanent. However, 'property' needs further explanation, at least in relation to intangible property, and the various lawful excuses for taking need to be set out in the rule. Even with such explanation, much of the rule remains open-textured so that it takes a textbook to explore its nuances fully.

Sometimes lawmakers find it irresistible to refrain from supplementing the basic law with additional provisions to deal with ambiguities and uncertainties as they are identified. At its most extreme this can produce a law which even legal specialists cannot fully understand. A particularly striking example is the UK Financial Services Authority (FSA) Handbook which sets out detailed regulations made under the Financial Services and Markets Act 2000, itself a hugely complex piece of legislation. The FSA Handbook is an enormous set of documents. For Release 093 of September 2009 the Glossary alone runs to 350 pages, and the High Level Standards section (a small part of the whole) is 444 pages long. The full Handbook amounts to many thousands of pages—I did not have the strength to count them all in 2009, nor to update these numbers since, though they have undoubtedly grown. On the assumption that the release number relates back to the inception of the FSA in 1997, it appears that major changes to the Handbook are made on average eight times each year. Each part of the Handbook contains cross-references to other parts, so that a full understanding of any part requires some mastery of the whole. It seems highly unlikely that any single person has a complete understanding of the entire regulatory regime and how it applies to all the regulated activities.

This would not be as much of a problem as it appears if the application of the FSA Handbook were confined to UK-regulated financial institutions. These institutions undertake regulatory 'conversations' with the FSA in its role as regulator, as a result of which they develop an understanding of how the Handbook applies to the activity under discussion. The conversations also lead to changes to the regulatory regime.[1] However, the Handbook's rules also apply to non-UK financial institutions whose activities are 'capable of having an effect in the United Kingdom'[2] but who are not included in these regulatory conversations. Worse, they often apply to online actors who are not established financial institutions, but who merely offer payment or other services which fall within the scope of the regulation. These actors have no realistic way of discovering the law which applies to them because it is too complex to be understood by anyone who is not a participant in the regulatory conversations.

Over-complexity is not confined to laws which regulate specialized sectors of activity. The EU data protection regime is of general application, triggered when any person becomes a controller or processor of personal data, and clearly illustrates how excessive detail makes the law hard to understand. It consists not simply of the Data Protection Directive[3] and its national implementing laws, but also of a large mass of reports, recommendations, guidance notes from regulators, and the like. As at July 2011 the UK Information Commissioner's website listed sixty-four different guidance documents under the heading 'Practical application', together with 104 'Detailed specialist guides'.[4]

A law which requires such a large volume of material to explain it is clearly very complex, and we should therefore not be surprised that those who are subject to the law often fail to understand it. It is commonplace that organizations regularly cite data protection concerns as a reason for refusing to do something which is perfectly lawful.[5] Lawyers may be able to understand how to comply with data protection law (or more accurately, some of them may understand how to comply with some of it), but this does not seem to be true of those whom the law regulates.

A further problem with over-complex laws is that it is often only possible to understand the overall legislative aims by working through the complex interlocking of the law's detailed requirements. Even if the detail is understood, the larger aims of the law are often obscure. This can produce severe compliance difficulties where a new technology or business model is adopted, as in many cases the application of the detailed requirements to the new activity will be difficult, or impossible, to work out.[6] This uncertainty can only be resolved if the aims of the law are set out somewhere in a way which is readily understandable.

---

[1] See *The proper uses of precision*, p 143.

[2] UK Financial Services and Markets Act 2000, s 21.

[3] Directive 95/46/EC on the protection of individuals with regard to the processing of personal data and on the free movement of such data, OJ L281/31, 23 November 1995.

[4] <http://www.ico.gov.uk/tools_and_resources/document_library/data_protection.aspx>. The Information Commissioner has recognized the difficulties this causes and has produced a new, plain English, Guide at <http://www.ico.gov.uk/for_organisations/data_protection/the_guide.aspx>. However, this Guide does not replace the other guidance documents but merely seeks to explain them more simply. A full understanding still requires that all the other guidance materials be read.

[5] See eg 'Police Chief Admits Huntley Records Were Wiped Out', *The Times*, 19 December 2003; 'Medical Research Need Not Fall Foul of the Law' (letter by Richard Thomas, Information Commissioner), *The Times*, 20 January 2006.

[6] This issue is discussed at length in Ch 10.

One obvious consequence of laws which are too complex to be understandable by those to whom they apply, examined further in Chapter 9, is that they may be ineffective in achieving their aims. Those who accept the authority of such a law can do no more than tick off their compliance with the various detailed obligations, even if this results in their behaving in a way which does not accord with what the lawmaker was aiming at.

Contradictory Rules

Contradictory rules are also, in the main, a product of complexity. Although contradiction is not a necessary consequence, where laws and regulations consist of a mass of technical detail the scope for internal contradiction or clashes with other complex laws is greatly increased.

An example of unintended internal contradiction is found in the UK Regulation of Investigatory Powers Act 2000, which makes a distinction between the content of a communication, which can only be intercepted under a warrant,[7] and data about a communication (not including its content), which can be demanded by notice given by a designated person.[8] Each of these processes is governed by a detailed Code of Practice which has statutory force.[9]

As Walden points out,[10] the dividing line between these two categories of data is often hard to draw, in part because the concepts derive from pre-internet communication technologies which made their separation far clearer.[11] It is therefore uncertain which regime applies, and potentially both might apply with contradictory results:

Communication service providers will face legal, procedural and operational uncertainties with regard to their obligations to obtain and deliver up data that has been requested by an investigating agency [and] law enforcement agencies will be faced with greater legal uncertainties in respect of the appropriate procedures to be complied with when carrying out an investigation or risk any data obtained being excluded.[12]

Contradictory rules can also arise where two different pieces of legislation address the same activity. A particularly striking example of this occurred in 2003 when the

---

[7] UK Regulation of Investigatory Powers Act 2000, s 1.

[8] Ibid, s 25.

[9] Interception of Communications Code of Practice (34 substantive pages) given force by the Regulation of Investigatory Powers (Acquisition and Disclosure of Communications Data: Code of Practice) Order 2007 SI 2002/1693; Acquisition and Disclosure of Communications Data Code of Practice (56 substantive pages), given force by the Regulation of Investigatory Powers (Acquisition and Disclosure of Communications Data: Code of Practice) Order 2007 SI 2007/2197.

[10] Ian Walden, *Computer Crimes and Digital Investigations* (Oxford: Oxford University Press, 2007) 4.244–4.256.

[11] For an explanation of some of the technological complexities see Alberto Escudero-Pascual and Ian Hosein, 'The Hazards of Technology-Neutral Policy: Questioning Lawful Access to Traffic Data' (2004) 47 *Communications of the ACM* 77.

[12] Walden (n 10), 4.256.

UK FSA attempted to impose the requirements of the e-Money Directive 2000[13] on mobile telephony companies.[14] Under the directive, issuers of e-money were prohibited from engaging in non-financial service activities.[15] At that time mobile telephony companies were starting to allow customers to make payments using the prepay float on their accounts. The FSA interpreted this as issuing e-money, and sent letters to those companies requiring them to obtain authorization as electronic money issuers. This placed the companies in a difficult dilemma—if they complied, they would be prohibited from continuing to offer telephony services and would thus be in breach of their telecommunications licence terms as well as being forced out of business. If they continued to offer telephony services, they could not seek authorization as electronic money issuers. The companies dealt with this problem in a commercially realistic way. They defied the FSA, which eventually backed down and left the issue to be resolved as part of a then forthcoming review of payment services regulation at EU level, which eventually resolved the contradiction by removing the prohibition.[16]

Contradictions of this kind are particularly likely to arise in cyberspace because of technological change. At the time the e-Money Directive was developed, the main available e-money technologies all envisaged that the funds would be stored on a smart card which would be in the physical possession of the user.[17] Within a few years though, internet and mobile communications became sufficiently fast and reliable to enable the development of the accounted e-payments business model. Under this model both payer and payee hold accounts with the service provider, and payments are made by simply debiting the payer's account and crediting the payee's account. The model only works if real-time messaging between payer, payee, and service provider is possible, and thus only became usable by non-banks when the internet and mobile telecoms networks provided the necessary communications facilities. The accounted model was adopted by the mobile telephony providers, and

---

[13] Directive 2000/46/EC of the European Parliament and of the Council on the taking up, pursuit of and prudential supervision of the business of electronic money institutions, OJ L 275/39, 27 October 2000 ('e-Money Directive 2000').

[14] UK FSA, Electronic Money: perimeter guidance (February 2003).

[15] e-Money Directive 2000, Art 1(5).

[16] Directive 2009/110/EC of the European Parliament and of the Council of 16 September 2009 on the taking up, pursuit and prudential supervision of the business of electronic money institutions amending Directives 2005/60/EC and 2006/48/EC and repealing Directive 2000/46/EC, OJ L267/7, 10 October 2009, Art 6(1)(b). In theory this directive, together with the Payment Services Directive (Directive 2007/64/EC of the European Parliament and of the Council on payment services in the internal market amending Directives 97/7/EC, 2002/65/EC, 2005/60/EC and 2006/48/EC and repealing Directive 97/5/EC, OJ L 319/1, 5 December 2007), creates a coordinated system of regulation for non-credit institution payment services. However, the dividing line between e-money issuers and other payment service providers is by no means clear, and this opens the way to further contradiction.

[17] See the original drafting of Art 1(3)(b) in the 1996 proposal, which defined e-money a being '(i) stored electronically on an electronic device such as a chip card or a computer memory' and '(iii) generated in order to be put at the disposal of users to serve as an electronic surrogate for coins and banknotes' (Proposal for a European Parliament and Council directive on the taking up, the pursuit and the prudential supervision of the business of electronic money institutions, COM (1998) 0461 final, OJ C317, 15 October 1998).

this gave rise to the conflicting application of regulation. Because law changes at a far slower rate than technology, such contradictions can persist for substantial periods of time—in the case of e-money this particular contradiction, which came to light in 2003, remained unresolved until the new regulatory regime came into force in 2011.

Precision

These problems of over-complexity and contradiction are often caused by a law-maker's attempt to set out rules as precisely as possible. Across all fields of law there is a clear trend for rules to become increasingly detailed. As an example, the UK Companies Act 1948 consisted of 462 sections and 18 schedules, whereas the 2006 Act runs to 1,300 sections and 16 schedules. Much of that increase is because of an attempt to spell out the law's requirements in exhaustive detail, rather than as broad obligations of principle. In 1948 the provisions relating to auditors occupied only seven sections of the Act;[18] in 2006 a full sixty-five sections were needed,[19] perhaps ten times as much detail.

Law-making which aims at detailed precision has three main characteristics. First, it attempts to regulate the behaviour of the law's subjects primarily by reference to objective and/or quantitative measurements. The aim is to make compliance with the law achievable by meeting these measurements. So far as possible, the law's subject is not required to make qualitative judgements about matters such as fairness or reasonableness.

Secondly, in many cases, compliance with the law can be achieved, either wholly or in large part, by completing check lists. This could fairly be described as a 'tick-box' approach to compliance.

Finally, although it is clear *what* the subject is required to do to comply with the law, it is often unclear *why* the law imposes those obligations. The lawmaker's normative aims can easily be obscured by the detail of the law. This is a particular problem in cyberspace because compliance with a law is largely dependent on the cyberspace actor's acceptance of its authority. The cyberspace technologies, and business models used by actors, are subject to continual change. This creates uncertainty as to whether the law applies at all to new developments, and if so how its detailed requirements should be complied with.[20] If the cyberspace actor is able to understand the normative aims behind the law's requirements, and accepts those aims as authoritative, then he is at least likely to attempt to comply with the spirit of the law. If those aims are not apparent from the text of the law then at best they can only be inferred by specialist legal advisors, and thus are unlikely to influence the acceptance of authority by a cyberspace actor who does not take, or cannot afford, specialist advice.

---

[18] UK Companies Act 1948, ss 159–61 and Sch 8 (ss 1–4).
[19] UK Companies Act 2006, ss 475–539.
[20] For further discussion of this issue see Ch 11.

Even if the law's normative aims are understandable and accepted as being appropriate by the cyberspace actor, he is unlikely to accept the law as imposing meaningful obligations on him if compliance with those obligations will not achieve the law's aims. Failure in this respect, examined further in Chapter 10, has been particularly common in those laws which aim to regulate cyberspace activities and which adopt a precision law-making technique.

The examples which follow illustrate these failings of the precision law-making approach.

Electronic signatures

Clearly it is not possible to apply a manuscript signature to online communications because there is no paper document on which the signatory can write his or her name. There are, at present, two main techniques for effecting an electronic signature for electronic communications. The first is to add information identifying the signatory to the communication, usually in the form of a typed name or a scanned image of a manuscript signature. This is an evidentially weak form of signature because an electronic communication can be edited without trace, and thus if, for example, the identity of the signatory is in dispute extrinsic evidence will be needed to prove his identity. Nonetheless, the English courts (among others) have acknowledged that these forms of information addition can create valid signatures in cases where identity is undisputed.[21]

The second is to use the mathematics of encryption to take a set of numbers which evidences the content of the electronic document[22] and encrypt them using a secret key to create a 'digital signature'. This secret key is logically related to a public key in such a way that (a) only the public key can be used to decrypt, and thus check, the signature and the integrity of the communication, and (b) the identity of the holder of the secret key can be determined via an electronic ID certificate issued by a trusted third party, a certification authority, which has identified the signatory and confirms his or her possession of the secret key.[23]

The common law has for centuries taken the view that a signature is a mere matter of evidence, rather than a formal act prescribed by law,[24] and will therefore accept either of these e-signature methods as valid. However, in civil law jurisdictions signatures often ascribe formal significance to the act of writing one's name on

---

[21] *Mehta v J Pereira Fernandes SA* [2006] EWHC 813 (Ch), [2006] 2 All ER 891; *In re a debtor (No 2021 of 1995)* [1996] 2 All ER 345.

[22] This set of numbers is created by a 'hash' function, a mathematical process which can be demonstrated as being highly unlikely to produce the same result from different documents.

[23] For a grossly oversimplified explanation of the mathematical basis of digital signatures, see Chris Reed, 'What *Is* a Signature' (2000) 3 JILT, <http://www2.warwick.ac.uk/fac/soc/law/elj/jilt/2000_3/reed/>, Part 4.3. The seminal mathematical paper on the topic is RL Rivest, A Shamir, and L Adleman, 'A Method of Obtaining Digital Signatures and Public Key Cryptosystems' (1978) 21 *Communications of the ACM* 120; although the implementation of digital-signature technologies in practice has required the development of more complex techniques, the elegant method proposed in this paper still lies at the heart of all those technologies.

[24] Chris Reed (n 23), Part 3.

a paper document. Because this physical act is not possible online, it was by no means clear that e-signatures could be used to achieve the same formal effects, and thus produce a legally valid signature.[25]

In an attempt to resolve this problem within the EU, the e-Signatures Directive[26] was enacted. The directive created a two-tier system: (a) what have become known as 'simple' electronic signatures, defined in Article 2(1) as 'data in electronic form which are attached to or logically associated with other electronic data and which serve as a method of authentication'; and (b) 'advanced' electronic signatures[27] which, if the identity of the signatory is evidenced by an appropriate ID certificate, are equivalent to digital signatures.

The legal validity of a simple electronic signature is left to national law, the directive providing merely that Member States are to ensure that signatures of this type are not denied validity, enforceability, and effectiveness solely on the grounds that they are in electronic form, or are not certified or created with a particular security device.[28] An advanced electronic signature, on the other hand, is granted by Article 5(1) the same legal effectiveness as a handwritten signature provided it is based on a 'qualified certificate' and created by a 'secure-signature-creation device'. These terms are described in precise detail.

The definition of 'advanced electronic signature' in Article 2(2) contains four elements,[29] all of which are in theory objectively verifiable[30] by a technical expert. A 'qualified certificate' meets the requirements of Annex I and is provided by a 'certification-service-provider' who fulfils the requirements of Annex II. Annex I sets out ten data elements which the certificate must contain, and Annex II contains twelve requirements which the provider must meet, only three of which have

---

[25] See Minyan Wang, 'The Impact of Information Technology Development on the Legal Concept: A Particular Examination on the Legal Concept of "Signatures"' (2007) Int JL&IT 253, 259–63 (Germany and China); Stephen Mason, 'The international implications of using electronic signatures' (2005) CTLR 160, 164 (France).

[26] Directive 1999/93/EC on a Community framework for electronic signatures, OJ L13/12, 19 January 2000.

[27] Defined in Art 2(2) as:

an electronic signature which meets the following requirements:

(a) it is uniquely linked to the signatory;
(b) it is capable of identifying the signatory;
(c) it is created using means that the signatory can maintain under his sole control; and
(d) it is linked to the data to which it relates in such a manner that any subsequent change of the data is detectable.

[28] Art 5(2).

[29] These are that:

(a) it is uniquely linked to the signatory;
(b) it is capable of identifying the signatory;
(c) it is created using means that the signatory can maintain under his sole control; and
(d) it is linked to the data to which it relates in such a manner that any subsequent change of the data is detectable.

[30] Or at least, to the extent that anything related to evidence of this kind is objectively verifiable. Such an expert would be able to give an estimate of the probability that each of the four requirements is met, which in the case of a reputable, commercial e-signature technology is likely to be 0.99 or better.

any real qualitative element.[31] Annex III sets out four matters which a 'secure-signature-creation device' must ensure, all of which are technically verifiable.

Thus, to sum up, the directive contains a check list of thirty items which, if met, bring the signature within Article 5(1). At first sight, it would seem that this provides a clear and objective test which, if a particular digital-signature technology ticks all thirty boxes, enables both the signatory and relying party to be certain that the signatures it produces have the same legal force as manuscript signatures. The aim of the legislation is clearly to enable a relying party to answer objectively the question whether the signature is legally valid. If before accepting the signature the relying party had to investigate the accuracy of the data in its certificate, or the effectiveness of the technical processes used in maintaining security, the law would not have achieved anything.[32]

In practice, this apparent certainty is illusory. These purportedly objective tests are not objective. To decide if a particular e-signature technology can be accepted as producing the equivalent to a handwritten signature, the relying party needs first to consult a legal specialist to identify which parts of the thirty-item checklist are important and what they mean in the context of the particular transaction. Then a technical expert needs to be consulted to produce an opinion on whether those requirements of the checklist have been met. Finally the legal expert needs to review the technical expert's opinion, to produce a further opinion as to whether a court would be convinced by the technical expert's argument.

If this is certainty it is a very uncertain type of certainty, and it is not surprising that the law has failed to achieve its aim of encouraging the pan-European use of digital signatures.[33] Cyberspace actors have understood that compliance with the law, by ticking off the thirty boxes, will not necessarily produce the normative result aimed at by the law, which is that the signature should be accepted conclusively as equivalent to a manuscript signature. They have therefore adopted lower-cost technologies which offer nearly as much evidential certainty as the advanced electronic signature but are, in particular, much easier to use in practice.

---

[31] These are the requirements to:

  (a) demonstrate the reliability necessary for providing certification services; . . .
  (b) verify, by appropriate means in accordance with national law, the identity and, if applicable, any specific attributes of the person to which a qualified certificate is issued; . . .
  (c) use trustworthy systems to store certificates in a verifiable form . . .

[32] The aim of the directive is that qualitative questions should arise only after the use of the signature, when determining the *consequences* of a failure on the part of signatory or certification service provider. For example, if the signatory's identity is misstated then under Art 6 the certification service provider is liable to a relying party unless there was no negligence on his part, and determining negligence of course requires a qualitative judgement.

[33] Jos Dumortier et al, *Study on the Legal and Market Aspects of Electronic Signatures* (KUL, 2003), <http://ec.europa.eu/information_society/eeurope/2005/all_about/security/electronic_sig_report.pdf>; Report from the Commission to the European Parliament and the Council on the operation of Directive 1999/93/EC on a Community framework for electronic signatures, COM (2006) 120 final, 15 March 2006, 5–8.

Data protection

For my second example I take the current European Data Protection regime, established in 1995.[34] The subject matter of data protection is personal privacy in data, an element of human rights, and one might therefore expect the obligations imposed by the directive to be drafted in terms of broad and fundamental principles. At first sight this appears to be true.

The primary obligation placed on data controllers[35] is to comply with the data protection principles when processing personal data. These are set out in Article 6(1) of the directive and, taken together with the obligation in Article 17 to take reasonable precautions to maintain data security, constitute a cogent and concise statement of the social purposes at which the law aims and the general obligations placed on those who control and process personal data.

However, the directive supplements these general obligations with others which are framed in much more precise terms. A closer examination of these obligations indicates that they are drafted in such a way as to permit forms of compliance which have no real connection to the wider aims of the law.

First, Article 18 of the directive requires most data controllers to notify their national supervisory authority before processing personal data. The second data protection principle, set out in Article 6(1)(b), requires that the purposes notified be legitimate. This clearly means more than that they should simply not be unlawful, as it is unlikely that a controller would notify an unlawful purpose.[36] 'Legitimate' must therefore be read in the light of the overall aims of the law, which are explained clearly in recital 2:

> Whereas data-processing systems are designed to serve man; whereas they must, whatever the nationality or residence of natural persons, respect their fundamental rights and freedoms, notably the right to privacy, and contribute to economic and social progress, trade expansion and the well-being of individuals.

It is a reasonable conclusion that the controller is supposed to assess the purposes to be notified against these aims, and that purposes which run counter to those aims are not legitimate.

However, the implementation of the directive in UK law via the Data Protection (Notification and Notification Fees) Regulations 2000[37] substitutes an objective approach for this qualitative assessment. Regulation 4 requires the Information Commissioner to decide the form and detail required for notification, and the online notification form[38] implements a process which is largely one of box-ticking. Applicants are presented with templates in which the purposes are already filled in,

---

[34] Directive 95/46/EC on the protection of individuals with regard to the processing of personal data and on the free movement of such data, OJ L 281/31, 23 November 1995.

[35] Defined in Art 2(c) as the person who 'determines the purposes and means of the processing'.

[36] eg it seems implausible that the collection of data on planned holiday dates, processed for the purpose of deciding which houses to burgle, would ever be notified.

[37] SI 2000/188, made under Data Protection Act 1998, s 22.

[38] <https://www.ico.gov.uk/onlinenotification/?page=7.html>.

using a broad list of generic purposes which are singularly uninformative.[39] There is no obligation for the controller to expand on them or add further purposes; although both of these are possible, it is rare to find a notification which departs from the standard list provided by the website.

As a supplement to the notification requirements, Article 20 of the directive obliges Member States to undertake prior checking where processing is 'likely to present specific risks to the rights and freedoms of data subjects'. Such prior checking would act as a qualitative control on the notified purposes if it actually took place, but there is surprisingly little information as to how much, if any, checking occurs. It is, however, certain that no such checking is undertaken by the UK Information Commissioner. Section 22 of the Data Protection Act 1988 only requires checking where the controller proposes to undertake 'assessable processing', as specified in an order made by the Secretary of State. No such order has been made.

The most comprehensive study appears to have been carried out by Charlesworth in an Appendix to a report on privacy impact assessments undertaken for the UK Information Commissioner in 2007.[40] From the table on page 5 of that Appendix it is possible to conclude that nine of the states investigated are likely to undertake prior checking,[41] six may do so,[42] ten either have no provisions for checking or in practice do not undertake it,[43] and there is no data available for the remaining two.[44] In other words, in somewhere between one-third and two-thirds of European countries, notification is a purely objective exercise, not subject to qualitative constraints.

Secondly, in order to process personal data lawfully the processing must be justified by one of the reasons listed in Article 7.[45] A data controller who relies on any of

---

[39] eg one of the standard registered purposes for law firms is 'The provision of legal services, including advising and acting on behalf of clients', which conveys no real information about how the law firm intends to use the data.

[40] Andrew Charlesworth, 'Broad Jurisdictional Report for the European Union', Appendix H to Linden Consulting Inc, *Privacy Impact Assessments: International Study of their Application and Effects* (October 2007).

[41] Denmark, France, Germany, Lithuania, Luxembourg, Netherlands, Poland, Slovakia, Sweden. This conclusion is drawn from the fact that these national laws include detailed provisions about the kinds of processing which are subject to prior checking.

[42] Austria, Greece, Italy, Latvia, Malta, Portugal. The laws of these states contain generic statements rather than detailed provisions.

[43] Belgium, Bulgaria, Cyprus, Estonia, Finland, Hungary, Ireland, Romania, Spain, UK.

[44] Czech Republic, Slovenia.

[45] The justifications are:

    (a) the data subject has unambiguously given his consent; or

    (b) processing is necessary for the performance of a contract to which the data subject is party or in order to take steps at the request of the data subject prior to entering into a contract; or

    (c) processing is necessary for compliance with a legal obligation to which the controller is subject; or

    (d) processing is necessary in order to protect the vital interests of the data subject; or

    (e) processing is necessary for the performance of a task carried out in the public interest or in the exercise of official authority vested in the controller or in a third party to whom the data are disclosed; or

    (f) processing is necessary for the purposes of the legitimate interests pursued by the controller or by the third party or parties to whom the data are disclosed, except where such

these criteria must, it would be thought, need to form a qualitative judgement as to whether it is necessary for him to process the personal data for that reason.

However, paragraph (a) of Article 7 permits processing where 'the data subject has unambiguously given his consent'. This has led to a practice whereby data controllers who interact with data subjects online, for example e-commerce businesses selling via a web page, secure consent by means of a check-box on the web page (often pre-ticked) accompanied by a link to a privacy policy and terms and conditions. A data subject who checks the box (or, more likely, fails to uncheck it) has thus consented to the proposed processing. It is, of course, notorious that online users rarely read privacy policies. Nonetheless, these controllers have obtained unambiguous consent, and have thus complied with Article 7. There is no need for them to undertake any further qualitative assessment of whether their data collection and processing is justified under the directive.

This is, of course, not the way that the directive was intended to operate when Article 7 was devised. Online collection of personal data was not generally feasible when it was enacted in 1995, and even less so when the directive was first proposed in 1990.[46] There was an unstated assumption that informed consent could only be obtained by some formal process, most likely involving receipt of explanatory documents, which would enable the data subject to 'weigh the risks and advantages of the intended processing'.[47] In the online world it is clear that data subjects rarely conduct this exercise, and the nature of online interaction via web pages which contain multiple check-boxes and buttons removes any special formality from the process of giving consent.

Other categories of data controller still need to make qualitative judgements about the necessity of their processing,[48] but they are increasingly undertaking online data collection where possible because of the efficiencies gained by reducing manual document processing. Although the problem of obtaining consent via online tick-boxes is beginning to receive attention[49] it is hard to see how the process could be modified to meet the aims of the law.

Australian internet censorship

Although the examples examined so far are drawn from EU legislation, the use of precise law-making techniques to regulate cyberspace is a global phenomenon. The provisions of the Singapore Electronic Transactions Act 1998, which regulate

---

interests are overridden by the interests for fundamental rights and freedoms of the data subject which require protection under Article 1 (1).

[46] Proposal for a Council directive concerning the protection of individuals in relation to the processing of personal data, COM (90) 314 final.

[47] Ibid, 26.

[48] See eg the UK Information Commissioner's Employment Practices Code and related supplementary guidance, <http://www.ico.gov.uk/for_organisations/topic_specific_guides/employment.aspx>.

[49] See Article 29 Working Party, 'Opinion 5/2009 on Online Social Networking', WP 163, 01189/09/EN, 12 June 2009; UK Information Commissioner, 'Collecting Personal Information Using Websites', Data Protection Good Practice Note v2.0, 5 June 2007.

electronic signatures, are at least as complicated as the EU directive, and the US Digital Millennium Copyright Act 1998 is even more precise and complex than its EU counterparts. As a final example it is worth examining the Australian Broadcasting Services Amendment (Online Services) Act 1999, which inserted a new Schedule 5 into the Broadcasting Services Act 1992.

The aim of this legislation was to control the online availability of obscene and indecent material in Australia by subjecting that content to the same censorship regime as for broadcasting and film.[50] Under the Act, an obligation was imposed on ISPs not to permit access to such material.

However, the Act set out two methods of compliance. One required ISPs to exercise qualitative judgement, but the other merely required them to undertake a non-judgemental and objectively verifiable activity. The method which required judgement was for the ISP to refuse to host information classified by the censor as unsuitable, and to block access to it if hosted by another. This would prevent the material being available to Australian internet users, and was what the Act aimed to achieve. An ISP which elected to comply in this way would, however, face serious difficulties. Classified material the file name of which had been changed, or which was available from domains other than that from which it was originally classified, would still be subject to the obligation, but the only way in which an ISP could identify this would be by viewing the material and making a value judgement about its nature.

The alternative method of compliance was to provide customers with technology which claimed to filter out undesirable content. If an ISP did this, it knew with precision that it had complied with the law, and thus had no liability under the Act in respect of hosting or providing access to classified material. Australian ISPs seized on this method of compliance and entered into bulk licensing deals with producers of content-filtering software. It is notorious that such software is not very effective, and easy for expert users (such as children) to circumvent. The law has thus had little effect on the accessibility of 'adult' content in Australia, which remains much the same as elsewhere in the world.[51]

Precision and normative failure

The precise law-making approach does, of course, have potential advantages. It aims to provide certainty to those subject to the law, and such certainty is welcome where

---

[50] s 10 of the Schedule defined as 'prohibited content' any internet content which had been classified by the Australian Broadcasting Authority (ABA) as X or RC (refused classification), in essence content equivalent to films which depict sexual content in a way which is unsuitable for minors; or been classified with an R classification (otherwise unsuitable for minors), if the material was made available other than via a control method which restricts children from obtaining access. Additionally, the ABA was required, on request from any person, to classify any other content (including material hosted outside Australia), and once classified the provisions above would apply. Australian ISPs could be required by the ABA to take down prohibited content or, if it was hosted outside Australia, to prevent access to that content.

[51] However, the Australian government is renewing its efforts to introduce internet content filtering via what has been described as the Great Australian Firewall—see Ch 7, n 50.

a person needs to decide whether to take a particular course of action in such a short time frame that it is not realistic to ask a legal decision-maker for a ruling.

An example of such a need is the liability of intermediaries for unlawful material which they host. Article 14 of the Electronic Commerce Directive provides that if the intermediary receives notice that unlawful material is being hosted, the intermediary will lose immunity from liability unless it acts 'expeditiously' to take down or remove access to the material. How is the intermediary to make a decision whether to keep the material available if the person whose site is being hosted asserts that the material is lawful? The directive gives no guidance at all, with the result that a sensible intermediary will override the protests of the site owner and disable access for fear of becoming liable to the person who complained.

Contrast this with the position of a US host who receives a complaint that material infringes the complainant's copyright. Under the Digital Millennium Copyright Act 1998[52] the intermediary has a similar immunity, which is also lost on notice of unlawfulness. However, the US Act contains precise technical provisions[53] as to how the immunity is affected if the owner of the hosted site contests the allegation of infringement. If these procedures are followed the host has certainty whether it is potentially liable to the complainant, and does not need to take a view on whether to risk leaving the material accessible.

This is a situation where precision furthers the aims of the lawmaker. Protecting the rights of a copyright owner needs to be balanced against the interests of free speech. Any uncertainty on the part of a host about whether there is a potential liability risk will lead to the chilling of free speech, and so clear protections, drafted in precise terms, are required.

The disadvantages of aiming at precision are less obvious, but more dangerous. In my view, one of the most unfortunate consequences of the search for certainty has been a real weakening of the normative effect of some parts of cyberspace law. This weakening occurs in at least three ways.

In the case of a law which aims to enable or encourage an activity, the law is ignored by avoiding that activity. Electronic signature law, as we have seen, is a good example. Compliance with the detailed technical requirements of the e-Signatures Directive is so expensive and uncertain in outcome that enterprises have sought and found alternative ways of doing business. Laws which fail in this way weaken the authority of the lawmaker, and thus taint the authority of other laws from the same source. From the cyberspace actor's perspective, if the e-Signatures Directive failed to produce a law which was meaningful in the obligations it imposed, there is a likelihood that other directives also set out meaningless obligations which can similarly be ignored.

In the worst case, the law is actively disobeyed. We saw this in the application of the e-Money Directive 2000 to UK mobile telephony companies. It imposed obligations in respect of registration and the use of funds which they felt to be pointless, in terms of achieving the law's aims, and which were practically impossible to

---

[52] Implemented as 17 USC § 512.
[53] 17 USC § 512(g).

comply with given the technologies which those companies were using to effect payments for their customers. This, together with the contradiction with the telecommunications regulatory regime, was sufficient to persuade them to reject the authority of the law as being meaningless for them.

More insidiously, a precision law-making approach can induce the law's subjects to ignore the normative aims of the law, and instead seek to do no more than to comply with the detailed, tick-box requirements, even if such compliance does nothing in respect of the law's aims. This might be described as complying only with the letter of the law, whilst ignoring its spirit. The Australian Broadcasting Services (Online) Amendment Act 1999 is a clear example of such behaviour, as is the notification regime for data controllers under the UK Data Protection Act 1998. A law which imposes apparently pointless obligations, in terms of its normative aims, is one to which only lip-service will be paid rather than respect.

The proper uses of precision

Precise rules are prevalent where primary legislation establishes a regulator which is empowered both to make rules and enforce them. Systems of this type are most commonly used to regulate those sectors of activity which operate as markets, such as the financial services sector, telecommunications, and energy utilities, but are sometimes adopted for social regulation as in the case of broadcasting. The most common approach to this kind of law-making is a co-regulatory model, under which primary legislation sets out comparatively general objectives to be achieved while the detailed implementation of those objectives as rules is carried out by a sectoral regulator, established by the primary legislation. The aim is to produce rules which describe as precisely as possible the conduct required from regulatees, reducing to a minimum the need for judgement or discretion on the part of both regulatee and regulator when assessing compliance.

The most salient feature of this regulatory model is the method through which the detailed rules are developed and applied. This proceeds via a series of regulatory conversations,[54] through which regulatees negotiate the content and application of the rules with the regulator. These conversations are possible because the regulatory model generates an interpretive community,[55] which consists of the regulator together with those specialists within each regulated entity who work on regulatory compliance and have a deep understanding of the issues involved and the existing rules. By its very nature, the conversational model of regulation does not seek to fix on a once-and-for-all rule-set, but instead sees the achievement of the regulatory objectives as a moving target which requires constant adjustment of the rules to take account of new behaviours and other relevant factors.

Regulatory objectives are achieved not only via the content of the rules but also through the ways in which they are enforced. The regulator has discretion over enforcement, either formally or de facto, and usually has a range of methods through

---

[54] Julia Black, 'Talking About Regulation' (1998) Public Law 77.
[55] Julia Black, *Rules and Regulators* (Oxford: Clarendon Press, 1997), 30–7.

which the rules can be enforced once a decision has been made to do so.[56] Thus the meaning in practice of the obligations set out in rules may be somewhat different from what their wording would suggest. This lack of concordance between published rule and its enforcement is not objectionable because of the conversational nature of the system. Regulatees know the difference between the wording of the rule and its practical implementation and can therefore frame their activities accordingly.

The fact that this regulatory model has been adopted very widely, and has persisted over time, permits us to conclude that the rules it generates cannot be so very defective. However, it should be noted that the empirical work of Braithwaite[57] suggests that precise rule-making can be less effective at achieving regulatory objectives than a rule-set which is open-textured, accompanied by regulatory conversations which focus on meeting the broad regulatory objectives rather than on detailed rule compliance. Sparrow, examining how regulation is implemented by agencies, notes that there is an inevitable element of discretion in its enforcement which makes the rules open-textured in practice.[58] His ideas about enforcement aimed at achieving desired outcomes, rather than merely seeking rule-compliance, are currently being embodied in the implementation of Canadian financial services regulation.[59]

The laws from cyberspace examined above are all primary legislation, rather than the products of a regulatory system. And yet the rules as drafted by the lawmaker seem to attempt a similar degree of precision to those found in the rules produced by regulators. Nor do these laws relate to the activity of markets, where it could be argued that detailed precision is needed to enable participants to make rapid decisions. Why might the lawmaker have made this choice?

Adopting this regulatory model could perhaps be sensible if the lawmaker's aim is to facilitate a market for a new activity.[60] In the cyberspace field, many governments have announced as policy goals the encouragement of innovation and the widespread adoption of information technology. The consequences of innovation and technology adoption have never been predictable, and a favoured technique has therefore been to attempt to establish a market through which the technology can be adopted and developed. This has normally been done by introducing law which purports to encourage use of the technology by removing legal uncertainty.[61] It is

---

[56] Malcolm Sparrow, *The Regulatory Craft* (Washington: The Brookings Institution, 2000).

[57] John Braithwaite, 'Rules and Principles: A Theory of Legal Certainty' (2002) 27 Austl J Leg Phil 47.

[58] Malcolm Sparrow (n 56). See in particular 4–6, 17–25, and 238–54.

[59] CL Ford, 'New Governance, Compliance, and Principles-Based Securities Regulation' (2008) 45 Am Bus LJ 1.

[60] Note, however, Julia Black's doubts as to the efficacy of using law for this purpose: 'for policy makers, an assumption that law can be used to stimulate financial market development is a helpful one to adopt . . . Lawyers may be more sceptical than policy makers of the likely success of this venture' (Julia Black, 'Forms and Paradoxes of Principles Based Regulation', LSE Law, Society and Economy Working Papers 13/2008, <http://ssrn.com/abstract=1267722>, 6; this thought is, however, omitted from the version published in (2008) 3 Capital Markets Law Journal 425).

[61] See eg European Commission, Proposal for a European Parliament and Council directive on a common framework for electronic signatures, COM (1998) 297 final, 13 May 1998, 3:

> In order to ensure the functioning of the Internal Market and to support the rapid development of the market in terms of user demand and technological innovation, prior authorization

therefore not too surprising that such law takes the form of detailed technical provisions that address the known uncertainties at the time, rather than attempting to specify a desired social and commercial outcome which the market might not achieve.[62] However, this justification fails if, as is true for most of cyberspace law, there is no market to be regulated.

A second possibility is that the influence of economic theory on political thought has led some lawmakers to prefer a detailed style of law-making which attempts to define compliance in objective terms. This understanding of economic theory was recently summarized by the journalist Anatole Kaletsky as follows:

The defunct economists today are the people who took control of the subject in the 1980s, with theories that closely coincided with the spirit of the Thatcher-Reagan revolution. Their three main ideas transformed the politics, as well as the economics, of the next 20 years. The first idea, known as 'rational expectations', maintained that capitalist economies with competitive labour markets do not need stabilising by governments.

The second idea—'efficient markets'—asserted that competitive finance always allocates resources in the most efficient way, reflecting all the best available information and forecasts about the future.

The third idea stated that economics, previously a largely descriptive study of human behaviour, had to become a branch of mathematics, using assumptions on human behaviour that were clear enough to be expressed in algebraic formulae. Economic problems that could not be analysed with mathematics were deemed unworthy of consideration.[63]

Although economists might reasonably claim that this is a distortion of their work, there is some evidence that politicians and lawmakers understood it in this way.[64]

---

has to be avoided. As a means to gain the confidence of consumers, voluntary accreditation schemes for certification service provider aiming at providing enhanced levels of security is considered to be useful. As far as such measures are required by the market, they could give a clearer or more predictable level of legal security for both the certification service provider and the consumer.

[62] The dangers of regulating an as yet non-existent market with the degree of precision appropriate to an established market are demonstrated by the first e-Money Directive (Directive 2000/46/EC of the European Parliament and of the Council on the taking up, pursuit of and prudential supervision of the business of electronic money institutions, OJ L 275/39, 27 October 2000). It is clear that its framers had no particular vision of how e-money should operate or, with the exception of imposing a consumer protection requirement to redeem e-money in the possession of a user, the nature of the legal relationships which an e-money system would necessitate. Instead they assumed that the 'invisible hand' of the markets would produce the results desired (if any), or at least that the results (whatever they turned out to be) would be desirable ones. The directive is generally agreed to have stifled the development of e-money in Europe—see Proposal for a directive of the European Parliament and of the Council on the taking up, pursuit and prudential supervision of the business of electronic money institutions, amending Directives 2005/60/EC and 2006/48/EC and repealing Directive 2000/46/EC, COM (2008) 627 final, 9 October 2008, 2. The 2000 Directive has been replaced from 2011 by a regulatory regime which imposes far more open-textured rules on the sector—Directive 2009/110/EC of the European Parliament and of the Council of 16 September 2009 on the taking up, pursuit and prudential supervision of the business of electronic money institutions amending Directives 2005/60/EC and 2006/48/EC and repealing Directive 2000/46/EC, OJ L267/7, 10 October 2009.

[63] Anatole Kaletsky, 'Three Cheers for the Death of Old Economics', *The Times*, 28 October 2009.

[64] See eg Lord Harris of High Cross, *Morality and Markets* (London: Centre for Policy Studies, 1986).

Those on the political left criticize the right for its faith in the workings of markets[65] while those on the right criticize the making of law which seeks a kind of mathematical precision through excessive detail.[66]

Even if this view of economic theory were accurate, it would only justify precise law-making if the activities regulated by the law were influenced primarily by economic considerations. This is obviously not the case for data protection, where the main aim is to protect the social value of privacy. Even in the case of e-signatures, which might well be used to validate some economically significant transaction, economic considerations of this type only influence the decision whether to enter into the transaction at all, rather than the decision as to which form of signature (if any) should be used. We have seen that the main economic calculation made about e-signatures seems to be that the most strongly legally validated form of advanced e-signature is too expensive.

More important than any justification for precise law-making, however, is the question of its efficacy. We thus need to ask if the regulatory model can be applied successfully to activities in cyberspace. I suggest that the answer is no for three reasons.

First, in many of those areas of cyberspace activity which lawmakers wish to regulate, there is no interpretive community, and no prospect of its development. The law relating to e-signatures demonstrates this clearly. If we ask which cyberspace actors might want or need to sign an electronic document, the answer is 'All of them'. Even if we limited our inquiry to, say, the largest e-commerce companies, it would not be possible to find 'e-signature compliance' professionals on their staffs, nor would those businesses see it as useful to establish such positions. A regulatory conversation is not possible if there is no one to speak to.[67]

The fact that there is no interpretive community also has the consequence that any mismatch between the law's aims and its actual text cannot easily be remedied through the use of enforcement discretion. The absence of regulatory conversation means that the enforcer is able only to guess as to how best to exercise enforcement discretion to achieve the law's aims. Because of the complexity of cyberspace activities, that guess is more likely to be wrong than in the physical world. Those who are

---

[65] 'What failed was the right wing fundamentalism that says you just leave everything to the market and says that free markets should not just be free but values free' (Speech of Gordon Brown to UK Labour Party Conference 2009, <http://www.guardian.co.uk/politics/2009/sep/29/gordon-brown-labour-conference-speech-in-full>).

[66] 'Regulations based on achieving outcomes, rather than just blindly following box-ticking procedure, will actually work better' (Ken Clarke, speech to UK Conservative Party Conference 2009, <http://www.conservatives.com/News/Speeches/2009/10/Ken_Clarke_Britain_will_be_a_decent_place_to_do_business_again.aspx>).

[67] This point is perhaps implicit in Julia Black's more recent work, where she writes that the success or failure of principles based regulation 'depends on how it is implemented and on the institutional context which surrounds it. Critically, that institutional context has to be characterized by the presence of a high degree of mutual trust between participants within the regulatory regime' (Julia Black (n 60), Capital Markets Law Journal 426). Where, as in much of the law of regulation of cyberspace, there is no institutional context at all, it is therefore unsurprising that this form of regulation produces problems.

attempting to frame their activities so as to comply with the law will have no easy way to discover how it is likely to be enforced, and this will inevitably produce a reduction in the law's normative effect.

Secondly, even if an interpretive community can be identified the results of the regulatory conversation will not produce effective law if that community is not a core part of the regulated entity. In financial services, regulation shapes the products of the industry and regulatory compliance is fundamental to business success or failure, so that the content of regulation is a matter which receives attention at the highest levels. Similarly, modern telecommunications is heavily shaped by regulation, as are many of its key business transactions such as interconnection with other networks[68] and the quality of service it is required to provide to its customers.[69] By contrast, those elements of cyberspace law where an interpretive community might be found are peripheral to the core business activities involved. It may be that an interpretive community of data protection officers is evolving,[70] but there is no commercial sector for which data protection is a core activity rather than simply a cost of doing business. The danger in such a situation is of disconnect between the core business and those involved in regulatory compliance, so that the regulatory conversation is confined to the silo of its interpretive community rather than involving the enterprise as a whole. Conversations are not taking place with those who control the business, and who are the real addressees of the law. This disconnect seems already to have happened in the field of UK employment regulation, with the consequence that HR departments are held in contempt and are seen as internal barriers to core activity.[71]

Thirdly, and perhaps most important, the conversational regulatory model posits fluidity in rule-sets, allowing them to evolve rapidly as circumstances change. By contrast, laws for cyberspace have attempted to establish the full rule-set at the outset, with no provision for refinement through a regulator. This is clearly the case for the e-Signatures Directive, but is also true for data protection law. The UK Information Commissioner's Office is primarily an enforcement body;[72] it has powers

---

[68] See Ian Walden (ed), *Telecommunications Law and Regulation*, 3rd edn (Oxford: Oxford University Press, 2009), Ch 8.

[69] See Chris Marsden, *Net Neutrality: Towards a Co-regulatory Solution* (London: Bloomsbury Academic, 2010).

[70] In February 2010 the UK National Association of Data Protection Officers decided to consult on establishing an accreditation scheme (<http://www.nadpo.org.uk/article.php?article=MTE=>). No information is available about membership numbers for NADPO, but the IAPP Global Privacy Summit in April 2010 is forecast to attract more than 1,500 delegates (<https://www.privacyassociation.org/>).

[71] See eg Luke Johnson, 'The Truth about the HR Department', *Financial Times*, 30 January 2008; Stefan Stern, 'What is HR Really For', *Management Today*, 29 April 2009; Sathnam Sangara, 'Human Resources Departments: I've Never Understood the Point of Them', *The Times*, 5 October 2009.

[72] The ICO's description of its data protection functions is clear on this:

> Our main functions are **educating and influencing** (we promote good practice and give information and advice), **resolving problems** (we resolve eligible complaints from people who think their rights have been breached) and **enforcing** (we use legal sanctions against those who ignore or refuse to accept their obligations).

<http://www.ico.gov.uk/about_us.aspx.>, emphasis in original.

to produce recommendations and endorse codes of practice[73] but not to change the rules.

Is precision unavoidable?

The work of McBarnett and Whelan in the fields of tax law and accounting standards[74] identifies that there are pressures from regulatees towards precise law-making,[75] which may be hard to resist. These pressures arise from the phenomenon of 'creative compliance', where legal advisers and accountants invent structures and transactions which comply with the precise terms of the rules while at the same time completely avoiding their intended effect.[76] Rules are redrafted to overcome a particular creative compliance strategy, and those rules are then used by advisers to produce new creative compliance schemes. This positive feedback loop drives the rule-set towards ever-increasing detail and precision.

McBarnett and Whelan point out[77] that this process may not be inevitable even for tax laws and accounting rules. There are two reasons why the drive towards precision may be easier to resist, or may even not exist at all, in other fields of primary law.

The first is that tax law shares a common structural feature with regulatory systems. That feature is that the law consists of a rapidly changing body of rules whose evolution is driven, in large part, through conversations within an interpretive community. Creative compliance strategies are devised by a discrete community of tax lawyers and accountants, who communicate regularly with the tax authorities over questions of interpretation of existing rules and the content of new rules. These communications have all the characteristics of Black's regulatory conversations, and indeed the 'discourse of resistance'[78] which produces the pressure towards increased precision arises from the content of those conversations.

---

[73] UK Data Protection Act 1995, s 51.

[74] Doreen McBarnett and Christopher Whelan, 'The Elusive Spirit of the Law: Formalism and the Struggle for Legal Control' (1991) 54 MLR 848. See also Doreen McBarnett, 'Law, Policy and Legal Avoidance: Can Law Effectively Implement Egalitarian Policies?' (1988) 15 Journal of Law & Society 113.

[75] McBarnett and Whelan express these as pressures towards formalism, but it is clear from the context that they are also referring to the concept described as precision in this article. Precision and formalism are of course Siamese twins—there is little point in going to the trouble of expressing rules in precise details if they are not also to be applied in their precise terms. Formalism has been described as 'the view that rules are legally binding because they are rules rather than because of any substantive justification for them. Historically, the term "formalism" has meant more than that, but exactly what it meant is far from clear' (Curtis Bridgeman, 'Why Contracts Scholars Should Read Legal Philosophy: Positivism, Formalism, and the Specification of Rules in Contract Law' (2008) 29 Cardozo L Rev 1443, 1449). An understanding of the subtleties of the term can be gained from F. Schauer, 'Formalism' (1989) 97 Yale LJ 509, who points out that one aim of formalism is to reduce the rule-enforcer's choice by limiting him to the terms of the rule, and E. J. Weinrib, 'Legal Formalism: On the Immanent Reality of Law' (1988) Yale LJ 949, discussing the aim that the law should be understandable on its own terms alone, without reference to external normative sources.

[76] Doreen McBarnett and Christopher Whelan (n 74), 849.

[77] Ibid, 871.

[78] Ibid, 856–60.

The second is that tax laws, and to a lesser extent accounting standards, are more prescriptive than normative. Tax law in particular prescribes what the taxpayer *must* pay as a consequence of his chosen behaviour, rather than how he or she *ought* to behave.[79] To achieve this end, the obligations of the taxpayer have to be spelt out in great detail. Precision in law-making is mandated by the prescriptive nature of the law, and thus calls to increase the accuracy of these already-precise rules are necessarily hard to resist.

By contrast, the rules relating to the crime of murder, or liability in negligence, are far from detailed to begin with. The basic rule in negligence can be summarized quite shortly: a person who owes a duty of care to another must take reasonable care to avoid injuring that other.[80] A full understanding of the rule requires extensive study of cases and explanatory texts, but none of these set out the rule with greater precision. Guidance on how the rule is likely to be applied in particular circumstances can be gained by such reading, but the rule remains as vague and open-textured as before.

Making Meaningful Law

All this tells us that the lawmaker needs to avoid making laws which are over-complex or contradictory, and that precision law-making techniques should be confined to those fields of activity where an interpretive community is likely to develop and thus be able to assist the enforcer of the law to refine its application and meaning. This will help to avoid making rules which are meaningless to cyberspace actors. But it does not explain how to make laws more meaningful, and thus increase the likelihood that their authority will be accepted.

Some assistance may be derived from reminding ourselves why the defects analysed above create the risk that laws will be perceived as meaningless. This happens because the cyberspace actor, from whose perspective we are examining the issue, is unable to understand the normative aims of the law, or unable to accept them because they conflict with other normative aims which have a stronger claim, or perceives himself as being obliged to undertake actions which are unlikely to advance those normative aims.

This suggests that a law whose text makes its normative aims clear, in as simple a manner as is possible, is more likely to be respected than one which attempt to impose a multitude of precisely defined obligations whose connection with the law's aims is obscure. This requires drafting in open-textured terms, using words like 'reasonable', 'fair', or 'necessary'. These concepts are used regularly in laws regulating human behaviour in the physical world, as we have seen in relation to theft

---

[79] Thus the rule in *Furness v Dawson* [1984] AC 474 does not provide that taxpayers should not engage in artificial tax avoidance activity, but instead states that steps in a transaction which have no business purpose apart from the avoidance of tax should be disregarded, which may (or may not) produce the effect that the scheme's purpose is nullified.

[80] *Donoghue v Stevenson* [1932] AC 562.

and negligence. There are few voices calling for these obligations to be explained in greater detail so as to reduce uncertainty.

In fact, as we saw for both data protection and e-signatures, a highly detailed set of obligations can produce as much uncertainty as a simpler, but more open-textured rule. Those who are familiar with data protection law might care to consider whether a greatly simplified regulatory regime, whose main provision would be that collection or use of personal data is only permissible if the data controller reasonably believes that his use does not contravene the data protection principles,[81] would be more or less likely to achieve the normative aims of the law than the current legislation.

---

[81] See Ch 13 for a more detailed explanation of how such a simplified reframing of data protection law might be undertaken.

9

Mismatch with Cyber Reality

Attempting to impose rules which clash with strongly established norms, or making law in such detail that the cyberspace user is not able to understand or comply with it, are not the only ways in which laws can be rendered meaningless. Law needs to regulate the reality which is faced by those who are subject to the law. It is obvious that a motoring law which was clearly designed for the regulation of horse-drawn transport would be perceived by motorists as having little meaning for them. And yet lawmakers commonly attempt to regulate cyberspace activities based on assumptions which only hold true in the physical world.

One reason why this happens is that the lawmaker is an unwitting prisoner of history. Much of the law which regulated the pre-cyberspace physical world developed piecemeal, and focused on the technology of the time by regulating proxies for the activity in question rather than the activity itself. As an example, criminal activity in relation to debt obligations, such as funds in a bank account, was for centuries dealt with under the English law of theft. This was possible because the debt obligation was transferred by means of paper instruments, which are physical property, and thus the wrongdoer could be charged with theft or fraudulent obtaining of the paper instrument.[1] The underlying debt obligation, the transfer of which was the true mischief, could not be stolen because it was not physical property, but this did not matter because the crime was still committed in respect of the paper proxy for the debt. When electronic recordkeeping and communication arrived, however, it became possible to 'steal' funds without taking any piece of paper.[2] As a consequence English law required amendment in 1996 to create a new offence which dealt with the true mischief rather than regulating a proxy for it.[3] We shall see below that the law of copyright regulates a proxy, and that this explains many of the difficulties the law has in coming to terms with cyberspace.

A second reason for the mismatch is that the lawmaker believes it understands how a cyberspace activity works and so, probably unintentionally, embeds that business

---

[1] Or at least until a series of cases on electronic analogues of cheques and bills led the courts to review their understanding of the nature of the property in financial paper documents—see Russell Heaton, 'Cheques and Balances' (2005) Crim LR 747.

[2] *R v Preddy* [1996] 3 All ER 481.

[3] UK Theft (Amendment) Act 1996.

model[4] into the law. Unfortunately this understanding is often erroneous. It seems to be a common belief that the business model used in the physical world translates directly to cyberspace. Most readers will know that to be incorrect. Even if an accurate business model is embedded in the law, it is notorious that cyberspace business models evolve very rapidly, so that in this case it will be only a very few years before the law fails to match the reality.

The Regulation of Proxies

From its inception, copyright was a legal right to control copying.[5] It has since expanded to encompass other acts, such as communication to the public[6] and the bypassing of Digital Rights Management (DRM) and other technical measures aimed at preventing copying,[7] but the control of copying lies at the heart of the law.

If, though, we ask *why* copyright law grants the right to control copying we see a different picture. Copying, per se, is not the point. The purpose of the right is to enable the right-holder to control *use* of a work, usually by preventing that use (by means of copying) if the user has not paid for the right to do so.

The Berne Convention, supplemented by the TRIPS (Trade-related aspects of Intellectual Property Rights) agreement and the WIPO (World Intellectual Property Organization) Copyright Convention, sets out the internationally agreed scheme for copyright. The works protected are set out in a list[8] which includes works in the form of text, pictures, and video.[9] These works are very different things in the physical world, and the methods of copying them in physical form, in whole or in part, also differ between works. Similarly the ways in which they might be used, with or without copying, differ. However, once these works are translated into digital form (or more commonly these days, created from the outset in digital form), these differences disappear. In cyberspace all that there is consists of *information*, and all the ways in which information can be used require it to be copied.

Information is by its nature a *non-rivalrous* good. Its possession, use or enjoyment by one person does not prevent any other person from also possessing, using or enjoying it. This means that if a creator wishes to monetize a work which is in the form of information, or to restrict its use for some other reason, something needs to be done to make the work *excludable*, or in other words to ensure that it cannot be consumed unless the creator agrees. One possibility is to modify the information

---

[4] I use 'business model' here in its widest sense, as meaning 'the way in which something works'. It is by no means intended to be limited to commercial activities.

[5] Mark Rose, 'The Public Sphere and the Emergence of Copyright: Areopagitica, the Stationers' Company, and the Statute of Anne' in Ronan Deazley, Martin Kretschmer, and Lionel Bently (eds), *Privilege and Property: Essays on the History of Copyright* (Cambridge: Open Book, 2010), Ch 3.

[6] WIPO Copyright Treaty 1996, Art 8.

[7] Ibid, Art 11.

[8] See eg UK Copyright, Designs and Patents Act 1998, ss 3–8.

[9] Terminology and the precise boundaries of works differ between jurisdictions. Thus, for example, UK copyright law protects 'films' (ibid, s 5(1)) whereas US law protects 'audio-visual works', of which 'motion pictures' are a subcategory (US Copyright Act 1976, §§ 101, 102(a)(6)).

content of the work, for example by using a DRM technology, in such a way that it cannot be consumed without such agreement, usually granted in return for payment. This can only ever be a temporary solution, though, because advances in computing technology, coupled with the ingenuity of those who believe information should be open, inevitably result in counter-technologies which are able to make the work non-excludable.[10]

The alternative route to excludability is for the law to grant rights to the creator of an information work which enable him to control some or all uses of that work. For most information works the current legal scheme is found in the law of copyright and neighbouring rights (such as performance right). These rights are purely legal constructs, which aim to restrict the fundamental openness of information in order to achieve benefits for creators, and as a consequence for society as a whole. Despite the advocacy of some commentators there is no 'natural' right to control the use of information,[11] and the shape and scope of rights in information works is set out purely as a matter of law and can (in theory at least) be changed by modifying the law.

Intellectual property laws grant information rights which fall into two broad categories. The first is rights to control use of information *created* by the right-holder, and these are primarily, though not exclusively, concerned with economic return. The second is rights to control use of information *about* the right-holder, which can be seen as aimed at protection of the personality.[12] I shall concentrate here on the economic rights category.

These economic rights embody a society's choice about the proper balance between the benefits to society from granting those rights and the costs of diminishing the openness of information. The fundamental shape of the rights is based on a balance which was set long before the arrival of digital information and open communication networks. There is no doubt that the advent of cyberspace has tilted the

---

[10] As examples, DeCSS was developed to remove the copy control mechanism on commercial DVDs, and HYMN (Hear Your Music aNywhere, <http://hymn-project.org/>) successfully circumvented Apple's Fairplay DRM. Legal action against distributors of DeCSS (*Universal City Studios v Reimerdes*, 111 F Supp 2d 294 (SDNY 2000), aff'd, 273 F 3d 429 (2d Cir, 2001)) and a cease and desist letter in the case of HYMN (<http://hymn-project.org/forums/viewtopic.php?t=2496>) had some effect on the availability of the technologies, but in neither case prevented copy-circumvention tools from remaining available.

[11] Arguments that copyright is a natural right are normally based either on John Locke's 'labour-desert' theory of physical property (John Locke, *Two Treatises on Government* (1689)—Second Treatise) or Hegel's conception that an individual who has invested his internal will into an external object thereby invests it with an aspect of his persona (GWF Hegel, *Philosophy of Right* (1821)). Proponents of copyright as a natural right extend these propositions about physical property by analogy, thus creating an argument for why the state should grant rights to creators of works, and also an argument that the form those rights should take is as property rights. This is advocacy, not deduction. Even if society accepts that creators of information works should own some property in them, that property right need not necessarily take the shape of a right to control copying.

[12] Moral rights are the main category of such rights, which operate on the basis that the work itself makes a statement about its author, thus giving the author the right to have the work attributed to him and to object to its derogatory treatment. In addition the laws of trade marks, passing off, and unfair competition also offer protection for some aspects of trade personality. Outside the field of intellectual property there are further rights, such as those under defamation and privacy laws, which protect other aspects of the personality.

balance substantially in favour of right-holders, and numerous scholars have made arguments that rebalancing is needed.[13] This, though, is not my concern here.

Instead I want to explore some of the reasons why the authority of copyright law is so little accepted by cyberspace users. My contention is that those users believe that the obligations imposed on them by copyright are arbitrary, rather than meaningful in terms of the law's aims. I believe that one of the primary causes of this lack of meaning is that the law regulates a proxy, copying, rather than the use of works.

The precise aims behind the existence of copyright are far from clear, obscured as they are by its long and piecemeal evolution.[14] However, it is not an unfair summary of its main aims at the present time to say that copyright grants limited rights to creators so as to allow them to make an economic return, thereby encouraging further creations, and also so as to permit creators to protect those aspects of their personality which are expressed in their creations from impairment through use of the creation by others. The return to society from the grant of these rights is that others can benefit from access to the protected works.

However, copyright law attempts to achieve these aims by granting to creators the right to control *copying*. Even a moment's thought reveals that copying has no direct connection with the law's aims. Instead, copying is a mere proxy for *use* of the creation, which is what the creator needs to control if the law's aims are to be achieved.

When copyright was first devised, and indeed until a mere fifty years or so ago, all copies had to take the form of personal property. Personal property is both rivalrous and excludable, so that controlling the making of and dealings in this personal property also, indirectly, controlled use of the creation. Cyberspace breaks the link between copies of information creations and any personal property on which that information is recorded. As a consequence a third party may copy information without making any use of the creation which is legally significant,[15] or alternatively may use the creation for economic gain without copying it.[16]

This means that in cyberspace, and to a large extent in the physical world as well, the control of copying has ceased be an effective proxy for control of use.[17] Recent developments in copyright law recognize this, and have extended copyright to

---

[13] See eg Pamela Samuelson, 'Intellectual Property and the Digital Economy: Why the Anti-circumvention Regulations Need to Be Revised' (1999) 14 Berkeley Tech L J 519; Jessica Litman, *Digital Copyright* (Amherst: Prometheus Books, 2001); Martin Senftleben, *Copyright, Limitations and the Three-Step Test: An Analysis of the Three-Step Test in International and EC Copyright Law* (The Hague: Kluwer Law International, 2004); Giuseppe Mazziotti, *EU Digital Copyright Law and the End-User* (Berlin: Springer-Verlag, 2008).

[14] For an interesting discussion of the combination of mixed and unstated aims of the Statute of Anne 1710 see Elizabeth F Judge, 'Kidnapped and Counterfeit Characters: Eighteenth-century Fan Fiction, Copyright Law and the Custody of Fictional Characters' in Reginald McGinnis (ed), *Originality and Intellectual Property in the French and English Enlightenment* (Routledge, 2009), 22–68.

[15] *Religious Technology Centre v Netcom On-Line Communications Services Inc*, 907 F Supp 1361 (ND Cal, 1995).

[16] Chris Reed, 'Controlling World-Wide Web Links: Property Rights, Access Rights and Unfair Competition' (1998) 6 Indiana Journal of Global Legal Studies, 167. Note that copying will still take place, though not by the user for gain but rather by the ultimate consumer.

[17] For a more detailed explanation of this issue see Ashley M Pavel, 'Reforming the Reproduction Right: The Case for Personal Use Copies' (2010) 24 Berkeley Technology Law Journal 1615, 1634–6.

encompass acts which do not necessarily require copying. Creators now have the exclusive right to communicate a work to the public[18] and also to prevent the use of technologies which overcome access and copy-protection technologies.[19] These do not solve the problem, though, as they are mere additions to an edifice which is based on what turns out to be a false premise, that what needs to be controlled is copying.

This offers at least a partial explanation for copyright's lack of authority in cyberspace. Users may not be familiar with all the nuances of national copyright laws, but they do understand the basic bargain between creators and society which copyright embodies. Their understanding is that personal, consumptive uses of works fall outside the scope of copyright, with the possible exception of those uses which have the potential to damage the creator's commercial exploitation of a work. This is how the bargain works in the physical world; I need no permission from the right-holder to read a book, look at a painting or photograph, or watch a film or television programme.

None of these is true in the digital world, though. It is not possible for a cyberspace user to make a personal, consumptive use of a work without copying it. Because copyright regulates the proxy of copying, not the use itself, digital technology has extended the right to encompass control of all these uses. Users understand that this was not what the law aimed to achieve and thus, with some justification, consider this purely technological extension of the law to be meaningless to them.

The focus on copying also makes it very difficult, perhaps even impossible, to correct the mismatch between copyright law and cyber-reality. The principle that at least some non-commercial uses of works should be permissible is accepted via the three-step test in Article 10 of the WIPO Copyright Treaty. Article 10 allows signatory states to grant exceptions to copyright provided that these 'do not conflict with a normal exploitation of the work and do not unreasonably prejudice the legitimate interests of the author'.

However, because our current copyright system regulates copying rather than use, courts and legislators have been persuaded to take a restrictive view of when such exceptions should apply. If we start from the proposition that *all* copying requires the permission of the right-holder, irrespective of the kind of use involved, then there can be no objection to the right-holder imposing conditions in return for the grant of such permission. The most common condition is payment. This leads to an understanding that the 'normal exploitation' of a work is by means of charging for making a copy. If this is the starting point, any unlicensed use which requires a copy to be made (as do all uses in digital form) must always be in conflict with normal exploitation.[20]

---

[18] WIPO Copyright Treaty 1996, Art 8.

[19] Ibid, Art 11.

[20] See eg the reasoning of the courts in the Mulholland Drive litigation in France, *Stéphane P, UFC Que Choisir v Société Films Alain Sarde*, TGI de Paris, 3ème ch, 30 April 2004; *Stéphane P, UFC Que Choisir v Universal Pictures Video France*, Cour d'Appel de Paris (4ème Chambre, 22 April 2005); *Société Studio Canal v Perquin et UFC Que Choisir*, Court de Cassation (28 February 2006).

The obvious solution[21] is to restructure copyright law so that it allows creators an appropriate measure of control over the *use* of their works. In other words, copyright should no longer be about copying! But of course there is no prospect of fundamental copyright form in the near future. The current shape of copyright is defined by international instruments, most importantly the Berne Convention, WIPO Copyright Treaty, and TRIPS Agreement. Changing these instruments requires consensus among the majority of national governments, and right-holders have an entrenched position of influence so far as changes are concerned.[22]

In the long term, though, change will need to come. The copyright system already fails to cope adequately with the challenges of digital technologies and cyberspace, and it is hard to see how it can be modified to cope simply by the accretion of new rights. A law based on controlling copying seems to me to be a law which is necessarily unable to evolve in a way which will impose meaningful obligations on cyberspace users. And unless those obligations are meaningful, and thus obeyed voluntarily by the majority of cyberspace actors, copyright will be widely ignored by users of works and cyberspace will continue to be full of law-breakers.

Embedded Business Models

Law-making for cyberspace is not something which can be undertaken purely in the abstract. Lawmakers need to develop an understanding of how cyberspace is actually being used, or how they expect it to be used, in order to identify the behaviours which their laws should attempt to influence. Thus cyberspace laws will always be based on some model of technology use, a *business model*. 'Business' is used here in the wider sense of activity,[23] rather than as a limitation to commercial uses of cyberspace, though of course a great deal of cyberspace regulation is found in the commercial sphere and applies mainly to commercial actors.

Problems arise where the business model is used not merely to identify the activities which should be regulated but is in addition embedded in the law. In effect, such laws attempt to mandate cyberspace users to adopt that business model. But it is well-known that business models in the cyberspace arena change almost as fast as the technology itself changes, and that predictions of the ultimate business model or models which will be adopted for a new cyberspace activity are rarely accurate. Thus regulation which contains an embedded business model is at risk of becoming meaningless to users in a very short space of time. The worst case, of course, is if the business model has from the outset no connection with cyber-reality, in which case

---

[21] Numerous other solutions have of course been proposed, but these either work within the current framework of treating copying as the regulated proxy, or propose the substitution of a different proxy; eg Pavel proposes that communication to the public should be the relevant proxy (Ashley M Pavel (n 17, 1639 ff), and see also Paul Edward Geller, 'Beyond the Copyright Crisis: Principles for Change' (2008) 55 J Copyright Society of the USA 165.

[22] See Jessica Litman (n 13).

[23] See *Shorter Oxford English Dictionary* definition 9: 'That about which one is busy; function, occupation'.

it is unlikely ever to be accepted by cyberspace actors as having meaning for their activities.

Outside the field of cyberspace it is common to find business models embedded in the law. Thus, for example, the UK Partnership Act 1890 section 1(1) provides 'Partnership is the relation which subsists between persons carrying on a business in common', with a view of profit and the remainder of the Act sets out the consequences of establishing such a relationship, as between the partners themselves[24] and in relation to persons dealing with the partnership. The modern shape of UK companies regulation, which was established in the second half of the nineteenth century,[25] is based on an embedded business model under which the company has a discrete legal identity, is owned by its shareholders, and is controlled in its day-to-day operations by its directors.

However, these are both examples of regulation which was devised long after their respective business models became established by use. By the time these laws were enacted the evolution of these business models had stabilized to such an extent that embedding them in the law did not cause major difficulties. It is instructive that the pre-1862 companies legislation, which was largely reactive to the problems which emerged as new uses of the corporate structure and new structures themselves were adopted, was amended constantly without much real success in achieving an effective system for their regulation.[26]

In the cyberspace field, lawmakers are not noted for their patience. It has been commonplace to regulate as soon as the potential implications of a new technology are noticed, and well before the business models under which that technology will be used are established. Such attempts to regulate a future which, it is clear, will contain a substantial degree of change can only be successful if the regulation is able to adapt to the new business models which will inevitably emerge. Unfortunately, much of cyberspace law fails to achieve this necessary flexibility because elements of an inappropriate business model are unconsciously embedded in the regulation.[27]

---

[24] However, s 19 permits the partners to agree on different relations between themselves than those set out in the Act, thus providing a high degree of flexibility and future-proofing.

[25] The UK Companies Act 1862 is generally seen as the starting point for the modern corporation. See BJ Davenport, 'What did *Russell v Northern Bank Development Corporation Ltd* Decide' (1993) LQR 553, 557–8; Michael Lobban, 'Nineteenth Century Frauds in Company Formation: *Derry v Peek* in Context' (1996) LQR 287, 288:

> in the mid-century, the courts ... had seen all those who signed a deed of settlement as partners with liability to creditors. After 1862, they took a different approach, seeing the company more as an abstract entity. On the one hand, shareholders were no longer seen as partners who had pledged their credit to the world at large. With the vague definition of the company member given in the 1862 Companies Act, it was no longer possible simply to see allottees whose names were on the register as partners. On the other hand, directors were increasingly seen as agents of the company (but not of the individual shareholders) ...

[26] See Michael Lobban, ibid, 289–317.

[27] The harmful consequences of intentionally favouring a particular business model have been recognized by Boss, initially in relation to e-signature legislation, where she states that the goals of such laws should be to 'remove the barriers to electronic commerce, treat electronic communications on a par with paper communications, and not to favor one technology over another (technology neutrality) nor one

Replicating physical world business models

Business model problems often arise because laws for the physical world also have models embedded in them. These laws will apply, of course, to conduct in cyberspace which falls within the scope of the law, and thus carry their physical world business model with them.

It is unsurprising, then, to find that the EU data protection regime is increasingly disconnected from cyber-reality because it pre-dates cyberspace and is based on a model of data processing which no longer applies. The 1995 Directive[28] is based on the 1981 Council of Europe Convention for the Protection of Individuals with regard to Automatic Processing of Personal Data,[29] which itself has its origins in the Swedish Data Act of 1973[30] and the German Lande of Hesse's Data Protection Act 1970.[31] At that time, computers were rarely found outside universities, central and local government departments, and large corporations. Although there were signs that the use of computing technology might become more widespread,[32] the business model on which these early laws were based was dictated by the limitations of the

business model over another (implementation neutrality)' (Amelia Boss, 'Searching for Security in the Law of Electronic Commerce', (1999) 23 Nova L Rev 585); see also Amelia Boss, 'The Uniform Electronic Transactions Act in a Global Environment' (2001) 37 Idaho L Rev 275, 292. The concept of implementation neutrality may have originated in the US contributions to the discussions on the UNCITRAL Model Law on Electronic Commerce, which proposed inclusion of the concept in the Model law—'Implementation Neutrality—Any rules should neither require nor hinder the use or development of new or innovative business applications or implementation models': *US Proposal for 'International Convention On Electronic Transactions'*, A/CN.9/WG.IV/WP.77, 25 May 1998, Chapter II—and influenced US policy on e-commerce law development:

> The market is very much in the early stages of experimentation with respect to business models for electronic commerce. The United States believes it is not wise at this time to attempt to identify a single model that these transactions will use or to develop a legal environment using a single model. Indeed, such an approach would prevent the market from testing different possible approaches and prematurely impose a particular model on all electronic commerce, inevitably limiting its growth. Therefore, at the current state of development, the legal framework should support a variety of business models so that the market is able to experiment and select the models that best fit particular types of electronic commerce. [US Government Working Group on Electronic Commerce, *First Annual Report* (November 1998), 14]

See also HR Subcommittee on Cts and Intell Prop, Hearing on HR 1714, Electronic Signatures in Global and National Commerce Act, 106th Cong (30 September 1999), Testimony of Pamela Meade Sargent, Commissioner for the NCCUSL, 5. These discussions of the concept appear to have focused on laws which intentionally favour a particular business model, and thus to have overlooked the possibility of unintentional embedding. It has not been possible to find an express recognition of the need for business-model neutrality, intentional or unintentional, outside the US literature.

[28] Directive 95/46/EC on the protection of individuals with regard to the processing of personal data and on the free movement of such data, OJ L281/31, 23 November 1995.

[29] ETS No 108, Strasbourg, 28 January 1981.

[30] Datalagen, 1973:289.

[31] Hessisches Datenschutzgesetz, Gesetz und Verordungsblatt I (1970), 625.

[32] The first commercial microprocessor, Intel's 4004, was launched in 1971 and the Apple II, the first genuinely mass-market personal computer, came on to the market in 1977. ARPANET, the defence research project which grew into the internet, started in 1969 but did not lose its military research basis until the early 1980s.

current technology.[33] Thus these laws made a number of assumptions about how an organization which processed personal data would operate. The first was that it would have only a limited number of computers, usually only one, which had limited or no connectivity to other computers. The second was that each of its working[34] datasets would be stored in a single physical location, in most cases as a single set of punched cards or magnetic tapes or disks. The final assumption was that direct access to the computer and datasets would only be allowed to a small core of technical staff.

This business model explains why the 1981 Council of Europe Convention concentrates its provisions primarily on the 'automated data file' and the 'controller of the file'.[35] Article 3, which sets out the scope of the Convention, contains seven references to files and only one reference to the processing of personal data. The data security obligations of Article 7 apply only to the file, and the subject access provisions of Article 8(a) and (b) similarly apply only to files. It is clear that the drafters of the Convention had the business model set out above very much in mind, and to some extent embedded that model implicitly in the Convention.

By 1995, when the Data Protection Directive was enacted, it was clear that the processing of personal data was being undertaken very differently from the 1970s model. Many businesses were operating networks of personal computers, allowing staff to store data locally as well as to access central data files, and a rapidly increasing proportion of the population had access to a personal computer at home.[36] This was also the year when the internet is thought to have entered the consciousness of the general public,[37] but although this development must have been known to the European Commission it was too late for the directive to be amended to take account of the new possibilities for processing personal data online.

The legislative history of the directive shows a recognition that the underlying business model for personal data processing was changing. The original 1990 proposal followed the Council of Europe Convention by drafting in terms of the file,[38] but the importance of this concept was reduced in the Commission's modified

---

[33] As an example, I studied computer programming at the University of Keele in 1975, working on an Elliott 803 computer—see <http://bil.members.beeb.net/elliott.html>. This was the Department of Computer Science's primary machine. It had only 8Kb of RAM and no possibility of network connectivity, as the sole I/O mechanisms were punched card/tape or magnetic tape. Only trained technicians were permitted to operate it directly. My thanks are due to Colin Reeves, former Head of Department at the University of Keele, for correcting my memories of this system.

[34] Backup datasets would most likely be held in a different location, but could only be accessed by physically bringing them to a suitable computer.

[35] Both defined in Art 2.

[36] US home computer access rose from 8% in 1984 to 24% in 1994—National Science Foundation, *The Application and Implications of Information Technologies in the Home: Where Are the Data and What Do They Say?* (February 2001), 11, citing US Bureau of the Census data.

[37] Probably based on the founding of the World Wide Web Consortium in September 1994. General public use of the internet was made possible by the 30 April 1993 announcement by CERN that it was placing the basic World Wide Web technology into the public domain and the launch of the Mosaic graphical browser by the National Center for Supercomputing Applications in the same year.

[38] Proposal for a Council directive concerning the protection of individuals in relation to the processing of personal data, COM (90) 314 final, Art 1(1): 'The Member States shall ensure, in accordance with

proposal of 1992[39] and eliminated in the final text.[40] In spite of these amendments, however, three elements of the 1970s business model remain embedded in the directive.

First, the law retains the concept that an organization, rather than its individual staff, determines whether personal data will be collected and for what purposes. This is seen most clearly in the notification provisions of Articles 18 and 19, which require a controller to notify the relevant national authority of a number of matters, including types of data to be collected and the purposes for which they will be processed, and not to commence processing prior to such notification. In the modern, distributed processing model the collection of data can be initiated by individual staff. It is rarely feasible for an organization to prevent individual decisions to collect and process data being made, nor is it easy to establish systems which ensure that they are reported centrally so that notification can be made. In practice this problem is largely overcome by notifying very wide and general categories of data and processing, but even so it is almost certain that every large organization is in breach of these obligations because of the activities of some of its staff.

The concept of controller itself is also an echo of the 1970s, containing an implicit assumption that there is central control of personal data processing and that the organization's staff merely undertake that processing in accordance with central instructions. Under Article 2(d) the controller is defined as 'the natural or legal person, public authority, agency or any other body which alone or jointly with others determines the purposes and means of the processing of personal data'. If this were applied strictly to, say, a modern university, it is clear that almost every member of academic staff, and a large proportion of non-academic staff, would be controllers because they act autonomously in determining the purposes and means of processing personal data.[41] This would mean that each of these staff would have obligations to register, notify, provide information to data subjects, receive and act on subject access requests, and so on.

The third element is the assumption that data can only be accessed via possession of a physical copy of the dataset. This is implicit in Article 25, which provides:

the transfer[42] to a third country of personal data which are undergoing processing or are intended for processing after transfer may take place only if . . . the third country in question ensures an adequate level of protection.

---

this Directive, the protection of the privacy of individuals in relation to the processing of personal data contained in data files.' The concept of 'data file' is used throughout this draft.

[39] The concept of 'personal data file' was retained primarily in relation to manual processing—COM (1992) 0422, 15 October 1992, Explanatory Memorandum, 2.

[40] Except for manual data, to which the directive applies only if that data forms part of a 'filing system'—Arts 2(c), 3(1).

[41] The university itself may also be a controller of that personal data, on the basis that it acts through its staff and thus their decisions are also its own decisions.

[42] Although the term 'transfer' is used 29 times in the recitals and articles of the directive, it is never defined.

It is clear that if a physical copy of a dataset[43] containing personal data is given to a person in a third country, a transfer will have taken place. However, it was only in 2003 in the case of *Lindqvist*[44] that the European Court of Justice (ECJ, now CJEU) determined whether permitting remote access from a third country to personal data held on a server in the controller's country would infringe Article 25. The court decided that including personal data in a web page amounted to 'processing', but that its availability worldwide via the internet was not a transfer of that data to persons accessing the website. Unfortunately the court did not give reasons for this decision, which nonetheless appears to confirm that Article 25 is not applicable to remote access to data. It seems that the 1970s business model is so firmly embedded in this part of the directive that the courts are unable to adapt it to cyberspace usage.

Business models are embedded in much of the rest of the world's cyberspace regulation, perhaps to an even greater extent than that of the EU.[45] This is seen particularly clearly in the field of e-signatures, where early legislation was usually inspired by the ANSI X.509 business model and thus embedded many features of that model.[46] In this case, though, the business model was not a legacy from the physical world and so e-signatures are discussed in a later section.

One of the most troublesome business models, which seems to hold a strong fascination for lawmakers, is that of the offline publishing industry. Under the offline model those who make information available to the public, namely publishers, undertake a process of selecting the material which they will make available and exercise editorial control over its contents to ensure, amongst other things, that the published information complies with national controls on content such as defamation and indecency laws. Regulators have consistently failed to resist the temptation to attempt to apply this model to online intermediaries such as ISPs, based on the only similarity with publishers that each makes information accessible. Perhaps the most interesting examples of this phenomenon are the US Communications Decency Act 1996[47] and the Australian Broadcasting Services Amendment (Online Services) Act 1999.

The intention of the Communications Decency Act was to introduce new criminal offences of knowingly creating, sending, transmitting, or displaying obscene or

---

[43] Or a part of a dataset—see recital 58.

[44] Case C-101/01, 6 November 2003, OJ C7/3, 10 January 2004.

[45] Whatever its other flaws, the EU's technocratic legislative process, which often bases first drafts of directives on theoretical research and allows a period of years for consultation and amendment, tends to eliminate the most egregious flaws in legislative proposals unless they are the subject of political disagreement and subsequent compromise.

[46] In the late 1990s the majority of US States adopted or proposed e-signature laws, many of which were X.509-based. The danger of embedding this particular business model, particularly in relation to liability, was recognized in a number of articles—see eg Brad Biddle, 'Legislating Market Winners: Digital Signature Laws and the Electronic Commerce Marketplace' (1997) 34 San Diego L Rev 1225, 1226; Thomas Smedinghoff and Ruth Hill Bro, 'Moving with Change: Electronic Signature Legislation as a Vehicle for Advancing E-Commerce' (1999) 17 J Marshall J Computer & Info L 723, 752. This legislation is now pre-empted by the US Federal Electronic Signatures in Global and National Commerce Act 2000 (usually known as 'E-Sign') which is not based on the X.509 model.

[47] 47 USC § 230.

indecent materials to minors, or knowingly permitting the use of telecommunications systems for these purposes. As a counterbalancing element, the legislation provided protection for 'Good Samaritan' activities on the part of ISPs. The aim was to over-rule *Stratton Oakmont Inc v Prodigy Services Co*[48] and thus permit ISPs to introduce blocking or filtering technology without assuming the role of editor or publisher, which would otherwise make them responsible for the third party content.[49] However, the new criminal offences were struck down in *ACLU v Reno*[50] as infringing the First Amendment protection for freedom of speech, leaving the immunity provisions of section 230(c) to stand alone. The relevant part is subsection (1) which states: 'No provider or user of an interactive computer service shall be treated as the publisher or speaker of any information provided by another information content provider.' The effect of this, discussed further below,[51] is to give a broad immunity from civil liability to ISPs and other intermediaries.

Australia's attempt to apply the publishing business model to ISPs took a different approach, by trying to impose the same censorship regime as for films. The Broadcasting Services Amendment (Online Services) Act 1999 inserted a new Schedule 5 into the Broadcasting Services Act 1992, section 10 of which defines 'prohibited content'[52] which ISPs must not host. Content which has not yet been classified, including content hosted outside Australia, is 'potential prohibited content'.[53] On request from any person this must be classified by the Australian

---

[48] 23 Media L Rep 1794 (NY Sup Ct, 25 May 1995).

[49] The Senate conference report on § 230 states:

> This section provides 'Good Samaritan' protections from civil liability for providers or users of an interactive computer service for actions to restrict or to enable restriction of access to objectionable online material. One of the specific purposes of this section is to overrule *Stratton Oakmont v Prodigy* and any other similar decisions which have treated such provid-ers and users as publishers or speakers of content that is not their own because they have restricted access to objectionable material. The conferees believe that such decisions create serious obstacles to the important federal policy of empowering parents to determine the content of communications their children receive through interactive computer services. [S Conf Rep No 104-230, at 435 (1996)]

[50] 929 F Supp 824, 830–838 (ED Pa, 1996), affirmed 117 S Ct 2329 (1997).

[51] See *Consequences of embedding* p 170.

[52] 'Internet content' is defined in the Australian Broadcasting Services Act 1992, Sch 5, s 3 as information that:

> (a) is kept on a data storage device; and
> (b) is accessed, or available for access, using an Internet carriage service;

> but does not include:

> (c) ordinary electronic mail; or
> (d) information that is transmitted in the form of a broadcasting service.

This is prohibited content under s 10 if it has been classified by the Australian Broadcasting Authority (ABA) as X or RC (refused classification), in essence films which depict sexual content in a way which is unsuitable for minors, or has been classified with an R classification (otherwise unsuitable for minors), if the material is made available other than by a 'restricted access scheme', essentially a control method which restricts children from obtaining access such as filtering software.

[53] Ibid, Sch 5, s 11.

Broadcasting Authority (the ABA), using the same tests as for films and video games.[54] If a complaint is made that potentially prohibited content is being hosted in Australia or is accessible via an Australian ISP, and it is classified as prohibited content by the ABA, then the ABA can issue a take-down notice to the ISP[55] or, in the case of content hosted outside Australia, give notice requiring the ISP to prevent access to that content.[56] Failure to comply with such a notice by the end of the next business day is a criminal offence. Fortunately for Australian ISPs, as we saw in Chapter 8, the law offered them an alternative method of compliance which did not require them to operate this censorship regime.

Both these laws were enacted on the assumption that, like offline publishers and film distributors, an ISP is capable of examining the content it makes available, accessing its compliance with legal standards, and making the editorial decision whether to make that content available. At the time this was simply untrue. It is, of course, purely speculative to suggest what the result would have been had these laws been applied as the lawmaker intended. For what it is worth, my view is that the mismatch with cyber-reality would have been so great that the laws would have achieved little respect from cyberspace actors. To the extent that the laws were complied with at all, that compliance would have been as 'creative' as possible, paying only lip-service to the law's normative aims.

Even so, the interest of lawmakers in imposing this business model on cyberspace has not dissipated. The Australian government still seems determined to apply its censorship model,[57] although quite how this is to be achieved is uncertain. The ISP business model has also evolved somewhat—technological advances now enable intermediaries to peer into content, rather than dealing with information purely in terms of its addressing data, and the commercial pressures towards providing varying levels of transmission service quality are requiring them to do so.[58] Some court decisions have imposed further pressures by attempting to evolve ISP immunity into a less absolute and more nuanced form.[59] Even so, the kinds of inspection of content and decision-making which might be possible in the near future are still ill-matched to the offline publishing business model.

---

[54] Ibid, Sch 5, s 13.

[55] Ibid, Sch 5, ss 30–9, 82–3.

[56] Ibid, Sch 5, ss 40–51, 82–3.

[57] See the December 2007 announcement by the Telecommunications Minister Stephen Conroy (<http://www.abc.net.au/news/stories/2007/12/31/2129471.htm>), and the October 2008 report that the government had modified its plans and would now introduce mandatory filtering of certain categories of content (<http://www.heraldsun.com.au/news/mandatory-censorship-on-web/story-0-1111117883306>).

[58] Chris Marsden, *Net Neutrality: Towards a Co-regulatory Solution* (London: Bloomsbury Academic, 2010), Ch 4.

[59] See, *inter alia*, *Barnes v Yahoo*, 565 F 3d 560 (9th Cir, 2009); *Hermès International v Feitz* (Case RG 06/02604, Tribunale de Grande Instance Troyes, 4 June 2008); *SABAM v Scarlet SA* (Brussels Court of First Instance, 29 June 2007, 24 October 2008, Case C-70/10, 24 November 2011 (CJEU)); *Internet Auction I* (German Bundesgerichtshof, Case I ZR 304/01, [2005] ETMR 25).

Guessing wrong

Where an activity is new, so far as the law is concerned, then a lawmaker who is not content to wait until the business models have become established will need to make an educated guess about how the activity will be undertaken. If that guess is embedded in the law and turns out to be wrong, it is inevitable that the law will prove to be something of a failure.

When the EU Databases Directive was proposed in 1992,[60] database technology was comparatively well advanced and, in particular, the commercial methods of exploiting databases had largely ceased to evolve. Databases were then, and still are, exploited in one of two ways: by providing online access on a subscription basis (usually via dial-up in 1996 rather than online, as today), or by supplying a copy of the database to be installed on the user's computing equipment in return for a licence fee (although this is an increasingly rare method of exploitation). Although these aspects of the business model were stable, however, the directive unintentionally embedded in its drafting a further element: an assumption that the business of database makers would be to seek out and make available third party data, rather than exploiting their own data.

Under Article 7(1) the directive grants a *sui generis* right to prevent unauthorized extraction and/or reutilization to:

the maker of a database which shows that there has been qualitatively and/or quantitatively a substantial investment in either the obtaining, verification or presentation of the contents . . .

Until 2004, the general consensus was that these words covered databases both of content originating from third parties, and content originating from the maker of the database.[61] Organizations which generate data, such as stock exchanges and market research companies, spend large amounts of money and effort in collecting, checking, and storing their data, and there seemed no doubt that this would amount to a 'substantial investment' for the purposes of Article 7(1).

---

[60] Proposal for a Council directive on the legal protection of databases, COM (92) 24 final, OJ C 156/4, 23 June 1992.

[61] This was clearly the original aim of the legislator. The explanatory memorandum to the 1992 proposal, COM (92) 24 final, 25, paras 3.2.7 and 3.2.8 makes it clear that the directive was intended to protect *all* databases against parasitic competition. Specific provisions were included to require the maker of a database who was also the only source of that data to grant compulsory licences (Art 8(1)–(3)) thus confirming that those 'single source' databases were to be covered by the *sui generis* sight. The later deletion of these compulsory licensing provisions, coupled with the insertion of the 'investment' requirement as a way of distinguishing valuable from trivial databases, produced the unintended business model embedding identified here. Certainly the European Commission held this view of the directive's intended scope throughout: 'databases which qualified for copyright protection under the "sweat of the brow" regime would no longer be protected. In exchange, and in order to compensate for the loss of the "sweat of the brow" protection, the "*sui generis*" form of protection for "non-original" databases was introduced as an entirely novel form of intellectual property' (DG Internal Market and Services Working Paper, 'First Evaluation of Directive 96/9/EC on the Legal Protection of Databases', Brussels, 12 December 2005, 8).

In that year, however, the ECJ decided the case of *British Horseracing Board Ltd and ors v William Hill Organization Ltd*.[62] The claimant (British Horseracing Board, or BHB) maintained a large database of information relating to horse racing, and the defendant had copied parts of it indirectly from sources published under licence from BHB, for use in the defendant's betting business. Initially in the UK the case proceeded on the assumption that the BHB database was protected by the *sui generis* right,[63] and concentrated on whether William Hill's use infringed that right. Various questions about the proper interpretation of the directive were referred to the ECJ,[64] including two which asked for a ruling on the proper interpretation of 'obtaining' and 'verification' in Article 7(1). In its judgment, the ECJ concentrated on these two questions. It made a distinction between *creating* and *obtaining* data, and held that any investment in the creation of data should not be taken into account in deciding whether the investment in making a database was substantial. When the UK Court of Appeal applied this ruling to the facts,[65] the outcome was that the investment in the BHB database was almost all in its creation, and that therefore the database received no protection via the *sui generis* right.[66]

The effect of this decision is that most databases which consist of data generated by their maker will fall entirely outside the directive's *sui generis* protection. The implicit and clearly unintended[67] effect of the drafting, that the database industry's role was to collect and make available third party data rather than to generate such data itself, was found by the ECJ to be reflected in the language of Article 7(1) and the recitals and thus to limit the scope of the *sui generis* right.

The effect of this embedded business model has not rendered the directive completely meaningless for cyberspace users, but it has clearly reduced its meaning substantially for any database maker which generates its own data. Further questions about the protection of these databases are still to be resolved,[68] and both makers and users of databases are likely to rely far more on contracts to govern their rights and obligations than on the law established by the directive.

---

[62] Case C-203/02, 9 November 2004. See also *Fixtures Marketing Ltd v Oy Veikkaus Ab*, Case C-46/02, 9 November 2004; *Fixtures Marketing Ltd v Svenska Spel Ab*, Case C-338/02, 9 November 2004; *Fixtures Marketing Ltd v Organismos prognostikon agonon podosfairou AE (OPAP)*, Case C-444/02, 9 November 2004.

[63] [2001] EWHC 516 (Pat) para 21.

[64] Set out at Case C-203/02, 9 November 2004, para 22.

[65] [2005] EWCA Civ 863 (CA).

[66] For a more detailed discussion of this judgment see Chris Reed, 'Database Protection' in Chris Reed and John Angel (eds), *Computer Law*, 7th edn (Oxford: Oxford University Press, 2011), Ch 8.

[67] DG Internal Market and Services Working Paper, 'First Evaluation of Directive 96/9/EC on the Legal Protection of Databases', Brussels, 12 December 2005, 13, states that the effect of the decisions in *British Horseracing Board Ltd v William Hill* and the *Fixtures Marketing* cases (Cases C-46/02, C-338/02 and C-444/02, all of 9 November 2004): '[goes] against the Commission's original intention of protecting "non-original" databases in a wide sense'.

[68] eg some elements of databases which fail to benefit from the *sui generis* right might still be protected by copyright—this question has been referred by the English courts to the ECJ in *Football Dataco Ltd v Yahoo* [2010] EWCA Civ 1380.

Even the most carefully drafted laws can run into business-model problems. For example, the e-Signatures Directive[69] took particular care to avoid embedding any one of the various e-signature business models which were then under development. However, its aim of legislating for a type of e-signature which would be accepted in all Member States and beyond required it to include provisions relating to the liability of the entity (the certification-service-provider) which certifies the signatory's identity and other attributes.[70] By issuing such a certificate, the certification-service-provider is subject to negligence-based liability to any person who relies on the accuracy of the certificate's contents,[71] or that the person named in the certificate controlled the technology used to create the signature,[72] or that the certification-service-provider's register of revoked certificates is accurate.[73]

These liability provisions contain an implicit assumption that these matters are under the certification-service-provider's control, ie that it performs identity and attribute checks before issuing the certificate, verifies that the signatory controls the technology, and operates the register of revoked certificates. These liability provisions derive from the ANSI X.509 standard,[74] which assumed an open rather than a closed PKI model,[75] and thus that the applicant for a certificate would provide proof of identity direct to a certification authority (a certification-service-provider in the directive's terms). This assumption was based on an operational business model described in RFC 2527[76] under which a signatory would purchase a single signature certificate from an independent certification authority and would use that certificate to validate all his e-signatures.

As e-signature schemes have been developed in recent years it has become clear that this model is not commercially viable. What happens in practice is that third parties, such as corporations or trade associations, identify a need for their employees or members to use electronic signature technology. In that case the third party enters into an agreement with a certification authority under which the third party will act as a registration authority. The registration authority, which already has a relationship with potential signatories, then identifies individuals and their attributes and provides the necessary identification information to the certification authority, using technology provided by the certification authority. The signature

---

[69] Directive 1999/93/EC on a Community framework for electronic signatures OJ L13/12, 19 January 2000.

[70] Ibid, Art 6. These attributes might include the signatory's employment or professional status, the extent of his authority to bind his employer, etc.

[71] Ibid, Art 6(1)(a).

[72] Ibid, Art 6(1)(b) and (c).

[73] Ibid, Art 6(2).

[74] See R Housley, W Ford, W Polk, and D Solo, Internet X.509 Public Key Infrastructure: Certificate and CRL Profile, RFC 2459, January 1999, <http://www.ietf.org/rfc.html>.

[75] An open PKI (public key infrastructure) is where the signatory obtains a certificate from a certification authority and uses that single certificate for all his communications. In a closed PKI, all signatories are members of the same organization, company or group, and certificates are issued only for the purpose of signing communications within the group.

[76] S Chokhani and W Ford, Internet X.509 Public Key Infrastructure Certificate Policy and Certification Practices Framework RFC 2527, March 1999, <http://www.ietf.org/rfc.html>.

certificate issued by the certification authority thus certifies that the signatory has identified himself to the registration authority, and not directly to the certification authority.

This modern business model does not map accurately to the liability provisions of X.509-based legislation such as the directive. As explained above, those laws place liability for inaccurate information in the certificate on the certification authority, whereas the body which has failed to take proper identification evidence is the registration authority. The consequences of this mismatch will be explored later.[77]

The e-Signatures Directive also provides in Article 6(3) and (4) that a certification service-provider may establish use limitations and transaction limits[78] in the certificate. However, it does not explain the legal basis on which such limitations will be binding on the relying party, or even provide that they will be binding at all. This is also based on RFC 2527, whose description of the liability of Certification Authorities to relying parties assumes that limitations contained in a published certificate policy[79] will be binding, either in contract or tort.[80] It is far from certain that this is a correct statement of the law, because it assumes that relying parties will receive from their software, or will seek out, information about these matters before relying on a certificate. Given that the appropriateness of the scheme of liability allocation in the directive is based on the enforceability of these limitations, it is surprising that national implementing legislation[81] does not deal at all with the issue of use limitations and reliance limits, apparently sharing RFC 2527's assumption that these will be binding in contract or tort.

The scheme of advanced electronic signatures has found little favour with cyberspace users, for reasons explained in the preceding chapters, and so these defects in the liability regime have received little attention. If, though, there had been an appreciable demand for such e-signatures it is conceivable that these problems might have reduced the meaning of the EU's laws to such an extent that cyberspace users sought alternatives. There is, for example, no barrier to EU-based users obtaining

---

[77] See *Consequences of embedding*, p 170.

[78] Thus eg the certificate might be usable only to sign purchase orders for the signatory's employer (a use limitation) up to a maximum value of X (the transaction limit).

[79] The normal practice would be for the signature certificate to contain a link to the certificate policy, thus enabling the relying party to investigate the limitations and, possibly, enabling his signature-checking technology to discover and flag these limitations.

[80] RFC 2527 is an operational description, not a legal analysis, and thus these points are presumed but not explained. The contractual analysis would be that the relying party has received notice of the limitations, via the link in the certificate to the certificate policy, and that the issue of the certificate is a unilateral offer by the certification authority to be liable to relying parties on the terms of the certificate policy. That offer is accepted by the act of reliance, forming a contract between the certification authority and the relying party. Given the high degree of automation in e-signature validation, it is by no means clear that a court would accept this analysis. The tortious analysis would be that the certification authority is liable to relying parties for fraud or negligent misrepresentation (see American Bar Association, *Digital Signature Guidelines* (Chicago: ABA, 1996), 22), and in either case will only be liable to the extent that it was reasonable to rely on the certificate in those circumstances. Reliance outside the terms of the certificate policy, assuming the relying party has sufficient notice of it, would be unreasonable under English and most US State laws.

[81] See eg for the UK, Electronic Signatures Regulations 2002, SI 2002/318.

their signature certificates from a Singapore certification authority and using them in purely European transactions.[82]

Rigging the market

On occasion lawmakers take a deliberate decision to embed a business model in the law, in an attempt to ensure that the regulated activity develops in a particular way. I have explained in Chapter 8 the touching faith of lawmakers in the ability of law to influence the development of markets, rather than vice versa, and it is clear that if the market fails to follow the law's lead then a mismatch will result.

In the case of the e-Money Directive 2000,[83] there are two elements of embedded business model, one accidental, based on the anticipated way in which the technology would be used, and the other deliberate. The first element is the assumption that e-money would be used in a similar way to cash, and would therefore consist of an electronic equivalent of notes and coins which would be held in the possession of the customer, rather than merely recorded as accounting data as is the case for value held in bank accounts.[84] Thus recital 3 of the directive states, 'electronic money can be considered an electronic surrogate for coins and banknotes, which is stored on an electronic device such as a chip card or computer memory and which is generally intended for the purpose of effecting electronic payments of limited amounts',[85] and the definition of electronic money in Article 1(3)(b) is:

monetary value as represented by a claim on the issuer which is:
  (i)   stored on an electronic device;
  (ii) issued on receipt of funds of an amount not less in value than the monetary value issued;
  (iii) accepted as means of payment by undertakings other than the issuer.

---

[82] The Singaporean regulatory regime is recognized under the mutual recognition scheme of Art 7 of the directive, with the result that Singapore-issued certificates are legally equivalent to those issued by a European provider.

[83] Directive 2000/46/EC of the European Parliament and of the Council on the taking up, pursuit of and prudential supervision of the business of electronic money institutions, OJ L 275/39, 27 October 2000 ('e-Money Directive 2000').

[84] The origins of the technological concept lie in the late 1980s—see eg David Chaum, Amos Fiat, and Moni Naor, 'Untraceable Electronic Cash' in Shafi Goldwasser (ed), *Advances in Cryptology: Proceedings of CRYPTO '88* (Berlin: Springer-Verlag, 1990), 319–27—and the first operational system, Mondex, was invented by Tim Jones and Graham Higgins in 1990 with in-house trials at NatWest in 1992 (see <http://www.mondex.org/mondexuk.html>).

[85] Certainly, at the time the directive was proposed the main available technologies all envisaged that such a device would be in the possession of the user. This interpretation is supported by the original drafting of Art 1(3)(b) in the 1996 proposal, which defined e-money as being '(i) stored electronically on an electronic device such as a chip card or a computer memory' and '(iii) generated in order to be put at the disposal of users to serve as an electronic surrogate for coins and banknotes' (Proposal for a European Parliament and Council directive on the taking up, the pursuit and the prudential supervision of the business of electronic money institutions, COM (1998) 0461 final, OJ C317, 15 October 1998).

The rapid spread of internet access to consumers has meant that much simpler e-payment technologies have become workable—for example, the world's largest non-bank[86] online payment service, PayPal, holds funds on its internal accounting system and effects payments by simple book transfers. Only in the last few years have stored-value e-money systems, the primary technology envisaged by the directive, begun to achieve commercial significance.[87] We saw in previous chapters how this mismatch between the business model assumed by the directive and the accounted models actually adopted led to a conflict between the UK FSA and mobile telephony companies. The fact that those companies simply refused to comply with the law shows clearly that they saw it as meaningless for them, and was one of the factors which led to the repeal and replacement of the directive.

The deliberately embedded element was that issuers of e-money should be regulated as financial institutions, adopting the regulatory mechanisms which had been devised to ensure that custodians of financial assets would not put the value of those assets unreasonably at risk. Without considering whether this was the most appropriate way of regulating a pure payment technology with almost no custodian-ship element and which, at the time, had not been put into commercial operation to any appreciable extent,[88] the Commission proposed a text under which e-money would be authorized and supervised by a national financial supervisor,[89] meet minimum capital and liquidity requirements,[90] limit investment of the float to specified low-risk vehicles,[91] and engage only in 'the provision of closely related financial and non-financial services'.[92]

The justification for these restrictions was to some extent so as to protect consumer holders of e-money, but the main reason for imposing them was to 'preserve a level playing field between electronic money institutions and other credit institutions issuing electronic money'[93] by limiting the ability of e-money issuers to compete with established financial institutions. For these policy reasons, therefore, the directive embedded a business model under which e-money issuers were required to be regulated institutions, engaging solely[94] in the business of issuing and

---

[86] PayPal became a Luxembourg bank in 2007, but its funds transfers are not made via the established interbank networks and technologies.

[87] A small number of increasingly active stored-value e-money businesses is now visible. Hong Kong's Octopus Card has more holders than the population of Kong Kong, and its success has inspired Transport for London to begin a project to introduce e-money functionality to the Oyster Card. The Proton stored-value card is widely used in Belgium, and the Chipknip card appears to be taking off in the Netherlands.

[88] 'At the present juncture, electronic money is not a widespread phenomenon' (Opinion of the EMI Council on the issuance of electronic money, 2 March 1998 para 1). See also ECB, *Report on Electronic Money* (August 1998), 9–10.

[89] Authorization was required by e-Money Directive 2000, Art 1(4) and the supervision provisions contained in Arts 4–6.

[90] Ibid, Art 4.

[91] Ibid, Art 5.

[92] Ibid, Art 1(5).

[93] Ibid, recital 12.

[94] With the exception of related minor technical activities which could not be a significant source of income—ibid, Art 1(5).

redeeming e-money. The mismatch with cyber-reality which resulted made the law so meaningless that the successor legislation abandons the model almost entirely.[95]

Consequences of embedding

The most serious consequence of embedding the wrong business model in cyberspace law is its effect on the behaviour of those who are subject to the law. Cyberspace actors adopt behaviours which they believe will enable them to comply with cyberspace regulation, but these have often been very different from what the lawmaker originally intended. Much of that behaviour has no meaning, in terms of achieving the law's aims, and it is thus unsurprising that cyberspace actors (if they comply with the law at all) do so only as a formal exercise.

We identified above three embedded business model elements in the Data Protection Directive: that an organization rather than its staff as individuals would determine the processing of personal data; that individuals would not exercise sufficient autonomous control over these matters to be data controllers themselves; and that access to and use of personal data required possession of a physical copy of the dataset. The consequences of the mismatch between this model and reality, where possession and control of data is widely distributed and online access is, for most purposes, indistinguishable from use of a local copy of a dataset, has three main consequences.

First, the requirement to notify to a controller's national authority the types of personal data which will be held and the purposes for which they will be processed has become almost meaningless. Organizations no longer have detailed knowledge of the personal data processing undertaken by their staff, and in some cases even their 'big picture' understanding of that processing may be inaccurate. In order to permit theoretical compliance with the directive, notification is made using broad, uninformative categorizations of data types and processing purposes,[96] which fail to achieve the directive's aim that data subjects should easily be able to discover what kinds of data an organization might hold about them and how the organization intends to use that data.[97] Notification has become a purely internal compliance function, undertaken for its own sake rather than for any useful end.

The second consequence is that compliance with the letter of the directive is in many respects impossible in practice for any but the smallest organization. For example, Article 11 requires a controller who obtains personal data from a source

---

[95] Directive 2009/110/EC of the European Parliament and of the Council of 16 September 2009 on the taking up, pursuit and prudential supervision of the business of electronic money institutions amending Directives 2005/60/EC and 2006/48/EC and repealing Directive 2000/46/EC, OJ L267/7, 10 October 2009.

[96] See eg the UK Information Commissioner's *Notification Handbook*, 12–14, <http://www.ico.gov.uk/upload/documents/library/data_protection/forms/notification_handbook_-_complete_guide.pdf>.

[97] Compare eg the Barclays Bank UK notification (<http://www.esd.informationcommissioner.gov.uk/esd/search.asp>) with the bank's privacy policy for personal customers (<http://www.barclays.com/privacy/per_info.html>). The former is a multi-page document containing uninformative terms of art; the latter is a single page which explains in clear language what the bank will do with the customer's data.

other than the subject to inform the subject of various matters at the time of recording the data or disclosing it to a third party. In, say, a university it is highly likely that some academics will have produced their own databases of information about their students' academic progress. Whether those students are informed about this will depend entirely on that academic's knowledge of data protection law. It is not feasible to devise central systems or processes to ensure that the university as a whole complies with Article 11. All large organizations experience similar compliance problems. As a second example a subject access request under Article 12 will be met by disclosure of the relevant records from an organization's central computer systems, but it is unlikely that the organization will be able to identify whether individual members of staff hold further information on their own computers or, even if this is discoverable, to devise an effective system for disclosing that information. It is fortunate that in practice most data subjects are satisfied with disclosure of central records only.

This situation is not unworkable because organizations and their staff normally comply with the spirit of the law, to the extent that they are aware of it. However, a system of regulation with which full compliance is impossible clearly has the potential to produce undesirable normative effects.[98]

Thirdly, the concept of protecting data subjects against the transfer of their personal information to 'data havens', based on controlling the possession of datasets, has become meaningless in the online age. *Lindqvist*,[99] if it is correctly decided and not reversed by future legislation, means that the complex legal structures which have been developed to make offshore outsourcing possible[100] will no longer be required if the dataset can be stored within the EU and simply accessed remotely by the outsourcing service provider. The apparent aim of Article 25, that personal data held in the EU should not be processed in another country which does not provide an adequate level of protection for that data, has been defeated by a change in business model.

The Databases Directive embeds a simple business model concept, that databases are made by intermediaries who collect third party data and make it available rather than by those who collect or generate data themselves directly. The effect of Article 7(1), as explained in *British Horseracing Board Ltd and ors v William Hill Organization Ltd*,[101] is to prevent most databases whose content was generated by their maker from benefiting from the *sui generis* right. This is exactly the opposite of the original intention of the legislator.[102]

---

[98] There is even, in the longer term, the danger that those subject to the regulation will cease to recognize it as having any normative force—see Fuller, *The Morality of Law*, rev. edn (New Haven: Yale University Press, 1964) Chapter II.

[99] Case C-101/01 6 November 2003, OJ C7 10 January 2004, 3, discussed at p 161.

[100] See eg Roger K Baker, 'Offshore Cyberspace Outsourcing and the 8th Data Protection Principle—legal and regulatory requirements with reference to financial services' (2006) 14 Int J L & Info Tech, 1.

[101] [2001] EWHC 516 (Pat) (High Court); [2001] EWCA Civ 1268 (CA); Case C-203/02, 9 November 2004 (ECJ).

[102] See DG Internal Market and Services Working Paper, 'First Evaluation of Directive 96/9/EC on the Legal Protection of Databases', Brussels, 12 December 2005, 8.

It is not possible for the maker of an unprotected database to prevent indirect extraction or reutilization by limiting access to online customers and imposing contractual restrictions on them, as Article 8(1) provides:

The maker of a database which is made available to the public in whatever manner may not prevent a lawful user of the database from extracting and/or re-utilizing insubstantial parts of its contents, evaluated qualitatively and/or quantitatively, for any purposes whatsoever.

The only option remaining is to create a special-purpose corporate vehicle, to which the data is licensed for a fee and which itself compiles the data into a database. Provided such a vehicle *makes* the database, rather than merely receiving a ready-made copy from the data creator, the licence fees will amount to a substantial investment in obtaining the data and should thus qualify the database for *sui generis* right under Article 7(1). Such a corporate vehicle serves no commercial purpose other than overcoming the defects in the directive caused by the embedded business model.

The liability provisions of the e-Signatures Directive embed a certification model under which the certification-service-provider itself performs checks on the identity and other attributes of the signatory and also confirms that the signatory possesses the signature-creation key. The effect of this is that the person who actually performs these functions, the registration authority, has no direct liability to a relying party.[103] This mismatch of business models creates real uncertainty as to the certification-service-provider's liability. There are two possible ways in which the courts might decide a claim against a certification-service-provider.

First, because liability under the directive is negligence-based,[104] a certification-service-provider might be held to have no liability at all to a relying party. Both UK[105] and US[106] negligence cases have held that where a function is properly delegated to a third party it will not be negligent for the delegator to rely on the performance of that third party unless there are reasons to suspect improper performance. This interpretation, if correct, would mean that the directive has in practice failed to achieve its aims so far as liability is concerned.

By contrast, if the negligence liability imposed on certification-service-providers by the directive is a non-delegable duty,[107] then liability can be reallocated from the certification-service-provider to the registration authority by means of indemnity provisions in the contract between them. These will normally extend beyond relying party losses and encompass some of the certification-service-provider's own risks. To counterbalance the extra risks which a registration authority thereby accepts, it is

---

[103] At least under the directive and its national implementing legislation, though of course there might be residual liability under general principles of tort law in some jurisdictions.

[104] The actual standard under e-Signatures Directive, Art 6 is that the certification-service-provider has a defence if he proves he did not act negligently; this is still a negligence standard, but with reversed burden of proof.

[105] See eg *Prendergast v Sam & Dee Ltd* (1988), *The Times*, 24 March 1988.

[106] See eg *Independent School District No 454, Fairmont, Minnesota v Statistical Tabulating Corporation*, 359 F Supp 1095 (ND Ill, 1973).

[107] See for UK law the principles set out in *Wilsons and Clyde Coal Ltd v English* [1938] AC 57.

likely to insist on use limitations which prevent the certificates being used outside the confines of the closed PKI for which the contract was negotiated. This need to allocate liability risks through contract, rather than imposing them by law on the party who can obviate the risks, makes it less likely that existing closed PKIs will be extended to create the form of open PKI for Europe envisaged in the directive, so again the directive will have failed in its aims.

It is worth noting that the uncertainties as to the liability position are made worse by the directive's failure to specify clearly whether, and on what legal basis, any use limitations and transaction limits are binding on relying parties. This failure derives from assumptions about the way in which certification-service-providers and relying parties will communicate during the signature-verification process, and thus how the law of contract and tort will view these limitations, and is a further consequence of implicit business-model embedding.

Where regulation has been based on the liability model for offline publishers and broadcasters, the unintended consequences have been far more striking. Because parts of the original US Communications Decency Act were unconstitutional, these were struck out by the Supreme Court leaving only the provisions granting immunity from civil suit. In subsequent litigation it has been held that the Act provides a complete immunity from all civil claims.[108] The aim of the legislation was to make ISPs police the internet and reduce the volume of indecent material available; the outcome has been exactly the opposite, and ISPs do no policing at all.[109] Similarly, the Australian Broadcasting Services Amendment Act had been intended to apply cinema censorship rules to online content. However, ISPs have no obligation in respect of prohibited content if they operate a 'restricted access system',[110] and have therefore universally adopted the simplest method of achieving this by supplying filtering software to their customers. Filtering software is notoriously ineffective, particularly as its filtering parameters can be adjusted by technically knowledgeable users such as children. So far as an outside observer can ascertain, little or no censorship of online content occurs in Australia, but providers of filtering software have found an important and continuing market.

Business model-neutral regulation

If embedding business models in cyberspace regulation potentially produces structural defects which can make the law meaningless to cyberspace actors, it would seem obvious that we should try to make business model-neutral laws. Achieving this aim is, however, more difficult than stating it.

---

[108] See eg *Zeran v America Online, Inc*, 129 F 3d 327 (4th Cir, 1997), 1998 US 4047 (cert denied) and *Blumenthal v Drudge and America Online, Inc*, 992 F Supp 44 (DDC, 1998) (defamation); *Doe v America Online Inc*, 718 So 2d 385 (4th Cir, 1999) (negligence).

[109] 'While it appears to this Court that AOL in this case has taken advantage of all the benefits conferred by Congress in the Communications Decency Act, and then some, without accepting any of the burdens that Congress intended, the statutory language is clear: AOL is immune from suit . . .' (*Blumenthal v Drudge and America Online Inc*, 992 F Supp 44, 52 (DDC, 1998)).

[110] Defined in Australian Broadcasting Services Act 1992, Sch 5, s 4.

A counsel of perfection would be to abstain from law-making until the business models adopted for a new field of cyberspace activity have become established, thus reducing substantially the danger of unintentionally embedding features of an incompatible business model. Such a policy of masterly inactivity[111] is difficult to sustain in the face of the pressures on lawmakers. All the EU directives discussed above were enacted to resolve the situation of differing and incompatible national laws, as was the US E-Sign Act. Both the US Communications Decency Act and the Australian legislation resulted from a moral panic which created political pressures to do 'something'. Masterly inactivity can be effective if these pressures are absent; the US took a policy decision in 1996 not to regulate e-money until it became a significant factor in the payment services market,[112] and this has proved a wise decision as the current e-money business models are very different from those envisaged at that time and are still evolving.

The main challenge is to find ways to avoid embedding business models in law unintentionally. Deliberate embedding of a business model, as in the EU e-money regime, at least gives the lawmaker the opportunity to consider what the consequences might be. Where the embedding is both implicit and unconscious there can be no chance to do this.

Lawmakers therefore need to begin by articulating the cyberspace business model which they believe will be adopted by those to whom the law will apply. This will enable important checks to be made. First, the business model should be compared with current uses of the technology to identify errors and omissions. As an example, although the internet had not entered the public consciousness during the period 1990–5 when the Data Protection Directive was under discussion, it was well known that organizations were sharing data cross-border via proprietary networks rather than physically transferring datasets between those countries. Articulating this fact would have raised the question whether such sharing amounted to a 'transfer' of data, and thus avoided embedding in the directive the assumption that physically transferring copies of datasets was the only way in which cross-border use would be undertaken.

Secondly, predicted changes in the technology and its use can then be researched, and their effects on the underlying business model analysed. In relation to e-signatures, the concept of involving a registration authority in the certification process had been identified by 1999,[113] and even before that date experts were arguing that the closed PKI model would be more commercially successful than the open model.[114] Identifying this as a potential development in the e-signatures business model would

---

[111] A term originally used to describe British foreign policy in the mid nineteenth century, particularly in relation to Afghanistan—see John Wyllie, 'Masterly Inactivity', (July–December 1869) XII *Fortnightly Review* 596—but which has proved invaluable ever since to justify policy decisions not to act.

[112] Federal Reserve Bank Governor Kelly, 'Developments in Electronic Money and Banking', Cyberpayments '96 Conference, Dallas, 1996.

[113] See S Chokhani and W Ford (n 76), although the role of Registration Authorities is not fully articulated.

[114] See Brad Biddle (n 46), although Biddle does not separate the functions of certification authority and registration authority.

have raised the question of what liability the e-Signatures Directive should impose on registration authorities. Similarly, the e-Money Directive's embedding of the stored value business model for e-money was based on the predominant technologies of the time, but accounted e-payment systems were already in operation[115] and the mass penetration of the internet to private users was clearly predictable.[116] This should have alerted the lawmaker to the possibility that the accounted e-payment model might soon become viable, and thus led them to consider whether such payment services should, and could, be encompassed by the directive.

The next step is to avoid the temptations of analogy. The fact that an existing sphere of activity operates successfully under its current regulation does not mean that a new activity, whose anticipated business model has common features with that of the existing activity, can successfully be regulated in the same way. The US Communications Decency Act and the Australian Broadcasting Services Amendment Act provide striking examples of how spectacularly this approach can fail. The danger of regulating by analogy will be much reduced if the business model of the new activity is properly articulated, because if this is done the differences between the two business models should become apparent.

The final step which regulators need to take, once they have a clear (and ideally reasonably mature) business model in mind, is to ensure so far as is possible that the regulation does not either (a) mandate those subject to the regulation to adopt the particular business model, or (b) favour that model over alternative models which might later be developed. This is a similar approach to that which aims at achieving technology-neutral regulation, a topic which will be examined in Chapter 11.

Once a clear and accurate business model for the activity to be regulated has been developed, lawmakers will have sufficient information about that activity to attempt to draft it in business model-neutral terms. There are a number of techniques which would assist this process.

First, it is essential to identify and enunciate the regulatory objectives. It is surprising how seldom this is done in any depth, and how easy it is to assume that controlling some aspect of the business model will achieve the intended regulatory objective without questioning that assumption. For example, the Data Protection Directive does not explain what it aims to achieve by the prohibition in Article 25 on transferring personal data outside the EU. Is it the transfer itself which is the

---

[115] PayPal was founded in 1998, though previous unsuccessful attempts to commercialize accounted e-payments had been made—see eg First Virtual, which was founded in 1994 but ceased to provide e-payments in 1998, <http://computing-dictionary.thefreedictionary.com/First+Virtual>. Also in 1998, the distinction between stored value e-money and accounted e-payments was explained in ECB, *Report on Electronic Money* (August 1998), 7 (using the term 'access product').

[116] US home internet penetration had risen from 2% in 1994 to 26% in 1998—National Science Foundation, *The Application and Implications of Information Technologies in the Home: Where Are the Data and What Do They Say?* (February 2001), 11, citing US Bureau of the Census data for 1998 and Clemente, *State of the Net: The New Frontier* (New York: McGraw-Hill, 1998) for 1994. The possibility that accounted e-payments might eclipse stored value e-money was recognized in ECB, *Report on Electronic Money* (August 1998), 9: 'However, it is possible that advances in the technology used for access products may reduce the comparative advantages of electronic money products and, consequently, their growth rate.'

problem, or is the aim to ensure that personal data originating within the EU do not lose the privacy protections set out in the directive when they are processed in a third country?[117] Assuming the latter to have been the regulatory aim, then if this had been expressed it would have been clear that data whose storage remained within the EU, but which was processed outside, presented a potential problem. The difficulty could have been resolved either by defining 'transfer' to include such remote processing or by imposing an obligation on the controller to ensure that any processing outside the EU did not deprive the data of those protections unless the place of processing also provided adequate protection. The latter would have been preferable because it addresses the aim more directly, and should thus work for future technologies or business models which might fall outside a revised definition of 'transfer'.

Similarly, the objective of the liability regime set out in the e-Signatures Directive appears to have been to give a remedy to a relying party who suffers loss as a consequence of inaccurate information in a signature certificate. However, this is not stated anywhere in the legislative history of the directive, which simply and without comment sets out a minimum level of liability for certification-service-providers. Had the regulatory aim been enunciated, the legislators should have been alerted to the possibility that this information might in practice be verified by persons other than the certification-service-providers, and thus that the verifying person might more appropriately bear the liability. This would have been a more nearly optimum solution because (a) it is the person who verified the information who was negligent and is therefore responsible for the loss, and (b) this approach regulates the behaviour of the verifier rather than the person who merely has the status of certification-service-provider, the quality of whose processes may play no role in determining whether the verification is accurate.

The likelihood of embedding a business model unintentionally is also greatly reduced if lawmakers address human activities directly, rather than by framing their laws in terms of proxies for that behaviour. In many of the examples considered in this chapter the laws made provision for establishing or regulating matters such as institutions, structures, or status. This implicitly assumes that those proxies will exist in the cyberspace business model, and that they will perform the roles expected by the lawmaker. The consequence is to reduce the meaning of the law for those who adopt a business model in which those proxies do not exist, or engage in different behaviours where those proxies play different parts. As we have seen, registration authorities take over functions which in the e-signatures model were performed by certification-service-providers, individual staff members take decisions about personal data processing which the data protection model presumed would be the preserve of the employer, non-financial institutions identify a business case for providing ancillary e-payment services, and so on. Even when business models change, the activities usually continue and thus regulating activities, and particularly their consequences, tends towards business-model neutrality.

---

[117] The closest to an explanation which can be found in recitals 56–60 of the directive is in recital 59: 'particular measures may be taken to compensate for the lack of protection in a third country in cases where the controller offers appropriate safeguards . . .', which suggests the second aim rather than the first.

Lawmakers should also avoid the temptation to frame their laws with excessive precision. We saw in Chapter 8 how this can reduce the meaning of laws for cyberspace actors, by creating conflicts with other obligations or otherwise making compliance difficult or even impossible. Excessive precision can also reduce the meaningfulness of laws by embedding inappropriate business models. To take just one example from the laws examined in this chapter, there was no need for the drafters of the Databases Directive to define the concept of 'making'. The meaning of this term would have been perfectly clear to the database industry and the courts. By defining 'making' a database in terms of 'obtaining, verification or presentation'[118] of its contents, the drafters limited the qualifying requirement of substantial investment to the money and effort spent on those activities alone. Had they resisted the temptation to explain 'making', *British Horseracing Board Ltd and ors v William Hill Organization Ltd*[119] would almost certainly have been decided differently and the original intention of the directive would have been preserved.[120]

Finally, lawmakers need to be more sceptical that passing laws is an effective way to ensure that what they intend to happen will in fact happen. This concentrates their attention on the intended consequences of their law-making, and perhaps leads them to believe that unintended consequences are unlikely. In cyberspace, lawmakers have a poor track record even so far as achieving their intended consequences is concerned. The Databases Directive aimed to correct the 'very great imbalance in the level of investment in the database sector both as between the Member States and between the Community and the world's largest database-producing third countries . . .'[121] by creating a uniform protection regime for databases in the EU, but the level of EU database production has not increased over the pre-directive level.[122] The e-Signatures Directive states confidently that 'a clear Community framework regarding the conditions applying to electronic signatures will strengthen confidence in, and general acceptance of, the new technologies',[123] but at the time of writing there is little or no use of e-signatures outside closed PKIs, and no sign of cross-border use within the EU. The Communications Decency Act has vastly reduced the likelihood that US ISPs will discourage indecent communications. The e-Money Directive aimed 'to provide a regulatory framework that assists electronic money in delivering its full potential benefits and that avoids hampering technological innovation in particular',[124] but only a handful of electronic money institutions

---

[118] Databases Directive, Art 7(1).

[119] Case C-203/02, 9 November 2004.

[120] Interestingly, the original Proposal for a Council directive on the legal protection of databases, COM (92) 24 final, OJ C 156/4, 23 June 1992, did not contain any investment requirement to qualify for protection. All database makers were to receive protection from 'unfair extraction' for commercial purposes (Art 2(5)), thus leaving it to the courts to decide whether, taking into account the exceptions to Art 2(1) set out in Art 8, the extraction was unfair. 'Making' was not explained anywhere.

[121] Databases Directive, recital 11.

[122] DG Internal Market and Services Working Paper, 'First Evaluation of Directive 96/9/EC on the Legal Protection of Databases', Brussels 12 December 2005, 4.

[123] e-Signatures Directive, recital 4.

[124] e-Money Directive, recital 5.

are authorized in the EU and e-money represents a tiny proportion of payment transactions.[125]

As we have seen throughout this book, lawmakers do not have the ability simply to issue commands to cyberspace actors and impose sanctions on those who do not obey. Instead their laws must seek to persuade cyberspace actors to comply. Lawmakers must therefore make a convincing case that they have authority to regulate this cyberspace activity, and do so by means of law whose content imposes meaningful obligations on cyberspace actors. Regulating proxies and embedding inappropriate business models in the law are effective only in reducing the meaning of the law for those actors, and thus its authority for them.

---

[125] In Belgium, which appears to have the highest European level of e-money usage, in 2003 2.5 million users spent less than US$1.8 million daily, and the figures for Germany (US$0.2 million) and the Netherlands (US$0.65 million) are proportionately lower per user—BIS Committee on Payment and Settlement Systems, *Survey of Developments in Electronic Money and Internet and Mobile Payments* (March 2004), Table B, 197 ff.

10

Aims and Effectiveness

The primary purpose of law is not to create employment for lawmakers and legal advisers, though a cynic might find a deal of evidence to the contrary. Rather, law's purpose is to order society by influencing humans to behave in socially desirable ways.

We saw in Chapter 7 that if a cyberspace actor is to accept the authority of a law, he needs to accede to that law's social aims. If the lawmaker cannot persuade actors that those aims are desirable, the law is likely to have little authority. But even where the social aim of the law *is* accepted, its authority may still be weak or non-existent if cyberspace actors cannot see that compliance with the law is likely to achieve that aim.

It is probably unhelpful to attempt to assess effectiveness at the level of the individual obligations imposed by a law, although it is obvious that this is what a lawmaker should aim at. Cyberspace actors will usually decide whether to accept a law's authority by taking it as a whole. If it appears likely to be generally effective at achieving its aims, then actors may even comply with individual provisions which are apparently ineffective on the assumption that the lawmaker has a clearer understanding of how the social aim is best achieved.[1] Even if the actor does not obey apparently ineffective individual provisions, compliance with the remainder of the law is still likely. However, if the law, taken as a whole, does not convince the actor that it will achieve its aims, then it is likely that none of its provisions will be accepted as having authority for him.

This suggests that we should examine the question of effectiveness at the level of the law system. A law system is the set of obligations which attempt to achieve a particular aim or connected set of aims; it might consist of only part of an enactment, the enactment as a whole, or a collection of linked laws.

It seems to me unarguable that a law system which fails to achieve *any* of its social aims is completely ineffective. It must therefore follow that a law system which achieves only *some* of its aims falls short of the highest standard of effectiveness. It is, of course, unrealistic to expect perfection in any law system, but the aspiration towards complete effectiveness is important. A law system which contains a high

---

[1] See Joseph Raz, *The Authority of Law*, 2nd edn (Oxford: Oxford University Press, 2009), 21–5. For a more extensive discussion of the reasons for rule-following see Frederick Schauer, *Playing by the Rules* (Oxford: Clarendon Press, 1991).

proportion of ineffective rules is, at best, in need of major improvement. A failure to achieve some minimum proportion of effective rules would seem to make it fair to describe the law system as having failed, because ineffective rules will reduce the law's authority until, at some point, it loses all authority. Vaver makes this point in relation to intellectual property laws:

Good economic laws must have at least three characteristics: they must be (1) clear; (2) just; and (3) efficient. These features have their intrinsic merits for all laws; they are critical for economic laws if commerce is to proceed as smoothly and predictably as possible. A failure in any aspect is costly and lessens the respect law should attract. The public will pay and be restricted more than it ought in return for the benefits the laws claim to offer it. People will then tend to ignore or avoid the law, and will resent those who support it and who tell them off.[2]

Thus effectiveness is important. But how can we assess the effectiveness of the law systems which presently claim authority over cyberspace?

Principles of Effectiveness

Surprisingly little work has been done on how best to assess whether a law system is effective in meeting its aims, though of course there is extensive writing on the effectiveness of particular legal provisions. The leading analysis of the principles which make a law system effective is Fuller's *Morality of Law*.[3]

In spite of the book's title, Fuller makes it clear that what he is examining is the essential elements which a legal system must possess if it is to be effective in 'the enterprise of subjecting human conduct to the governance of rules'.[4] Those elements are what he describes as the minimum internal morality of law. This is not a morality in the Natural Law tradition of Aristotle, Aquinas, and Hobbes, but rather a morality of aspiration, as opposed to duty.[5] In other words, it does not prescribe what must be done, but instead sets out aims which lawmakers should aspire to achieve. The more nearly those aims are achieved, the more likely the law system will produce effective law.

By means of his parable of Rex the King, Fuller elucidates eight guiding principles of internal morality.[6] The first three of these are that laws should be in the form of general rules rather than individually addressed directives; that they should be made known rather than kept secret; and that they should not, as a general rule, be retroactive. A law system which consistently failed to abide by these principles would be equally as ineffective in the physical world as in cyberspace. The same is true

---

[2] D. Vaver, 'Reforming Intellectual Property Law: An Obvious and Not-so-obvious Agenda' (2009) IPQ 143, 144.

[3] Lon Fuller, *The Morality of Law*, rev. edn (New Haven: Yale University Press, 1969).

[4] Ibid, 96.

[5] Ibid, 5–9.

[6] Ibid, 33–8, under the heading 'Eight ways to fail to make law'. The eight principles are examined in detail at 46–91.

of Fuller's eighth principle that there should be congruence between official action, particularly enforcement action, and the declared rules.

Principles four to seven, however, have a particular importance for our discussion. It appears to be far more difficult for lawmakers to comply with these principles when making laws for cyberspace. The fourth and fifth principles are that the law's rules should be understandable by those who have to comply with them, and that the rules should not be contradictory. These are related to the ways to make meaningless law which we examined in Chapter 8, and we saw there a number of examples of cyberspace laws which contravened these principles. This was primarily because they were framed in over-complex terms and adopted an approach to law-making which aimed at precise specification of the law's demands.

For much the same reasons many laws in cyberspace contravene Fuller's seventh principle, that rules must not be changed so frequently as to obstruct efforts at compliance. Laws which specify compliance requirements precisely and in excessive detail are likely to require frequent amendment. It seems to be an inevitable consequences of legislating objective and quantitative requirements that continual updating is required to take account of changes in social or business conditions, and perhaps also of advances in understanding the complex effects of laws drafted in this way.

Frequent change must necessarily increase the burden on the law's subjects, both in keeping up to date with their obligations and changing their operations in accordance with the revised law. At some point, the cumulative effect of constant changes will adversely affect the authority of the law for those who need to implement those changes. Anecdotally, there are few organizations whose staff believe their HR department performs an important function, and the employment policies which HR departments produce in response to legal and regulatory change are often seen as barriers to be evaded rather than as normative guidance about proper employment behaviour.

In cyberspace, data protection is in danger of following the same route. The UK Data Protection Act 1998 has seen thirty-three statutory instruments amending or supplementing the rules since the passage of the Act.[7] In addition, there is a constant stream of guidance and other interpretive material which issues from the Information Commissioner's Office, as we saw in Chapter 8. All this detail is, at least theoretically, very helpful in enabling data controllers and processors to comply with the law, but a law which requires such regular amendment and constant explanation is likely to be less well understood, and thus its authority less well respected, than a law which is stable over time.

Fuller's sixth principle is that lawmakers should not make laws which it is impossible to obey. Lawmakers rarely, if ever, set out to achieve impossibility, and from the perspective of their own legal systems they rarely do so. However, the law system which applies to a particular cyberspace activity is not usually the law made by a single national lawmaker, but rather that set of national laws which applies, at the

---

[7] Source: BAILII search (<http://www.bailii.org>) May 2011.

least, to the various national communities of which the cyberspace actor is a member. A national lawmaker which does not look outside its national boundaries runs the risk that it will impose obligations which can only be obeyed by disobeying the laws of some other lawmaker. In this situation it is impossible for the cyberspace actor to comply with all the rules of the law system, and he will need to choose which to disobey.[8] We have already seen an example of this in the dilemma faced by SWIFT, the financial telecommunications service, which could only comply with US antiterrorism laws by breaking EU data protection law.[9] Similarly, the financial-institution advertising controls discussed in Chapter 5 make it practically impossible for a bank to operate a website without contravening some country's law.

If many of the law systems which regulate cyberspace fail to meet a substantial proportion of Fuller's principles of morality, it would seem likely that they are ineffective in persuading cyberspace actors to comply with them, and thus ineffective in achieving their social aims. Is there any way of testing whether this is true?

And is there, also, any way to discover whether the substantive content of these laws, which is not a matter addressed by Fuller's principles, is effective at achieving its aims? Certainly it is possible to envisage a law system which meets all the elements of Fuller's tests but which is clearly an ineffective system because it achieves nothing at all. Let us suppose that the dictator of Ruritania, inspired by Rex the King, decides to produce a comprehensive code for the regulation of e-commerce. Unfortunately the dictator has also been influenced by the example of the megalomaniac villains in Bond films,[10] and so the code says nothing about the formation and validity of online contracts, how to comply with legal requirements for signatures, the obligations of online sellers, or the protection of online consumer buyers. Instead the law requires all those engaged in e-commerce to wear Ruritanian national costume, and demands that all online sellers should include a sound file of the Ruritanian national anthem on each website page. This law is clear, non-contradictory, easy to comply with, and will not need regular amendment. However, it cannot reasonably be disputed that the dictator's code is a failed law system for e-commerce because it does not achieve its aim of regulating e-commerce effectively.

Empirical Testing

The fact that examples of ineffective laws can be found demonstrates, unsurprisingly, that the cyberspace law systems are not perfect. But are these failings equally common in physical world laws, or does the nature of cyberspace mean that it is more difficult to make effective law?

---

[8] Murray's concept of regulatory gravity may help us predict the actor's choice—see Ch 6, n 56.

[9] See EU Article 29 Data Protection Working Party, 'Opinion 10/2006 on the Processing of Personal Data by the Society for Worldwide Interbank Financial Telecommunication (SWIFT)', 01935/06/EN, 22 November 2006.

[10] These villains, at least in the earlier films, always attempt to achieve their aims via the most unlikely means conceivable.

A methodology for answering this question, though not the answer itself, has been proposed by Schmidt.[11] He suggests that an empirical measurement of law system quality might be achievable:

> The quality of a law system is not only related to its success in fulfilling the requirements of the design and the design's competitive edge, it is also related to its capacity to attract people, interested to manage, to work and to take part in it. Without this capacity the law system fades from existence. So an additional and existential measure for law-system quality is the capacity to attract and sustain 'membership', in its capacity to generate willingness to participate . . . Consequently we can summarize our quest for rational understanding what the quality of law systems is in one sentence: *law-system quality is a function of our willingness to participate in it and our willingness to participate is an individual function of interchange values.*[12]

Although Schmidt does not put it in this way, he is highlighting the link between the community which a law system regulates and the authority of that law system. If membership of the community dwindles, so does the authority of the law. The quality of a law system consists in more than just its effectiveness in achieving its aims, but it would seem hard to construct an argument that it is possible for a law system to be of low quality but still effective. Thus Schmidt's methodology enables us to make some assessment of effectiveness.

Schmidt identifies the range of options available to those who are currently part of the law system under analysis and those who are outside it,[13] and proposes that if data are available as to the choices they made, those data can be used to calculate an empirical value for the quality of the law system.

Of course, such data are not readily available, if at all, but by estimating likely values for some law systems Schmidt concludes that a subset of the option variables is likely to be a good guide to quality.[14] First, a positive net inflow of participants to the law system suggests it is of high quality, whereas a net outflow suggests the opposite. In the case of the e-Money Directive 2000,[15] we know that there were

---

[11] Aernout Schmidt, 'Radbruch in Cyberspace: About Law-system Quality and ICT Innovation' (2009) 3 Masaryk University Journal of Law and Technology 195.

[12] Ibid, 206 (emphasis in the original).

[13] Ibid, 208:

[I]ndividuals participating in the law system have the following behavioral options:

(1) to use (u),
(2) to comply (c),
(3) to evade (e),
(4) to try and leave the law system (l),
(5) to revolt (r),

and those outside the system have the following options:

(1) to try and join the law system (m),
(2) to try and team up with the system (t),
(3) to try and fight the law system (f).

[14] Ibid, 212.

[15] Directive 2000/46/EC of the European Parliament and of the Council on the taking up, pursuit of and prudential supervision of the business of electronic money institutions, OJ L 275/39, 27 October 2000 ('e-Money Directive 2000').

few who joined the e-money law system by becoming authorized e-money issuers. The European Commission's evaluation of the directive suggests that an important reason for this was the law itself, because the obligations it imposed on issuers were too onerous and too uncertain:

Shortcomings of the Directive in terms of meeting its objectives primarily have to do with uncertainty over its scope and applicability, and/or with the perceived (dis)proportionality of the regulatory framework ... questions about if and how the legal framework should apply to certain schemes (certain account-based schemes, electronic vouchers) and issuers (MNOs [mobile network operators], transport providers) have led to a considerable degree of legal uncertainty ... While the EMD [e-Money Directive] has not excluded any storage devices for technical reasons, whether it has actually encouraged, hampered, or made no difference to innovation depends mainly on the perceived appropriateness of the regulatory framework, and on the degree of legal (un)certainty regarding its applicability ... While the limited practical experience to date makes it difficult to assess whether a level playing field exists between ELMIs and traditional credit institutions, there are concerns that some of the requirements and restrictions for ELMIs may be excessive.[16]

We also know that at least one of the major players, PayPal, chose to leave the e-money law system and join instead the system of ordinary banking regulation.[17] Even without empirical data there seems little doubt that the EU's law system for e-money was of poor quality and thus to a large degree ineffective in achieving its aims.

There are numerous other examples of law systems, established specifically to regulate cyberspace activities, where cyberspace actors have simply declined to join the system and accept the authority of its rules. The EU e-signatures regime has been discussed in previous chapters, and we saw that the majority of cyberspace actors who had the opportunity to use advanced electronic signatures decided not to do so. Australian ISPs declined to join the law system to censor cyberspace content, but instead provided ineffective self-censorship technologies to their customers.[18] It seems to me that such widespread reluctance to join law systems is uncommon in the physical world, although I have no empirical data to demonstrate this.

Schmidt's second measure is the proportion of participants who attempt to evade or avoid the provisions of the law system. This proportion is inversely related to the quality of the law system. In the physical world widespread evasion seems to be common only in respect of speeding laws and, in some countries, tax laws. By contrast, evasion seems to be common in cyberspace. The take-up of the system for VAT registration for non-EU online businesses selling into the EU has been minimal,[19] even

---

[16] An ELMI is an electronic money institution. *Commission Staff Working Document on the Review of the E-Money Directive (2000/46/EC)*, SEC(2006) 1049, 18 July 2006, 9. See also Proposal for a directive of the European Parliament and of the Council on the taking up, pursuit and prudential supervision of the business of electronic money institutions, amending Directives 2005/60/EC and 2006/48/EC and repealing Directive 2000/46/EC, COM (2008) 627 final, 9 October 2008, 2.

[17] Tom Stevenson, 'PayPal becomes a bank to fight off Google', *Daily Telegraph*, 15 May 2007 <http://www.telegraph.co.uk/finance/markets/2808982/PayPal-becomes-a-bank-to-fight-off-Google.html>.

[18] See Ch 8, pp 140–1.

[19] See Ch 6, pp 93–4.

though the penalties for evasion are substantial (though unlikely to be enforceable). Most strikingly, the law of copyright as it applies to music and video downloads exhibits such a high degree of evasion by those subject to the law[20] that, on this measure, it appears to be almost completely ineffective in its aim to prevent the making and sharing of unauthorized copies. In the e-commerce field avoidance of the provisions of foreign law through terms and conditions and the structuring of operational methods is widespread,[21] and we saw in Chapter 3 that some US publishers are avoiding the UK's defamation law system by blocking online access to their sites from UK IP addresses.[22]

Finally, Schmidt tells us that a high proportion of participants who revolt against the law system, coupled with outsiders who fight against it, is also an indicator of low quality. The strong opposition by users to the laws relating to copyright in online music and video is a good example of this phenomenon,[23] as is the defiance of the UK Financial Services Authority by mobile telecommunications providers over e-money regulation. At the time of writing, there appears to be a high level of both internal and external opposition to the most recent Australian online censorship proposals.[24]

Although no overall conclusions as to the quality of cyberspace law systems, compared to their physical world counterparts, can be reached by this method, there is clear evidence that many of these law systems are of low quality, and thus of doubtful effectiveness.

Reasons for Ineffectiveness

It is, I suppose, conceivable that a law might have aims which would be accepted by cyberspace users as being worthy of obedience, and yet be drafted in such a technically incompetent way that it completely fails to achieve those aims. Such laws are few and far between. Instead we find ourselves in the situation where lawmakers devise their laws with care and technical competence, often on the basis of substantial research, but still manage to produce laws which are unable to achieve their aims.

My contention is that these laws are ineffective because they have no authority in cyberspace. Either the authority of the lawmaker to impose obligations is denied, or

---

[20] See Ch 7, pp 124–6.

[21] Thomas Schultz, 'Carving Up the Internet: Jurisdiction, Legal Orders, and the Private/Public International Law Interface' (2008) 19 EJIL 799.

[22] 'Libel Threat to Force US Papers Out of Britain', *The Times*, 8 November 2009.

[23] This opposition is largely at an individual level, but it is worth noting that the Swedish Pirate Party won a seat to the European Parliament in 2009 and Pirate Parties have been formed in other countries—<http://en.wikipedia.org/wiki/Pirate_Parties_International>. There are numerous examples of opposition in reform proposals—see eg Electronic Frontier Foundation White Paper, *Let the Music Play* (2008), <http://www.eff.org/wp/better-way-forward-voluntary-collective-licensing-music-file-sharing>.

[24] Participant opposition is organized by, *inter alia*, Electronic Frontiers Australia, <http://www.efa.org.au>; the Digital Liberty Coalition, <http://dlc.asn.au/>; and GetUp!, <http://www.getup.org.au/campaign/SaveTheNet>;, while external opposition is co-ordinated by NetChoice, <http://www.netchoice.org/>.

the rules themselves are not accepted as having authority because the cyberspace user does not understand them to impose any meaningful obligations on him.

We saw in the previous chapters that cyberspace actors will not understand laws to be meaningful if they clash with the norms under which the actor is already operating, unless the law is successful in replacing those norms with its own norms. The US Communications Decency Act 1996 is an illuminating example here. The intention of this legislation was to introduce new criminal offences of knowingly creating, sending, transmitting, or displaying obscene or indecent materials to minors, or knowingly permitting the use of one's telecommunications systems for these purposes. As a counterbalancing element of the legislation, section 230 provided protection for 'Good Samaritan' activities on the part of ISPs, allowing them to introduce blocking or filtering technology without assuming the role of editor or publisher and thereby becoming responsible for the third party content.[25]

These new criminal offences clearly clashed with the free-speech norm, which in the US is entrenched in law as the First Amendment to the Constitution. They were therefore struck down in *ACLU v Reno*[26] as infringing the First Amendment. The outcome was a law which achieved almost exactly the opposite of the lawmaker's aims. No criminal offences were created and ISPs were encouraged to refrain from acting as Good Samaritans for fear of losing the immunity. In subsequent litigation it has been held that section 230 provides a complete immunity from civil actions for defamation,[27] even where the ISP pays the author for the right to provide access to the defamatory material,[28] and even from a claim alleging negligence in failing to prevent continued solicitations to purchase child pornography made via the ISP's system.[29]

Even if the First Amendment did not exist, there must be real doubt whether the Act would have been effective to achieve its aims. ISPs would have been under severe pressure from their customers to act in accordance with the free-speech norm. They might well have resisted taking steps to comply with the Act, leaving the US authorities with a difficult decision about whether enforcement was likely to be successful. At that time it was impossible in practice for an ISP to inspect the traffic it carried, so that a defence of lack of knowledge would have had a good prospect of success. Even if ISPs had attempted to censor their traffic, cyberspace actors who rejected the

---

[25] The Senate conference report on § 230 states:

> This section provides "Good Samaritan" protections from civil liability for providers or users of an interactive computer service for actions to restrict or to enable restriction of access to objectionable online material. One of the specific purposes of this section is to overrule *Stratton Oakmont v Prodigy* and any other similar decisions which have treated such providers and users as publishers or speakers of content that is not their own because they have restricted access to objectionable material. The conferees believe that such decisions create serious obstacles to the important federal policy of empowering parents to determine the content of communications their children receive through interactive computer services. [S Conf Rep No 104-230, at 435 (1996)]

[26] 929 F Supp 824, 830–838 (ED Pa, 1996), *affirmed* 117 S Ct 2329 (1997).
[27] *Zeran v America Online, Inc*, 129 F 3d 327 (4th Cir, 1997), 1998 US 4047 (cert Denied).
[28] *Blumenthal v Drudge and America Online Inc*, 992 F Supp 44 (DDC, 1998).
[29] *Doe v America Online Inc*, 718 So 2d 385 (4th Cir, 1999).

authority of the law would have access to anonymizing proxies as tools to circumvent such censorship. In my view it is unlikely that the Act could have been effective.

Laws which are over-complex, contradictory or impossible to obey, usually because their maker has attempted to be too precise in specifying their obligations, can also lack effectiveness and thus meaning. We have already seen in Chapter 8 that in the field of data protection, the requirement to notify the types of personal data which will be held and the purposes for which they will be processed has become an almost meaningless box-ticking exercise. Compliance does little or nothing to ensure that the data controller processes personal data for appropriate purposes, which is what the law aims to achieve. The same can be said for the Australian internet censorship law, whose consequence has been the supply of ineffective filtering software to internet users rather than the intended blocking of proscribed categories of content.[30]

Laws which do not accord with the realities which cyberspace actors face, because they are based on assumptions which do not hold true in cyberspace, will also be ineffective if they are perceived by cyberspace actors as meaningless. Private individuals largely ignore their obligations under copyright law, and the EU Databases Directive fails to protect those single source databases which the law was intended to cover. Neither has proved effective in cyberspace. The prohibition in data protection law of the transfer of personal data to 'data havens' outside the EU[31] which do not provide adequate data protection is based on an assumption that use of a dataset depends on its possession. *Lindqvist*[32] made it clear that mere access from a third country to personal data held on a server in the controller's country will not constitute a transfer, and so the prohibition is now largely pointless.[33]

All these are negative features of cyberspace laws, which in combination can reduce their authority for cyberspace users to the point that the law system becomes ineffective. Their common factor is that they concentrate on the lawmaker's own aims and perceptions, and thus ignore the cyberspace actor's perspective. Once the lawmaker accepts that its main focus must be on securing the respect of the cyberspace actor for its laws it becomes much clearer how these defects can be avoided, and thus more likely that the law will be effective in achieving its aims.

---

[30] Ch 8, *Australian internet censorship*.

[31] Directive 95/46/EC on the protection of individuals with regard to the processing of personal data and on the free movement of such data, OJ L281/31, 23November 1995, Arts 25 and 26.

[32] Case C-101/01, 6 November 2003, OJ C7/3, 10 January 2004.

[33] Opinion of the European Data Protection Supervisor on the Communication from the Commission to the European Parliament and the Council on the follow-up of the Work Programme for better implementation of the Data Protection Directive, OJ C 255/1, 27 October 2007, at para 42 notes that this is 'a logical and necessary consequence of the territorial limitations of the European Union', and that Art 25 'will not provide full protection to the European data subject in a networked society where physical borders lose importance'.

Cyberspace Law-making Aims

If you are shooting at a target which is too far away for your arrow to reach, it would not be surprising that you failed to hit it. This is where many cyberspace lawmakers are going wrong. Often they concentrate on telling the cyberspace actor what to *do*, not realizing that they have even less control over behaviour in cyberspace than they have in the physical world. Sometimes they aim at an invisible target which might not even be there—the various aims to establish markets in e-money and e-signatures through legislation are clear examples.

Aiming at the achievable is a far more sensible strategy, though it requires lawmakers to accept the unpalatable truth that there are practical limits on their law-making powers. What those aims should be ought by now to be clear.

First, the lawmaker has to achieve respect for its authority in cyberspace. Its primary aim must therefore be to identify those cyberspace actors who have joined the physical world community which already accepts the lawmaker's authority, and work out how to exclude the rest of cyberspace from its authority claims. It must also aim to work within the normative framework which already has authority for actors, because otherwise the actor will be faced with competing claims to authority and might well reject the claims of the lawmaker.

Secondly, the lawmaker must aim to make the law's content meaningful for the cyberspace actor. Many of the problems we have seen in this part of the book could be avoided if the law aimed to tell the actor the proper way to behave, rather than issuing instructions about what to do. The lawmaker must remember that laws addressed to legal advisors are less likely to be meaningful, because even large corporations cannot afford the time and expense of taking advice on every law which might apply to them in cyberspace. Speaking directly to the actor will convey far more meaning.

11

Future-proofing

Let us suppose that a lawmaker is able to persuade cyberspace actors of its authority to regulate their activities, and that it does so by way of imposing obligations which an actor accepts as meaningful in the context of its activities and the law's aims. If my argument so far is correct, such laws will achieve a high level of voluntary compliance in cyberspace.

However, society, business models, and technologies all change. At some point, these changes will be extensive enough to render laws meaningless to their subjects. When this happens lawmakers need to address the matter again by amending the law to take these changes into account.

Cyberspace presents real challenges to lawmakers here. Even if it does not produce change in society itself, which seems unlikely, cyberspace technologies and business models evolve with bewildering speed. For cyberspace laws to retain their meaning, and thus their authority, they need to be as future-proof as possible.

Technology Neutrality

Technology neutrality has long been held up as a guiding principle for the proper regulation of technological activities, particularly where information and communications technologies are involved. The liberalization of the telecommunications market, first in the US and then in Europe, led to calls for the new regulatory regimes to be technology neutral,[1] and technology neutrality has continued to be a pervasive concept in that field, influencing among others the debates on convergence with

---

[1] The earliest discoverable use of the term describes the aims of the US Electronic Communications Privacy Act 1986—see John R Kresse, 'Privacy of Conversations over Cordless and Cellular Telephones: Federal Protection under the Electronic Communications Privacy Act of 1986' (1987) 9 Geo Mason UL Rev 335. See also Nicholas W Allard and Theresa Lauerhass, 'Debalkanize the Telecommunications Marketplace', (1991–2) Cal WL Rev 231 for an early use of the term.

broadcasting,[2] voice over IP,[3] universal service,[4] spectrum allocation,[5] and net neutrality.[6]

In July 1997 the US government published its *Framework for Global Electronic Commerce*, which stated that when regulating online activities, 'rules should be technology-neutral (ie, the rules should neither require nor assume a particular technology) and forward-looking (ie, the rules should not hinder the use or development of technologies in the future)'.[7] The following year the term was used in EU legislative proposals for the first time[8] and has been adopted in relation to most EU technology legislation ever since.[9] Technology neutrality for online law has also been espoused extensively by national legislators and international organizations.[10] The desirability of technology-neutral regulation has become part of the general wisdom, and is rarely questioned.

One of the main reasons why lawmakers seek to produce technology-neutral laws is to reduce the risk that those laws will become outdated by technological change,

---

[2] See eg Herbert Ungerer, 'Access Issues under EU Regulation and Anti-Trust Law: The Case of Telecommunications and Internet Markets' (2000) 5 International Journal of Communications Law and Policy, <http://www.ijclp.org/>; Niloufer Selvadurai, 'The Regulation of the Information Society in the European Union' (2004) 10(6) CTLR 130.

[3] See eg Shaun, Montana, 'An Approach to the International Regulatory Issues of IP Telephony' (2002) 8 BUJ Sci & Tech L 682, 704; James B Speta, 'Deregulating Telecommunications in Internet Time' (2004) 61 Wash & Lee L Rev 1063.

[4] See eg Allen S Hammond IV, 'Universal Service: Problems, Solutions, and Responsive Policies' (2005) 57 Fed Comm L 187; Thomas Roukens, 'What Are We Carrying across the EU these Days? Comments on the Interpretation and Practical Implementation of Article 31 of the Universal Service Directive' (2006) 15-SPG Media Law & Policy 201.

[5] See eg Patrick S Ryan, 'Wireless Communications and Computing at a Crossroads: New Paradigms and their Impact on Theories Governing the Public's Right to Spectrum Access' (2005) 3 J Telecomm & High Tech L 239.

[6] See eg Richard E Wiley, 'A New Telecom Act—Remarks' (2006) 31 S Ill U LJ 17.

[7] 1 July 1997, <http://www.technology.gov/digeconomy/framewrk.htm>.

[8] Opinion of the Economic and Social Committee on the Proposal for a Council Recommendation concerning the protection of minors and human dignity in audiovisual and information services, OJ C 214 10 July 1998, 25 para 3.2.5: 'Regulation should be "technology-neutral": as few as possible new regulations, policies and procedures should be specific to the new services'; recitals to the Proposal for a European Parliament and Council directive on the taking up, the pursuit and the prudential supervision of the business of electronic money institutions, COM (1998) 0461 final, OJ C317, 15 October 1998, 7: 'this Directive introduces a technology-neutral legal framework that harmonises the prudential supervision of electronic money institutions to the extent necessary for ensuring their sound and prudent operation and their financial integrity in particular'.

[9] See eg Amended proposal for a European Parliament and Council directive on a common framework for electronic signatures, COM (99) 195 final; Proposal for a directive of the European Parliament and of the Council concerning the processing of personal data and the protection of privacy in the electronic communications sector, COM (2000) 0385 final, OJ C 365 E, 19 December 2000, 223; Communication from the Commission to the Council, the European Parliament, the Economic and Social Committee, and the Committee of the Regions, 'Electronic Communications: The Road to the Knowledge Economy', COM (2003) 65 final; Proposal for a Decision of the European Parliament and of the Council on establishing a multiannual Community programme on promoting safer use of the Internet and new online technologies, COM (2004) 91 final.

[10] Bert-Jaap Koops, 'Should ICT Regulation be Technology-Neutral' in Bert-Jaap Koops et al (eds), *Starting Points for ICT Regulation: Deconstructing Prevalent Policy One-liners* (The Hague: TMC Asser Press, 2006), 77, 77–9.

and thus lose their meaning and authority for those to whom they apply. Unfortunately they have often failed in this attempt. At least part of the reason for this failure is that the concept is not properly understood by lawmakers. It was only in 2006 that Koops published his essay on the subject,[11] the first proper analysis of the use of the concept outside the telecommunications sector. Although there are numerous references to the desirability of technology neutrality in earlier writings,[12] these do no more than attempt a brief definition of that concept without seeking to explore its deeper meaning and implications.

Meanings of 'technology neutrality'

The first discoverable extension of this term from telecommunications regulation to the wider field of ICT regulation appears to be in the US government's *Framework for Global Electronic Commerce*, quoted above. Here, technology neutrality is used to mean that 'the rules should neither require nor assume a particular technology'.

Only a few days later, the Bonn Ministerial Conference Declaration of 6–8 July 1997 used the term in a different way, declaring in its principle 22:

Ministers stress that the general legal frameworks should be applied online as they are off-line. In view of the speed at which new technologies are developing, they will strive to frame regulations which are technology-neutral, whilst bearing in mind the need to avoid unnecessary regulation.[13]

This is primarily an espousal of the principle of offline and online equivalence, which we have already examined in Chapter 7 and to which we will return later in this chapter. It seems likely though, given the reliance on the principle of technology neutrality in later law-making,[14] that the EU authorities also thought it desirable to make laws which were technologically neutral in the sense used by the US government.

Thus technology neutrality requires that legal rules should not favour or discriminate against a particular technology, but this formulation contains an ambiguity.

[11] Ibid.

[12] See eg Erik S Knutsen, 'Techno-neutrality of Freedom of Expression in New Media beyond the Internet: Solutions for the United States and Canada' (2001) 8 UCLA Ent L Rev 87, 95 ff; Joanna Gray, 'Draft Secondary Legislation on Financial Promotion: A Technology-neutral Investment Marketing Regime' (2001) 22 Comp Law 150; Tapio Puurunen, 'The Judicial Jurisdiction of States over International Business-to-Consumer Electronic Commerce from the Perspective of Legal Certainty' (2002) 8 UC Davis J Int'l L & Pol'y 133, 174; Richard W Downing, 'Shoring Up the Weakest Link: What Lawmakers around the World Need to Consider in Developing Comprehensive Laws to Combat Cybercrime' (2005) 43 Colum J Transnat'l L 705; Laura Hildner, 'Defusing the Threat of RFID: Protecting Consumer Privacy through Technology-specific Legislation at the State Level' (2006) 41 Harv CR-CL L Rev 133; Chad A Kirby, 'Defining Abusive Software to Protect Computer Users from the Threat of Spyware' (2006) 10 Computer L Rev & Tech J 287, 303 ff.

[13] <http://europa.eu.int/ISPO/bonn/Min_declaration/i_finalen.html>.

[14] See eg Communication from the Commission to the European Parliament, the Council, the Economic and Social Committee, and the Committee of the Regions, 'Towards a New Framework for Electronic Communications Infrastructure and Associated Services: The 1999 Communications Review', COM (1999) 539 final, 10 November 1999, 14: 'Technological neutrality means that legislation should define the objectives to be achieved and should neither impose, nor discriminate in favour of, the use of a particular type of technology to achieve those objectives.'

Clearly, a rule which states that only technology A can be used to comply with it[15] favours that technology and discriminates against all others, so it is clear that technology neutrality has to avoid specifying a particular technology as the means of compliance. What, though, of a rule with which technology A can comply without modification, whereas technology B can only comply if feasible, but expensive, modifications are made? Such a rule does not favour technology A directly but it does *indirectly* discriminate against technology B.

This ambiguity should focus our attention on the aims of the legislator. If the aim is to regulate the activities of users of already-existing technologies which are used for similar ends then technology neutral regulation will adopt the first of these approaches, attempting to treat use of each type of technology in equivalent ways. Thus the EU regulation of commercial communications imposes restrictions whose stringency increases with the intrusiveness, cost to the recipient, and potential deceptiveness of the communication, rather than allowing the use of some communications technologies and forbidding or restricting others.[16] If, however, the aim is to define the legal consequences which arise from the use of technology, such as whether a valid signature has been made[17] or when and where a communication has been received,[18] then the legislative solution must necessarily concentrate on the characteristics which are required to achieve that legal consequence. Some existing technologies may already possess those characteristics, whereas others do not. In these circumstances, a technologically neutral solution will not prevent the latter type from being modified to achieve those characteristics, but will inevitably favour technologies which do not need such modification.[19]

To complete our understanding of the concept of technology neutrality, it is clear that we must identify what further aims are intended to be achieved by use of the concept. Koops has undertaken this analysis and identifies four main legislative purposes:[20]

1. the achievement of particular effects, in terms of peoples' behaviour or the outcomes of activities
2. functional equivalence between different modes of activity, in particular offline and online
3. non-discrimination between technologies with equivalent effects
4. future-proofing of the law in two senses: drafting of laws in a way which is flexible enough not to hinder the future development of technology; and

---

[15] eg the German Digital Signature Act (Signaturgesetz) 1997.

[16] Directive 2002/58/EC concerning the processing of personal data and the protection of privacy in the electronic communications sector (Directive on privacy and electronic communications), OJ L 201/37, 31 July 2002, Art 13 and recitals 40–5.

[17] Directive 1999/93/EC on a Community framework for electronic signatures OJ L13/12, 19 January 2000.

[18] Australian Electronic Transactions Act 1999, s 14; US Uniform Electronic Transactions Act 1999, § 15(b) and (d).

[19] See the discussion at p 197, *Potential neutrality*.

[20] Koops (n 10), 83–90. This summary does not match Koops' analysis precisely but is, the author hopes, conceptually equivalent.

achieving sustainability in the sense that the law should not require over-frequent revision to cope with technological change.

The last of these is most commonly cited as the reason why legislation should be technologically neutral, though there is as yet little evidence that much legislation has been future-proofed successfully in this way.

Assuming for the moment that technology neutrality is worth attempting, we must now examine the three main legislative techniques which can be adopted.

Technology indifference

Some laws and regulations apply in identical ways, whatever the technology. The law of murder gives an obvious example. Professor Plum's guilt is unaffected by his choice between strangling the victim with the rope in the conservatory or bludgeoning him with the lead piping in the drawing room. Such laws are *indifferent* to the technology used, because they apply to behaviour of the actors involved and the effects of that behaviour[21] and not to the means through which the actors behave or by which those effects come about.

In the information- and communications-technology field, one of the most apparently technology-indifferent legal provisions is the right to authorize communication of a work to the public,[22] granted to authors by copyright law.[23] The reason for the introduction of this right in 1996 was the increasing quantity of online information provision,[24] but the right is by no means limited to online communication.

---

[21] Koops (n 10), 83–6.

[22] WIPO Copyright Treaty 1996, Art 8: 'authors of literary and artistic works shall enjoy the exclusive right of authorizing any communication to the public of their works, by wire or wireless means, including the making available to the public of their works in such a way that members of the public may access these works from a place and at a time individually chosen by them'. It is worth noting that the Berne Convention of 1979 is not technology-indifferent on this point, in most cases limiting the right to 'communication to the public by wire'—see Arts 10, 11bis(1), 14(1). Only the rights to prevent the communication of performances (Art 11(1)) or recitations (Art 11ter(1)) are technology-indifferent.

[23] Copyright law is often said to be generally technology-neutral, using that term in the sense of technology-indifference:

> Copyright law has by and large been formulated according to principles of 'technological neutrality.' It has focused on the nature of the use of the work, rather than the medium by which the use is accomplished, or the physical facilities or equipment involved. Thus, the law has granted to authors the rights to reproduce the work, to adapt it, to perform it publicly, and to communicate it to the public. The primary exception to this technological neutrality has been the separation of a broadcasting right from the general right of communication to the public. [(Shira Perlmutter, 'Convergence and the Future of Copyright' (2001) 24 Colum-VLA JL and Arts 163)]

[24] See Proposal for a European Parliament and Council directive on the harmonization of certain aspects of copyright and related rights in the Information Society COM (97) 628 final, 10 December 2007, 20:

> Technological developments have made it possible to make protected works and other subject matter available in new ways which differ significantly from traditional methods of exploitation. This is particularly true with respect to the exploitation of intellectual property online over the networks, and notably 'on demand'.

If the works of Shakespeare were still in copyright I could infringe his rights in *Hamlet* in numerous offline ways, for example via the use of older technologies such as semaphore-flag communication or Morse-code radio transmissions.

At first sight, the right to authorize communication of a work to the public appears to exhibit technology neutrality in all the senses analysed above. Further thought reveals, however, that the concept of 'communication' implicitly makes an assumption about the intention of the communicator. If I write a letter and post it, I have clearly communicated its contents to the recipient. If, though, I draft a letter and then accidentally drop it in a public place, where it is read by a third party, I will not have communicated it to that third party because I had no intention (yet) to communicate it to anyone. If I write a letter to a newspaper, which prints it, both I and the newspaper will have communicated it to the public because we intend to do so. But if I head the letter 'Not for publication', and the newspaper still prints it, then only the newspaper will have communicated it to the public. Similarly, if a notice is posted on a notice board which I control, I can only be held responsible for its communication once I know (or perhaps ought to know) of its existence and fail to remove it.[25]

The difficulty in cyberspace arises because communication is effected by the cyberspace technologies, in some cases without there being any need for the actor involved to form any intention about the particular communication. Thus the role of intermediaries is to store, copy and/or forward all the information they receive, and to do this automatically, normally without examining its semantic content. This has already raised the question whether 'copying' for the purposes of copyright law is a factual description or an intentional activity,[26] and similar questions will need to be answered for the right to control communication to the public. If the right to control communication to the public is infringed by communication which is unintentional, in this sense, then the right is not technologically indifferent because it imposes more stringent obligations on the users of cyberspace technologies.

As Perlmutter has written:

Even rights deliberately written to be technologically neutral are quickly called into question by the rapidity of today's technological developments. There ensues a tremendous diversion of time and energy in debating the precise borders of each right. Which rights are implicated by a particular type of dissemination—for example, 'making available' online? Reproduction? distribution? rental? communication?[27]

Thus although a genuinely technology indifferent rule is likely to be future-proof to a high degree, achieving technology indifference is not easy. The rule needs to be addressed to the human actor, and even then it is important to ensure that the rule

---

[25] *Byrne v Deane* [1937] 1 KB 818.

[26] See *Religious Technology Centre v Netcom On-Line Communications Services Inc*, 907 F Supp 1361, 1374 (ND Cal, 1995) and the extensive jurisprudence and legislation, in the US and elsewhere, addressing this issue, discussed in Chris Reed, *Internet Law: Text and Materials*, 2nd edn (Cambridge: Cambridge University Press, 2004), Ch 4.

[27] Shira Perlmutter (n 23), 173.

does not include unstated assumptions about the intention of the actor when specifying the behaviours, or outcomes of behaviours, to which the rule applies.

Implementation neutrality

Often a lawmaker will desire to confine the scope of its regulation to the uses of a particular type of technology. This will usually be because the introduction of that technology indicates that the prior regulatory settlement can no longer apply appropriately to its use, but rewriting the regulatory settlement from scratch in technology indifferent terms is too difficult an exercise. Here the law must by definition be specific to that technology. However, it is often possible to frame that law in such a way that it does not favour one or more *implementations* of that technology over others. This type of technology neutrality has been described as 'implementation neutrality'.[28]

The implementation-neutral approach has been widely adopted in relation to the signature of electronic documents. There are many ways in which such a signature might be attempted, the most common being: typing the signatory's name into the electronic document; adding a scanned image of the signatory's manuscript signature to the document; encrypting the document (or more normally, a mathematical message digest of the document) with the signatory's secret key, using an encryption method which enables the recipient to validate the signature by decrypting with the sender's public key; or capturing some biometric characteristic of the signatory, such as his signature metrics, iris print, or voice print, and encrypting that biometric data with the message digest of the document.

Most jurisdictions which passed laws to enable electronic signatures to be treated as legally valid forms of signing a document have done so in a way which does not exclude any of these signature methods from being valid. This is comparatively easy in common law jurisdictions because case law has established over the years that the precise form a signature takes is not decisive.[29] A signature is any process which, when applied to a document, produces sufficient[30] evidence: (a) of the identity of

---

[28] This terminology seems first to have been recorded by Professor Amelia Boss; see Amelia Boss, 'Electronic Commerce and the Symbiotic Relationship Between International and Domestic Law Reform' (1998) 72 TLNLR 1931, 1971; 'Searching for Security in the Law of Electronic Commerce' (1999) 23 Nova L Rev 585.

[29] Thus eg in English law, valid signatures have been made by initialling a contract (*Hill v Hill* [1947] Ch 231), making a mark on a will (*in re Clarke*, 27 LJPM&A 18), printing a name on a letter (*Schneider v Norris*, 2 M&S 286) or using a rubber stamp facsimile of a manuscript signature (*Goodman v J Eban Ltd* [1954] 1 QB 550).

[30] It is obvious that the electronic signature methods described above are not equivalent in terms of their evidential weight. The test for evidential sufficiency is not an absolute standard, however. The question is whether the signature method used provides sufficient evidence of these matters in the particular case. Thus an email on which I have typed my name, where I do not dispute that I typed it, is sufficient proof of all these matters and is thus signed by me. By contrast, if I deny sending the email, the fact that my name is typed on it is not—on its own—sufficient evidence of identity, intent to sign, and adoption of contents so as to constitute my signature. Were there additional evidence, eg from my service provider's records, that the email came from my computer and that the computer was under my control, this might be sufficient to validate the typed name as my signature.

the signatory; and (b) that the signatory intended to sign the document and thus adopts its contents.[31] Any e-signature law which imposes as the sole requirement for validity that evidence of these matters must be produced is implementation-neutral as between the available e-signature methods.

Thus the UNCITRAL Model Law on Electronic Signatures 2001, Art 2(a) states:

'Electronic signature' means data in electronic form in, affixed to or logically associated with, a data message, which may be used to identify the signatory in relation to the data message and to indicate the signatory's approval of the information contained in the data message.

Similarly, implementation-neutral drafting can be found in the US Electronic Signatures in Global and National Commerce Act 2000 15 USC 7001, § 106(5); the Singapore Electronic Transactions Act 1998, sections 2 and 8; the Australian Electronic Transactions Act 1999, section 10(1); the UK Electronic Communications Act 2000, section 7; the EU e-Signatures Directive,[32] Arts 2(1) and 5; and numerous other laws.

It is perhaps worth noting here that implementation neutrality is very close to technology indifference—indeed, Article 2(a) of the UNCITRAL Model Law could easily be redrafted to apply to both electronic and non-electronic signatures.[33] In the case of signatures, a technology-indifferent approach would require each legislature to consider whether any exceptions were required to preserve any differences from the evidential approach which existed for particular types or uses of manuscript signatures.[34] For this reason, no country has chosen to introduce new legislation which extends beyond signatures in electronic form, and thus a technology-indifferent approach has been ruled out.

In other fields of activity it may only be possible to impose functionally equivalent obligations on users of different kinds of technology by regulating each type of technology specifically. In this case the closest approach to technology indifference is that of implementation neutrality. For example, the issuance of e-money is so fundamentally different an activity from the printing of banknotes and minting coins that it would clearly be difficult, if not impossible, to regulate both activities by means of the same legal rules. The EU e-Money Directive 2000[35] aimed to be implementation neutral as between different e-money technologies,[36] but we have seen in

---

[31] Chris Reed, 'What *Is* a Signature' (2000) 3 JILT, <http://www2.warwick.ac.uk/fac/soc/law/elj/jilt/2000_3/reed/>.

[32] Directive 1999/93/EC on a Community framework for electronic signatures, OJ L13/12, 19 January 2000.

[33] eg, '"Signature" means a process applied to, or information in, or affixed to, or logically associated with, a document, which may be used to identify the signatory in relation to the document and to indicate the signatory's approval of the information contained in the document.'

[34] In eg English law, a memorandum of a contract for the sale or disposition of interests in land under the Law of Property (Miscellaneous Provisions) Act 1989, s 2 requires a personal (ie manuscript) signature—*Firstpost Homes Ltd v Johnson and ors* [1995] 1 WLR 1567.

[35] Directive 2000/46/EC of the European Parliament and of the Council on the taking up, pursuit of and prudential supervision of the business of electronic money institutions, OJ L 275, 27 October 2000, 39.

[36] Recitals to the Proposal for a European Parliament and Council directive on the taking up, the pursuit and the prudential supervision of the business of electronic money institutions, COM (1998)

Chapter 9 that it failed to do so because it embedded a business model which was rapidly outdated by cyberspace communication.

It is worth noting that the extent of neutrality as between different technology implementations depends very much on the definition of the technology to be regulated. Thus a law which controls the carrying of weapons is likely to be neutral as between different types of armament, whereas a law which regulates the carrying of guns will potentially favour those who prefer knives or bows and arrows. The choice in the e-Money Directive to regulate the issuance of e-money, rather than the provision of e-payment services, was one of the reasons why this legislation was not implementation-neutral.

Potential neutrality

Sometimes a lawmaker will take the view that a particular attribute of a technology, or method of its use, is essential to achieve the legal result which the lawmaker is aiming for. Unless all existing and potential implementations of the technology exhibit that characteristic or are used in that way, implementation neutrality will not be available as a legislative technique. In these circumstances, the lawmaker can achieve some level of neutrality between different technology implementations by drafting the legal requirements in such a way that non-compliant implementations can be modified to become compliant.

Again, e-signature law provides a good illustration of this approach. E-signatures are used primarily in online dealings, and the question of the identity of the online counterparty is a perennial issue.[37] A document may appear to be signed electronically by Alice, but how can the recipient be sure that Alice is really Alice? The answer to this conundrum is for a trusted third party to take evidence of Alice's identity (usually via inspecting a passport or some other official document) and then issue an electronic certificate which confirms her identity and links her with the e-signature mechanism. Identity certification was from an early stage built into digital signatures, ie those which rely on asymmetric public/private key encryption,[38] but not into the other e-signature methods.

As we have seen above, the common law jurisdictions have tended to favour a purely evidence-based approach which does not mandate identity certification.[39] However, civil law countries have traditionally treated offline signatures as a requirement of form, rather than a matter of evidence, and therefore considered independent

---

0461 final, OJ C317, 15 October 1998, 7: 'this Directive introduces a technology-neutral legal framework that harmonises the prudential supervision of electronic money institutions . . .' It is clear from the context that 'technology-neutral' is used here in the sense of implementation neutrality.

[37] See Chris Reed (n 26), Ch 5.

[38] See RFC 2459 and 2527 (<http://www.ietf.org/rfc.html>) and ANSI X.509 for technical descriptions.

[39] Though the earliest e-signature laws required identity certification as a prerequisite for validity of the signature, in common law as well as in civil law jurisdictions. See eg Utah Digital Signature Act 1996 (Utah Code, § 46-3), German Digital Signature Act (Signaturgesetz) 1997, and Ordinance (Signaturverordnung) 1997.

evidence of the identity of a signatory to be an important factor if electronic signatures were to be given legal validity.[40] Thus the EU e-Signatures Directive, Article 5(1) introduced the concept of an advanced signature based on identity certification. This type of e-signature '[satisfies] the legal requirements of a signature in relation to data in electronic form in the same manner as a handwritten signature satisfies those requirements in relation to paper-based data' and is admissible as evidence.[41]

This provision enabled digital signatures to comply with little or no modification, but the main competing technology, biometric signatures, was not designed to include third party identity certification. As a consequence, Article 5(1) of the directive favours the former as against the latter. This apparent lack of technology neutrality has been noted,[42] but is not the point. Once the legislators had decided that identity certification was necessary to achieve the formality necessary to grant e-signatures legal validity (at least in civil law countries), that choice would necessarily discriminate against non-certified e-signature technology. The question is whether neutrality could potentially be restored by modifications to the technology discriminated against, and it is clear that there is no insuperable barrier to incorporating identity certification into biometric signature technologies.[43] The fact that this has not been undertaken is explained by the lack of economic demand for e-signatures of either kind, and not because of the law's discriminatory effect.

Had the directive imposed a requirement to meet a technical standard in order for an e-signature to achieve legal validity[44] it would have not have been potentially technology-neutral legislation. Because, however, its requirements are at least theoretically achievable for non-digital-signature technologies, the directive exhibits some minimum level of technology neutrality.

---

[40] See recital 20 of the directive: 'national law lays down different requirements for the legal validity of handwritten signatures; whereas certificates can be used to confirm the identity of a person signing electronically; advanced electronic signatures . . . can be regarded as legally equivalent to handwritten signatures only if the requirements for handwritten signatures are fulfilled'.

[41] It is noteworthy that the UK's implementation of the directive in the Electronic Communications Act 2000 and the Electronic Signatures Regulations 2002, SI 2002/318 does not enact Art 5(1) expressly, because as already explained, under English law *all* signature methods have equivalent legal effect except where a personal signature is required.

[42] See eg Susanna Frederick Fischer, 'Saving Rosencrantz and Guildenstern in a Virtual World? A Comparative Look at Recent Global Electronic Signature Legislation' (2001) 7 BUJSTL 229, 236; Report from the Commission to the European Parliament and the Council on the operation of Directive 1999/93/EC on a Community framework for electronic signatures, COM (2006) 120 final, 15 March 2006, s 2.3.2.

[43] It is even theoretically possible to produce a manually typed signature to an electronic document which complies with Art 5(1)—cameras could simultaneously record the typing and the face of the typist, and the output of those cameras could be encrypted with a message digest of the document and a third-party-certified picture of the signatory in a way which meets the directive's other requirements. This would be a cumbersome and ultimately pointless exercise, as the encryption process would most easily be performed using digital-signature technology, but the fact that it is technically achievable demonstrates that Art 5(1) is at least *potentially* technology neutral in the sense discussed here.

[44] As was the case for the German Digital Signature Act (Signaturgesetz) 1997 and Ordinance (Signaturverordnung) 1997.

A similar approach was taken in those parts of the EU Electronic Commerce Directive[45] which regulate online contracting. For example, Article 11(2) provides:

Member States shall ensure that, except when otherwise agreed by parties who are not consumers, the service provider makes available to the recipient of the service appropriate, effective and accessible technical means allowing him to identify and correct input errors, prior to the placing of the order.

At that time many e-commerce technology platforms did not provide this functionality, and Article 11(2) therefore discriminated against these implementation of the technology. In spite of this the directive has not been criticized for its lack of technology neutrality. The legislative aim was to ensure that the technology was operated in the specified manner, and the offending platforms were modifiable, and have since been modified, to enable online sellers to comply with Article 11(2).

Can Technology Neutrality Achieve its Aims?

Future-proofing means producing law and regulation which can continue to apply to new technological developments without constant amendment. 'Regulation that is based on specific technology can quickly become outdated, and may lead to inefficient investment by market players.'[46] It should be clear that technology-indifferent regulation avoids this trap, unless a technological advance is so disruptive that it effectively overturns the implicit assumptions on which that regulation is based.[47] Doubts have been expressed, however, whether the other techniques for attempting technology neutrality are capable of sufficient foresight to achieve future-proofing:

it has to be said that technological neutrality is not always desirable. Applied to a regulation, it means that the regulation will apply to new technologies, the invention or development of which cannot be foreseen. The pre-regulation of those technologies may produce undesirable consequences and even prevent the deployment of new technologies.[48]

These doubts may not be well founded. Although there are many examples of laws becoming outdated by innovations in cyberspace, in most cases their failure to achieve the original legislative aims was caused primarily by changes in the underlying

[45] Directive 2000/31/EC on electronic commerce OJ L 178, 1, 17 July 2000.

[46] Communication from the Commission to the European Parliament, the Council, the Economic and Social Committee, and the Committee of the Regions, 'Towards a New Framework for Electronic Communications Infrastructure and Associated Services: The 1999 Communications Review', COM (1999) 539 final, 10 November 1999, 14, n 6. See also Koops (n 10), 87–9, using the term 'sustainability'.

[47] Satellite broadcasting might be an example, producing a complete disconnect between the geographical location of the broadcaster and recipient of the broadcast, and thus overturning the regulatory settlement for broadcasting which was based on geographical location. This was resolved in the EU by applying the regulation of the country of uplink—Directive 89/552/EEC, now replaced by Directive 97/36/EC and to be replaced from 2008 by the Audiovisual Media Services Directive art 2(4) (24 May 2007 draft).

[48] Daniel J Gervais, 'Towards a New Core International Copyright Norm: The Reverse Three-step Test' (2005) 9 Marq Intell Prop L Rev 1.

business models for use of these technologies, rather than by over-specific regulation of particular technologies.[49] From this, one might conclude that if other aspects of the legislation are satisfactory, a technology-neutral approach can provide a useful degree of future-proofing to the law.

However, it is common for lawmakers to assert that achieving technology-neutral regulation will encourage the development and uptake of the regulated technology. In this they often exhibit a charming, if naive, idealism about what law-making can achieve which is not always identifiable in their other activities. Many of the legal instruments which attempt to regulate online activities specifically claim that they will encourage those activities.[50] It must, however, be doubted whether legislation on its own can ever achieve this aim. Some technologies, of which e-money is a prime example, have been solutions in search of a problem ever since their invention.[51] Others, such as e-signatures, have so far failed to find widespread acceptance because the cost of the technology infrastructure outweighs the potential benefits of its use, though in the case of e-signatures this may change as the costs of identity theft continue to rise.[52] In neither case did regulation do much, if anything, to encourage use of the technology. By contrast, digital music downloading has flourished in spite of the fact that the vast majority of downloads are in breach of the law. Technologies are adopted because of their perceived benefits, rather than because they are legally sanctioned.

---

[49] Chapter 8, and for a more detailed analysis see Chris Reed, 'The Law of Unintended Consequences—Embedded Business Models in IT Regulation' (2007) 1 JILT, part 2, <http://www2.warwick.ac.uk/fac/soc/law/elj/jilt/>.

[50] Some of these claims are particularly extravagant, such as the assertion in the Proposal for a European Parliament and Council directive on the taking up, the pursuit and the prudential supervision of the business of electronic money institutions, COM (1998) 0461 final, OJ C317, 15 October 1998, 7 that the proposed legislation:

> will create legal certainty, encourage new market entrants, encourage competition, and contribute generally to the development of electronic commerce.

Other examples might include the European Parliament resolution of 17 July 1998 (A4-0189/98) on the proposed e-Signatures Directive; Australian Broadcasting Services Act 1992 s 4(3)(c) (as amended); Communication from the Commission to the European Parliament, the Council, the European Economic and Social Committee, and the Committee of the Regions, 'Radio Frequency Identification (RFID) in Europe: Steps towards a Policy Framework' COM (2007) 96, para 3.5.

[51] The origins of the technological concept of stored value e-money lie in the late 1980s—see eg David Chaum, Amos Fiat, and Moni Naor, 'Untraceable Electronic Cash' in Shafi Goldwasser (ed), *Advances in Cryptology: Proceedings of CRYPTO '88* (Berlin: Springer-Verlag, 1990), 319–27—and the first operational system, Mondex (<http://www.mondex.com>), was invented by Tim Jones and Graham Higgins in 1990 with in-house trials at NatWest in 1992. Initially stored value e-money was proclaimed to be a solution to the problem of low-value payments where giving change was difficult, such as car parking, then as a solution to the problem of payment over the internet, and most recently as a technology for mobile telephony payments. In each case, simpler technologies have proved commercially more effective.

[52] UK government estimates of this cost were £1.3 billion per annum in 2002, rising to £1.7 billion in 2006—see <http://www.identity-theft.org.uk>—though it is unclear what proportion of the cost is due to online activities.

Achieving the aims of technology neutrality necessarily requires it to be possible to draft the law in technology-neutral terms. Some authors doubt whether this is ever achievable:

Language cannot be completely technology-neutral; it is impossible to draft legislation with sufficient precision and clarity that addresses every possible future technical variation.[53]

Others are more sanguine about the prospects of success:

Where regulation is drafted in technology neutral terms (for example, 'any means of transport', 'any means of communication', 'any means of human reproduction', or the like), a literal interpretation will keep the law connected to the technology.[54]

The most important element in determining whether technology-neutral drafting is possible is the extent to which the legislator not only understands the workings of the technology, but more importantly can predict how it will be used by cyberspace actors. We have seen in previous chapters many examples of failure in this respect. One example is the EU Databases Directive,[55] whose drafters wrongly assumed that the generation of valuable information, and its dissemination via databases, would be undertaken by different entities. We saw in Chapter 9 how this drafting led the courts to deny protection to most single-source databases. Similarly the assumption in the EU e-Signatures Directive that certification-service-providers would themselves take evidence of a signatory's identity created a liability gap because this function is most commonly performed by a different entity, a registration authority.

Even if this matter is properly understood, drafting in technologically neutral terms is a challenging exercise. By definition the law cannot be very specific about the subject matter that it regulates, which at least avoids the risk of excessive detail and precision which we saw in Chapter 8. The main danger seems to be that the drafter will go too far in the other direction. Escudero-Pascual and Hosein point us to the laws regulating the interception of communications data,[56] where an unsuccessful attempt to achieve technology neutrality has resulted in a law whose meaning is so vague that its application to the technology is often a matter of guesswork. In the House of Lords debate on the UK Regulation of Investigatory Powers Bill 2000, the Earl of Northesk was provoked to remark:

One of the many difficulties I have with the Bill is that, in its strident efforts to be technology neutral, it often conveys the impression that either it is ignorant of the way in which current technology operates, or pretends that there is no technology at all.[57]

The line between excessive and insufficient detail is a fine one in any case, and attempting technology-neutral drafting makes it easier to miss the target.

---

[53] Lyria Bennett Moses, 'Understanding Legal Responses to Technological Change: The Example of In Vitro Fertilization' (2005) 6 Minn J L Sci & Tech 505, 578.

[54] Roger Brownsword, 'Regulating Human Genetics: New Dilemmas for a New Millennium' (2004) 12 Med L Rev 14, 31 (footnotes omitted).

[55] Directive 96/9 on the legal protection of databases OJ L77, 27 March 1996, 20.

[56] Alberto Escudero-Pascual and Ian Hosein, 'The Hazards of Technology-Neutral Policy: Questioning Lawful Access to Traffic Data' (2004) 47 *Communications of the ACM* 77.

[57] *Hansard*, House of Lords, 28 June, 2000 (Committee Stage), col 1012.

One real danger of the technology-neutrality approach is that it can tempt legislators into regulating prospectively, before it is properly understood how a new technology will be used and what problems the regulation will actually need to solve. The results of a rush to make law are not always flexible enough to deal with the technology as it develops. Lawmakers need to understand that they are not regulating technology as an end in itself, but rather the commercial and social consequences of actors adopting that technology. It is unsafe to make law before these consequences are apparent and understood:

> In the mid-90s, and still oft quoted today, technological neutrality is preached as a standard by which regulation in this field should be measured. Yet, technology is not neutral, ICTs are fundamentally altering the landscape and creating unique issues that policy-makers have to be prepared to address. One principle that would seem to stand the test of time, however, is that of allowing law to lag behind developments, rather than try to anticipate markets. The focus of the Electronic Signatures Directive on certification services, as the basis of a trust industry perceived critical to the mass take-up of electronic commerce, seems, to date, to be an example of how policy-makers can effectively regulate a market to a standstill.[58]

The most nearly future-proof law is perhaps one which manages to achieve true equivalence between the online regulation of an activity and its offline regulation. We saw in Chapter 7[59] that such laws are likely to concentrate on the intention of actors and the outcome of their behaviours, rather than on the behaviours themselves or the means used to carry them out. Such a law will necessarily be technology-indifferent, and thus achieve technology neutrality without further effort on the lawmaker's part. We also saw, though, that in most cases a complete reconsideration and reform of the offline law would be needed. Lawmakers have limited time and resources, and so are only likely to attempt this in a minority of instances.

Non-future-proof Laws

Finally, we need to recognize that it is often too early, or too difficult, to attempt to future-proof the law. If the technology, or the ways in which it will be used, are not fully understood then a *technology-specific* approach is likely to produce better law. Specificity is often rejected at the outset because technology neutrality has been hailed so loudly as the only correct way to proceed in cyberspace. Provided the law's normative aims are sufficiently clear to receive respect from cyberspace users, and not (for example) obscured by excessive detail, such an approach can provide increased certainty as to the scope of the law and what needs to be done to comply with it.[60] As a consequence, the level of compliance is likely to be higher, and the

---

[58] Ian Walden, 'Regulating Electronic Commerce: Europe in the Global E-conomy' (2001) EL Rev 26(6) 529, 546.

[59] Ch 7, *Mental states and the outcomes of behaviour*.

[60] As an example from a different field of technology, the UK Road Vehicles (Construction and Use) Regulations 1986 SI 1986/1078 appear to be so clear in their application that there is only one case since 2000 which turns on the interpretation of those regulations (*Lord-Castle v DPP* [2009] EWHC 87 (QB)).

compliance costs lower, than would be the case if legal advice were needed as to the meaning and application of the law regulation. A further benefit of technology-specific regulation is that its effects will not spill over into other fields of activity, forcing unwanted behavioural change in those fields.[61]

Technology specificity does, of course, have a cost. It is immediately apparent that technological change will challenge such regulation, and that it is very likely that the regulation will not cope adequately with that change. This forces the law-maker to reconsider the regulation at regular intervals,[62] thus ensuring that the law keeps pace with technological and other changes. This may not be so great a disad vantage as it might at first appear—as we have seen, purportedly technology-neutral regulation is not necessarily good at coping with change either.[63]

The major part of this cost is the legislative time and effort required to keep technology-specific regulation up to date. Perhaps, though, this is an inevitable con-sequence of a world in which technological change occurs rapidly and in seemingly unpredictable directions.[64] As Brownsword has noted in relation to the equally problematic technology of genetics:

[If] there is a genuine question about whether (and, if so, where) the new technology falls within the spirit and intent of the regulatory scheme . . . it is entirely appropriate that

---

[61] See Lionel Bently, 'Copyright and the Victorian Internet: Telegraphic Property Laws in Colonial Australia' (2004) 38 Loy LA L Rev 71, 176:

> The experience of the 1870s may, however, remind us that technology-specific laws can be valuable, particularly where the goal is not outright prohibition. As we have seen, the goal of the prohibition on copying news was to facilitate the organization of economic relationships for dissemination and, in turn, to provide a legal mechanism for cost sharing. There was no need to extend the laws beyond news sent by telegraphy, nor necessarily to anticipate that later technologies of transmission would involve the same problems. Moreover, the impor-tance of limiting the telegraphic property laws to news sent by electronic telegraph was to enable existing journalistic practices of appropriation, typically with attribution, to continue unaffected. The telegraphic property laws were formulated narrowly to meet the particular problem with a corresponding solution and to leave others alone.

> Today, the drive for 'technologically neutral' laws, such as those that would broaden the notion of 'reproduction,' comes equally with the danger of bringing perfectly acceptable social practices into the realm of law, unintentionally replacing traditions with negotiations, and unnecessarily juridifying life worlds. A review of the story of the telegraphic property laws reminds us that technological neutrality is not always ideal.

[62] The Road Vehicles (Construction and Use) Regulations 1986 have been amended more than 20 times since their enactment.

[63] '[A] good technology-neutral solution of today is not guaranteed to make sense in relation to a future technology simply because it is technology-neutral' (Dan Jerker B Svantesson, 'The Characteristics Making Internet Communication Challenge Traditional Models of Regulation: What Every International Jurist Should Know about the Internet' (2005) 13 Int'l J L & Info Tech 39, 64).

[64] 'Our perspective of the sustainability of laws is influenced greatly by the past, and law-making processes are still largely the same as they were in the pre-ICT era. But time is a relative matter. The rate of change in current society is much higher than it used to be, and it might therefore be necessary to adapt our requirements of sustainability accordingly. In the industrial era, there may have been a require-ment that laws should be sustainable for a period of, say, twenty or thirty years, but such a period seems much too long in the ICT era . . . It seems pointless these days to require telecommunications laws to last for decades, and the same holds for many other ICT laws' (Koops (n 10), 89).

regulatory resource should be committed to further debate and decision concerning the new technology.[65]

The problem, of course, is that legislators are reluctant to re-examine issues which they believe they have already solved. Although technology-neutral law is clearly a desirable thing to aim at, lawmakers must not treat it as a substitute for investing the effort necessary to decide whether their regulatory objectives have been achieved, and to remedy the law's inevitable defects.

---

[65] Roger Brownsword, 'Regulating Human Genetics: New Dilemmas for a New Millennium' (2004) 12 Med L Rev 14, 32.

PART IV

LAW-MAKING

12

Revisiting the Modalities of Regulation

In Chapter 1 we touched briefly on Lessig's analysis of the modalities of regulation. His model places the individual in the centre of a set of regulatory pressures, exerted by law, social norms, markets, and the architecture of the space in which the individual acts. The combined effect of these pressures is what controls, or at least strongly influences, the behaviour of the individual. The architecture of cyberspace consists of the computer code which determines the shape and functionality of that space. This differs from the other three modalities in an important respect—it exerts *ex ante* control over behaviour, rather than influencing the will of the individual through incentives or through sanctions or consequences after the fact, and thus offers a potentially perfect form of behavioural control. Lessig concludes that it is inappropriate for such a strong instrument of control to operate in secret, embodying only the choices made by private bodies such as corporations, and subject to influence by the demands of government.[1] Instead choice needs to be returned to the user, in effect re-establishing democratic control over code.[2]

Although Lessig's thesis initially generated substantial interest, it has had far less influence on subsequent theoretical work than might have been expected, and almost no influence on the practice of lawmakers. Mayer-Schönberger writes:

It is perhaps surprising ... that few in legal academia have subjected Lessig's work to a thorough examination ... Lessig's views are either referred to and cited with slightly muted

---

[1] Mayer-Schönberger summarizes the argument neatly:

Lessig believes that governments will desire to rebuild cyberspace as an architecture of control—in part to reclaim the control that governments may have lost over cyberspace due to its decentralized, packet-switched nature, and in part because of the general tendency of governments to desire control over society. As a result, governments will move from directly constraining behavior with East Coast Code to indirectly constraining behavior with laws that regulate West Coast Code. Such indirect regulation is much less transparent and thus less likely to face the stiff public opposition that has kept the government within our society's system of checks and balances. Lessig is also worried that the plasticity of software allows governments to constrain behavior more easily and to a greater extent than they could through law alone. Corporations will work with government to change the architecture of cyberspace because they, too, profit from a more controllable space. [Viktor Mayer-Schönberger, 'Demystifying Lessig' (2008) Wis L Rev 713, 718]

[2] This can be top-down control, via democratically made law, or bottom-up control through the use of open-source code which permits the individual to modify the code if its controls are unsatisfactory.

appreciation—as an appropriate, but not too ostentatious nod towards the star—or used as building blocks for new instantiations of a Lessigian narrative.[3]

It seems to me that this is because whilst it was obviously true (once pointed out) that code can perform a regulatory function, even at the time it was by no means clear that the use of code to regulate behaviour in cyberspace would develop as Lessig predicted. With the benefit of a decade's hindsight we can see that code's role has not so far developed in that way, nor does it seems likely to do so.

Lessig's predictions were erroneous because his thesis contains two fundamental flaws. The first is a misunderstanding of the ways in which the modalities of regulation interact. The second, and more fundamental, is his belief in the perfection of control which is possible via code.

The Interplay between the Modalities of Regulation

In Lessig's visualization of his model[4] the individual is represented as a dot surrounded by the four regulatory influences. Each of these exerts regulatory pressure on the individual, represented by arrows. The dot is in a similar situation to a cork floating on the ocean, tossed hither and thither by external forces—indeed, Lessig describes it as 'pathetic'.[5] The individual's freedom of action is highly constrained by these pressures.

In a sophistication of the model Lessig then adds further arrows of regulatory pressure, emanating from the modality of law and influencing the other three modalities.[6] In other words, he asserts that law can be used to control the way that markets work, to establish or change social norms, and to mandate the workings of the code which makes up the architecture of cyberspace.

If Lessig's model is accurate then the lawmaker's task is, conceptually at least, a simple one. All that needs to be done is to decide first what behaviour the individual dot should be coerced into, and then to determine which of the regulatory modalities needs to be modified in order to effect that coercion. Laws can then be devised to achieve that modification, and thus the desired behaviour. But is this how regulation actually works?

Mayer-Schönberger makes two criticisms of Lessig's thesis. The first, which though convincing is not relevant here, is that Lessig's preferred solution of user choice between technologies, facilitated by laws which remove information asymmetries so as to facilitate a properly informed choice, is unlikely to lead to the results which Lessig desires.[7] The second builds on earlier criticisms by Post,[8] that Lessig takes a deterministic view of markets which is not borne out by the way in which they

---

[3] Viktor Mayer-Schönberger (n 1), 714.
[4] Lawrence Lessig, *Code and Other Laws of Cyberspace* (New York: Basic Books, 1999), 88.
[5] Ibid, 87.
[6] Ibid, 93.
[7] Viktor Mayer-Schönberger (n 1), 728–36.
[8] David G Post, 'What Larry Doesn't Get: Code, Law, and Liberty in Cyberspace' (2000) 52 Stan L Rev 1439.

actually operate in cyberspace. Mayer-Schönberger identifies that this determinism also clouds Lessig's view of the way in which technology develops. Not only do consumer choices not inevitably lead to market preferences for the freedom Lessig is seeking, but also those market preferences often fail to produce technological architectures which give effect to those user choices:[9]

Such a view of technological innovation has been thoroughly criticized in the science and technology literature as omitting the myriad of individual actors and mechanisms that influence the development and use of technological innovations over time. Detailed studies from Bakelite, to light bulbs, to bicycles, to dikes, to the electrical power system, to the telephone have shown that the interplay between technology and society is both vastly more complex and bidirectional than Lessig's model, with societal processes (much beyond the simplistic metaphor of the invisible hand of commerce) influencing technology as technology influences society.[10]

In place of a one-way flow of coercive communications, we find instead a complex network of interactions between individual cyberspace users, code producers, lawmakers, and markets. Communication and feedback through that network results in an evolutionary development of technology, rather than simply determining its shape as a result of pressure from a 'higher' authority (such as markets or law). As an example, cookies were developed by code producers to solve a range of problems but were then used by e-commerce providers for a different purpose. Users objected to some of those uses on privacy grounds, and technologists then modified cookie technology to address those concerns. 'This happened without a legal threat and against obvious economic rationality.'[11]

What this tells us is that that the relationship between the modalities of regulation is not a linear one, as Lessig proposes. Instead there is continuous communication and interaction between them, through which process the regulatory settlement evolves, rather than being imposed. Indeed, the term 'settlement' is somewhat misleading—at some point an evolutionarily stable situation will be reached, but this will persist only until some disruptive technology disturbs the settlement and restarts the evolutionary process. The story of the development of encryption controls in Chapter 2 is an example of such evolution, and we have seen in several places in this book how the disruptive technologies of cyberspace have restarted evolution of the copyright settlement, which is clearly far from reaching a stable settlement at present.

Murray's work takes us even further though. In *The Regulation of Cyberspace*[12] he tells us that the subject of regulation is not the individual alone, but instead the whole mass of individuals to whom the regulation applies. This mass is also an intercommunicating network, and collectively can apply substantial pressure on markets, law and code. The subject of regulation is no mere 'pathetic dot', but rather an

---

[9] Viktor Mayer-Schönberger (n 1), 736–45.
[10] Ibid, 739.
[11] Ibid, 743.
[12] Andrew Murray, *The Regulation of Cyberspace* (Abingdon: Routledge-Cavendish, 2007).

active matrix of dots[13] which act, collectively, as a powerful player in the shaping of the regulatory settlement. The combined weight of this collective regulatory pressure can result in the rejection of some innovation in law or code,[14] or can subvert or modify the expected effect of that innovation.[15]

Thus an accurate diagram representing the forces which, in combination, produce the current regulatory settlement would connect each element to every other element with two-way arrows. Laws influence markets, norms, and code, but these in their turn influence law, and of course each other. The collective preferences and choices of cyberspace users influence all four of these modalities. Any apparently stable balance in these forces is merely temporary, and the consequences of change at any part of the network are inevitably unpredictable.[16]

It is worth considering the active matrix of cyberspace users in a little more depth. Clearly, markets are in fact the outcome of the aggregate choices of these users, acting either as suppliers or consumers. Law and code constrain those choices, and thus help shape the market, but we have seen at numerous points in this book that law is powerless to establish a market on its own,[17] or to constrain it in ways which that aggregate of choosers will not accept.[18]

More importantly, though, the matrix of cyberspace users is also the source of social norms. What, after all, is a norm but the collective view of a grouping about how its members *ought* to behave? It has been a central theme of this book that norms play by far the most important role in regulating cyberspace.

The role of norms in securing compliance with the law is underestimated generally,[19] and almost universally in relation to cyberspace. Although Lessig accepts that norms play a role, and that law can influence norms (though not, seemingly, vice versa),[20] for the most part in *Code and Other Laws of Cyberspace*, norms are little more than background noise.[21] Even Murray's more sophisticated and nuanced

---

[13] Andrew Murray, *Information Technology Law: The Law and Society* (Oxford: Oxford University Press, 2010), 68.

[14] Ibid, 69–70 (anti-pornography laws and DRM code).

[15] eg, the response of e-commerce businesses to the EU's taxation regime for information products which we examined in Ch 6, or the new uses for cookies explained above by Viktor Mayer-Schönberger.

[16] Andrew Murray (n 12), citing WR Ashby, 'Variety, Constraint and the Law of Requisite Variety' in W Buckley (ed), *Modern Systems Research for the Behavioural Scientist* (Chicago: Aldine, 1968).

[17] See eg the examples given in Ch 11.

[18] See eg the example of music file sharing in Ch 1.

[19] eg although HLA Hart in *The Concept of Law*, 2nd edn (Oxford: Oxford University Press, 1994) accepts that obedience to the law is dependent on general acceptance of the social norm that it should be obeyed (112–18), his primary distinction is between norms, which are obeyed only because of social pressure, and law, which is obeyed because it emanates from official law-making sources. We saw in Ch 7 that, in cyberspace at least, whether or not rules are obeyed is largely dependent on norms, and not on the status of those rules as laws.

[20] Lawrence Lessig (n 4), 92–3.

[21] See ibid, Ch 12, which discusses free speech. Norms receive very little attention, and then only to explain how the norms *restricting* free speech are rendered powerless by cyberspace code.

modelling of cyberspace regulation sees the role of norms as primarily that of self-regulation within communities.[22]

But, as I hope to have demonstrated in Parts II and III, <u>cyberspace actors are likely to obey those laws which they think ought to be obeyed</u>, and <u>ignore those whose authority they do not accept</u>, or whose obligations they find meaningless. This is <u>irrespective of whether those laws are actually applicable or enforceable against them.</u>

The Limits of Code's Control

This discussion of the modalities of regulation would be largely irrelevant if code were able to achieve the perfect control over cyberspace users which Lessig envisages.[23] Undesired behaviour would not be possible, and so our main concern would focus on the processes through which code controls are devised. Law, markets, and (perhaps) norms might exert pressure on code writers, but the individual cyberspace user would be relegated to impotence, except insofar as he might be able to influence laws and markets. As Murray writes:

in the man-made environment of the digital sphere our ability to change the design of that place with a few well placed keystrokes means that the use of architecture as a modality of control . . . is increasingly in evidence and is increasingly effective.[24]

The short history of code in cyberspace indicates, however, that perfection of control may be unachievable. One reason for this is inherent in the nature of code itself. In theory at least, any code control is capable of circumvention by other code. The second reason is that the modalities of markets and norms (and perhaps, though to a lesser extent, law) have so far proved stronger than the desires of code writers.

The subversion of code controls by code has been apparent for many years. Even before the advent of cyberspace, worms[25] and viruses[26] were well known. Once email became widely used, spam-message writers began their long-running battle with writers of email filtering code and spammer databases, a battle which shows no sign of reaching any conclusion. DVD makers introduced the CSS (Content Scrambling System) technology in 1996 to prevent digital copying of DVDs, and in 1999 the DeCSS counter-code became available.[27]

---

[22] Andrew Murray (n 12), Ch 5.

[23] Lawrence Lessig (n 4), 6.

[24] Andrew Murray (n 13), 70.

[25] The experimental Creeper code, written in 1971, is said to have been the first worm—Richard E Schantz, 'BBN's Network Computing Software Infrastructure and Distributed Applications (1970–1990)' (2006) 28(3) *IEE Annals of the History of Computing* 72, 74.

[26] Cohen claims to have written the first virus in 1983—Fred Cohen, 'Computer Viruses: Theory and Experiments' (1987) 6 *Computers and Security*, 22.

[27] The alleged author of DeCSS, Norwegian programmer John Johansen, was acquitted of hacking charges in relation to DeCSS in 2003, and his acquittal upheld on appeal later that year—Bogarting Appellate Court, 22 December 2003. For a fuller account of the DeCSS saga see Andrew Murray (n 12), 192–200.

Conflicts of this kind are technological instances of evolutionary arms races.[28] The standard biological example is the race between gazelles and cheetahs. Gazelles which run faster than other gazelles are less likely to be eaten, and therefore leave more offspring. The same is true of faster cheetahs, as a slow cheetah catches no gazelles and starves before reproducing. Thus over time both populations become faster runners. The race ends when one population is unable to evolve to keep up with the other, in which case the loser population may become extinct, or more likely (as in the case of gazelles and cheetahs) when an evolutionarily stable state is reached. In our example this occurs when for both sides the costs of running faster, in terms of energy required, balance the risk of being eaten (or not eating).[29]

At present, code arms races are not halted by these kinds of internal constraint, because the available speed of computer processing increases continually and its cost decreases also. Thus spam is still with us, and encryption security needs constantly to be improved because those seeking to crack encryption technologies have more computing power available to do so each year.

However, code arms races have regularly been ended by external constraints, either from the market or from norms. In the case of DeCSS, for example, it was not possible for the DVD makers to devise counter-technologies because this would have rendered the installed customer base of DVD players redundant, and thus severely damaged the market for DVD sales. The use of DeCSS clearly contravenes the prohibition on overcoming technical protection measures, introduced by Article 11 of the WIPO Copyright Treaty,[30] but the difficulties in enforcing this prohibition against users has meant that, in practice, CSS is largely redundant.

In the case of Apple's Fairplay DRM, which was introduced in 2003 and imposed technical restrictions on copying downloads from the Apple iTunes Store, the arms race continued for a number of years, with various anti-Fairplay technologies countered in successive releases of iTunes.[31] However, in 2007 Apple announced that Fairplay would be abandoned, and iTunes downloads supplied with no copy restrictions.[32] Publicly, Apple claimed to be motivated by the effort required to keep ahead in the arms race and the potential risks if it lost what was likely to be a prolonged and uncertain battle.[33] It seems probable also, though, that a combination of the strong social norm that purchasers of music should be free to copy it to all their music-playing devices,[34] together with the likelihood that competing DRM-free music

---

[28] On biological arms races see Richard Dawkins, *The Extended Phenotype* (Oxford: Oxford University Press, 1982), Ch 4.

[29] There is actually a far wider range of potential outcomes than this simplistic explanation suggests—see ibid.

[30] See eg *Universal Studios v Reimerdes*, 111 F Supp 2d 294 (SDNY, 2000) and *Universal City Studios v Corley*, 273 F 3d 429 (2nd Cir, 2001), decided under the US Digital Millennium Copyright Act.

[31] See <http://en.wikipedia.org/wiki/FairPlay#Circumvention>.

[32] <http://www.apple.com/pr/library/2007/04/02Apple-Unveils-Higher-Quality-DRM-Free-Music-on-the-iTunes-Store.html>.

[33] 'DRMs haven't worked, and may never work, to halt music piracy' (Steve Jobs, 'Thoughts on Music', 6 February 2007, <http://www.apple.com/uk/hotnews/thoughtsonmusic/>).

[34] See Ch 2.

would very soon become available on the market,[35] were also important factors in this decision.

This leads us to the second reason why code fails to achieve perfect control over user behaviour. Code's controls do not operate in a regulatory vacuum. They are influenced by the other modalities of regulation, and most strongly by the norms of cyberspace users. If users had thought that copying DVDs and music downloads was morally reprehensible, neither DeCSS nor the various anti-Fairplay technologies would have been adopted by users.

On a number of occasions Facebook has been confronted by the outrage of its users and thereby forced to modify its code. In 2007 it launched Beacon, an advertisement system which, when a Facebook user transacted with a partner company, immediately posted details of the transaction to that user's Facebook newsfeed. As a consequence, these details were immediately sent to other Facebook users who subscribed to that newsfeed.[36] User opposition grew rapidly, and within a month the code was changed to make Beacon an opt-in system, rather than opt-out.[37] As a result of the settlement in a class action brought by Facebook users, Beacon was finally discontinued in 2009 and a Privacy Foundation for Facebook was established.[38]

A mere eighteen months later in February 2009, Facebook generated more controversy when it unilaterally deleted a section from its terms which read:

You may remove your User Content from the Site at any time. If you choose to remove your User Content, the licence granted above shall automatically expire, however you acknowledge that the Company may retain archived copies of your User Content.

The effect of deleting this term would have been that Facebook would have unlimited rights to use content indefinitely, under the licence granted when users signed up. This licence permits use by Facebook for any purposes whatsoever. Once a journalist discovered the change and alerted users, over 38,000 of them joined a Facebook group to protest at the change[39] and there was substantial adverse publicity in the media. Within a few days, Facebook was forced to announce that it was reinstating the term.[40]

Facebook has a track record of attempting to use code to share the data of its users as widely as possible,[41] but in large part these code controls have been opposed

---

[35] See 'EMI Takes Lock Off Music Tracks', < http://news.bbc.co.uk/1/hi/technology/6516189.stm>.

[36] As an example it is reported that one user purchased a diamond as a present for his wife, and was naturally upset when she immediately learnt about it via Facebook, <http://www.insidefacebook. com/2010/03/18/facebooks-beacon-settlement-approved-by-judge/>.

[37] Mark Zuckerberg, 'Thoughts on Beacon', 5 December 2007, <http://blog.facebook.com/blog. php?post=7584397130>.

[38] Order of Judge Seeborg, C 08-3845 RS, 17 March 2010. See 'Case Comment: Lane v Facebook Inc: United States—privacy—internet' (210) 16(1) CTLR N5.

[39] Nick Graham and Helen Anderson, 'Are Individuals Waking Up to the Privacy Implications of Social Networking Sites?' (2010) 32 EIPR 99, 101.

[40] BBC News, 'Facebook "Withdraws" Data Changes', 18 February 2009, <http://news.bbc.co. uk/1/hi/technology/7896309.stm>.

[41] See eg BBC News, 'Facebook Faces Criticism on Privacy Change', 10 December 2009, <http:// news.bbc.co.uk/1/hi/technology/8405334.stm>; BBC News, 'Facebook U-turns on Phone and Address Data Sharing', 18 January 2011, <http://www.bbc.co.uk/news/technology-12214628>; BBC News,

successfully by users as being contrary to the social norms which they expect to govern their use of the service. Law has, of course, played a part, through the criticisms made by the EU's Article 29 Working Party[42] and a decision of the Canadian Privacy Commissioner,[43] but norms have proved equally effective, and far faster, in countering code controls.

Lessig offers us three examples[44] of areas in which code can exert its perfect control: intellectual property, privacy, and free speech. The Facebook example illustrates how imperfectly code controls privacy, and we have seen numerous examples throughout this book of code's failure to protect intellectual property rights. Is this also true for code controlling free speech?

Lessig's main example here is pornography. He discusses the ways in which cyberspace technologies could be used to control access to pornography, for example access by children, and to filter content in accordance with the preferences of individual users (or, of course, of governments).[45] Unfortunately for Lessig's thesis, neither of these technologies has developed sufficiently to enable effective control.

The identification technologies which Lessig envisaged could be used to control access by children are the identity-certification part of the e-signature infrastructure we have previously examined. As already noted, this infrastructure has simply not developed, for largely market-related reasons.[46] There is at present no effective system for online age verification which could be used to control access by means of code.

Content-filtering technologies work either by searching for linguistic semantics, ie evaluating the words used on a web page, or by trying to identify images whose proportion of skin-tone colours suggests they might be pornographic. Neither of these is terribly successful. Word-based filters result in a high level of over-blocking (the 'Scunthorpe problem',[47] most amusingly illustrated recently when an email from the Mayor of Dudley, a town in the English West Midlands, was flagged by software as offensive because it described his favourite local meal, faggots[48]) and have been widely criticized as unintentionally impairing free speech.[49] For very similar reasons, skin-tone filtering finds it difficult to distinguish between pornographic images and holiday beach photographs:

Flaws in the design and delivery of filtering technology result in filtering products that are unable to evaluate content effectively. While technology has a place in preventing access or

---

'Germans Question Facebook Tagging Privacy, 3 August 2011, <http://www.bbc.co.uk/news/technology-14391788>.

[42] Opinion 5/2009 on online social networking, 01189/09/EN WP 163, 12 June 2009.

[43] *CIPPIC v Facebook*, Case 2009-008, <http://www.priv.gc.ca/cf-dc/2009/2009_008_0716_e.cfm>.

[44] Lawrence Lessig (n 4), Chs 10–12.

[45] Ibid, 176–82.

[46] See Ch 7, n 69.

[47] <http://en.wikipedia.org/wiki/Scunthorpe_problem>.

[48] A type of meatball, traditionally eaten with mushy peas. 'Black Country Councillor Caught Up in Faggots Farce', *Birmingham Mail*, 24 February 2011.

[49] See eg Electronic Frontier Foundation and Online Policy Group, *Internet Blocking in Public Schools* (2003), 25–72, <http://web.archive.org/web/20070913184401/http://www.eff.org/Censorship/Censorware/net_block_report/net_block_report.pdf>.

pornographic material, the tools available today are not sufficient to serve as the sole arbiter of suitability.[50]

Far from code being able to control free speech, it appears that its primary capability is that of making free speech possible. It is noteworthy that those jurisdictions which censor speech extensively do so by means of continual human surveillance, the results of which are of course implemented in code.[51]

An important reason for code's failure to control free speech is the strongly entrenched free-speech norm. In the system operated by the UK Internet Watch Foundation (see Chapter 4), code is used by UK ISPs to block subscriber access to some websites containing sexual images. However, the system does not attempt to enforce the UK's laws relating to unlawful sexual content generally. Blocking is restricted to sites which contain images of child sexual abuse; other websites of a sexual nature remain unblocked, even if viewing or downloading their content amounts to an offence under UK law. This limited level of code control is the result of a normative assessment that the UK conception of free speech does not extend to images of child sexual abuse, but that it is likely to be contravened by any more extensive attempt to block unlawful material. And markets inevitably play a role as well. The economic cost of blocking child sexual-abuse material is a not unreasonable burden for ISPs, and thus their subscribers by way of charges, to bear. A more extensive attempt to block unlawful content would be far more costly, and would lead to the same kinds of disagreement about where those costs should fall as we saw for the UK Digital Economy Act scheme to deter file sharing.[52]

Law's Limits

I began this book by explaining that law is not, in cyberspace at least, a particularly effective mechanism for controlling the behaviour of cyberspace users. Nor, as we have seen elsewhere, is it able to establish markets on its own,[53] nor is it particularly successful in setting norms.[54] Some readers might be left wondering why we go to so much effort to make laws if they are incapable of achieving the results we want from them.

The answer is that law achieves many important things, but it does not do so by issuing commands which are inevitably obeyed. Most lawmakers would like it work

---

[50] Stefan C Dombrowski, Karen L Gischlar, and Theo Durst, 'Safeguarding Young People from Cyber Pornography and Cyber Sexual Predation: A Major Dilemma of the Internet' (2007) 16 *Child Abuse Review* 153, 164.

[51] See Yutian Ling, 'Free Speech and Privacy Online: A Legal-based and Market-based Approach for Internet Companies in China', (2010) 27 Santa Clara Computer & High Tech LJ 175, 179–87; Christopher Stevenson, 'Breaching the Great Firewall: China's Internet Censorship and the Quest for Freedom of Expression in a Connected World' (2007) 30 BC Int'l & Comp L Rev 531; Jonathan Zittrain and Benjamin Edelman, 'Internet Filtering in China' (2003) 7 *Internet Computing*, 70.

[52] 'Digital Economy Act: Further Delay to Illegal Downloading Measures', *The Guardian*, 28 March 2011.

[53] See eg Ch 11.

[54] See Ch 7.

in this way, and some appear, through wishful thinking, to believe that it does, but in reality law is a far more subtle and limited enterprise. It influences the behaviour of individuals, and also influences the other modalities of regulation (and is in turn itself influenced by them).

Law reinforces already-held social norms in two ways. First, by transposing these norms into law it makes a public statement that compliance with the norms is particularly important for the proper function of the lawmaker's community. Thus the norm that we should not kill each other is reinforced by the laws of murder and manslaughter, and the norm that we should keep our promises is given increased force, for certain types of promise, by the law of contract.

Law further reinforces the norms which it entrenches by prescribing state-sanctioned consequences for non-compliance. These might influence the behaviour of an individual who does not subscribe to the norm, so that he complies with it nevertheless. If he fails to do so, the law's enforcement mechanisms may be used to resolve the resulting disorder in the community.

This function of reinforcement, coupled with the social norm that the law should be respected, also gives law some limited power to establish norms. If a community disagrees over the proper content of a norm the law can resolve that disagreement. It is also possible, as we saw in Chapter 7, for law to influence the evolution of a norm in a particular direction, though only in gradual steps[55] and not in a direction which conflicts excessively with already-established norms.

Law also influences markets. It establishes a stable basis for their transactions without which they would be unlikely to operate effectively, as we saw in the case of eBay.[56] It also specifically regulates their conduct in some instances, such as the financial markets, though we have seen recently how difficult it can be for the regulation of a market to achieve its regulatory objectives, financial stability in that case. What cyberspace laws like the e-Money and e-Signatures Directives tell us is that law seems powerless to establish markets.

In theory law could also influence code, but there are remarkably few examples of it doing so. ICANN's Uniform Domain Name Dispute Resolution Policy[57] is an obvious instance, but the subject matter of the Policy, domain names, are pure code creations, and it is therefore unsurprising that enforcement of decisions under the rules is purely a matter of code. We find similar implementation of 'laws' through code in other pure code environments, such as virtual worlds and other online communities,[58] but outside that specialist area the main interaction of code and law is found in content-blocking lists, such as that maintained by the UK Internet Watch Foundation. In general the initial shape of code tends to be set by

---

[55] Dan M Kahan, 'Gentle Nudges vs Hard Shoves: Solving the Sticky Norms Problem' (2000) 67 U Chi L Rev 607.

[56] See Ch 1, pp 7–8; Jack Goldsmith and Tim Wu, *Who Controls the Internet? Illusions of a Borderless World* (New York: Oxford University Press, 2006), Ch 8.

[57] See Ch 6.

[58] Chris Reed, 'Why Must You Be Mean to Me?—Crime and the Online Persona' (2010) 13 New Criminal Law Review 485, 496–505.

markets, and its subsequent development influenced mainly by markets and norms.[59]

Cyberspace lawmakers cannot pretend that these limits on what law can achieve do not exist. Successful cyberspace law-making will need to understand law's limitations, and work within them.

---

[59] See the example of Facebook above.

13

Making Laws for Cyberspace

The main thrust of this book so far has been to persuade the reader of the need to shift perspective, from the lawmaker's intentions to the cyberspace actor's normative understanding. By making this shift I hope I have been able to shed light on the reasons why some laws work in cyberspace, in the sense of influencing actors to obey their rules, while others do not.

But the book is about law-making in cyberspace, and individual actors do not make laws.[1] This last chapter therefore needs to turn back to the lawmaker. In the light of this different perspective, how should lawmakers direct their enterprise of making laws which are effective in cyberspace?

Recognizing Limits

Lawmakers have traditionally proceeded on the basis that their law-making powers are limited only by the rules of their own legal system. These limits might be set out in a constitution, or in legislation,[2] or via case law or conventions which are applied by the courts. These internal limits recognize the rival claims of other lawmakers to similarly unlimited power through the rules of the lawmaker's state on applicable law and jurisdiction, though this category of limits on law-making power is somewhat grudgingly accepted and often ignored in practice. From the lawmaker's perspective the fact that its laws are useless, bad or even wicked, does not prevent them having authority so long as their collective effect is not so egregious as to induce citizens to rise up and overthrow the state.

If, though, the lawmaker desires to make law which is more widely obeyed than by its citizens alone, it needs to abandon its internal perspective and look at the matter from the point of view of those whom it desires to do the obeying. It then immediately becomes clear that there are severe constraints on what the lawmaker can do in the way of cyberspace law-making.

---

[1] However, as we have seen, the collective responses of individuals do influence the content of laws, and in a purely cyberspace community the collective consensus among actors about the norms which should apply in that community might become the effective law system for it—see Ch 7.

[2] See eg the UK Human Rights Act 1998, s 3 of which provides that legislation is to be interpreted by the courts in a way consistent with the Act.

Markets are one obvious constraint. They often fail to respond in the ways predicted or desired by the lawmaker, as we have seen in relation to e-signatures and e-money. Often markets simply ignore the law as irrelevant. For example, the demand from US citizens for online gambling is substantial, and efforts by US lawmakers to curb the provision of online gambling proved largely ineffective to reduce that demand until they undermined the economic basis of online gambling by making it difficult for US gamblers to place wagers or receive their winnings.[3]

The code of cyberspace also places constraints on lawmakers. There is no theoretical obstacle to a lawmaker forbidding the use of TCIP/IP or the HTML protocol by persons within its jurisdiction, but the effect of such a law (if obeyed) would simply be to cut that state off from internet connectivity.[4] More realistically a lawmaker might desire some categories of website to take age verification from all their users, so as to exclude children from accessing those websites, but there is currently no code infrastructure which makes this possible.

The most powerful constraint on law-making, as I have tried to demonstrate in the course of this book, is norms. Lawmakers benefit greatly from the social norm that laws should be obeyed, but this is part of the wider normative framework which guides the activities of cyberspace users. It is only one part of the full set of norms which such users apply, and does not necessarily override those other norms. Thus cyberspace users will not be likely to obey a law unless they accept that the lawmaker has authority over their activities, nor will they comply with a law whose content appears meaningless and thus unworthy of respect. Even if a law meets these tests, cyberspace has developed norms about the free exchange of information which may be sufficiently strong to override the norm that this law should be obeyed.

Murray proposes that lawmakers should devise their laws in the light of these constraints by means of a careful and scientific methodology:

First, regulators must produce a dynamic model of the regulatory matrix surrounding the action they wish to regulate (including a map of the communications networks already in place). From this they may design a regulatory intervention intended to harness the natural communications flow by offering to the subsystems, or nodes, within the matrix, a positive communication which encourages them to support the regulatory intervention. Finally they must monitor the feedback that follows this intervention. If the intervention is initially unsuccessful they should consider modifying it slightly and continuing to monitor the feedback in the hope of producing constant improvements. If successful, the positive feedback generated will reinforce the regulatory intervention, making it much more likely to succeed.[5]

In my view this methodology, theoretically justified though it might be, is not merely difficult (as Murray acknowledges) but in practice completely impossible to carry out. The complexities of interaction between cyberspace users, the norms each

---

[3] See Julia Hörnle and Brigitte Zamitt, *Cross-border Online Gambling Law and Policy* (Cheltenham: Edward Elgar, 2010), 114–18.

[4] See the discussion of the UN-devised OSI protocol for network communications, which was the preferred solution of many governments until ousted by the success of TCP/IP, in David G Post, *In Search of Jefferson's Moose* (New York: Oxford University Press, 2009), 140–1.

[5] Andrew Murray, *The Regulation of Cyberspace* (Abingdon: Routledge-Cavendish, 2007), 250.

community espouses (bearing in mind that there are a myriad of communities in cyberspace), the normative demands of all the lawmakers with claims over that activity (and not merely the demands of *this* lawmaker), and the operations of markets and code, would result in a model which is so complex that the effects of a regulatory intervention cannot be predicted. Indeed, the model might turn out to be chaotic,[6] which would give it little value in predicting the outcome of a regulatory intervention. Even if this were not so, following this methodology would make such large demands on lawmaker resources that very little law would be produced (though some readers might applaud that outcome, of course).

The best that can be managed is to develop a heuristic[7] approach to law-making. The suggestions which follow are therefore not certain to result in cyberspace laws which *will* be obeyed, but I am convinced that they greatly increase the *probability* of this happening.

Starting Points

The first step is for the lawmaker to make the perspective shift and examine the law-making proposal from the point of view of the cyberspace actor. The proper question should be, 'Will this law persuade the cyberspace actor to comply with it?' We have seen that this can be unpacked into two further questions: (a) will the actor respect that lawmaker's authority over this area of cyberspace activity? and (b) will the actor recognize the obligations set out in the law as having some sensible meaning? Sensible meaning requires not only that the law should be understandable and possible to obey, but also a clear connection between its obligations and the law's normative aim, so that obeying them is more than a mere compliance exercise and has some prospect of achieving that aim. The ways in which the lawmaker might answer these questions satisfactorily are explored under the next two headings.

Clearly these questions can only be answered if the lawmaker understands the environment in which the cyberspace actor is operating. It will be important to identify the other normative pressures on the actor, which will consist not only of generally accepted cyberspace norms but also the rules made by that lawmaker, and by other lawmakers, which claim to apply to the actor's activities. An investigation of all the world's laws is clearly impracticable, but it is a comparatively simple task to identify salient examples; most of these are cited and analysed in the growing corpus of texts on the law in cyberspace.

---

[6] A chaotic system is one in which tiny changes in one value can produce substantially different outcomes which vary depending on the starting state of the system. The weather is a typical example—glider pilots like myself know that a mere 0.5 degrees Celsius change in surface temperature can radically change the amount of cloud, which therefore changes the temperature further, and as a consequence cloudbases might rise or fall, the chance of rain will be very different, and so on. For those interested in chaos theory a suitable lay introduction is James Gleick, *Chaos: Making a New Science* (London: Penguin, 1988).

[7] This term comes from the artificial intelligence community, and might most simply be described as working via rules of thumb, derived from experience, which have been demonstrated to increase the chance that objectives will be achieved.

Norms are not the only part of the cyberspace landscape which needs to be understood. Lawmakers also need to identify how actors are actually conducting the activity in question in cyberspace, rather than assuming that it will be undertaken in the same way as in the physical world. The market's incentives for particular activities may also differ in cyberspace, and so these too need to be investigated. Finally the limitations placed on actors by code need to be understood, so that the lawmaker can frame its rules in a way which does not make compliance excessively difficult.[8]

Research on these matters is not particularly difficult or time consuming, but may be a novelty for some lawmakers. Where a lawmaker is regulating physical-world activities in its territory then the existing normative landscape is, in theory at least, already known. The ways in which activities are undertaken are likely to be common knowledge, unless they are unusually specialized. And of course, cyberspace's code constraints do not apply directly in the physical world.

The final starting point is for the lawmaker to recognize that law in cyberspace rarely achieves *control* of a user's activities. The primary aim must instead be to influence and persuade, which means that issues of control and enforcement should be considered mainly in relation to the minority who will refuse to comply with the law voluntarily. The technique of specifying the behaviour which must be engaged in, or avoided, in order to comply with the law may work in the physical world, but in cyberspace behaviours are altering constantly, even if the underlying activity remains in essence the same. This is too low a level at which to attempt to regulate. Lawmakers need to focus on the higher levels of cyberspace activity, perhaps on the intentions of actors and/or the outcomes of their activities, without concerning themselves with the precise behaviours which result from those intentions, or which lead to those outcomes. It is also important to recognize that, for those who do not obey the law voluntarily, enforcement by means of sanctions against them may be excessively difficult, either because detection is made more burdensome through the lack of identification in cyberspace or because the actor's person and assets are outside the lawmaker's jurisdiction.[9] Lawmakers therefore need to consider other options, which might include regulating the environment in which actors operate so as to make non-compliance more difficult. We saw above that this is how the US authorities succeeded, in part at least, in reducing online gambling with its residents, and the UK Internet Watch Foundation's blocking of child sexual abuse images[10] is a further example.

---

[8] See eg the guidance issued under the UK Financial Services Act 1986 about the enforcement policy of the Financial Services Authority in respect of non-UK financial advertising via websites. This guidance was that the primary aim of a financial institution should be to avoid 'issuing' advertisements in the UK, and that an advertisement would be issued if it was visible in the UK—Financial Services Authority, *Treatment of Material on Overseas Internet World Wide Web Sites Accessible in the UK But Not Intended for Investors in the UK*, Guidance 2/98 (1998), paras 11–12, 15. The code through which the internet operates made this almost to achieve in practice, though there was some comfort in the further guidance that an institution which had no dealings with UK residents would be unlikely to be subject to enforcement proceedings.

[9] See Ch 4.

[10] See ibid.

Regulating a Community

If a cyberspace actor resides in the lawmaker's physical territory, or has assets located there, then in general the actor is likely to accept that the lawmaker has authority to regulate his cyberspace activities.[11] But this is not necessarily so for cyberspace actors whose only connection with the lawmaker is via cyberspace.

The problem arises from the general rules of each legal system about the applicability of that system's laws. As we saw in Chapter 3, those rules tend to produce the result that laws are applicable to any person, wherever they might be located, whose activities have effects within the jurisdiction which fall under the ambit of the law. Thus if a law is applicable to a cyberspace actor it makes a claim to authority over that actor. But of course, all the applicable laws of all the other countries of the world make similar claims.

In practice such claims are rarely asserted by means of enforcement against the cyberspace actor unless he has assets in the jurisdiction,[12] but the very existence of these overlapping and potentially contradictory claims to authority is distinctly anti-normative. Post writes:

It's not, to my eyes, a satisfying resolution of the problem. It turns law, and the question of legal obligation, into something that looks more like a game—Three-Card Monte, or Jurisdictional Whack-a-Mole: If you (or your assets) pop up in Singapore, ... *Wham!* Singaporean law can be—can *legitimately* be—applied to you. Once posted to the Web, your daughter's junior high school letter is indeed subject to Brazilian and Japanese and Kenyan (and Malaysian and Mexican and Latvian ...) law simultaneously, because it may indeed be having 'significant effects' in each country, and each country can therefore legitimately apply its coercive powers against the school or its officers or the newsletter editors (if it turns out to be in a position to do so). Yahoo!'s obligation, and your daughter's school's obligation, to comply with those laws is defined by the likelihood that it has assets in any one of them, or that any of its officers might travel to any of them.

It's a strange kind of law ... law that only gets revealed to the interacting parties *ex post facto*, and which can therefore no longer guide the behaviour of those subject to it in any meaningful way.[13]

Post's preferred solution is that lawmakers should abandon all their claims to authority over cyberspace, and recognize a right to self-determination for cyberspace actors: 'their right—perhaps even their *inalienable* right—to govern themselves as they see fit'.[14]

This proposition is more than a little idealistic. Quite how states are to be persuaded to abandon the law-making jurisdiction they currently have is not explained, in particular because they do have legitimate claims to protect their citizens against harm,

---

[11] I say 'in general' because there is always the possibility that the actor interacts only with those from a different jurisdiction in the field of activity which the law claims to regulate. If so, the actor is likely to give greater weight to the law-making authority of that other jurisdiction.

[12] Jack L Goldsmith, 'Against Cyberanarchy' (1998) 65 U Chi L Rev 1199, 1216–7.

[13] David G Post (n 4), 168.

[14] Ibid, 185.

even harm suffered in cyberspace. The interregnum until the various cyberspace communities established their internal law systems would be likely to be prolonged, particularly given the difficulties experienced by those communities which have already tried the experiment of self-government.[15]

However, there is an incentive for states to *reduce* substantially their claims to authority over cyberspace. A claim to regulate everyone is palpably nonsensical, as states do not have the power to make such a claim a reality. States who make such a sweeping claim lose much of the benefit of the social norm that laws should be obeyed.

Thus a lawmaker which reduces the claims of its laws, so that they apply only to the group of cyberspace actors who are likely to recognize themselves as forming part of the lawmaker's community, is likely both to reduce the normative confusion in cyberspace and to increase the normative force of its laws *within* that community.

But how is such a reduction to be achieved? The answer is theoretically simple, but more complex in its implementation. Lawmakers need to identify the community of cyberspace users which they have a legitimate claim to regulate, and then to restrict the applicability of the law to that community.

Criminal law tends to apply in three circumstances: if either victim or perpetrator is physically in the jurisdiction when the crime is committed; if the crime is against property located in the jurisdiction; or if the perpetrator commits an act, including using property or equipment, within the jurisdiction which constitutes a significant element in the commission of the crime. The first two of these are unproblematic; no fraudster or thief, for example, could reasonably complain that he was not a member of, or making attacks against, the lawmaker's community if these were the justifications for applying the law.

However, the third justification requires more careful thinking on the part of the lawmaker. As an example, suppose that an English perpetrator commits acts of harassment or blackmail against an Australian victim by means of private messages communicated via a bulletin board hosted in the US. The criminal activities of the perpetrator have no significant effect on the US community, and so any claim by the US to assert authority over the activity would be excessive. Even if harassment were committed via open messages on the bulletin board, this affects the US community no more than any other community whose members participate in discussion, and so again an authority claim would be unwarranted. On the other hand, an Australian hacker who uses a computer located in England to attack a computer in the US will, in the current state of the law, commit a crime in England.[16] This seems to me to be an appropriate assertion of authority; there is international consensus[17] that states

---

[15] See Jennifer L Mnookin, 'Virtual(ly) Law: The Emergence of Law in LambdaMOO' (1996) 2.1 *Journal of Computer-Mediated Communication*, <http://jcmc.indiana.edu/vol2/issue1/lambda.html>; Chris Reed, 'Why Must You be Mean to Me? Crime and the Online Persona' (2010) 13 New Criminal LR 485.

[16] UK Computer Misuse Act 1990, ss 4(2) and 5.

[17] Commonwealth Model Law on Computer and Computer Related Crime 2002, s 4; Council Framework Decision 2005/222/JHA on attacks against information systems, OJ L 069/67, 16 March 2005.

should take steps to sanction the use of computers in their territory to attack other states, and the perpetrator is aware that he is using the intermediary computer in question (even if he does not know in which state it is located) and is thus subjecting himself to the laws of that community. By examining this question from the perspective of the person who will be subject to the law, a lawmaker should be able to decide whether an assertion of authority is justifiable, and likely to be accepted by the community over which authority is claimed.

Contract law, outside the field of consumer dealings, already adopts an approach which is compatible with this principle. The applicable law will be either that chosen by the parties or, in the absence of choice, the law of the state where the person undertaking the main performance of the contract resides.[18] In either case the parties know in advance the national community involved, and have clearly joined that community through the terms of their contract and thus subjected themselves to its contract laws.

Laws protecting consumers, in their current state, present some of the clearest examples of lawmakers' excessive claims to authority. States, quite legitimately, believe they have a duty to protect their citizens against improper trading practices,[19] and because their law-making is undertaken through the lens of their own law-making powers they fail to recognize that these laws claim authority over sellers who, also quite legitimately, do not accept that they form any part of the lawmaker's trading community. States do not, in fact, claim authority to regulate all the physical world trading with their residents. If a European resident travels to New York and goes shopping there, no European state would claim to apply its consumer protection law to those shopping transactions. Consumers are far more perceptive online than their laws often give them credit for being, and are usually well aware of the difference between a 'foreign' purchase, where they run the risk of losing their national protections, and a 'normal' purchase (even from a foreign seller) where they do not. Lawmakers can deal with this problem by applying their consumer protection laws only to sellers who target the lawmaker's consumers. As explained in Chapters 5 and 6, a seller who targets the consumers of a particular state online has clearly joined, albeit temporarily, the trading community of that state. Because of this, the trader is likely to recognize the authority of that state's lawmaker over its transactions, and thus to grant the necessary protections voluntarily. It must be borne in mind that enforcement of these consumer laws, either by the consumer or by some authority on behalf of the consumer's state, is excessively costly. If traders cannot be persuaded into voluntary compliance, the law is merely symbolic of the state's concern for its consumers.

---

[18] See eg Regulation (EC) No 593/2008 of the European Parliament and of the Council of 17 June 2008 on the law applicable to contractual obligations (Rome I), OJ L177/6, 4 July 2008, Art 4.

[19] See eg Recommendation of the OECD Council Concerning Guidelines for Consumer Protection In the Context of Electronic Commerce (OECD, 1999), Guideline I:

> Consumers who participate in electronic commerce should be afforded transparent and effective consumer protection that is not less than the level of protection afforded in other forms of commerce.

It achieves no practical purpose, and may even do harm by reducing the respect of cyberspace actors for that state's other laws.

Laws which claim to regulate some activity for what might be described as the 'general good' of the state in question, such as privacy or obscenity laws, also run the risk of making excessive claims of authority, again because they are devised without considering the perspective of the cyberspace user. As suggested for consumer protection, the claims of these laws to applicability in cyberspace can usefully be limited through a targeting approach.[20] It is worth noting that the *Yahoo! v LICRA*[21] controversy would not have arisen had the French anti-Nazi laws limited their application to communications targeted at French residents. This would also match the aims of the law, which are to protect the French community against a resurgence of the evils it suffered through its Nazi occupation during the Second World War. Postings on the yahoo.com auction site targeted no country in particular (unless they were so predominantly from US sellers that they targeted the US community), and so it is not surprising that an assertion of the authority of French law was perceived by posters, and Yahoo! itself, as making excessive claims.

Thus although there is no single route to limiting the applicability of a law to the appropriate community, we can see that there is a range of techniques which can be used effectively. All these have been tested in practice and appear to work. The difficulty for the lawmaker is not in selecting the appropriate technique, but in making the perspective switch to examine the question from the cyberspace actor's viewpoint. Once this is done, the problem is a long way towards being solved.

Norms and the Content of Law

Even if the authority of a lawmaker is accepted, the content of a particular law may be so defective as to achieve no normative respect. Such laws are unlikely to be complied with. We examined the reasons for this in some depth in Part III, and the results are summarized briefly here.

The first thing which the lawmaker needs to avoid is creating conflict with the other rules which constitute the cyberspace user's law system. I argued in Chapter 6 that cyberspace users adopt a subject rule of recognition to determine which subset they will obey out of the multiple laws claiming authority over them. These laws make up the largest part of the normative framework within which the user frames its activities, and are further supplemented by the social norms which have developed within that community of cyberspace users.

If the lawmaker's new rules conflict with that established normative framework then they will only be obeyed if they convince the user to substitute them for the rules which conflict. More likely, though, they will be rejected by the user as meaningless because it is not possible to comply with them whilst also complying with the

---

[20] See eg Article 29 Data Protection Working Party, 'Opinion 8/2010 on Applicable Law', 0836-02/10/EN, WP 179 16 December 2010 ('WP179'), discussed in Ch 6.

[21] Discussed in Ch 3.

set of norms which the user has already accepted as authoritative. This tells us that the lawmaker needs to research the norms which currently apply to those cyberspace users it considers to be part of its community, and then to frame the new law to work within that framework.

Laws may be able to modify existing norms by means of gradually extending their scope in the lawmaker's desired direction, provided the extension does not depart so far from the existing norm as to create an irreconcilable conflict with it.[22] But if the lawmaker cannot work within the existing normative framework then its only choices are to modify its law-making plans, or to go ahead with them in the knowledge that compliance with the law will only be achieved via the difficult task of enforcing the law at a level which is stringent enough to persuade cyberspace actors to comply with it.[23]

A second pitfall is making a law which is not understandable by cyberspace actors. Problems arise here because laws are addressed not only to those to whom they are applicable, but also to courts and other officials charged with enforcing them and, increasingly, to internal or external advisers. The trend has been to concentrate on this last group of addressees, explaining the law to them in increasing detail. The consequence is that the law is expressed in such complex terms that its subject is often unable to understand the obligations it imposes, even in general terms,[24] without turning to specialists for advice. Compare, for example, the UK Partnership Act 1890 with the EU Electronic Signatures Directive 1999.[25] Section 1(1) of the 1890 Act provides, 'Partnership is the relation which subsists between persons carrying on a business in common with a view of profit.' In most cases it will be clear to individuals, including cyberspace actors, whether they have formed a partnership. By contrast, Article 5(1) of the directive, which explains the requirements for a signature to be treated as equivalent to a written signature, are completely opaque:

Member States shall ensure that advanced electronic signatures which are based on a qualified certificate and which are created by a secure-signature-creation device:

(a) satisfy the legal requirements of a signature in relation to data in electronic form in the same manner as a handwritten signature satisfies those requirements in relation to paper-based data; and

(b) are admissible as evidence in legal proceedings.

We saw in Chapter 8 that specialist legal and technical advice is needed for a signatory to know whether an electronic signature meets these requirements. As I hope to demonstrate below, this level of complexity is unnecessary.

---

[22] See Ch 7, pp 126–8.

[23] See Ch 4.

[24] Of course it has not, for several centuries, been possible for a law's subject to understand these obligations fully. This is why we have the profession of lawyer. But it has, until comparatively recently, normally been possible for the individual to understand the general framework of obligations to which he is subject.

[25] Directive 1999/93/EC on a Community framework for electronic signatures, OJ L13/12, 19 January 2000.

Cyberspace actors cannot be expected to take legal advice each time they become a temporary member of some foreign community. It may be every subject's duty to obey the law, but there should be a corresponding duty on the lawmaker to explain the law in a way which facilitates obedience. Failure to do so loses the benefit of the norms that laws should be obeyed and, in the case of cyberspace actors, makes it very likely that such laws will be ignored as meaningless to their activities. This is particularly likely if the lawmaker adopts techniques which are appropriate for a regulatory community, such as the financial services sector, and attempts to apply them to cyberspace activities where no such community exists.

A third defect in cyberspace law-making is where the law is framed in terms which have no apparent connection to what the cyberspace actor actually does. If the actor cannot see the connection between the law's demands and his behaviour in cyberspace he is likely to reject the law's claims as meaningless. This problem tends to arise where the law, as designed for the physical world, regulates proxies rather than the behaviour or effects which the law seeks to influence,[26] or assumes a particular business model of the way the regulated activity will be carried out.[27] If those proxies or business models are replicated in the law as it applies to cyberspace, but the cyberspace activity uses those proxies in different ways or adopts a different business model, then again the law will appear meaningless to the cyberspace actor and thus lose its normative force.

What all these pitfalls have in common is that they are legacies of the conception that a lawmaker is a supreme source of authority, as a consequence of which its commands will be obeyed. If this were true, none of the problems identified in this book would have occurred. Cyberspace actors would have abandoned their compliance with norms which conflicted with legal commands or, faced with contradictory commands, simply abandoned their online activities as impossible to undertake lawfully. There would be no different business models or use of proxies in cyberspace as opposed to the physical world, though it is hard to see how cyberspace would exist at all in the absence of copying. Meaning in the law would be irrelevant, as cyberspace actors would simply follow the lawmaker's commands blindly.

Of course this was never true in the physical world, and it is even less so in cyberspace. Lawmakers need to convince cyberspace actors that they *ought* to behave in accordance with the lawmaker's aims. There is thus a need to explain to the actor — and not merely to his (probably non-existent) legal advisors—the normative aims of the law. These aims must therefore be consistent with the actor's existing normative framework, understandable both in terms of what is required of the actor and also how that is likely to achieve those aims, and achievable in the context of what the cyberspace actor actually does (as opposed to what the lawmaker thinks he might be doing). Ideally the law will be sufficiently future-proof to survive changes in cyberspace technologies and business models, and we saw in Chapter 11 that laws which are excessively complex and over-precise are most likely to fail in this respect. Framing laws in terms of intentions and outcomes, rather than prescribing behaviours, not

---

[26] eg in copyright law, which regulates copying rather than use.

[27] Such as data protection's implicit assumption that processing is centralized within an organization.

only makes their normative aims clearer but increases the chance of coping with an uncertain future.

'Good' Cyberspace Laws

A theory of how best to make laws for cyberspace is all very well and good, but can it actually be used to produce better laws? As I write I can hear the reservations of lawmakers, particularly in two areas. First, they will say, surely it is true that cyberspace is a highly complex and technical arena. That being so, we must need complex and technical laws to capture all the details we wish to regulate. Secondly, do we not need to provide cyberspace actors with certainty about their legal duties? There are constant complaints about how uncertain the legal environment of cyberspace is, and the least we can to is to make our laws as certain as we can.

I propose to address these reservations in two stages. First, I will try to show, by taking some of the laws whose failings I have most strongly criticized earlier in the book, that it is possible to reframe them in accordance with the principles set out above, and without losing any of the fundamental elements of those laws. The result will necessarily be, or at least will *appear* to be, more generic and less certain than the existing laws, and I will address that point in the final section of this chapter.

In doing this, I will adopt three guiding principles. First, the extent of the law's application to cyberspace users must be made clear, and that scope must be limited to those cyberspace actors who will understand themselves to be part of the law-maker's community. Secondly, the normative aims of the law must be expressed, so that they can guide the actor's online activities. Finally, the law will be expressed so far as possible in terms of the actor's intentions and outcomes, with desired or prohibited behaviours explained in general terms and as little focus as possible on detailed behaviours.

This is an exercise in reframing, not redrafting, but I hope the reader will be able to see with sufficient clarity how these proposals might be transposed into their national law.

Data privacy

My main criticisms of the EU's data protection regime[28] in the preceding chapters are that it imposes obligations on data controllers whose meaningfulness is (at best) doubtful, is based on an outdated business model which does not map to cyber-space, and is unclear in its extraterritorial application to cyberspace actors. Its aims, though, are good.

Dealing with the last criticism is comparatively easy. Clearly the law should apply to those cyberspace actors who process personal data using a permanent

---

[28] Directive 95/46/EC on the protection of individuals with regard to the processing of personal data and on the free movement of such data, OJ L 281/31, 23 November 1995 ('Data Protection Directive 1995').

establishment[29] in the EU, in other words, those using a physical presence in the jurisdiction for their data processing. It should also apply to those who target the personal data of EU residents for collection or processing, following the principle suggested by the EU Article 29 Working Party.[30] However, the examples of targeting given by the Working Party go far beyond that group of cyberspace actors which might reasonably be said to have joined the EU community temporarily while collecting or processing data:

the fact that a data controller collects personal data in the context of services explicitly accessible or directed to EU residents, via the display of information in EU languages, the delivery of services or products in EU countries, the accessibility of the service depending on the use of an EU credit card, the sending of advertising in the language of the user or for products and services available in the EU.[31]

Whether a cyberspace actor is targeting the personal data of EU residents is a question of the actor's mental state. These factors might be evidence that the actor has such a mental state (though, as an example, the use of English can surely not be evidence that a US actor is targeting the UK and Ireland) but cannot be used to determine the applicability of the law without over-asserting the authority of EU law in cyberspace. This difficulty can be resolved by providing that if a cyberspace actor takes reasonable precautions to avoid collecting data about EU residents then it is not targeting the EU,[32] thus permitting the actor to demonstrate its actual mental state so far as targeting is concerned.

Those cyberspace actors which collect personal data globally present a policy dilemma. On one view they are targeting nowhere in particular; on another they are targeting every jurisdiction in the world. In practice the largest players, such as Google, will recognize their community membership and thus be likely to comply voluntarily with the law in any case. By contrast small players will be ignorant of all but their home data privacy laws, so the provisions of foreign law such as the EU data protection regime will have little influence on their behaviour. Claiming law-making authority over all these cyberspace actors would be unlikely to be seen as excessive, even if in practice it achieved little in terms of securing obedience to the law.

So far as the normative aims of the law are concerned, these are clearly set out in the data protection principles,[33] to which should be added the obligation to take

---

[29] This is a term of art in EU law, requiring the use of premises and staff to undertake the processing, both located in the jurisdiction. See 'Freedom to Provide Services and the Interest of the General Good in the Second Banking Directive', Commission interpretative communication SEC(97) 1193 final, 20 June 1997, for a more detailed explanation of the concept.

[30] Article 29 Data Protection Working Party, 'Opinion 8/2010 on Applicable Law', 0836-02/10/EN, WP 179, 16 December 2010.

[31] Ibid, 31.

[32] This is the approach adopted by the US in relation to financial advertising, discussed in Ch 3, *Selective enforcement*. See Securities and Exchange Commission, *Statement of the Commission Regarding Use of Internet Web Sites to Offer Securities, Solicit Securities Transactions or Advertise Investment Services Offshore*, Release Nos 33-7516, 34-39779, IA-1710, IC-23071; International Series Release No 1125, 23 March 1998.

[33] Data Protection Directive 1995, Art 6(1).

reasonable security precautions in respect of personal data.[34] The normative difficulty with the Data Protection Directive 1995 is thus not that it fails to set out its aims, but that the translation of those aims into detailed obligations produces a law whose obligations are often meaningless to cyberspace actors.

The solution I would propose is to abandon all the detail. Instead the law should impose on the cyberspace actor broadly defined obligations to comply with the data protection principles. These might look something like the following:

Personal data may only be collected or used where the data controller reasonably believes that his collection or use does not contravene the data protection principles.

Personal data may only be disclosed to another if the data controller reasonably believes that other will use them in accordance with the data protection principles.

This formulation is likely to be far more meaningful to the cyberspace actor for three reasons. First, it is expressed in terms of the actor's belief that he is complying with the law, which is a matter within the actor's own knowledge and understanding. The requirement that this belief be reasonable directs the actor's attention to the normative aims of the law and the actual uses he makes of personal data, rather than to mere check-box compliance. Secondly, it is adaptable to any business model used in cyberspace because the actor's belief that he is complying with the data protection principles is not affected by his choice of business model. It avoids metaphysical concepts such as the 'export' or 'transfer' of data, and instead concentrates on the likely behaviour of the recipient of that data.[35] Finally, in my view a law cast in these terms would be more likely to achieve its normative aims because, by not prescribing behaviour but instead leaving it to the actor to decide how best to act, the actor will be likely to develop (and keep under review) internal compliance behaviours which are understood by its staff in terms of those aims, rather than seen as a purely bureaucratic exercise.

In theory there would be no need for a law in these terms to make any provision about the data subject's consent or other reasons why processing personal data would be fair, nor about sensitive data relating to matters such as health or sexual orientation, nor giving the data subject a right to object to processing. All these are matters which a cyberspace actor would necessarily take into account in deciding whether he held a reasonable belief that his processing complied with the data protection principles. However, it is highly likely that the EU lawmaker would decide at least to issue guidance on all these matters.

We saw in Chapter 8 that the current requirement under the directive to notify the types of data collected and the purposes for which they will be processed has descended into a mere box-ticking exercise which serves no normative purposes. However, the aim that data subjects should be able to discover what uses are likely to be made of their data is an important one. The simplest solution is to require the

---

[34] Ibid, Art 17.

[35] There is no reason why the current 'white list' of countries whose law provides adequate protection could not be retained, raising a presumption that a recipient in those countries would comply with the data protection principles, though this presumption would not be met if the discloser knew different.

cyberspace actor to develop a data privacy policy which it reasonably believes complies with the data protection principles, and to make that policy readily available to data subjects (most obviously via the actor's website). This has a number of advantages in addition to reducing the compliance burden on actors: the development of the policy becomes an exercise in normative reflection, not box-checking; it is far more likely to convey meaningful information to the data subject than does the current notification system;[36] and it make the information available where the data subject is most likely to seek it out.

This recasting is not, of course, complete. Decisions would still need to be made about how best to enforce the law's obligations, including the proper balance between civil claims by data subjects and enforcement action by officials. Subject access would also need to be considered, though the current provisions of the directive would need little modification to fit within this new law.

Overall, though, I would contend that this recasting captures the essential elements of the current data protection regime. And because it directs the minds of cyberspace actors to its normative aims, rather than compliance gymnastics, in my view it would be likely to lead to a greater level of respect for data privacy than does the current law.

Content-control laws

All states have laws which limit the communication of certain types of information content. Some of these are for the protection of the community as a whole, as in the case of obscenity or hate-speech laws, whilst others protect private rights, such as the law of defamation. For obscene content it may be unlawful both to possess it[37] and to communicate it to others.[38] For hate-speech and defamation, the unlawful act usually consists of communication of the content. A state will normally only claim authority to regulate possession of content within its physical jurisdiction, so I will concentrate here on laws which attempt to control the communication of content.

Laws of this type tend to make their normative aims very clear, and are also expressed in terms of obligations which, generally, convey meaning to cyberspace users. Because they usually pre-date cyberspace there were initial uncertainties as to how the particular communications concepts used in the law should be applied to the online environment—for example, many cyberspace users appear to have believed that for defamation purposes 'publication' occurred only once, when content was posted to a newsgroup, discussion board, or website.[39] However, *Gutnick v*

---

[36] See Ch 9, n 97.

[37] Though usually if there is also a intent to distribute the content, except in the case of child sexual-abuse images where mere possession can be sufficient. See Gavin Sutter, 'Online Intermediaries' in Chris Reed (ed), *Computer Law*, 7th edn (Oxford: Oxford University Press, 2010), 305, 354–7.

[38] eg UK Obscene Publications Act 1959, s 2(1); Tennessee Code, § 39-17-902(a).

[39] This was probably based on the US single-publication rule that a particular edition of a book, newspaper, or broadcast is treated as a single publication, and continuing to make it available does not constitute a new publication on each occasion that a copy is issued—US Restatement (2nd) of Torts (1976) § 577A.

Dow Jones[40] alerted users to the fact that many national laws considered each act of communication to be a publication, and there seems now to be a fairly wide awareness that the application of content-control laws is often based on access to the content by persons in that jurisdiction.[41]

The problem with these kinds of law, so far as cyberspace is concerned, is that they are based on radically divergent national standards as to what content is acceptable. Untrue but non-malicious comment about public figures is acceptable in the US but potentially defamatory in the UK. Nudity is uncontroversial in Scandinavia but scandalous in Malaysia. We have seen at several points in this book that the national differences between content-control laws create severe compliance difficulties for cyberspace actors, and that they result in excessive claims of law-making authority by states which potentially damage the normative force of their other laws.[42]

These problems could be reduced, though not eliminated, by defining the applicability of these laws in relation to whether the communicator of the content is targeting persons in the jurisdiction. Thus, to take the well-known example of *Yahoo! v LICRA*,[43] if the French law had adopted this approach then it would have been open to the courts to decide that Yahoo!'s auction service was not targeting French residents because (a) the sale postings in question were in English, (b) the majority of sellers and buyers were not French, and (c) Yahoo! operated a (logically) separate auction service for French buyers and sellers via the yahoo.fr domain name.

The political difficulties in adopting such an approach are, of course, substantial. By ceasing to apply its laws to content which is not targeted to its residents, a state expressly accepts that it is powerless to protect those residents against content which is thought, in that state, to be so morally wrong that its availability should be restricted. But of course, states are in fact powerless to control such matters through the medium of law.

Content control is an arena where cyberspace has robbed the law of much of its power. But it is also an arena where code has the potential to offer a measure of control. Code has been used successfully to prevent content from being accessible to a state's residents, whether widely as in China, or narrowly, as in the UK via the Internet Watch Foundation's block list of child sexual-abuse image sites.

Using code in this way, whether on the basis of a legal obligation on ISPs or through some informal agreement between them and the state, is of course subject to pressure from the other modalities of regulation. To take pornography as an example, market demand appears to be so strong that anti-pornography norms have become much weaker in many countries, while free-speech norms have been immensely strengthened by the cyberspace communication technologies. As a consequence, democratic states will inevitably face difficulties in using code to control

---

[40] [2001] VSC 305, [2002] HCA 56 (Australia).

[41] This was always the US position for content other than defamatory statements—see eg the extradition proceedings from California to Tennessee for communicating obscene content in *United States v Thomas*, 74 F 3d 701 (6th Cir, 1996).

[42] See Ch 3, pp 30–4.

[43] See Ch 3, pp 45–6.

the availability of pornography,[44] except perhaps for those categories of pornographic content which are widely accepted to be beyond the pale.[45]

This change in the normative landscape reduces the ability of states to mandate code controls for content. Additionally, the increasingly liberal nature of these social norms makes it unattractive for states to attempt enforcement of content laws against their residents, even if the technical and human resources were available to do so. It seems that lawmakers may have to learn to live with the consequences, and limit their content-control efforts to the most egregious types of content. They may also have to recognize that restricting the availability of such content through code is all that can realistically be achieved. Attempts by a state to maintain more extensive content-controls risk damage to the normative force of its other laws.

Electronic signatures

Electronic signature laws do not suffer from the problems of excessive reach into cyberspace that we saw for our two previous examples. The law of a particular state will only apply to an electronic signature if the question arises whether the signed transaction is legally binding in that state, and it is hard to imagine situations where the relevant state whose law applies would not have been apparent to the parties when the transaction was entered into.

At a general level, there is also little difficulty for cyberspace actors in understanding the law's normative aims. The legal effect of all signatures is that they provide evidence of the signatory's identity and his agreement to and/or adoption of the content of the document which is signed. Electronic signature laws normally provide that an e-signature which produces sufficient evidence of these matters is a legally valid signature. Cyberspace actors will have no difficulty in finding these laws to be meaningful.

The problems arise, however, where laws provide for a type of e-signature which has the same legal force as a manuscript signature, and do so by requiring the identity[46] of the signatory to be certified by a third party. The legal regime for such signatures introduced by the EU e-Signatures Directive[47] has been criticized extensively in previous chapters for imposing such over-complex requirements for validity that it is excessively difficult for cyberspace actors to know whether their signatures comply with the law, and also for imposing a regime that embeds a business model which differs from that actually used in cyberspace.

---

[44] See eg the opposition to the Australian internet censorship proposals, Ch 10, n 24.

[45] Thus eg although the mere possession of 'extreme pornography' is an offence under the UK Criminal Justice and Immigration Act 2008, s 63, this content is not covered by the Internet Watch Foundation's block list, though the Foundation does provide a facility to report the possession of such images in the UK to the law enforcement authorities. See <http://www.iwf.org.uk/hotline/the-laws/criminally-obscene-adult-content/criminal-justice-and-immigration-act-2008>.

[46] And perhaps other attributes, such as the signatory's authority to bind his employer or sign as agent for a third party.

[47] Directive 1999/93/EC on a Community framework for electronic signatures, OJ L13/12, 19 January 2000.

The defects in the EU's e-signature regime are largely caused by the decision that issuing signature certificates should be a regulated activity. This led the EU lawmaker to adopt the lawmaking techniques which are used in other regulated sectors, without recognizing that the essential features which make such laws workable (and in particular continuing dialogue between regulator and regulatees) could not be applied successfully to players outside the regulatory system, such as signatories and those relying on signatures. In order to remedy these defects it is necessary to decouple the regulation of certification authorities, if any, from the law's provisions on signature validity and liability.

The conditions laid down by the directive for an e-signature to have the same legal validity as a manuscript signature need only minor modification, though extensive simplification, to make them meaningful to cyberspace actors. In revised form, these should be that the signature has the following characteristics:

1. that the accompanying certificate states that the signatory has been identified, and by whom, and is electronically signed by the issuer of the certificate
2. that the certificate also states that the signature-application technology was in the possession of the signatory when the certificate was issued, and that the issuer has checked that the signature-validation technology validates a signature so applied[48]
3. that the technology used to effect the signature provides adequate proof that the signature was applied by the signatory identified in the certificate, and that the electronically signed document has not been altered since the signature was applied.

Framed in this way, it would be for the person arguing in favour of the signature's validity to prove these three elements. At first sight this might seem unfair to the relying party, because none of these matters are within that person's control. However, as between signatory and relying party these matters could be dealt with by means of contractual warranties in a commercial relationship, and the relying party would also benefit from the liability provisions explained below. This is exactly the way that manuscript signatures are dealt with by current law—a handwritten signature might be forged, or applied without authority, and these are risks that any person relying on such a signature must take. There is thus a clear functional equivalence between both kinds of signature, and the normative aims of the law are identical in both cases.

A further aim of the directive, in which it did not succeed,[49] was to enable the relying party to accept an e-signature without any risk that further evidence of these matters would need to be provided in legal proceedings. The most obvious way for a revised law to achieve this aim is to modify the existing accreditation scheme for signature technologies and certification authorities, and to provide a legal presumption that a signature meets these conditions if it is made by using accredited technology and a certificate issued by an accredited certification authority. In order for this

---

[48] The directive is conceived in terms of encryption keys—see eg Art 2(4) and (7)—but there is no need for the law to entrench this particular e-signature technology.

[49] See Ch 8, pp 135–7.

to work the accreditation scheme has to be a 'black box', so that neither signatory nor relying party, nor the courts, need know anything but that the technology and certification authority are accredited.

The most effective way of establishing such an accreditation scheme is via the co-regulatory model, as used for financial services regulation. Rather than the requirements for accreditation being set in stone, as in the directive, instead they should be expressed at a higher level and elaborated in the scheme rules through the kinds of regulatory conversations we examined in Chapter 8. The accreditation body, technology providers, and certification authorities constitute exactly the kind of regulatory community which can make such a system work, and this will enable precise and detailed rules to be developed which have genuine meaning for all participants. It also enables the rules to be adapted as signature technologies evolve, thus providing a high level of future-proofing. These rules will, of course, have no meaning at all for signatories or relying parties, which is why the law should not involve them in any assessment of how effectively the scheme meets its regulatory objectives.

This reframing immediately makes it clear where potential liabilities might arise. There are three main functions to be performed:

1. Verification of identity and any other attributes of the signatory will often not be undertaken by the certification authority, and different attributes may be verified by different persons.[50] Thus liability for erroneous verification, for the purpose of incorporation in a signature certificate, should be placed on the person undertaking the verification.

2. The linking of these verifications with the signature-application technology, and the checking that the signatory possessed this technology and that a signature made using it was validated by the signature-validation technology, is undertaken by the certification authority. Thus liability for failures in these respects should be placed on the certification authority.

3. If an e-signature is held invalid because of defects in accreditation, either the loss must lie where it falls on the signatory or relying party, or the accreditation scheme must compensate the party suffering the loss. There is no 'right' answer to this choice, though clearly an e-signature accreditation scheme which offers compensation is likely to produce e-signatures which are more attractive to signatories and relying parties.

Whether these should be strict or fault-based liabilities is a matter for the lawmaker to decide.

As we have seen, though, merely making a law is no guarantee that the technology validated by the law will actually be adopted by cyberspace actors. Nonetheless, a reframing along these lines at least increases the chance of this happening. Under the directive's regulatory scheme there is no intermediate step between a cheap and easy-to-use technology which creates a valid signature, but one which may not have legal

---

[50] eg an English solicitor's identity might be certified by the Law Society, but authority to bind a law firm would be certified by that firm.

equivalence to a manuscript signature, and an expensive and cumbersome technology which creates signatures which do have such equivalence. By decoupling validity from accreditation, the market is given a route to creating signature technologies which have the potential to meet the validity requirements. This might give actors sufficient confidence to use them without the benefits of accreditation, even though it would not be certain that a non-accredited technology would satisfy the law. If this development occurred, the accreditation scheme could also evolve to bring these technologies within its ambit and thus increase user certainty.

Copyright infringement

We have seen throughout this book that copyright is singularly ill-adapted to cyberspace. In particular its provisions on infringement are far from meaningful for cyberspace actors, commercial as well as individual, because the regulatory settlement on which it is based has largely been developed by only two stakeholders: creators, and those who finance creations and undertake their exploitation.[51] Until there is a new regulatory settlement which encompasses users as well, there can be no serious prospect of reforming the law.

Even if such a settlement can be achieved, though, it will in my view be impossible to implement it in meaningful law whilst retaining the law's focus on copying. Copying is the primary mechanism by which the cyberspace technologies operate, so that revising the law in terms of copying would result in such a complex framework of exceptions that it would be unlikely to be understandable by, and thus remain meaningless to, the majority of cyberspace actors. A focus on copying also runs directly counter to the entrenched cyberspace norm that communication, and in particular sharing, of information should be unrestricted.

Given that copying is the basis of the law only because of the historical accident that it was a convenient proxy for regulating use of creative works, the obvious solution, as I have suggested in Chapter 9,[52] is to reframe copyright infringement in terms of the *use* of works. This reframing would be much more meaningful to cyberspace users. As they are constantly copying, it is inevitably hard for them to distinguish between permitted and prohibited varieties of the same act. However, it should be obvious to any cyberspace actor whether he is using a work.

A major part of copyright law's aims is to encourage creators by securing for them a return, and that return will be achieved through commercial exploitation of the work. It therefore seems axiomatic that, prima facie, uses of a work which amount to its commercial exploitation should amount to infringements.

Commercial exploitation must mean, of course, more than merely selling copies of a work or providing paid access to it. For example, the use of audio or visual works

---

[51] See Christopher Jensen, 'The More Things Change, the More They Stay the Same: Copyright, Digital Technology, and Social Norms' (2003) 56 Stan L Rev 531, discussed in Ch 7, *Community norms and copyright*.

[52] See Ch 9, pp 154–6.

in marketing or advertising is clearly a commercial exploitation.[53] Interesting questions arise in relation to intermediaries such as YouTube—a video of an amateur performance of a musical work is not a commercial exploitation by the poster of that video, but it is arguable that the intermediary's activity of hosting a video and making it available amounts to commercial exploitation if revenue is derived from advertising displayed to viewers of that video. The general benefits to society from hosting of this kind might justify treating it as non-commercial exploitation, even if it generates some revenue for the host—a relevant factor would clearly be the proportion of advertising and other revenues which the host derives from this source, compared to those from, for example, music videos licensed to the host by the rights owner, which are clearly commercial exploitations. Precisely how to resolve this issue depends on the terms of the regulatory settlement.

Hosting by intermediaries would not, of course, be the only exception to this right to control commercial exploitation. It is likely that the regulatory settlement would retain the right to quote with appropriate acknowledgement, perhaps some right to use works for commercial research, rights to parody, and so on.

A further advantage of reframing the law to concentrate on use, rather than copying, is that it would direct the minds of users (and judges) to the real issues involved, rather than to metaphysical questions about whether use involved copying. The recent decision of the English Court of Appeal in *Newspaper Licensing Agency Ltd and ors v Meltwater Holding BV and ors*[54] is a classic example of the intellectual gymnastics which are required under the current law. Meltwater operated the online equivalent of a press-cuttings agency, undertaken by screen-scraping news websites and providing its clients with email digests of all news stories containing the search terms specified by the client. The question before the court was whether those clients infringed copyright in the news stories. The court held that these digests would amount to infringements because they reproduced a substantial part of the story, an uncontroversial finding. What surprised many commentators was that the court also held that by receiving and viewing the emails, Meltwater's clients made copies of the digests and thus infringed the news websites' copyrights. The fact that the clients could have visited the websites and viewed the full content, without infringing copyright, was not discussed in the judgment. This is not to say that the court would necessarily have reached a different decision, but rather to point out that the concentration on copying led to an important factor being ignored.

By contrast, there seems to be no justification for granting right-holders the general right to control all non-commercial uses of a work, at least so far as uses in cyberspace are concerned. It is generally accepted at present that the return to society from the granting of rights in creative works is that those works should be available to society for useful purposes, and that some at least of those uses should not require payment to the right-holder. Non-commercial uses by definition generate no return

---

[53] As with all legal categories, problems arise at the penumbra—eg use of a work in advertising by a non-commercial organization such as a charity could legitimately be classified as either commercial or non-commercial exploitation.

[54] [2011] EWCA Civ 890.

in which the right-holder could share. However, this starting point would clearly need modification because some non-commercial uses have the potential to damage the right-holder's commercial exploitation of a work, and thus remove the benefits granted in the regulatory settlement.

The principle that some non-commercial uses are permissible is already accepted via the three-step test in Article 10 of the WIPO Copyright Treaty. Article 10 allows signatory states to grant exceptions to copyright provided that these 'do not conflict with a normal exploitation of the work and do not unreasonably prejudice the legitimate interests of the author'.

However, the copying business model embedded in our current copyright system has led courts and legislators to take a restrictive view of when such exceptions should apply. If all copying requires the permission of the right-holder, whatever the use which is being made of the work, then the right-holder can charge for such permission. Thus the 'normal exploitation' of a work is by means of charging for making a copy. From this starting point, any use which requires a copy to be made (as is inevitable for digital uses) must be in conflict with normal exploitation.[55]

If, though, we were starting afresh, we would need a new approach to deciding whether a non-commercial use conflicted with the right-holder's commercial exploitation. One possible source for such an approach is that of substitutability in the market, a concept borrowed from EU competition law. Definition of the applicable market is essential when assessing whether activities are anti-competitive, and the most important test for whether two products or services are part of the same market is whether a purchaser will substitute one for another. To put it more simply, the supply of bananas and apples constitutes two separate markets because a consumer, faced with a lack of bananas, will not buy apples instead.[56]

Translating this principle into cyberspace, a video made by an amateur musician of the song 'Under the Boardwalk' is unlikely to be treated as a substitute for the Rolling Stones' recording of the same song. Viewers of the video will not refrain from buying the Rolling Stones' version because the amateur performance satisfies their desire for the song, no matter how closely the amateur succeeds in replicating the Rolling Stones' performance. Thus this non-commercial use would not infringe the Rolling Stones' rights because it does not conflict with their commercial exploitation of their work.

Conversely, if a cyberspace actor rips a Rolling Stones CD to his computer and then makes an MP3 of 'Under the Boardwalk' accessible via some file-sharing platform, those who obtain a copy of it *will* treat it as a substitute for the copy available commercially. Thus file sharing (of commercial recordings at least) would remain an infringement even if it is undertaken on a non-commercial basis. On the other hand, an individual who rips his CD to make an MP3 file for use on his iPod would not be an infringer.

---

[55] See Ch 9, p 155.
[56] *United Brands v Commission*, Case 27/76, [1978] ECR 207.

Deciding whether a non-commercial use substitutes for licensed commercial exploitation is a more difficult task than might at first appear because many creative works have multiple creators with different interests and modes of normal exploitation. To continue with 'Under the Boardwalk' as our example, there are two sets of creators involved:

1. The Rolling Stones created the performance under consideration. They make revenue by (i) performing the song live, (ii) selling copies of their recording on CD or online, and (iii) selling merchandise such as T-shirts which refer to the recording or the album containing it. As discussed above, the amateur recording does not substitute for their version in the market in relation to any of these revenue streams, and thus does not conflict with their normal exploitation of the work.

2. The music and lyrics were composed by Arthur Resnick and Kenny Young, and the only way that they can exploit their creation is by way of licensing the making of recordings. It is thus less obvious that an amateur recording has no impact on the normal exploitation of their work.

One way for the lawmaker to deal with this second issue is by creating a list of exceptions, this time in favour of the right-holder. As we have seen, detailed law-making of this kind has a number of normative disadvantages, particularly here where the law is addressed to the non-commercial cyberspace user. Detailed exceptions inevitably introduce technical concepts which are hard for individuals to understand, and are therefore less likely to be accepted as authoritative under the subject rule of recognition they are using. We know that copyright is extremely hard to enforce against individual cyberspace users on any more than a symbolic scale,[57] and so it would in my view be more desirable to leave the principle in the broad normative terms in which I have expressed it.

In deciding whether the YouTube video we have been discussing infringes Resnick and Young's rights, our amateur musician (and, if it came to it, the courts) would consider the ways in which those rights currently generate revenue. If these remained unchanged from the current situation, the amateur would discover that no licence fee is charged for performing music privately, or for making a private recording. So far as the uploading to YouTube is concerned, again there is no licence available for this activity, as all the licensing agency schemes cover only the *distribution* of recordings on a commercial basis, calculated by reference to the number of copies which the maker intends to distribute. Our musician might consider that his uploading is analogous to performing the work in public, and would then discover that venues pay licence fees, but not the musicians who play in them. He, and the courts, would be likely to conclude that there had been no damage to Resnick and Young's commercial exploitation, and thus no infringement.

This is, of course, by no means the only way in which copyright law could be reframed. It does, however, correlate far more closely with how users of works behave

---

[57] See Ch 4, pp 50–5.

in cyberspace and what they understand themselves to be doing, and the obligations it would impose on them are thus more likely to be accepted as meaningful. It also works within the established framework of cyberspace norms about free communication, rather than diametrically opposing them. Whatever solution is ultimately arrived at for copyright, it will need to meet these conditions if it is to have any chance of being effective.

Certainty and the Normative Trade-off

Every reader of this book will have heard complaints from non-lawyers that the law is not clear enough. If only it explained precisely what they were required to do, obedience would be so much easier. Many lawmakers have responded to this criticism by writing highly detailed laws for cyberspace, in the hope that by so doing they will increase the likelihood that those subject to the law will comply more readily. How can I possibly argue that increased certainty in the law is not always a good thing?

The answer is found in the other common complaint from non-lawyers, that the law is too complex to be understood. The ideals which they desire are that the law should be both simple enough to be easily comprehensible, and certain enough that they know exactly how to comply with it. Unfortunately these ideals are wholly incompatible with each other.

All lawmakers know that there is a trade-off between simplicity and certainty. A choice therefore needs to be made between them. I think there should be general agreement that compromise, in the form of a law which is too complex to be understood easily but still contains major uncertainties of meaning, is the worst possible option.

We also need to recognize that certainty is very difficult to achieve. It requires the lawmaker to elaborate the cyberspace actor's required intentions, behaviours, and outcomes in some detail. We saw in Chapter 8 that such elaboration increases the chance of conflict with other laws, and can also obscure the law's normative aims. This latter point is important because there is an inevitable element of open texture[58] in any rule; at some point the law's subject is likely to be required to choose between alternative behaviours about which the law makes no detailed provision, and thus needs guidance from the normative aims of the law to make the correct choice.

By choosing certainty over simplicity, lawmakers also make a choice about the law's addressees. A highly detailed law can only be addressed to lawyers, in the shape of legal advisers and decision-making officials. This is because complex detail in the law requires legal training in order to understand and interpret its meaning and application.

---

[58] See Frederick Schauer, *Playing by the Rules* (Oxford: Clarendon Press, 1991), 36:

> Open texture is the ineliminable possibility of vagueness, the ineradicable contingency that even the most seemingly precise term might, when it confronts an instance unanticipated when the term was defined, become vague with respect to that instance. No matter how carefully we may try to be maximally precise in our definitions . . . some unanticipated event may always confound us.

The problem with addressing the law in this way, so far as cyberspace is concerned, is that the majority of cyberspace actors do not have legal advisers. Even if they are aware of the law's existence, they are unlikely to perceive it as imposing meaningful obligations on them, or even obligations they could obey irrespective of their meaning, because they will not understand the law. We also saw in Chapter 3 that because there are so many national laws which claim to apply in cyberspace, even multinational corporations cannot in practice take legal advice about all of them. Thus even the most sophisticated of cyberspace actors will be ignorant about a large proportion of their obligations under the law.

This tells us that there is a further trade-off between certainty and law's normative force. The more detailed and certain a law's provisions, the less likely it is to influence the behaviour of its subjects (other than those who are able to take legal advice on the matter). Is it wise for the lawmaker to make such a trade-off?

My argument throughout this book has been that, in cyberspace, law cannot operate as a mechanism for controlling the behaviour of cyberspace actors. This is because the trans-jurisdictional nature of cyberspace results in too many demands being placed on actors, such that they cannot comply with them all, and also because the difficulties of enforcement in cyberspace place overwhelming demands on any state's enforcement mechanisms. And in any event the law does not operate as a control mechanism in the physical world, so we can hardly expect it to do so in cyberspace.

This means that the lawmaker must concentrate on influencing the behaviour of cyberspace actors, rather than deluding itself that control and enforcement is realistically possible. By doing so it can take advantage of the social norm that laws should be obeyed. Of course, that social norm will only guide the cyberspace actor to comply with laws if he accepts the authority of the lawmaker, and we saw in Part II that lawmakers are most likely to have success here if they limit their claims of authority to the cyberspace members of their own regulatory community.

In order to influence that community, the lawmaker must address its laws to community members directly, and not to lawyers alone. This requires those laws to convey meaning to cyberspace actors by making their normative aims clear, and by imposing obligations which are understandable and possible to comply with, and which are perceived by the actor as relevant to those aims and likely to help in achieving them. Laws expressed in terms of high-level normative obligations are likely to achieve this; laws which aim too much at certainty are not.

This leads me to a conclusion which I find somewhat surprising. Laws for cyberspace should say little, if anything, about cyberspace technology. Law is about human behaviour, not the workings of technology. Lawmakers must focus on humanity if they are to make cyberspace a lawful space.

Epilogue

As I was writing the final words of the last chapter, I started to wonder what kind of book I had produced. It certainly wasn't the book I had set out to write.

Theories of cyberspace law tend to be of two sorts. One group concentrates on the legitimacy of claims to law making authority, whilst the other takes a field of substantive law and tries to identify fundamental principles which should shape the content of that law. Their questions are: who should make law and what should that law say? I discover that, for the purposes of this book, I am largely agnostic about both questions.

For my purposes, anyone whose rule-making authority is accepted by a non-trivial group of cyberspace actors is to some degree a lawmaker. Thus ICANN and the World Trade Organization clearly qualify, but so do eBay, YouTube, and Facebook. Two of the discussion boards I frequent have in the last year debated rule-making authority, one settling on a monarchy and the other an autocracy, and I am quite content with both regimes.

Similarly, I find it difficult to assert that there are obvious answers about the substantive content of cyberspace laws. There is no clearly 'right' way to regulate e-signatures or e-money, though there are ways to do so which are pretty pointless. Different societies have different views on such fundamental values as privacy and free speech, and it is not obvious to me that the privacy principles applied in, say, Sweden are vastly better or worse than those of the US.[1] China's approach to freedom of speech, which seems intolerably repressive from a UK perspective, appears to be acceptable at present to the vast majority of Chinese citizens. It would presumptuous of me to tell these communities how they should regulate themselves. Of course, I do have views about the proper shape of the laws which apply to me, and also about how cyberspace will force those laws (and Swedish, US, and Chinese law) to change, but this book is not about those views.

My objection to both these kinds of theory is their assumption that law just *works*, provided we have the right lawmaker, or the right substantive content. This is not my experience of law. In cyberspace much of it is regularly ignored, subverted, or complied with in unexpected ways. It seemed to me that the reasons were not understood, and thus worth exploring.

What I think I have ended up with is a theory of how law achieves effects in cyberspace, and, consequently, how law needs to be devised if it is to work there. It tells me, and I hope convinces you, the reader, that the legitimacy of the lawmaker

---

[1] I pick these countries because they are poles apart on two issues. In Sweden, personal tax returns are publicly available documents, a fact which appals most US citizens when they hear of it. Swedes are similarly outraged by the commercial collection and sale of personal information, which is perfectly acceptable in the US.

and the content of the rules it makes are interlinked issues, and that unless *both* achieve respect for their authority from cyberspace actors then the law will be a failure.

Theories about legitimacy or content are strongly normative. They assert who ought to be the lawmaker, or what the law ought to provide. In that sense my theory is not normative at all—at most it asserts that a lawmaker whose authority is not respected, or a law whose content lacks meaning, will not succeed in influencing the behaviour of cyberspace actors. It is, though, normative in other ways. It tells lawmakers how they ought to behave if they want to make law, as opposed to symbolic statements, and it tells them to focus on norms rather than commands.

I began by saying that I wanted cyberspace to be a space where well-meaning actors behaved in a proper manner. Law, if it is made properly, sets the standard. Badly made law produces nothing but confusion and normative failure.

Index

Printed in Great Britain
by Amazon